The Failure of Conservatism

in modern British poetry

Selected previous publications by Andrew Duncan

Poetry

In a German Hotel
Cut Memories and False Commands
Sound Surface
Alien Skies
Switching and Main Exchange *
Pauper Estate *
Anxiety Before Entering a Room. New and selected poems
Surveillance and Compliance
Skeleton Looking at Chinese Pictures
The Imaginary in Geometry
Savage Survivals (amid modern suavity) *
In Five Eyes *
Threads of Iron *

Criticism

The Poetry Scene in the Nineties (internet only)
Centre and Periphery in Modern British Poetry **
The Failure of Conservatism in Modern British Poetry **
Origins of the Underground
The Council of Heresy *
The Long 1950s *
A Poetry Boom 1990-2010 *
Fulfilling the Silent Rules (forthcoming)

As editor

Don't Start Me Talking (with Tim Allen)
Joseph Macleod: *Cyclic Serial Zeniths from the Flux*
Joseph Macleod: *A Drinan Trilogy: The Cove / The Men of the Rocks
        / Script from Norway*

* original titles from Shearsman Books;
** 2nd editions from Shearsman Books

The Failure of
Conservatism
in modern British Poetry

Andrew Duncan

Shearsman Books

Second Edition, revised and expanded.
Published in the United Kingdom in 2016 by
Shearsman Books Ltd
50 Westons Hill Drive
Emersons Green
BRISTOL
BS16 7DF

Shearsman Books Ltd Registered Office
30–31 St. James Place, Mangotsfield, Bristol BS16 9JB
(this address not for correspondence)

ISBN 978-1-84861-498-7

ACKNOWLEDGEMENTS
The publisher wishes to thank Shannon Eden for her assistance
in preparing this volume for the press.

Some parts of this book previously appeared in different
forms in *Angel Exhaust*, *fragmente*, and *Eonta*.
My thanks to the editors of those magazines.

We are grateful to the following for their permission
to quote from copyright material:

J.H. Prynne for excerpts from *Poems* (Hexham: Bloodaxe Books, 2015),
and for an excerpt from an uncollected piece originally published in *Prospect*;
Carcanet Press for excerpts from Christopher Middleton, 'Reflections on
a Viking Prow' in *Jackdaw Jiving: Selected Essays on Poetry and Translation*
(Manchester: Carcanet Press, 1998); to Allen Fisher, Ulli Freer and W.N.
Herbert for extended excerpts from their work; to Wolfgang Görtschacher
for excerpts from *Little Magazine Profiles: The Little Magazines in Great
Britain 1939-1993* (Salzburg: University of Salzburg Press, 1993).

Contents

The Failure of Conservatism in Modern British Poetry:
Style Time 1960-1997

Newly conservated

Are you doing what you were doing five years ago? Well, don't make a career out of it.
      – Mark E. Smith, heckling a heckler.

                        And in the
face of the 'new frankness' in immaculate
display in the highest places, why should
the direct question not be put: if any discrete
class with an envisaged part in the social process
is not creating its own history, then who is doing
it for them? Namely, what is anyone waiting
for, either resigned or nervous or frantic from
time to time? Various forms dodge through
the margins of a livelihood, but so much talk
about the underground is silly when it would re-
quire a constant effort to keep below the surface,
when almost everything is exactly that, the
mirror of a would-be alien who won't see how
much he is at home. In consequence also the
idea of change is briskly seasonal, it's too cold
& thus the scout-camp idea of revolution stands
in temporary composure, waiting for spring.

      from 'Questions for the Time Being',
      by J.H. Prynne, in *Poems*, 1999, p.112

Foreword
to the Second Edition

This is a re-issue of a book composed in 1993-5 (last draft 1997) and published in 2003. It was about the failure of conservative poets to write something worth reading and of conservative critics to move their halt line, their death line, beyond 1960. The subject matter was inherently controversial and the presentation caused some disagreements at the time of publication. While the consensus of scholars has progressively moved towards my interpretation, there is still room for a critical review of what I said back then. I have taken this opportunity, owed to the tolerance of a generous publisher, to amend some of its faults. I am aware that reissuing a book now 20 years old could be seen as a conservative act. I have tried to add more exact information and remove the generalisations.

FCon is not a one-volume history of modern British poetry. It was part of a four-volume work on modern British poetry when published. What eventually emerged was seven volumes. (I can't account for the three extra volumes. I just kept writing and trying to describe the material better.) The whole project is called *Affluence, Welfare, and Fine Words*.

What people most want is to find the good stuff without having to wade through the bad stuff. Imagine a TV series with 140 characters. How far do you have to go to give the viewers the ability to tell them apart? You have 140 modern poets of excellence. They are the scene, and the idea of any book is to get them across to the reader. It's no good printing-lists of facts. Obviously you do it by staging arguments, as provocative as possible so that the reader can only resolve them by reading the poems, and by delving into them learns or sharpens distinctions.

Because modern poetry is so little known, the booklist or shopping list is probably the most useful part of the book. Everyone I left out became my lifelong enemy. This list has cost a great deal of effort and soul-searching. After locating Kathleen Nott I had the problem that the 1960 book just wasn't so good, her books of 1947 and 1956 were the really excellent ones. I was worried about this but eventually I added a list of 1950s books which allowed me to get her name in there. I think the connoisseurs were unhappy to see the information about the good stuff made available to a profane public. The 'shopping list' of books of poetry in *FCon* was expanded by about 50 books over the years. I just didn't know enough in 1996. The 300 books are a formidable set of points for any theory to join up and cover. Writing about artistic ideologies, sets of stylistic structures which rise and unite several poets and fade, seemed adequate as thought material but could not also give salient accounts of all the 140 poets I was interested in. The apples push the (verbal) net out and it loses its shape. Yet this is a good way of capturing all those names, all those styles, in memory. The ideologies were beautiful even when they couldn't be realised.

I know people brandish the idea that 'there is no progress in art' and follow through to say 'therefore my poetry can't be out of date'. They wave Ernst Gombrich's *Kunst und Fortschritt* (Art and Progress). I can't explain why there is no progress in art and simultaneously conventional and old-sounding art is boring. I don't have to explain it. Gombrich did not say, 'Your poetry is not out of date'. The title should possibly have been, 'This device can't be 50 years out of date because I'm still using it'. The reply, from at least some parts of the public, was 'You *are* out of date, Bozo, because you have ignored every innovation of the last 50 years'. When we throw these accusations, they have to be right. Fairness depends on an accurate map of what was new.

The question of originality is too important to be dealt with at the unconscious level. Also, it involves the landscape as a whole; it is essentially about the relations between different poets within the large field of the other poets. In order to be fair to a poet being judged, you have to have a map of the public structure of stylistic conventions and changes. This is what *FCon* sets out to offer. You can't say that someone changed the norms unless you have a firm idea of what those norms were. By defining the creative phase you get closest to the creative core of a poet. Further, it is when you realise how conventional someone is that you become conscious of the convention and that something important about the scene swims into the foreground. Much of the detail of *FCon* is discussing what is up to date at several points in modern times, which has the further effect of locating what is out of date, weary, and clinging. This is not the way to make yourself popular. This volume only has to do that, it's not an evaluation of all the poetry in the period.

Classifying sensations does not get us to the end of our task. There is a deeper level of response that requires us to change. The goal is to get to the middle of a text and to have your centre where the centre of the text is. This produces an instability of viewpoint, a lack of solidity. I don't want to be a solid object. I think the idea of writing criticism is to identify the right psychological position to respond maximally to the art in question. This is a task that prevails over decades. This poetry responds to affection.

I took out the stuff about The Movement because no-one cares about them any more; they aren't worth attacking. I decided that all these flows of opinion are actually groups of people, and that therefore the attacks on conservatives had to go; instead I would empathise with them. Even if their empire seems to be made of rags and shadows. This will go down as the history that said that about 60% of the good poetry of the period came from the Underground or small-press area. This isn't a political statement, it's about aesthetic quality. Over 20 years, probably every year has seen the consensus move towards this position. A radical position becomes mainstream. It isn't either a claim to know the history of the underground. I collect a few hundred data points without covering the whole territory. I don't understand the history of the underground. Recently I have seen some generalisations about the underground, by participants, which I don't believe. This suggests that there is no consensus. So what is the history a history of? Dissidence is not a constitution. In contrast, I do have some texts. A few texts are patches of knowledge.

I notice a trend among critics of avoiding artistic judgments. I find this problematic. If the art is good, your experience of it is vivid. It is a strong memory, of definite shape. The judgement is the easiest thing to make. If there is no vivid experience to share, this game has to end because there is no ball to play with. We all have to go home. There is a case, isn't there, for throwing away poetry that yields no vivid sensations and no strong memories? It may be true that the more I express what I actually felt, the more people I alienate. This may also be the right route to take. There has been an unwritten rule since about 1974 (exact date missing!) that you can't publish a negative review of a female poet. This is a form of social anxiety. The consequence has been a withdrawal from honesty in the public sphere, where the rewards of honesty are meagre and anxiety is powerful. If the longer outcome is that people are scared to make honest artistic judgements, I have to protest. Inhibitions are not a form of prosperity. I don't care whether poetry was popular or not. I'm not interested. Poetry works as art or not at all. What is promoted as objectivity and professionalism is in fact a fear of displeasing influential and articulate people. Maybe professionalism is that, in its own right, abidingly.

One reviewer said he was desperately bored by the Scottish material. Dialectically, I decided to add a lot more about Scottish poetry. I briefly considered throwing out the English poets to make space. This was a projection of geographical bias; the reviewer was not interested in spending time in Scotland. It's the weather and the geology. Like a holiday destination. Maybe every aesthetic judgment is based on geographical perceptions and fantasies, defeating aesthetics. When I re-read *FCon*, I was amazed to see that the essay on George Mackay Brown had not made it into print. I experience a deep emotional regret about not writing enough, over the whole of *Affluence*, about him. So I have added an essay.

FCon was in part a critique of the mainstream and of poets or critics who rejected all the innovations that floated up after 1960. The first criticism I would make of it is that it seizes on the bad mainstream poetry and ignores the good mainstream poetry. A related problem is description of the bad poets in the innovative sector. I did not undertake this, largely to avoid confusing the message. Within *FCon*, specifically, this omission may have been misleading. I left out the poetry I find tedious. This does ask for a few words of explanation. There is no consensus about who is important, so let's start with the full set of poets who think their own work is Significant and who expect to find themselves covered (wrapped? uncovered?) in a book about modern poetry. That would be about 2,000 poets, I think. So in the end I wrote about the poets I like. Actually, I think some of my colleagues have written the history of tedious poetry. I don't believe the blurbs of books and I don't believe the opinions of the people who wrote the blurbs and massaged the market. Writing history is not just recycling what conservative (and even conniving) editors selected and silencing what they rejected. That is not the halt line.

Most of the poets discussed had careers after the cut-off point of 1997. I have decided not to describe these because I believe in frustration and believe it should be left intact. The basis of need is craving: to get why a poem published in 1986 was necessary, you have to reconstruct the limits of being alive in 1986, the need for new creativity, the heroic quality of original endeavour. To make everything available must mean satiation.

I see I have used a non-standard term: *mega-visual*. This refers to the production of oversized and blaring images, intrusive and authoritative, of which huge advertising hoardings and huge cinema screens are the most obvious examples. Yet the line goes back a long time. Both Nazi and Soviet art included an important mega-visual component, and this points back to antecedents in history painting for monarchs and others, public monuments, probably Roman imperial art, Pergamum, Egyptian royal art. The concept was developed by Peter Fuller.

The original edition did not thank anybody, because I was unhappy with the advice people had given me. This time I would like to acknowledge the contribution of Simon Smith and Harry Gilonis in compiling the original list of good books in 1995; and Paul Holman, Gavin Selerie, and John Goodby for precise and unusual information.

What Just Happened?

"It's also important to remember that in-group cooperation evolved
partly in response to competition between groups."
– *New Scientist*, 25/7/2015

Görtschacher's Time-Line of Poetry Magazines

It seems helpful to give a map of large-scale public movements, as
handholds. This account is based on the Austrian scholar Wolfgang Görtschacher's extraordinarily thorough study of little magazines, the most
detailed research yet done on our period. He names 4 periods: the 1950s;
the British Poetry Revival era of 1959-77, with a flourishing and creative
scene; a mass demise of magazines and conservative reaction from 1978
to 1985; and a period, hard to describe, from then up till 1993. In what
follows I paraphrase his account.

(1) The sterility and narrowness of the 1950s may have been related to the
scarcity of publishing outlets, as first paper shortages and then inflation
wiped out most of the little magazines. Wrey Gardiner records as one
of the reasons for giving up *Poetry Quarterly* in 1953: 'My printer's bill
was about ten times what it had been in 1940.' Malcolm Bradbury told
Görtschacher, 'The whole thing changed totally in the 1950s, because there
was this massive jump in printing costs. The whole world of magazines was
altered by the massive cost of printing one.' This was a decade in which
alternatives had literally disappeared.

(2) 'During the late 1950s and early 1960s an upsurge of little-magazine
and small-press activities occurred, which resulted in many British poets'
reception of American and Continental influences', followed by 'the
resurgence and proliferation of little magazines during the late 1960s'.
The expansion of higher education provided the social milieu for the new
magazines, and the 'Mimeograph Revolution' supplied the reprographic
capability: 'The proliferation of little magazines in the 1960s partly
occurred in consequence of technical developments, i.e. the conversion
from letterpress to offset printing, that enabled a single person to produce a
little magazine without any constraints as to aesthetic visual art.' This low-
cost technology ended, in the first half of the 1960s, the cultural dominance of London. An affluence of supply led to a luxuriation of styles. The
Arts Council's engagement with poetry, still trivial in 1964, took off in

1965-66. There was the 'heyday of little magazines in the late 1960s and early 1970s'; in the 1960s, there were 2,000 poetry magazines (p.503), but the numerical peak was in the early 1970s. These 'zines did tend to have low print quality, messy layouts, and stapled spines.

(3) The commodity boom of the 1970s multiplied the price of paper, and inflation eventually provoked consumer withdrawal: 'The late 1970s saw the greatest slaughter on the British little-magazine scene that had ever occurred.' 'The major cut in experimental magazines has produced lacunae of adequate forums...' A decrease in sales had (undiscussed) analogies in the decline of political enthusiasm. 'The swing back to conservatism that Jim Burns had ascertained in 1981 has manifested itself in most little magazines.' p.31. There is a drift towards photocopying, from low-grade typescript, and therefore to the A4 format, stapled.

(4) 'After a period of decline of little magazine activities during the late 1970s and early 1980s [...] the number of little magazines seems to have been catching up again with the heyday [of] the early 'seventies." In the second half of the 1980s, he says, 'This technical evolution [availability of microprocessors and desktop publishing (DTP)] and a reawakened enthusiasm for the arts – in consequence of the individual's retreat from public life to his self, motivated by a strong feeling of apathy towards politics in certain strata of British society – seem to have been responsible for [...] the second revival of little magazines after 1945.' The professionalisation of DTP packages and the advent of the desktop laser printer push little magazines and small presses to a new zenith of quality. '(L)ittle magazines have been booming since 1986, both in terms of sheer number of titles, contents, and quality of production...' p.211

We can check this 'fever chart' of gross activity levels in the poetry world against the chronology in Martin Booth's book, oriented more towards readings, which offers a decade of goodness and growth 1964-74 and a decade of decline and sterility 1974-84, which is when his treatment stops. Both readings and magazines are only here as measures of an overall metabolic rate of poetry: numbers and enthusiasm.

Census Of Books

I have sporadic counts for overall numbers of books being published: the Poetry Book Society checklist for 1960 gives 131 + 27 anthologies. Then

Poet's Yearbook for a year running 1976-7 gives 906 books + 68 anthologies. Then a count by the Arts Council gives 1944 books for 1995.

The number of titles has grown by a factor of thirteen. It is as if we are talking about two different eras here: the position of 1957 is irrecoverable. In between has come the arrival of lifestyle choice as the central thing in everyone's life, even if that also means the growth of commercialism to supply the disposables which the choice requires. Without much doubt, the change has been good for the reader but bad for critics who want their expertise to be intact in the face of data too rapid and diverse to assimilate. That is: you can have whatever poetry you want but you can't have the information that would let you get at it. These figures agree with what Görtschacher says. It is evident that reviewing takes account of the merest fraction of this deluge. The good part is that there may be a whole undiscovered country, and the book I am writing holds the key. The bad part is I also only know about a fraction of this material.

Poet's Yearbook runs, awkwardly, from June to June. Its volume for 1978 shows about 25% titles from High Street publishers and 75% from "small presses". The huge growth in output from small to micro-businesses is a key feature of the era. Were all the uncommercial concerns running radical, innovative, underground poetry? No, the two categories overlap but many of the artists were just unsuccessful mainstream poets. Conversely many advanced and unconventional poets had relations with commercial publishers.

In the period 1960 to 1997, it follows, there were something in the region of 28,000 volumes of poetry published in this country. The expansion itself caused strains and distortions associated with rapid growth. The public did not keep up with developments in poetics and a reaction of incomprehension to the new poetry was widespread. Let's just imagine that you have to read 1000 of these books, chosen at random (and not on the basis of a critic recommending them). You would probably think, as you sat down in a room full of books (locked from the outside of course), that most of them would be repeats: reruns of standard clusters of ideas and effects, made vague by the imprecise faculties of the second-rate, blunt instruments battering at an unresponsive clay. Is this a fair picture? it is something being imagined, but the weight of the term *mainstream* is that it is a turn-off, an idea of the tedious that operates to prevent you from reading a poem.

GOOD BOOKS OF THE 1950s

1950
Christopher Fry, *Venus Observed*;
George Barker, *True Confession of George Barker* (part 1);
Peter Hellings, *Firework Music* (no date but circa 1949 or 1950)

1951 Lynette Roberts, *Gods with Stainless Ears*;
Dorian Cooke, *Fugue for Our Time*;
Peter Yates, *Light and Dark*;
Charles Causley, *Farewell Aggie Weston*

1952
David Jones, *The Anathémata*;
Andrew Young, *Into Hades*;
W.H. Auden, *Nones*;
Kathleen Raine, *The Year One*;
Roland Mathias, *The Roses of Tretower*;
Edwin Morgan, *The Vision of Cathkin Braes*. (Young's poem was followed by a sequel in 1958 and it would be eccentric not to read them together.)

1953
Edith Sitwell, *Gardeners and Astronomers*;
Robert Graves, *Poems 1953* (*viz.* Collected Poems);
Adam Drinan, *Script from Norway*;
Patrick Anderson, *The Colour as Naked*

1954
Glyn Jones, *The Dream of Jake Hopkins*;
F.T. Prince, *Soldiers Bathing*;
Dylan Thomas, *Collected Poems 1933-52*; *Under Milk Wood*;
George Barker, *A Vision of Beasts and Gods*;
Roy Fuller, *Counterparts*;
Alan Ross, *Something of the Sea*;
Eithne Wilkins, *Oranges and Lemons* (in a magazine only)

1955
W.S. Graham, *The Nightfishing*;
Charles Tomlinson, *The Necklace*
1956 Hugh MacDiarmid, *In memoriam James Joyce*;
Kathleen Nott, *Poems from the North*;

Christopher Logue, *Devil, Maggot, and Son*

1957
Audrey Beecham, *The Coast of Barbary*;
David Gascoyne, *Night Thoughts*;
Terence Tiller, *Reading a Medal*;
Roy Fuller, *Brutus' Orchard*;
Ted Hughes, *The Hawk in the Rain*

1958
Alan Ross, *To Whom it May Concern*

1959
George Mackay Brown, *Loaves and Fishes*;
Christopher Logue, *Songs*;
Geoffrey Hill, *For the Unfallen*;
Peter Redgrove, *The Collector*

I haven't read the Yates volume but to be fair I have read his other books and this one is rare. *45-60*, ed. Thomas Blackburn, is the best anthology.

Anyone looking at surviving documents from the 1950s is likely to say that the scene was in a parlous state and that there was a revival. There is some dispute about when things got better. People like to instrumentalise the change, saying something like 'poetry revived when my publishing firm got started' or 'poetry was *so* monochrome until I arrived on the scene and then everything burst into bloom'. To some extent, the ability to ignore when the breakout actually happened depends on conservative critics who denied that it was happening and created an image of sterile conformism. For some people, the greyness of the 1950s lasted until the 1980s. The 'liberation event' is something which both managers and poets *urgently want to claim* as part of their personal trail of achievements and assets, and this is why it is claimed at dozens of different years. The repression process is never claimed as a first person act by any cultural manager but the amount of liberation cannot possibly be greater in quantity than the amount of repression which it undoes. The act of repression is itself repressed from memory. Still it was the 1960s when the numbers of poets and the scope of poetry expanded. It's like British 1950s pop music, British 1950s cinema. Everything got better in the 1960s. In the 1960s. Other claims are instrumentalisations. I don't think you can take a deluge and put it into a pipe and claim to own the pipe.

It would be unfair to depict the 1950s simply as the desert from which life started and not look at what was actually happening at that time. There were certainly people writing poetry. But as you speak of the big take-off in the 1960s, barriers being burst, etc., it is easier to speak of the 1950s as a greyed out decade. I think you can say a lot of people were frustrated.

The issue of mid-century cultural decline asks to be explained.

HOMOGENEITY

Kenneth Allott's standard anthology of mid-century poetry, titled *British Poetry 1918-60* (first edition 1950, though) is a summary of the poetic culture which mainstream poets in 1960 had access to. I counted that 40.8% of the poets included had studied at Oxford university. Some 40 years later, the entries for British poets in *The Oxford Companion to Twentieth Century Poetry in English*, edited by Ian Hamilton (1994), include 367 names of whom 111 studied at Oxford University – a mere 30%. That is, the 20th century draws to an end and Oxford is still dominant. This makes us ask if the standard kind of poem was actually being written by a standard kind of person. One way of reacting is to suggest fantastic levels of bias for Allott and Hamilton. That does not work very well, they were basically recording the standard picture. Another way is to feel gratitude – these writers made efforts to give us pleasure, they rose above simply recording personal experience and into literature. Another is to see it as the realisation in aesthetic terms of the power structure of a society.

I read a work on genealogy which looked at a large set of saints in a European country and reckoned that most of them were related to the royal family in the region they lived in. The spiritual hierarchy is intimately related to the ranking of men in the society of daylight and real estate. Rather than seeing social prestige as an accidental quality of a high proportion of the poets who achieved cultural prestige, we could see their literary success as a passive and smooth delivery of the social prestige to an audience who were highly sensitive to that kind of thing and who wanted to consume it. This delivery of relations of property and competitive success (in exams and so on) carried things which already existed – it would be truly perverse, in this circuit, to be anything except conservative. A critical attitude could only damage the commodity which was the essential charge of the reading experience. The poetry book would then be like a weekend in a tourist destination, to be exact Oxford. You would not start such a weekend by blowing up all the buildings.

Almost none of the people on the scene would tolerate this *delivery of prestige* as a statement of poetic intent. The Left sympathies prevail throughout, and there is no neo-conservative party in poetry, as in other arts. But it is debatable that this is the unconscious rule of the game. If you start to say that you want to make everything conscious, you must overturn the rules of poetry – the intuitive practices which are also the lair of conservative values. We have reached a crisis here – the poetry which challenges everything is the only valid response to the burden of inherited culture and wealth, but simultaneously the new language it produces is unrecognisable and uncomfortable for the existing audience. It would be necessary to invent a new marketing system and a new audience for it to live in. Actually, this is what happened; new language, new audience, new distribution network, all came about.

Everyone in the EngLit business shares the same staple culture, the same carbohydrate pack of texts and clever remarks. But people from Oxford have more of it. The textbooks used by schools and other universities are likely to be by Oxford graduates. The industry has a vertical structure: some places are closer to the apex than others. The apex is, probably, in a certain group of streets in Oxford. Thus the dominant poem reproduces the axis of domination of the literature industry. But there is a public which is not tied to universities. They are not expected to put their artistic feelings into organised prose. Reading the reviews may give a distorted view because there is this wider audience whose reactions are less organised (and more aesthetic), and less vocal.

The community believed it was open but was noticeably homogeneous. The identification we talked about was exceptionally easy to carry out because it was covering such a short distance. Is identification a form of narcissism? A lot of poets suspect that the reader – a certain reader, a group of readers, anyone – does not identify with their poems because they belong to the wrong social class or the wrong ethnic group. This is unverifiable and people who invest in that belief may be blocked off from criticising their own writing and so from improving it beyond the most basic level of assertion and recitation. It is helpful to discuss the act of identification but it may not be possible in the end to drag it out into the light of day. It belongs in the depths and it may explode if you bring it to the surface where pressure is low. I think the immigrant (or second-generation immigrant, etc.) people in the literary world do well to ask how the identification and intimacy constitutive for that world (which would dissolve without them) work in relation to ethnicity and how far the content of the work of art is an offered self which also has a sociological identity. I imagine that identification is the key institution in the culture we have ('we' may have a boundary here) and that it deserves study in the same way that the law does when you are interested in how society works. Every linguistic act involves categorisation as its basic component. With very few exceptions, Allott leaves out Scottish and Welsh poets. Perhaps he just felt unhappy outside Southern England. I don't think you can make identification a conscious act, but you can be clever about the things you can modulate.

Close reading may have functioned as a premature reprisal against attempts to define the literary act as ethnocentric. However, its popularity with its owners may have been unconsciously an admission that the act was indeed one of narcissism and group egocentricity. Allott used Close Reading to identify 40.8% of significant poets as being Oxford products. In fact close reading was a product of Cambridge, to a large extent. Empiricism is a key principle and I would not want to blank out its purpose. It was there to capture ideology, to drag it to the surface and destroy it by exposure to air. It did not follow that identification, liking, and trust were also detained. But those psychological events acted like ideology. The majority of all complaints in poetry politics are ones about, *you identified with him, gave him all your time, gave him all the space, and did not give all that to me.* That would hardly be so if these acts were not the central institutions

Cultural conversation is made more comfortable by homogeneity, but it also has the result that everyone talented is a dissident and an internal exile.

Kulturkritik

The complement of the m-stream is the culturally critical poet, the intellectual as poet.

The cultural critic does not present experience as an object of consumption but criticises it and makes it vanish while the shadow of a new and unlived possibility flickers across it.

The cultural critic does not offer personalities as identification objects but depicts social roles as the product of power relations and manipulations producing alienated behaviour cycles when their origins are crushed into unconsciousness by the mass of repetition.

The cultural critic takes the elementary structures of everyday life, simple hand-object loops like sewing, and recovers from them deep histories and the trace of history, the repeated action sequences which are typical for a society and which embody its deep cognitive programming.

The cultural critic is not lost in abstraction but sees in the fabric of everyday life conscious decisions buried by time and which can become the fabric of a truly radical intellectual activity.

For the cultural critic everything can be replayed, the past is not frozen. Where the phonetics of the language spoken in England could be Frisian rather than Anglian, where every temporal series is virtual and can be replayed by a set of transforms just as much as they are stored in categories and symbolic sets.

For this person the idealised Bavarian village running round the bottom of the glass from which you drink your Erdinger is as significant as the rent levels in the block opposite the pub.

For the cultural critic there is no discontinuity between the processes of radical philosophy and the crises of everyday life, of sexual choice, of being rejected, of afternoon shopping, of subjective freedom and anxiety.

The cultural critic can deal with the utterances of politicians and business satraps as effortlessly as with Danish avant-garde poets, and put up a good fight with Treasury experts.

For the cultural critic Blake's poetry and speculative thought are two forms of the same thing; for them the accepted history of society is the transcript of a speculative fantasy on the lines of Blake's; for them both the future and the past are the result of speculations, for whom the fitting of parts into a pattern is as real as putting clay into a mould to bake bricks.

For the cultural critic writing directly onto an object, say a flint nodule, is like thinking within the restrictions of a mathematical thesis whose known axioms produce unforeseen properties; and every mathematical theorem can be viewed as a three-dimensional object, in the object park; and a poem is like a collection of objects.

The cultural critic looks for a basic thermodynamic plausibility as the test of every hypothesis.

The cultural critic is devoted to improvisation – and has a vast stock of completed improvisations as a lexicon of esoteric forms.

For the cultural critic the design of appliances like electricity substations and personal computers is the product of serial intellectual, economic, and aesthetic acts. Which are subject to intellectual critique or admiration as much as the design of an estate.

For the cultural critic the poem is not pulled painfully from memory but drawn from a matrix of ideas which respond to intelligence and answer intellectual questions. It is the theory of itself.

The cultural critic lives in a liminal ground where intense limited stimulus fields allow a basis for concentration, and this allows the Utopian grounds to be seen palpably & resisting attacks; they are around us and we are in them. Where the symbolic descends into wrought physical objects and works them again.

The cultural critic lives on montage and can write texts with a thousand splices from 200 sources that produce a result unrecognisable as any of the source texts – a dimension faster, faster by an order of magnitude.

The cultural critic thrives on the cults of a thousand elective ancestors whose trajectory inspires and amazes.

Sigh. That's so wonderful. We are allowed to ask if any flesh and blood person actually lives up to that. The intellectual is deeply annoying. It's not enough to be right. That language of criticism and clarity and insistence is the sound of authority. You can't just use the language of the dominant the entire time or you will be as unpopular as politicians. As soon as you say *me anthropologist – you native* the bond of sympathy vanishes. But it is all about truth –once it's true it's irrelevant that it irritates you.

One of Adorno's essays was presented as a talk at a 1958 *Kultur-kritikerkongress*, a congress of cultural critics. Needless to say, Adorno wrote an essay where he criticised the idea of cultural criticism.

THE STANDARD POEM 1960-97

This period is short enough for one abiding poem-type to be described as its typical output. I have a 'site-type' which exhibits the kind of poetry I am talking about – a volume called *Poetry Dimension 2*, from 1974, which only includes one kind of poetry. The density of the poetry-writing group allowed a standard poem to last for 30 years, whatever out-groups were breaking out a few miles away. At one level this stability is a source of great frustration for people living through the period. It wasn't such a great commodity in the first place. At another level, this is where people of the time were – you have to go there to find them – and its persistence must indicate that somebody liked it.

In about 2005, my co-editor at *Angel Exhaust* described a first book he was reviewing by a young poet as being made up entirely of rewrites of well-known poems by poets of the day. They were from different poets, they were up to date, but each poem had an identifiable model, its surprise was something remembered. He wrote a really nice review of this not very bright poet, not mentioning the derivation of the ideas. I was impressed by his knowledge of the mainstream, he'd actually read all that junk. One function of the literary centre is to offer standard poems that will serve as models for most amateur poems. This is a public service, reassuring people that they are writing in the correct way. The lack of originality is vital to this function. Anxiety is always part of cultural attainment, and conformity is close to comfort. It may be that most poems written in 1969 (let's say) were realisations of standard models which people had seen in poetry magazines or in prize-winning books. I don't think we can list all the poem types of the era, but we can set out with two vulnerable poets, they're called Bill and Betty, they met at Oxford and graduated in 1959, married in 1960, and won second and first places in the Allott-Shallott Prize in 1961. Their friends reassured them that what they were doing was right. By writing in a validated and regulated way they were able to say, at every point, *Look, I've won the poem.* It would be churlish to dispute this verdict. Bill and Betty spent 40 years writing approvable poems. They won Allott-Shallott prizes again in 2001. It was like a friend of theirs who in 1956 bought a set of those excessively long wooden salad-servers, which were only ever used for serving salad and were a way of drawing attention to the flow of consumer goods, that new thing in the later 1950s when austerity was over, so that fresh vegetables were on sale and you could buy essentially unnecessary things. *Look, I've won the salad.* And lo, it was so. They had won the salad and their poetic gestures were approved by other people like them. And yet...

We spoke of a standard poem, and the poem was notably:

Unhedonistic. Lack of interest in style and structure can be seen as a dislike of play and so as part of this joylessness.

Anti-rhetorical. Rhetoric is felt to block empirical knowledge. There is an unconscious idea of reaching absolute truth by reducing language to one dimension, the strength of one cognitive faculty, something quite literal. Limits affecting cognition. The poetry is notably plain and similar to prose. An alternative means for the expression of emotion and emphasis has not been found.

Offers someone as central identification figure and makes a promise of reality. This means that the conventions of society are the cellular substance of the poem. The poem feels like natural language and unmodified social experience. The central figure is a Christian academic, a member of the professional classes. (Not being Christian or academic would be a revolt.) The poem offers the sound of a voice as an element of comfort; the continuity of the voice is what defines the poem as finished.

Brief. The poem fits into a slot in magazines which has a preset extent. It deals with a single incident or moment of insight, normally, to match this size limit. There is also a cognitive rhythm which is just right for picking up the information set out in such a poem. This is a boundary and poems which ignore it are *in breach*.

Respects boundaries. Linguistic tact means social tact which turns out to mean deep respect for property boundaries. However education offers a way up.

Unimaginative. The poem poses a writer in a situation which as it is not otherwise specified lapses back into the rules of conduct of twentieth-century England. Abdicating the ideas level means that the existing rules dominate the poem, which has less and less chance of escaping. The poem is lacking in hope. (It is only fair to add that empiricism was designed as a way of dispelling general ideas and so of a hope of getting out to a new situation.) Read in bulk, these poems are passive and defend existing values and relations.

Passes tests of moral fitness. The designated way of reading the poem is to fit its statements into a model of the writer's moral reactions and to accumulate these to form a moral diagram of the writer which would be compared with other writers in a grand test of fitness to serve. Because the poet selects the subject of the poem, this feels like an exam where the only candidate has set all the questions. Its results become less convincing for that reason. The planned response pattern includes utterances like 'unlike the modernist writers who flirted with totalitarianism, Bill shows an exquisite interest in ordinary people and yet is morally restrained enough to dislike them.' This kind of thing is not pleasurable to read but at least you know what you're supposed to do. The poet is invested in a role of social control, and other people generally appear in order to be judged.

Empirical. The poet strives for concrete details and to notice things. This focus on external detail is concomitant with an inability to write about ideas or emotions. The senses are felt to be the messengers of everything which is true and reliable.

Easy to assimilate. The poems are compatible with each other in shared contexts like anthologies or magazines. Once you have read 100 of them reading more is remarkably easy.

This poetry has almost all the virtues of prose and almost none of the virtues of poetry.

Two more comments. First, disenchantment. A preferred subject is the loss of religion, of collective feeling, of belief in an artist or political idea. The mass of reviews of poetry in the respectable magazines very rarely give it a grade higher than gamma+. The judicious and cold attitude of academics towards heated adolescents seems to have reproduced itself in poems by academics as scepticism towards art and experience. Secondly, the shift away from metre and towards the colloquial. There was an ideal of the formalist poem (as defined by Eric Homberger at pages 88-101) which the mainstream was moving away from in the early 1960s. He says in his chapter on the 1950s, 'In poetry, we call it an age of formalism, uniform to both England and America. By formalism we mean the interposition of *technical* imperatives between the poet and "reality".' The new thing, from maybe 1964, was to delete all technical imperatives – creating a new banality separate *both from academic poetry and from the innovative sector*. It is important that a core feature was actually disappearing within the period – which therefore cannot be homogeneous. It is less clear that the many individuals who moved from regular verse to irregular actually changed the sound of their poetic voice while doing so. It was not a violent transition.

'The poems display a sensuousness, a feeling for tangs, hardnesses, distances, for the muscularity of nature.' (Anon. in the TLS, reviewing *The Fugue and Shorter Pieces*, 1960, by John Holloway). This sums up so much of the wishes of the time. I like Holloway's poetry, but he was a Fellow of Queen's College, Cambridge, not a sailor or shepherd. This sensuous bias was the predilection of a group who were working mainly as teachers or critics and scholars, their profession did not involve objects at all. The sensuous thing seems inherently a wish or denial, and surely writing poetry of ideas would have been more attainable. The rubric of the volume (*Poetry Dimension 2*) as best poems of the year reminds us of another thing – the need to keep producing. There was a community of the poem and they would have been in disarray if the flow of poems had stopped. This supply could though be like a works canteen where you eat every day – but don't much like the food. It is The Daily Pittance.

Many of the poems could be described as written to fulfil remarks made in reviews in the *TLS*, *Poetry Review*, or *Critical Quarterly*. Those reviews form a coherent mass. The solidarity between reviewers, poets, and readers was very high. Unfortunately, the implication of this interpenetration was that when new poetry came to be written there would be a fierce struggle for it to get published and reviewed. Internalising one set of verbal patterns defined other patterns as Wrong and Impossible and not fit to publish. The effect of doing art together is to become homogeneous and surely that leads to being tedious. I can claim to be suffering from Post-tedium traumatic apathy disorder, a condition in which extreme boredom leads to a prolonged inability to react to stimuli. There is such a thing as loss of empathy through boredom. Empathy generally improves with age but experience of terribly tedious poetry turns it off and leaves you disastrously unable to navigate through a world filled with other people.

The mid-century decline had some connection with long-term developments within the core of Oxford literati and their shared norms. The data suggest that the 1920s generation at Oxford were awesomely talented and that the mid century decline of English poetry was inseparable from the weakness of their successors, which was due to a literary investment in models (W.H. Auden, John Betjeman) which didn't work out. The issues were to do with the detailed conventions for writing a poem and also for reading and approving it. The decay of the models may have had to do with the decline of the Anglican Church and with a withdrawal from modernism and early commitments. The dip was resolved by an adaptation of these models (which actually preserved some of their essential features), presumably during the 1980s and 1990s. The sense of superiority and urgent grand destiny felt by the Underground was only sustainable up till then, while conventional writers and commentators were suffering from this debilitating shortage of creativity. I suspect that both the mainstream and the Underground positions have collapsed, and that young poets now are faced by a strange and unexplained situation.

TRIUMPH OF THE MOBILE

Donald Davie's 1989 book on poetry from 1960-88 does not find any poets since 1960 to like. This is a failure of an obvious kind, but what he says about legitimacy is interesting. Davie believes he knows a contract or compact between poet and reader which (all) modern poets fail to keep to. That is, the compact is one-sided, he controls it, and he refuses to change it. Radical democratic politics was the basis for radical poetics, and the wish to dissolve boundaries and for *distributed powers* is the motive for writing in a modern way. The situation is, though, that each poet offers a speculative poetic grammar and the reader guesses what it is and applies it and the guess is confirmed by recognition of pattern within the parts and the whole of the poem. There is a capture spiral as the text reveals its structure to you. There is no written theory of modern poetry, you learn it directly, inside the texts, by intuitions which the text confirms. When your guess coincides with the poem, there are a million prickles of gratification, a million papillae tingling with the taste, a mirror effect where the approval of the poet is the gratification sought for. The closed pattern has opened itself to you. The modern thing heightens your powers of association, turns you into a volatile state, drifting around as a kind of self-vapour. But you had to be volatile to even set the process in motion, and there is a 'modern moment' where the reader just cannot see what they are supposed to do. The whole exercise is a puzzle. The gratification is a filter and this is how poetry becomes a minority pursuit. Variation is no longer defined as failure. Indeed the boundary between a poem and other kinds of language may be in this volatility and mobility – so, not in a link to Oxford and punts.

In this volume, I write about poetry as if it were understandable through chronology. Time is a way of explaining why a poet and a reader shoot right past each other and semantic webs tangle and ravel rather than forming a beautiful nervous textile. The grammar of a poem does not belong to the poet, it is a public arrangement. We could even call it an institution; the period was, politically, one of radical dissatisfaction with institutions, and radical reforms. It is subject to argument. The notion of volatility explains how I can find an atmosphere changing even within a five-year period, while also suggesting that time-bound moods can make strange styles easier to understand. You just need to be excitable and volatile. But the underground is not unified, it is not following one single time-line. There is not a *single* modern poem nor a *single* set of artistic rules. The alternative poetry is viral, it reproduces itself inaccurately in a million variants, generating new information which is itself the reward for reading.

Randall Stevenson's is the standard account. He writes about large-scale processes without trying to distinguish good poetry from bad. What I am doing is more like a restaurant guide, it selectively emphasises the good stuff. Stevenson also seems uneasy about the small press world, being generous about its importance while saying that evaluation of it has yet to happen. This area of blankness suggests that his standard history is not yet complete. So this theme of legitimation is still pervasive. I am not saying that you can *market* these unusual books, just that a history should include them as parts of its narrative and stage sets. I listed all the reviews in *Poetry Review* in our period. It came to over 1,100 poets as review subjects. There is a corps of professional reviewers, in the serious magazines. Academic historians have tended to go straight to those reviews, and history is based on them. But in the whole period the magazines had an unstated rule that small press books did not get reviewed. They were not 'for the trade' and bookshops did not want to stock them; it was hard for readers to find them. Librarians and bookshop owners wanted *sound* advice. So the available accounts mostly leave out the small press poetry in its entirety. The failure of conservatism is not just the artistic failure of mainstream poetry (for the most part and with very significant exceptions) but the cultural failure of conservative gate-keepers to receive, review, explain the reformed poetics of the time, and to concede that a new landscape existed.

If several thousand people thought their poetry was good enough to publish, that argues for a collapse of belief in authority. Most of that poetry was not good enough to publish. I am inclined to conceal this – it would be tragic if people found out that poetry is difficult. This is (also) an era where publishers forgot how to say No – the technology and incidence of costs coincided with aesthetic libertarianism and the two fed on the result.

WHAT JUST HAPPENED?

An 'actor' living in the scene often divides it into 'people who get with what I do' and 'people who don't like me and would not publish me'. This gives a binary division. If you mapped the dual divisions of a hundred actors onto one diagram, you would not find that they coincided. Hence the scene is not really binary. But the intuitive maps are what people steer by.

People are equipped to make cultural choices, and that equipment constitutes the history of poetry. There are turn-offs and turn-ons, rapid allover reactions to surface signs. They are a mechanism by which the memory of bad experiences is stored up to use in future choices: it is stored as reactions to stylistic features, and becomes their meaning. The features are important because they are the way we navigate through the oceans of literary text. I mentioned 28,000 books – people were saying no to most of them, so the NO decision is the key one, always, and it is based on stylistic traits. Poets may want to forget about style because it's all about their personality, which they intend to be liked – but the personality is hidden in language and the language is saturated in markers of style which readers intuitively react to.

This has been a period of poetry in which the retail economy only displays the mainstream, which is caught up in the recycling of prestige, and there is an outsider sector, an Underground which you can't find in the High Street, and is never reviewed in the magazines you can find in W.H. Smith, which attracts hundreds of poets who are unconventional both linguistically and personally, and which piles up an alternative literature (which is neglected by academic historians). Not every datum, every moment of literary activity, confirms this overall pattern, but it is robust enough to account for a great deal of what people were doing and feeling in the period –and it is the story which this book tells. The failure it describes is the artistic failure of the great majority of poets 'in the trade', writing conservatively to capture an existing market and getting lost in the rapid changes which were an effect of a market economy. I thought of writing a follow-up called *the success of conservatism* – the visible poetry scene is remarkably conservative and the most radical writers are still invisible to the market. It is not attractive to watch people spending so much time either writing theoretical proofs that a kind of poetry which they haven't read is incapable of moral integrity, or getting paranoid about the reluctance of the book trade to accept their goods, and the unworthiness of the managers and indeed the poetry world in general, but people are trapped in the patterns of the time, and to be free of them would be to depart from the time. Conversely, not to understand them is not to grasp the time. I have to give an account of what people actually felt and said. Mutual hostility was quite a big part of that.

One version of what happened is this. You start with the decline of priests. A wave of secularisation is washing everything away. The phase of secular intellectuals that prevails is pseudo-priests, they are still carrying out moral instruction and judgment, if without the sanction of Scripture. In poetry, you have Christian lay academics who want to be moral authorities. This is their legitimation as critics and as poets (the poems are for weekends). Then come a generation of Marxists who want to judge and control everything, including the imagination. They are acutely aware of being in competition with the 1950s academics, and they compete by being super-moralists. They construct a crystalline world of pitiless simplicity and virtue. In it, almost everything which actually exists is judged to be corrupt. Their students are on their side and even try to out-compete them with designer Marxisms. Then this programme collapses. The bubble bursts. There follows a regression to ludic poetry and to suavity. The intellectuals don't feel able to control events and have reason to doubt their ability to explain them. The word *post-modern* was popular to suggest a kind of salvation knowledge which the intellectuals still managed as a commodity.

Versions of the Chronology of Style

Because the notion of 'style history' refers to a public and collective practice, an eccentric view of it is wrong rather than 'personal'. I have therefore collected a number of accounts of things happening in poetry, in the period 1960 to 1997, and searched them for statements about style history. Everything starts with an individual book, and most critics are too happy identifying with a single poet, whose style is probably quite stable, to get into ideas about overall change. It is too tempting to rebadge your favourite poet as 'innovatory' simply as a way of saying you like them.

The search has involved full-scale treatments in books in the libraries I use. More views could be extracted from introductions to anthologies, book jackets, or reviews in magazines, but these were too difficult to marshal. Charles Tomlinson's reviews of the British scene in *Poetry* (Chicago) around 1960 are classics, but that is to name just one set of articles.

These books are being interrogated only for their views on the evolution of poetic style, and not for anything else.

Some books about modern British poetry that have been searched for versions of style:time change –

1960s
(1-2) British Council pamphlets *Poetry Today* by Geoffrey Moore and Elizabeth Jennings (1958 and 1961)
(3) Morgan, Kathleen *Christian Themes in Contemporary Poetry* (1965)
(4) Orr, Peter, ed., *The Poet's Voice* (radio interviews with poets) (1966)
(5) Alvarez, Alfred (certain essays in) *Beyond All This Fiddle* (1968)
(6) Jones, Glyn, *The Eagle Has Two Tongues* (1968)
(7) Dodsworth, Martin, ed., *The Survival of Poetry* (1970)

(We could add Tomlinson in *Poetry*, and a legendary article by Denise Levertov in *Kulchur* (1962). These are the first statements of the corruption of the mainstream thesis.)

1970s
(8) Lucie-Smith, Edward, notes in his anthology *Poetry since 1945* (1970)
(9) Miller, Karl, ed. *Memoirs of a Modern Scotland* (1971)
(10) Raban, Jonathan, *The Society of the Poem* (1971)
(11) Schmidt, Michael and Lindop, Grevel, eds. *British Poetry Since 1960*, (1972)

(12) Seymour-Smith, Martin, a section in *Guide to Modern World Literature* (1972)

(13-14) Thwaite, Anthony *Poetry Today* (3 editions, 1973-96, for the British Council); and *Twentieth Century English Poetry*, 1978

(15) Hamilton, Ian, *A Poetry Chronicle* (1973)

(16) Thurley, Geoffrey *The Ironic Harvest* (1974)

(17) Fulton, Robin *Modern Scottish Poetry: Context and Individuals* (1974)

(18-19) Grigson, Geoffrey, *The Contrary View* (1974); *Blessings, Kicks, and Curses* (1982)

(20) *Akros* 28 (1974) is a survey, of Scottish poetry from 1920-74, at book length; *Akros* issues 29-44 then provided long surveys of many individual poets. editor: Duncan Glen

(21) Mottram, Eric, catalogues to PCL Conferences 1974 and 1977

(22) Homberger, Eric *The Art of the Real* (1977)

(23) Holbrook, David *Lost Bearings in English Poetry* (1977)

(24) Fraser, G.S., *Essays on 20th C Poets* (1977)

(25) Fisher, Roy interviews (in: *Nineteen Poems and an Interview*, 1977; and *Gargoyle* 24). The most important theoretical statements of the period, now reprinted in *Interviews through Time*.

(26) Hobsbaum, Philip, *Tradition and Experiment in British Poetry* (1979)

(27) King, P.R. *9 Modern Poets: a Critical Introduction* (1979)

(28) Jones, Peter and Schmidt, Michael, eds., *British Poetry Since 1970* (1980)

1980s

(29) Raine, Kathleen, *The Poet's Journey into the Interior* (1982) (see also her magazine Temenos, *passim*)

(30) Hooker, Jeremy *Poetry of Place* (1982)

(31) Conran, Tony *The Cost of Strangeness* (1982)

(32) Ryan, M.P., *Career Patterns in British Poetry* (1982) doctoral thesis based on interviews with 30 poets

(33) Middleton, Christopher *The Pursuit of the Kingfisher* (1983)

(34) Easthope, Antony *Poetry as Discourse* (1983)

(35) Weatherhead, A. Kingsley, *The British Dissonance* (1983)

(36) Crozier, Andrew 'Thrills and Frills' (in: Sinfield, Alan, ed., *Literature and Society 1945-70*) (1983)

(37) Tomlinson, Charles, essay in volume 8 of the *New Pelican Guide to English Literature*, ed. Boris Ford (1983) (this is more or less identical with his essay in the previous edition, 10 years earlier)

(38) Riley, Peter, *Spitewinter Provocations*, interview, in *Reality Studios* 5 (1985)

(39) Mathias, Roland, *A Ride Through the Woods* (1985)

(40) Booth, Martin *British Poetry 1964-84: Driving Through the Barricades* (1985)

(41) Fisher, Allen *Necessary Business* (1985)

(42) Lucas, John *Modern English Poetry from Hardy to Hughes* (1986)

(43) Hooker, Jeremy *The Presence of the Past* (1987)

(44) Mole, John, *Passing Judgments: Poetry in the Eighties: Essays from Encounter* (1988)

(45) Essays on Scottish poetry in Cairns Craig, ed., collective work, *Scottish Literature*, vol. 4, *the 20th Century* (1988)

(46) Robinson, Alan, *Instabilities in Contemporary British Poetry* (1988)

(47) Jackaman, Rob. *The Course of English Surrealist Poetry* (1989)

(48) Davie, Donald *Under Briggflatts: British Poetry 1960-88* (1989)

Since 1990

(49) Morgan, Edwin *Crossing the Border* (1990)

(50) Allchin, Donald *Praise above all: Discovering the Welsh Tradition* (1991)

(51-52) Moore-Gilbert, Bart, and Seed, John, eds, *Cultural Revolution?* (1992); Moore-Gilbert, Bart, ed., *Cultural Catastrophe* (1994) both include essays on poetry by Robert Sheppard

(53) *Sglefrio ar Eiriau*, golygydd/edited by John Rowlands (two of the essays are about modern poetry in Welsh) (1992)

(54) Riley, Denise, ed. *Poets on Writing 1970-91* (1992)

(55-57) Crawford, Robert *Devolving English Literature* (1992); *Identifying Poets: Self and Territory in 20th Century Poetry* (1993); introduction to anthology *The Penguin Book of British Poetry Since 1945* (1998)

(58) Chevalier, Tracy, ed., *Contemporary Poets* (the St James Guide) (1992); previous editions contain some poets not included in this one; the 1970 issue was edited by Rosalie Murphy, the 1975 and 1980 issues by James Vinson, the 1985 issue by Vinson and D.L. Kirkpatrick.
This contains essential information about the external careers of hundreds of poets. Each poet makes a statement about their work.

(59) Görtschacher, Wolfgang, *Little Magazine Profiles 1949-93* (1993)

(60) Barry, Peter, and Hampson, Robert, eds., *New British Poetries: The Scope of the Possible* (1993)

(61) Corcoran, Neil, *British Poetry Since 1940* (1993)

(62) Jackaman, Rob *A Study of Cultural Centres and Margins in British Poetry Since 1950. Poets and Publishers* (1995)

(63) Acheson, James, and Huk, Romana, eds, *Modern British Poetry* (1995)

(64) Ludwig, Hans-Werner, and Fietz, Lothar, eds. *Poetry in the British Isles: Non-metropolitan Traditions* (1995)

(65) Kennedy, David, *Changed Relations* (1996)

(66) Gregson, Ian, *British Poetry and Postmodernism* (1996)

(67) Bush, Clive, *Out of Dissent* (1997)

(68) Docherty, Brian and Day, Gary, eds., *British Poetry from the 1960s to the 1990s: Politics and Art* (1997)

(69) Clarke, Adrian (papers in) *Millennial Dialogues and Three Papers* (1998)

(70) O'Brien, Sean, *The Deregulated Muse* (1998)

(71) Tuma, Keith *Fishing by Obstinate Isles* (1999)

(72) Fisher, Roy *Interviews Through Time*(2000)

(73) Marks, Alison and Rees-Jones, Deryn, eds. *Contemporary Women's Poetry: reading/writing/practice* (2000)

(74) Whyte, Christopher, *Modern Scottish Poetry* (2003)

(75) Stevenson, Randall, *The Last of England?, 1960-2000* (2004)

(76) Allen, Tim and Duncan, Andrew, eds., *Don't Start Me Talking. Interviews with Modern Poets* (2006)

(77) Barry, Peter, *Poetry Wars* (2006)

(78) Sheppard, Robert, *When Hard Times Made for Good Poetry* (2011)

(79) Caddy, David, *So Here We Are* (2012), letters from England for an American radio programme

(80) Pattison, Neil, Pattison, Reitha, Roberts, Luke, eds., *Certain Prose of the English Intelligencer*, (introduction by Neil Pattison contains a history of the group) (2012)

§

Especially useful volumes were those by Chevalier, Görtschacher, Mottram, Seymour-Smith, Thurley, Conran, Homberger, (Peter) Riley, (Roy) Fisher, *Akros*, Lucie-Smith, Crozier.

Scraping together what these authors say about Style Time, we can identify five principal versions of it:

THEORY A

From 1959-61 there was a breakout from an old, restricted style, spread through little magazines, and appealing to a new audience created by the expansion of the universities, and as this continued the new thing received a boost from the revolutionary urges of 1968 and the mass radicalisation of the succeeding years. It was severely constrained and deflected by events around 1977-9, notably a hangover of disillusion and a right-wing backlash, victorious in poetry, as not in the visual arts. Since then poetry has been split between a pop-conservative mainstream and the succession of the breakthrough, undergoing complex internal evolution in a cultural margin. In this margin, cohesion was as a group of friends, and through shared outlets, while the 'style rule' was to innovate constantly, questioning everything and relying on spontaneity.

THEORY B

Poetry was formerly in the hands of a little clique defined by education, residence, and loyalty (to themselves), and was restricted by this allegiance.

They had a complex game called culture, which involved rhetoric and erudition. Since 1945 (or, 1960, or 1970, or 1980, or 1910, or 1880) the arrival of new cohorts of educated and poetically active people has shattered these restraints and made poetry flatter in style, less demanding, more cheerful, more sensuous, and more diverse.

Theory C

There is no set of collective representations of how the parts of a poem should be governed, and so changes to this set are unreal (or inexplicable, or uninteresting). Assessing how innovative a poet is is irrelevant to judging their artistic merits. Fashion is a bad thing. Changes in the course of an artist's career are due to the workings of deeply inner temperament, fulfilling timeless patterns, rather than to changes in the wishes and beliefs of the audience.

Theory D

Poetry is a moral act and belongs within the defensive walls of a sanctified religion. Only a self-elected spiritual elite with access to the authorising works of the past can be trusted to control moral welfare, and so to control poetry. History went fundamentally wrong (in AD 449, or AD 1200, or AD 1520, or 1789, or 1914, or 1923, or 1945, or 1960), when it fell into the hands of levelling materialists, and time since then is essentially featureless. Modernity must be stamped out. It involves sex, and machines, and reasoning, and science, and democracy, and free verse. However, the timeless ('perennial') is available in the hands of a precious few masters.

This paranoid Christian strain would include Raine; Holbrook; Davie. I would like to add a benign Christian group, to include Morgan and Allchin.

Theory E

Several complex theses about the course of Welsh and Scottish poetry, within the aegis-thesis that English poetry became ineffective at some point, and that nationalism is the key knowledge that has made poets effective. This can also involve theories about territorial rootedness, and belonging to a community (that is, other than the literary one).

This current is represented by Conran, Hooker, and Crawford.

Theory F

This is the detailed account prepared by Eric Homberger of stylistic succession from 1939. 'The purpose [...] is to understand something of the mechanics behind the way a body of assumptions and practices became nearly universal'. He is only interested in the group which is defined by membership of the academic world of EngLit and which includes both English and Americans. Homberger's account of this insanely convergent group is uniquely satisfying. His book stops in about 1973, and he complains of 'balkanisation' making English poetic history impossible to write after that point. This is presumably the poets outside this exampassing elite pressing back on stage.

This survey has identified problems in the uneven flow of time that this book will hope to shed light on. Theories C and D give us nothing concrete to test; theory A is the one the book will address, and it will move in the ambit of works by Crozier, Görtschacher, Mottram, Thurley, Booth, Sheppard, Riley, Bush, and the collective works edited respectively by Barry and Hampson, by Denise Riley, and by Acheson and Huk. Theory B will be discussed briefly with regard to an essay by Crawford and Armitage; theory E will receive only partial coverage in this book, but is discussed in classic works by Conran and Hooker. The most effective studies of historical change within *Textmilieu* are by Conran, followed by Martin Booth, and in *Akros* issue 28. Theory F is complete as stated in Homberger's classic work.

Another group can be segregated because they identify oppositions in poetic theory without supplying a set of dates to go along with them; in this group I put works by Allen Fisher, Roy Fisher, Adrian Clarke, Raworth, (Denise)Riley (ed.).

There are largely three groups of critics: the ones with a critical understanding of time, based on style analysis, and impressed by innovation; the ones who identify each decade with two or three poets and reduce time to the style and personalities of those foreground figures, who hide all the background; and those who resent the 'star' theory and its exclusivity, but lack a critical theory of change and a sensitivity to style. Authors who do not perceive any collective change are unable to explain why the rules of poetry have shifted over the past 50 years, cannot give any explanation of how shifts in style relate to changes in economy and society, and cannot understand why poets argue about style. If you decide that only two or three poets per decade compose the subject, you write off the history of style along with all the other poems you have jettisoned as boring. The competing theories of the timeline of change are, therefore, few, and they can largely be reconciled with each other. The time curve that we accept for this work is theory A, and I rely on the broad consensus about it within a group of critics. Of course, there are other proposed chronologies.

THE CHRISTIAN ETHICAL VIEW OF THE POEM

Christian critics have a strong version of time, in which the centripetal relationship of every man to the man in Palestine in the first century AD is the universal centre and the life of every man is dependent on it, and every Christian text is modelled on it. Human behaviour that differs from this is a transgression, and the differences fit into the drama of a single soul, oscillating around the norm. Of course there is a calendar, but the feasts of the Church are given over to remembering parts of that single and eternal time sequence. Christianity, admirably, puts all humans on the same footing, so that typification, where one poet stands for all (and the poet of 1960 mystically 'is' the poet of 1920), is something they find sympathetic. The history of technique is here not available, because style is being used as a window on character and ethical progress. The drama of the loss of cultural creativity of the Anglican communion is attenuated by the psychological fact that the Anglicans don't feel any need of extra poetry written after 1700. The concentric view of time bonds naturally with a version of style in which archaic language (as well as hallowed models) is dominant; as progress is merely secular and there is a sacred knowledge.

In literary criticism with the Christian-ethical approach, there is a general lack of accounts of time, or technique, or the shared milieu, or links to politics or to other arts; this sums up the alienation of a later generation of students and academics from it. If you resist change you are naturally reluctant to write about it. A failure of formal analysis serves the art-political purpose of disguising this immobility. A flat ethical view of the world flattens out history in the cause of a timeless present of ethical guardianship. Sadly, the concept of a cultural field consisting of individual souls is turned by commercial considerations into one of a few individual souls – at a rate of two poets per decade.

Kathleen Morgan's book *Christian Themes in Contemporary Poetry* traces a Christian idea of poetry that is caught in the complex static pattern of the individual soul, and unable to deal with historical change and with collective representations other than religious doctrines. This allows us to guess that this focus on ethical tests seized in a narrative finished in the first century AD accounts for the lack of historical or stylistic analysis in *most of the works listed above*. It is fairly simple to get from Morgan to the ethical and anti-modern views of Holbrook and Abbs, a militant Christianity, the more aggressive and feeble for being outside the institutional framework of the Church, and rejecting what they see around them. Morgan's attitude, in 1963, is very similar to Canon Allchin's more recent work *Praise Above All: Discovering the Welsh Tradition*, which discusses David Jones amongst others, and is a theory of what poetry ought to be. Flattening out Welsh history, he regards historical change over the past eight centuries or so as superficial compared to the really deep truths. The 1960s produced a split in poetry criticism between the non-projective, materialist, comparative, and technical view, associated with intellectuals, the Left, and with working-class academics; and the identifying, humanized, ethical, approach, which was Christian in inspiration and conservative in results.

THE AGE CLASS

If we look at G.S. Fraser's collected *Essays on Twentieth Century Poets*, we will first of all be impressed by the breadth of coverage, and, if we read the text, by his sympathy and skill. But then we may note that the youngest poet in the book (with one exception) was born in 1910 and published his first book in 1944: a puzzle, since the volume of essays was published in 1977. One explanation would be that there was no interesting English or Scottish poetry in the period 1950-77; an explanation I dismiss on several grounds. Another explanation, noting the connection between the years of birth of MacCaig in 1910 and of Fraser (1915-80), has to do with the disrespect of the old for the young: the sociological inhibition on taking seriously the ideas and emotions of people a few years younger than you. One version has to do with the critic's sensibility drying up: but Fraser has no problem with poems published when he was well into middle age, so long as they were published by someone older than he was. An extension has to do with disappointment. Critics tend to be hypnotised by their own poetry, or by the poetry that they dream of writing. Fraser was an esteemed and widely-read poet when he was young, and until he was about 40; he did not pursue this line of writing, nor (within limits) did his readership expand. We could guess that, when much of his emotional energy was going into thinking about writing, his identification with other poets was intense, and so was his curiosity about the fine detail of their work, and consequently he was readily able to record what he had already noticed in an organised form. Losing interest, it may be, in his own career, he lost interest in the careers of other poets; with an exception, almost a prolongation of youth, for the figures he had already profoundly identified with. The faculty that forms identifications is, we are speculating, both weak and fickle, and governed by laws.

An important stage of Fraser's career was his involvement as a reviewer and anthologist, mainly in the 1940s, and so to a large extent with poets of his own age. See for example his anthology *Poetry Now*, of 1953. His collection of essays (both, in fact) omits his immediate contemporaries, but in earlier years his record of helping and publicising them was excellent – to the extent that his withdrawal from the New Romantic movement and espousal of a more austere and prosaic style helped to change the literary scene and end the former school. (His own 1940s poetry looked remarkably up to date in 1956.) One can speak of saturation and weariness as elements in his evolving response; he did not, in retrospect, consider the 1940s poets worthy of extended examination.

One of the rumours about the scene is that academics believe in a tiny canon (one significant poet per decade, roughly), detest having to form an opinion, refuse to write about anything that hasn't already got a long bibliography that they can copy opinions from, refuse to write about non-canonical authors because their colleagues won't read them and they (the essays) won't get onto reading lists and earn Brownie points (only books on the syllabus 'need' a secondary literature), and dislike reading poets they didn't read as undergraduates. The belief in a tiny élite of poets suited the lazy academic, but was also stimulated by the fanaticism of F.R. Leavis. However, the theory that no-one cares about people younger than they are tends to clear academics of much of this opprobrium, since their ingrained being-forty-years-out-of-date may be due to a biological dislike of, or indifference to, their juniors.

How general is this pattern? With the exception of Eric Mottram, I have not found a single critic who has a distinguished record of writing about the poets younger than them. (Of course, I am writing about poets younger than me – but this could be a form of faking the results.) Very similar patterns are found in the critical careers of F.R. Leavis, Geoffrey Grigson, Donald Davie, Martin Seymour-Smith. Besides which, I seem to find them in the tastes expressed in interviews, and in reviews generally.

Relations with contemporaries are characterised by an intense curiosity, since these are the people in the world most similar to oneself. This curiosity is partly independent of their ability to write poetry. Their successes may cause irrational jealousy. It is hard to be impressed by them, especially after meeting them when they were unknown and unsuccessful.

Relations with those one age-group older are characterised by envy, a desire for approval, resentment, imitation, irrational respect. These are the people one will write theses and reviews on. The struggle for individuation starts with them as literary models, who have to be burst and cast off, like a chrysalis, in a shadow duel. One expects their material help, flowing from their institutional power; their expectations induce tension and worry. Their opinions may induce distortions imprinting one's whole career.

Relations with poets one age-group younger are characterised by insouciance; they are only there to show respect and appreciation. This attitude may go along with writing poems that are increasingly slow and boring, as a function of one's swelling self-regard. One does not take their needs seriously. Why replace something that is not obsolete? They are expected to be grateful for material help which is rightfully theirs; an asymmetrical relationship. They are not expected to become intense and demanding on subjects that the elder group has compromised on and redefined as unimportant.

If the theoretical battles are being fought by people under 25 and still forming their style, and the prominent critics are in their 40s and uninterested by anybody younger than that, then textbooks, academic courses, and reviews in well-known magazines will all be irrelevant and pointing in the wrong direction. This in fact seems to be the case. This is one of the reasons for now re-examining the 1960s and 1970s.

THE IRONIC HARVEST

Geoffrey Thurley's *The Ironic Harvest* (1974) is a classic work. It covers the period roughly 1914-1972. Its real strength is in analysing the weaknesses of the mid-century English tradition, but the chapter on the 1960s is fragrant with new hope and spontaneity. Surprisingly enough, Thurley (1936-) is the only writer on this list who has an overall theory of English poetry (say, 1910-1970), integrated with intellectual and political changes, and explaining aesthetic successes and failures. In some ways, this is the best book on this list. His work is classical in its poise and tragic in its theme. He taught at Essex and may even be linked to the famous Essex School.

What we guess from Thurley is no less than that the goal of irony, detachment, and non-commitment is favoured by the professional classes because they are going to sell their analytical skills to the highest bidder and so cannot afford to have opinions. Thurley traces the history of detachment (the ironic harvest) as it affected the course of modern English poetry, suggesting that this overriding teleology was accepted uncritically and needs much deeper examination to recognise its full impact. He provides an underpinning for a traditional Leftist position, that the educated were supercilious, incapable of artistic creation because they were incapable of emotional commitment and regarded it as 'provincial'. If you have opinions, your employment opportunities are restricted. The craving for 'detachment' may be simply the carrying-out of the basic imperatives of possessive individualism, always calculating the odds and always preparing to abandon a loyalty group because some other group offers better conditions. People who write 'virtual' poetry wouldn't accept that they represent possessive individualism, but can we trust them?

Thurley favours existential poetry, in the sense of poetry to which the writer is emotionally committed, and in which his or her existence is at stake, without the guarantee of success; a poetry of risk and endurance. He correctly identifies the academic tradition of irony and withdrawal as the enemy of this strain, and writes the history of existential poetry, fragile because the forces in play were so much greater than the powers of the poets to affect fate. This seems like a puzzling abandonment of the powers of fantasy and virtuality. However, much of the most interesting modern poetry (written after Thurley finished his book) also follows these existential rules; the work of Denise Riley and Michael Haslam, for example. We can take it that Prynne is an existential poet, and that the writing of his poetry enacts risk and strain, where commitment and integrity are the values he most seeks.

O'BRIEN AND BARRY

I wanted to say some more things about O'Brien (*The Deregulated Muse*, 1998), since I underrated this book the first time. O'Brien does represent continuity with the 1950s and it is valuable to see someone still imposing the higher concepts of authenticity and moral integrity to the 1980s, when the subject seems to be outside the frame altogether. The most interesting aspect of the book is the thesis, barely even sketched but present in a few references, that poetry has deteriorated since the 1950s and that 1950s values are the ones to be imposed. This is not underpinned by good poetry from the 1950s, which he is unable to produce, and does not explain why modern poetry is excellent (although it can explain why it is bad). His belief that only Catholicism is authentic in literature is less credible. Given these preferences, he must find almost everything that has happened since 1960 radically unacceptable, and he does well to keep up a sense of authority and confidence even though he finds the material so thin in interest. He is an exceptionally organised writer, clear about his theses and orderly and efficient in presenting them. Another book could have been written that pushed left-wing writers on stage in order to show how an approach based on social commitment and a sense of ethical obligations can fuel modern poetry, and even to explore where it does not work. It would go on to explore how the withdrawal from social reality and from psychological coherence has weakened the poetry of 'post-modernism', which O'Brien does suggest. It was depressing in the 21st century to see how effective poetry by Geoffrey Hill and Christopher Logue was, and to think that the earnest moral questioning that they undoubtedly practised in the 1950s had given them the ability to write, almost half a century later, poetry that explained that politicians could be bad as well as good. This seemed to bear out O'Brien's idea: if you don't have a point of view your poetry is bound to be inconclusive.

Peter Barry, in his 2006 book on 'the battle of Earl's Court' already mentioned, ventured a proposal about the history of the whole scene after 1977:

> there is a widespread preoccupation by poets of all persuasions today with more-or-less experimental explorations of such things as: linguistic registers, implied voices, varieties of narrative technique and viewpoint, ways of using metaphor to undermine the 'real', and various ways of using myth. Consequently, it is rare today to find the kind of poetry in which 'a straightforwardly autobiographical speaker muses on aspects of his/her love-life, or domesticity or ruminates in relationships with god and nature.' This amounts to saying that the 'defeat' of the avant-garde in 1977 has taken the form of assimilating its lessons and adopting many of its methods. [...] This, I would suggest, is the 'hidden history' of contemporary British poetry.
>   (in *Poetry Wars: British Poetry of the 1970s and the*
>   *Battle of Earl's Court*, 2006, quoting material from Barry,
>   *Contemporary British Poetry and the City*, 2000, p.12)

However, in 1978 Douglas Dunn had published an editorial in *Poetry Review* (just after the 'battle') where he said that two poets

> seem to suggest in their work that it is possible to handle traditional expectations and the New in one practice of writing. Indeed, what else has English poetry been working towards during the past decade [*so from 1968 on, AD*] if not that?'.
>   (from *Poetry Review*, issue [number], 1978)

This may be a personal position rather than a disposition of the scene itself. It may all be a sound theoretical explanation of something that didn't happen. Because the wise want to rise above conflict, they admire compromise above all things. This may be a reason for artistic failure. If you asked 2,000 conservative poets if they had integrated as much modern technique as was necessary and tasteful, at least 1,991 of them would say yes. This is not style history.

In conclusion, I want to add that the sheer number of books coming out makes it easy for critics to pursue their appetites and completely miss each other: producing eventually two accounts of the times that don't overlap. I may be attacked for breaching a consensus, but really there is no consensus. People are looking at different things. The different views presented above do not disprove each other and retain their fascination.

FORM, TIME, FASHION

Because a writer can have a productive life of 40 years during which their style is rather stable, the scene of literary production can also seem stable. We habitually read collected poems that work as wholes. This creates an effect of non-change that screens out the change happening all around. Any year you look at has memorable poems being written by older writers. We live on an artificial surface of stability. But historical change is constant, and this becomes obvious when we look at what the youngest poets are doing at any point. If you look at poets making debuts year by year, for example, you get a glimpse of things that *are* changing. Things have changed since the 1950s.

Because of the human life-span, the styles of five previous decades (scarcely six, I think?) are still 'now' at any moment. George MacBeth's style is salient for the 1960s; I don't think anyone was writing like that in the 1950s, even if few people, in fact were writing like that in the 1960s. MacBeth's style seems to be 'the 1960s style' also because it wasn't especially his, and it resembles patterns in the other arts of the period (and not of other periods); if you see his style as utterly personal, it loses its candidacy as a style 'of the time'.

William Watson said in a lecture published in 1913 that

> Indeed I am more and more convinced that there exists a large though scattered body of cultivated, intelligent, serious, but silent lovers of fine literature, who are quite unswayed by ephemeral literary fashions, and quite indifferent to the critical catchwords which are so often made to do duty in place of the unchanging laws of taste and form.
>
> (from 'The Poet's Place in the Scheme of Life', in
> *The Muse in Exile. Poems.* 1913, p.25)

Many people are still saying just this; it is an idea of resisting change which resists change. If laws are 'unchanging', why should people read 20th-century poetry at all? Or even 19th-century poetry?

Everyone agrees that forms decay and grow old; the position of conservatives today isn't 'nothing has changed since the Middle Ages' but 'the forms I use were in use fifty years ago but of course they aren't out of date because I'm still using them'. There is a lack of public sensitivity to these delicate variations of poetic time, so that people who are expert in dating a film, a piece of clothing, or a pop record, and in labelling something out of date, have difficulty in dating a poem or in identifying its original moments.

I tried, in 1995, to define what was modern. The provocation for *Unit Structures* was a wish to define the boundary line of what magazines like *fragmente, Reality Studios, Parataxis, First Offense, Angel Exhaust* would accept. The line represented editorial practice but also the wishes of a certain public who might buy the magazines if they stayed modern. I asked how one knows that a certain poem is not going to appear in their pages. This list is applicable in 1995, when I drew it up. It's not quite true that any poem that did use these innovations was forbidden from appearing in the mainstream magazines. Geography is not quite that simple. Nor is it true that poems which use all or many of these innovations must be good.

UNIT STRUCTURES: POINTS OF TECHNIQUE REPRESENTING CHANGE FROM THE STANDARD AVERAGE POEM OF 1959:

(1) BACK TO ZERO

The keen awareness of illusion that followed 20 years of heated propaganda (from, say, 1936) induced some people to start an epistemological project in which nothing was assumed to be true. This has been called *kenosis*, or emptying-out. The consequent building of poems from simplified and incomplete world-models did at least bring out that all poems are simplified and incomplete world-models, unless by some chance they are as complex as the universe. (See 30, *Ostranenie*)

(2) COHERENCE

Formerly, all levels of the poetic text were convergent, isolating and heightening the emotional message or plea. This derives from an elemental necessity of self-presentation in social life, which poetry no longer feels obliged to copy. There is also the ethical aspect: the poet eschews self-aggrandisement, and does not wish unprincipled self-serving. This stopping of the music is related to the forfeiture of the sublime.

(3) DISSONANCE

The modern trait is to seek out dissonance whenever possible; as if we lived surrounded by a coherent surface of illusion and poetic experience was only available on the further side of it, where flaws disproved its version of space. There is also the didactic intent of showing how social reality is made by agreement (cf. *The Social Construction of Reality*, by Berger and Luckmann) and how meaning is consciously created.

(4) MEDIATIONS

The modern poem tends to interrupt the mediation process in order to interrogate the process by which symbolic meanings are formed. The primitive satisfaction of symbolic utterance is sacrificed in order to obtain glimpses of a process and to liberate volatile energies from beneath a bound structure. The process of emotional identification and internalising objects is made conscious.

(5) LEGATO VS. STACCATO

The modern poem tends not to have a forward sweep that carries every-thing away. This is partly because of the jettison of regular metre. Phrases tend to hang in their own time, relatively isolated and static. The short line generally has less rush, and less sensuous power, than the long one. Juncture becomes the dominant device.

(6) POLITICS IN POETRY

The modern poem is mandatorily political. Admittedly, this task is made easier by redefining everything as political. Incredibly, this is combined with a thorough rejection of ideology and of stable moral standards. Modernity relaxes all rules of personal morality while being severe and intransigent about how governments must behave (No bureaucracy! No hierarchy! No inequality!)

(7) MYTH & REALISM

The modern trait is to use myth, especially non-Classical myth, and especially with a justification in terms of the unconscious.

(8) RELIGION

The decisive shift of the past three decades has been the disappearance of the Christian religion from serious poetry. However, Third World religion, especially shamanism, is fashionable.

(9) MORALISING

The world of objects has been freed of its allegorical and moral significance. It is felt that the morality of Christian times was a closed circuit, valid within artificial stories and generating new artificial stories confirming it, never confronting the complexity of the real world and never admitting the weak basis of the knowledge of any leader who framed or taught it. It is felt that the consequences of actions are unknown, and that the preparation for such knowledge would be artists simply telling the truth for a few thousand years. Moral stories are seen as a form of fantasy. Social control is felt to be implemented in the wrong way. The punitive effect of poetry has gone away.

(10) TIMELESS BEAUTY, THE SUBLIME
The habit of saying 'beauty is…', or finding truths outside time, or eternally
recurring moments, has vanished. In fact, the pursuit of The Beautiful is
felt to be rather starry-eyed: the meal is possible without the pudding.
More serious attention is now given to the pursuit of natural forms, rather
than repetitive reminiscences of previous art or religion.

(11) USE OF PROVERBS AND THE CLASSICS
Poetry in the 1950s was sententious. It purveyed wisdom. It is no longer
OK to write poems illustrating proverbial truths, or providing scholia on
classical and familiar works of literature. This is seen as academic.

(12) IMPERSONAL AUTHORITY
The modern thing is to explode and disperse the stable, non-temporal
knowledge that art formerly possessed. If the reader can no longer predict
the course of the literary work from the first chapter, the poet cannot then
foresee the consequences of actions (see 28, *Determinacy*). Such knowledge
is seen as a weapon of social control, to be savagely attacked.

(13) TOPOGRAPHY, TOMBS, LOCAL ANTIQUITIES, LITERARY ANECDOTES,
    REREDOSES
All the bric-à-brac of antiquarian learning has been thrown out as a subject
for poetry. This is partly because it is so dependent: like a mussel clinging to
a rock. As a form of determinacy, it restricts the potential of the text. This
version of the past (so allied to archaism of language, the pricy romance
of feudal words) is detested because the most splendid and solid elements
of the past were expensive, and so belonged to the rich, and so give a
partial vision; the modern poet is only interested in the past for its critical
potential. The past is interesting for its limiting conditions, marking
where forces clashed, or were pent in, or wreaked dramatic changes; the
antiquarian approach only shows surfaces.

(14) IDENTIFICATION
Identification, the cardinal process of a previous artistic dispensation, has
been dethroned, as an assumption that had been too deeply buried, and as
an attractor which confined the domain of art and made its results resemble
each other too much. The aim of making the poet the 'ideal love object' for
a number of inexperienced and hopeful adolescents is now obsolete (having
been taken over by other arts). The forms of the perceptual world are felt
to have other values than simply being minted as tokens of something
previous and personal.

(15) HIGH AND LOW AFFECT
The modern poem tends to distrust emotion and its verbal outlets. The

1960s brought sensationalism and high libido in most artistic media, but not in poetry, where what is prevalent is the other 1960s fetish of coolness.

(16) Subjectivity and regression

The Medical Metaphor (see 31) suggests that the gradually growing world-model will at some point go through a stage of violent subjectivity, emotional drives as yet unmodified by moral inhibitions. The scenario of artistic rebellion implies resistance to paternal authority, which implies that the rebellious artist is strongly drawn towards the disputed methods and subject matter. In fact, the choice of artistic method is often felt to represent a duel between young and old, a symbolic overthrow of authority.

(17) Process vs. Self-expression

The chronology of this shift is hard to trace; self-expression as a principle goes back to Romanticism, if not the Renaissance, but was at a low in the 1950s, a time of impersonal severity and moral restraint. After working on one's poetry for several years, it is normal for the primitive autobiographical drive to come to an end. At this point, you have the time to devise new ways of working; a new generator of the unpredictable is needed, and this is supplied by chance or indeterminate procedures, combined with rules chosen to generate new decisions. Of course, if you believe only in autobiographical poetry, this temporary pause is not liberation, but a source of depression, neurosis, and eclipse. Process poetry, developed most notably by Allen Fisher, is an alternative set of decision rules to self-expression. The latter tends to convergence, and therefore repetition of effects.

The new at any point is contained in the negative space, or in the unconscious, spontaneous, sporadic style elements of the current artistic practice.

(18) Molecular and Peripheral Sensations vs. Coherent Self

Modern poems reject the mandatory autobiographical focus, and accept the incoherence of the self. If experience is presented as inconsistent, this is not a failure of self-interrogation, but empirical sobriety. It is suggested that the process of verbalisation is one of centralisation and simplification, and that pure experience and words stand on opposite sides of an abyss. The polarisation implicit in intense emotion is felt as a distortion rather than an enhancement (see 22, *Eristics*). Exit from infantile emotional states is felt to supply the silence necessary to perceive other people and the outside world. The new poetic universe is full of orphaned shapes of indefinite meaning. The inventory of objects is much larger. Multiple parallel processes become visible within a life.

(19) NEGATIVE SPACE

Negative space is the space excluded from any picture enclosing space; by transfer, it is the zone excluded by any artistic or narrative system, or by a political system. The marginal becoming central is seen as the thrilling and virtuous event. This induces a new vision of central things as, functionally, the light-absorbing objects that create negative space. But what are the central things in Western art? Religion and the personality, at least in the first instance. Modern poetry is an exploration of the grey space exposed when these plot generators are systematically switched off.

(20) CONTINUOUS PRESENT

The pre-modern poem finds the poet in a kind of atemporal control room, integrating experience from undefined pasts in order to discover, or reinforce, timeless truths. The modern poet is typically immersed in a flux of experience, and assimilation or 'mastery' is by no means guaranteed. Storage is felt to deprive experience of essential vitamins – although a poem is a form of data storage.

(21) GROUP AUTONOMY

The implied group of the poem is a kind of prayer meeting indued with full sovereignty; a kind of constituent assembly. This is distinct from individual self-definition and from membership of a formal political movement. The embodied powers include particularly those of agreeing poetic expectations and the collective imaginary. The continuous present is embodied in the temporary group, and the poem is their group object. Part of the problem with the personality could be that it represents resistance to the group – specifically, identifications are seen as adhesions that disintegrate the group, sustaining the dominance of the past.

(22) ERISTICS

The techniques of formal argument that go back to the Greeks are thoroughly distrusted in modern poetry. It is felt that perception is more direct and more ambiguous. Formal argument is suited to law and theology, and perhaps needs a written code of rules to start from; this is concealed authoritarianism.

(23) RHETORICAL DEVICES

A number of rhetorical devices have been deleted from the inventory. These are numerous, but we can mention personalisation, apostrophe, allegory, abstracts as substantives, climaxing repetition, contrast, epic simile, creatures from mythology, and the set genres of poetry (eulogy, elegy, courtship, exequy, etc.) This purge goes back to around 1910 but was still relevant to stylistic dissent in 1960. It is part of the attack on mediations.

(24) Foregrounding Conventions

It is impossible to make symbolic utterances without using conventions, which are clearly an entrance point for errors and restrictions of scope. By boldly exaggerating them, one hopes to prevent them from precluding possibilities. If some of the rules of a text are imitations of reality, others are purely arbitrary and tautological, and it is good to know which is which. Lay bare the device, Shklovsky said.

(25) Non-European traditions

This is not mandatory, but almost any use of forms and ideas from outside Europe is fashionable and acceptable. This would include folk forms, felt to escape the terms of the high European systems. The new thing could be defined as non-Hellenistic poetics. This is part of the crisis of mediations. Examples are Indian and Chinese philosophy, Siberian mythology. The use of devices from African-American popular song (cf. Adrian Mitchell's use of blues conventions) is also acceptable.

(26) The Arrow of Time

The modern poetic community is agreed that progress is a feature of art, and consequently being out of date fills the audience with horror and indifference. This ultimate deterrent is not accompanied by clear collective perceptions of style and temporal sequence.

(27) Parataxis

Modern poems tend to eschew subordinate clauses (syntaxis or hypotaxis) in favour of parallel ones (parataxis). This inexplicitness of causal relationships stems from the collapse of organised knowledge. It suggests that the world is mysterious, indeterminate, and in need of active interpretation.

(28) Determinacy

The comparison would be with a text one knows exceptionally well, so that any fragment can be assigned to a precise place, any event entrains a series of events that precede and follow it, any inconsistency is spotted and rejected. This is a determinate, bound, structure. The new poem is indeterminate: at the level of prosody, at the level of autobiographical motivation, at the level of character governing behaviour, at the level of explanation, at the level of classifying phenomena. This may be simply to do with the inner state of the observer, no longer dominating the text as a bureaucrat does a filing system. Syntax has altered, because the classifying matrix that underlies distinctions and causal relationships has been dissolved, making all events strange, see (23, *Rhetoric*). Morality no longer fits into a text where the consequences of actions are uncertain. The new discourse is shifting and polyvalent, perhaps corresponding to the mystery that is supposed to envelop classical poetry.

(29) Disjunction and free association
(See 2, *Coherence*.) Rules of continuity have been radically changed, so that the sequence of ideas in a poem can be quite shocking and uninterpretable. This is probably not blind chance, but rather the introduction of a new set of combinatory rules that cannot yet be grasped or explained. Probably, our myths possessed a wild arbitrariness, and so an irrational and magical richness, which we don't see because they are too familiar. Tell me why coral was born from the blood of Medusa, and the winged horse Pegasus from her body, and I will tell you why images flow as they do in Tom Raworth. The more explicable the sequence of a poem, the more archaic it is.

One view of this fertility is that it expresses unconscious states. This acts to reduce many phenomena to a few; more genuinely modern is the view that the mind is composed of thousands of unrelated phenomena, and no such reduction is possible.

(30) Ostranenie (defamiliarisation, estrangement).
'without estrangement, no understanding' (H. Plessner) Things are presented as if seen for the first time; information is withheld, and the reader's frustration with the incomplete pattern is what gives the information its compelling appeal. The post-perceptual processing, of deduction, integration, composition, projection, affective identification, etc., is foregrounded – the mind reading through its own rules. This has been practised above all by Roy Fisher. It makes impossible the prevalence of identification. It derives its energies from contradictions.

(31) The Medical Metaphor
The modern poem is often animated by the project of solving emotional problems by confession, re-enactment, making conscious, and so on. This is limited by the supply of problems.

(32) Conditioning / Reconditioning – roles
It is assumed that behaviour is largely influenced by conditioning, in which art plays a large part. Some modern poetry assumes that this technology can simply be decentralised, and influencing machines made available to the domestic consumer; poetry is to state what the poet wishes to be true. This belief assumes, for one thing, that there is no underlying reality to falsify volition; and so that multiple behavioural tactics are equally valid in a given situation. Play is assumed to be part of behaviour acquisition, and so fantasy can be recruited as part of a self-realisation project.

This theory is quite widely rejected.

(33) RHYTHM

This is necessarily *vers libre*, on which a strong and incompetent attack was launched in the 1950s. The poet is expected to develop a rhythm specific to each incident in the poem. A system of multiple echoes, regularities, and displacements emerges, fit for stunningly beautiful effects and unnervingly hard to master. The underlying point throughout is emphasis, the movement of the speaker's attention. This stress on subjectivity could be a strain. However, the pulse of free verse need not be purple emotion, but can also be cool unwearying curiosity (see 29, *Disjunction and free association*).

(34) ON BEING IN LOVE

There is no doubt that any writing about being in love sounds old-fashioned and unintelligent. I view this with alarm, but it's a fact. Glancing allusions to habitual camaraderie hardly amount to love poetry. All the same, the mainstream has no brilliant love poems to show, and the 1950s were full of advice about moral obligations but excluded personal experience as too transient. This is a deep-rooted problem (see 29, *Disjunction and free association*).

The advantage of writing out so many points is showing that modernity is polycentric, and any single gesture of ostentatious modernity will expose itself as shallow and mechanical. These features are quite different from the practical skill of being able to write a good poem; they are also largely distinct from changes in literary theory, or in the human sciences in general, since the 1950s. They do not reproduce revered styles of the past (Surrealism, Imagism, Objectivism, etc.) although these have participated in their formation. They are hard to assimilate to a political standpoint, although a number of these features are highly compatible with an anti-authoritarian, libertarian socialist or even anarchist stance.

The first attempts of a new poetic weren't great and definitive in themselves; *torse 3* and *City* are revolutionary and subversive, but not passionate. All these points of technique make poetry more difficult to write. They empty out the field and make conscious decisions necessary at every step. I suppose they also make for more of a gap between professional and amateur poets. Most of the points are ways of guaranteeing diversity and preventing the re-use of ideas; they make poetry more divergent and harder to grasp, aggravating the problems of balkanisation that Eric Homberger complained of in 1977.

INNOVATION AS TERRITORIALITY

We could reduce innovation to the quality of *nov*, which can be marked and owned. *My nov is bigger than yours. He has a bigger nov than me, but we have an alliance and I acknowledge his seniority. If my nov gets smaller, I become less important and have fewer rights. The history of poetry is the history of nov. I want my nov to be as big as possible. Other people do not realise how big my nov is.*

This allows endless reminiscing and discussion of nuances. This territorial map of innovation is meaningful to very few people, and accepted, as a long social game, by even fewer.

As poetry is a communicative act surrounded by cooperation, subjecting it to the rules of competition is problematic. This theory of railway train-like progress is known as *historicism*, and it may be helpful here to give an account of historicism in the form in which it grips many agents of the avant-garde. Three essential components are that everything which is not avant-garde is kitsch, that artistic innovation is 'world-historical' and so more important than anything else, and that there is a timetable of formal innovation which always goes forward (and that disqualifies anything else as retro). A fourth tenet is that artists are engaged in a debate about the formal properties of the art object and that somehow the art is *about* its own formal properties. When the debate moves on, all older artistic practices become obsolete. This continual emptying is very exciting for young poets because it continually creates territory which they can stake out and occupy. The 'timetable' of advance allows for a zone of originality which can be demarcated and turned into private property. Thus the advance into undefined stylistic space is like the occupation of the U.S.A. by white Americans.

This sounds like a joke. It's no joke when one of these stormtroopers tells you you're out of date. What of yours you own, I own – only more so. Historicism promotes a total equivalence between writers, where everything is a public technique and every such technique is owned by everyone else. There is thus no individuality except in time – the last inch of advance is your own, prior to being overrun by the next person. If you destroy the sentence or the line of verse you can claim personal territory that if you stick with the sentence and the line of verse as known to the English language you can't claim. Withdrawal from the zones of known art including the most fertile and effortless ones is thus mandated by the territorial metaphor, and to stray outside the boundaries of owned (and sensorily derived) estate would invalidate the idea of ownership and so the whole bundle of historicist metaphors. Moving on thus implies wiping out the past and progression towards grey monochrome painting and white cube rooms was a logical extension of impulse. It was a process of becoming conscious in which climactically the objects of consciousness disappeared.

Why Change?

Time isn't a thing in itself, but an abstraction from our perceptions of change. The time we have to consider is not embodied in any system of the physical world, but only in human beings, making judgments and meanings as they constantly do. This version of 'time' can repeat itself, go in a loop, be in many different points on the same timescale at once, reverse itself, lose memory, jump stages: it is not separate from the environment inside the human bodies it is carried in. So time, which is linear and measured by clocks, may be the wrong word to use. We should think in terms of waves of excitability and suggestion being carried across human groups. The course of the waves reveals the internal structure of the group. Taste is transmitted by imitation; but people also use artistic choice for competition and differentiation.

Time is convergence. By sitting in a reading following the poet's voice you come into concord with the poem and with everyone else in the room. Over a long period, this means a deep convergence. You assimilate to someone's thought patterns until you can hear their voice even when they aren't there. This is very powerful and it means a shared state of mind. If I say '1970', it is apparent that there could be many different groups, all converged on their own centres, in 1970. Also, a milieu I internalise, which internalises me, could be rather stable over 30 years. So to name the time, 1970 or any other year, is not the same as naming the cultural horizon that is the home of a poem or a poet. Convergence is the key – not the calendar date. In theory a convergence could go on for 100 years. Any room full of people engaged in converging is likely to have at least one person who is violently dissimilating – the psychic equivalent of nausea.

One individual undergoes a change of aesthetic attitude perhaps in a single moment; a non-duration, like the moment when the tide turns. This non-duration is the substance of cultural change. Poetry does not become obsolete because it physically decays. It does so only because the community of the poem decides that something is obsolete. Community may be the wrong word, since internal splits, exclusion of dissidents, and self-exile by the embittered, are so predominant inside it, emaciating its inside; we can think rather of a turbulent series of intermittent central spaces, filled with signal and contact, always breaking up. To ignore the rules of the group is to be truly deaf. They are the landscape. Enthusiasm is transient because it uses up its own source. This biases the art world in favour of change and the new. Possibly freedom from poetic fashion is really just a lack of all excitement, thermally drained sluggishness. The flow of excitement in a poem depends on continually new images and sensations. A poem is frozen time, but perhaps it is also frozen change; a slope of words where nothing is the same at the end as it was at the beginning.

Suppose that what we are seeing, in the 'timeline' of poetry, is internal to the human organism; not exactly a chemical clock, it is a 'psychological clock', of specific content. The minimal conditions for such a 'time' existing are similarity and simultaneity across several organisms; we can guess that these imply a means of transmission. We derive 'time' from the simultaneity, rather than *vice versa*. There are two scales of time in flow, the chronological one, of days becoming years, and the stylistic one. This style time could be either cyclic or serial; since recurrence is one of its basic attributes (without this there would be no point recording works of art in storage media), we may suspect that non-repetitive seriality is an exceptional form for it to adopt. The factor that brings simultaneity across several organisms is not 'calendar time' but the update pulses that switch the organisms into the shared state. Time is composed of the pulses carrying impulse trains across the group. It is a flow composed of separate drops, like rain. The significance of these drops depends on political success. If we look at a poem, we see one of these drops; like a virus being a 'naked gene'. What time is made out of, the poem is made out of. Defining your relationship to recent history is meaningless unless you are connecting with the enthusiasm of the reading public; it is an arbitrary act that is also illegitimate and null.

Where is this 'virtual symbolic space' made and remade? The serially changing areas we could consider are: sociological patterns, e.g. of consumption; economic conjuncture; party politics; fashions in other arts; atmospheres of opinion in magazines and media; changes of ideas in the universities; shifts of taste in the little magazines; radical politics; business thought; advertising; international relations; technology; the Church; pop culture; the shops (and the designers); social groups such as the affluent suburbs, the socially mobile, the young, the big cities, the oppressed; America; France. It's clear that these are out of phase with each other, and that their content is different, so that equating events across them, as if there were some big thing that made ripples in all these channels, is doubtful; but at the same time one human is affected by all of them. But how does a poem excite a reader if it is not new? How can it avoid being merged with previous poems, to indistinctness, a kind of sonic mud, if it is not vitally different from those poems? Isn't the classic trait of poetry that it should provide excitement which is new but of brief duration? As for the contents of a poem, isn't it so that everything can be removed which does not add to the poem; that the vital part of each line is what is new in it; and that what is indispensable and exciting about the poem is what is new in it? Reading means acquiring information; if we already possess the information we are reading, our alertness drops rapidly and we try to skip through the text until something new happens.

If a slow rate of information makes us drowsy and torpid, a too high rate of flow can, by straining our memory, powers of construction, and ability to form hypotheses and interpretations, make reading too much effort, or too ambiguous. High uncertainty can also be high anxiety; conservatism is a response that avoids this. There is a kind of ridge where you fall one way or the other. Now, the information content of what we are reading need not consist only in the sequence of events it recounts, but also in rhythmical patterns, syntactic patterns, genre assumptions, the relation of the poet to the experiences being recounted, assumptions about how the world works and how experience is organised, dialect, and so on. In the official world of the post-Movement poet, there was only one kind of poem; the poet might visit different places, but the snapshot was always the same size and shape. The features I have just listed were frozen, not susceptible to variation, excluded from the zone of decisions.

There is a spectrum between petrified eternal objects and transient high-excitation objects. One of the ways in which thought advances is by speeding up its shutter, metaphorically, so that events and objects that occur very rapidly are caught and recorded; this new class of objects is in some ways trivial; its nature is to vanish rapidly and be replaced by something more accurate. It takes up lots of storage space, and we can see that to recognise only durable objects and events would take much less space. You need to retain this class of fine and volatile objects in order to perceive the possibility of an original poem, which must come out of the unlegitimated and uncategorised.

If you live in a small town and know one other person who writes poetry, the chances are that they won't be enthusiastic about a book at the same moment you are. Maybe they read it 20 years ago; maybe they dislike it. Having several people enthusiastic about the same thing at the same moment is a completely different experience. The requirement for a 'living network' privileges a few cities, and in those cities a few groups. This may annoy people, but it is a fact. The 'out of date' style correlates with isolation, self-satisfaction, conservatism, and (in fact) egoism. Language is dialogic and isolation makes it decay, slide into repetition and eccentricity. This quiet and passive existence is more typical of the provinces than of the great cities.

History was slanted against the no-innovations kind of poetry, because of the rather rapid and never slowing transformation of the middle class into a class of graduates with high intellectual expectations and a corporate belief in innovation, which alone could make their skills necessary. The optimistic temper of people becoming upwardly mobile through education led in the same direction. The values of the educated class have changed, and poetry, a wholly amateur art form, hasn't necessarily been able to keep up.

The old system didn't turn pale, die and blow away when a new poetry arrived. The internalised ideals and reading habits of perhaps 100,000 people, aged from 15 to 90, were unable to change very fast. New patterns were perceived by many as a threat destructive of property values – this in a culture deeply opposed to innovation. Readers mostly didn't want a poetry that made them insecure, that is by inviting them to learn new habits. The sense of loss was heavy. People only want a new future if it has a special place for them. The broad mass of modern poetry (i.e. the seven or ten thousand people who 'regularly write poetry') remains untouched by most of these; modernity isn't simply the common features of all poetry written in the past year, or ten years.

FAILURE OF EQUIVALENCE

The doctrine of equivalences is fascinating. Logically, it would mean that Kathleen Raine turned into Denise Riley and Riley then turned into Andrea Brady. I can imagine a film graphic, like the montage sequences in *CSI: Crime Scene Investigation*, where you would be shown all the parts mutating, structures dissolving or branching out, and finally see a new poet emerging complete. This doesn't work because finally one poet is not a rebuilt copy of another: human beings are too complex for that. Poets as subjects form projective identifications onto older poets. This is very important, and it comes to carry cultural substance because these internalised images are part of the process of writing poems in an unconscious and emotionally ramified way. But there are many other processes.

If you say something changed, it has to be basically the same thing – as opposed to two things replacing each other. But one poet is not basically the same thing as another. There was no Denise Riley in the 1950s. One thing is not a changed version of another unless it is essentially the same. One thing comes after another but this does not mean that one thing changes into another. Thinking about shifts across time is remarkably compelling and intriguing even if its intellectual basis is weak.

By using a features matrix, you can make comparison of poets objective to some extent. I looked at one point at a large-scale comparison, 500 poets from the 1950s compared to 500 from the 1990s. This was intractable. You can't (for example) compare female poets of the 1950s with female poets of the 1990s. These are just not comparable objects. To say that the position of female poets changed suggests that someone from 1952 was there in 1992 and their situation was steady enough for change to be observed. This is moonshine. If comparison is made possible by stripping out the details, it operates through a defeatured model and the more poets you involve the fewer features the model has. If the details of a poem are significant, this implies that the defeatured model is terminally unsatisfactory. Historicism relies on a doctrine of total equivalence that faces a number of objections.

Talking about the structures of reception as sustaining and stable agencies is meaningless. You cannot speak about how *Mop Mop Georgette* would have been published, reviewed, and received in 1952 because it did not exist then. Works of art are unique. Conversely, if works by female poets active in 1952 had been published in 1992 it is unlikely that they would have been received with post-reforms enthusiasm. Their nature prohibited that, because it was wholly integrated with the cultural situation of the time, and those books were not shaped by the cultural ambitions that would have made them vital in the 1990s. Talking about culture changing is fraught with difficulty. But we can deal with concrete works of literature, and with related groups of works. The closest equivalent of Riley in the 1950s is Kathleen Nott, also someone with philosophical training who levelled an intense scrutiny at feelings about love. But Denise Riley starts each poem from zero. There is no legacy nucleus.

INFORMATION ON
NON-STANDARD POEM MODELS

Besides the standard poem there are other models for poems. We will look at some of these. Theodor Mommsen says that, '[t]he oldest Etruscan writing shows no knowledge of lines, and winds like the coiling of a snake'; we have orthogonal and completely regulated printing conventions that are the most banal of all spatial possibilities. The coils could be the movement of a speaker in some cultic recitation. Roman writing is regular, orthogonal; the variant possibilities of Iron Age inscriptions are suppressed; classicism is an abridgement.

We have another convention of the now-moment of a poem being in one place, mimicking a speaker who utters a syllable and moves on to the next, with no overlap. But real life normally has a wash of different sounds under which we focus on a voice, creating an isolation; a poem could for example have two simultaneous speakers, two now-moments, and so shift the unknown to the question of what is concentration (and what *other* levels of perception are there). A speech group has a top stress that is its most prominent feature. This tends to be towards the centre of the group of syllables. They are the most important feature of the group and yet traditional metrics ignores them altogether. The speech group is the basis for the line of verse. The end of a speech group is the phonological basis for the line break. The line break is not signalled in English speech, the new centre takes over silently. The line break in verse is something artificial. It's a feature of an imaginary object on which the poem is inscribed, like a slab that has an edge and where lines turn at the edge. Poetry emphasises the ends of lines and speech emphasises the middle. Actors asked to speak verse ignore the line break and so get to something plainer and less valuable. As you listen to actors messing up every line break and thinking 'I've found the way to make this odd text live', you realise where the 'plainness = authenticity' garbage seeps from. They ought to be shot, of course. But the shots should be rhythmically spaced. Banal English poetry is following an impulse to eliminate artificiality.

Straight lines of print are the culmination of a project to reduce a three-dimensional object to a series of two-dimensional surfaces. Variant poems can be imagined as written on imaginary three-dimensional objects and retaining dimensionality. The variants defy description. The underlying pattern seems to be that anything expressive is a reduction of predictability, unambiguity, and speed of assimilation. The expressive dimension is a return of archaic circumstances and is tinged with the melancholy of remembering a long series of repressions and schematisations.

NOTIONS ABOUT THE NEW POETRY; POST-POUND

To explain changes happening in the 1960s, I want to introduce the notion of a data plot. This phrase is based on camera plot: a list of shots in a film, saying what scene we are looking at and where the film shifts to a new scene or a different camera. There is a poet named Meic Stephens, a Welsh nationalist activist who later became known for writing poems in the (Welsh-language) dialect of Trefforest (or *Gwenhwyseg*). In *Poetry Dimension 2* there is a poem by Stephens called 'Hooters' that deals with air-raids on the industrial districts of Glamorgan in 1940, when he was a young child. The use of the past tense signals that this is a memory, and in stanza seven we come back to the present, around 1974, with the poet hearing an ambulance siren that reminds him of air-raids. In stanzas five and six we have another time-frame, not exactly specified, as the sirens remind him of the pit sirens sounding for a mining accident. A fourth element is a mythical comparison starting, 'The dogs of Annwn barked for me then', referring to dogs in folklore who howled before a death and possibly carried souls off to Hell (Annwn). Thus we have a data plot with four dates. We could mark each line with a colour to show which date it belongs to. We could equate each of these with a camera and the poem would be three shots spliced together (film does not do metaphor so arguably you would not define the Annwn bit as a 'shot'). If you related some lines to the wrong date the poem would be very confusing. I want to suggest that the data plot of the standard poem is very simple, that this is part of its aesthetic of plainness and is one of the ways by which we identify a poem as being mainstream. One of the features of the underground poem would be that its data plot is more complicated. Eric Mottram, poet and cultural critic, published in 1989 a book called *Peace Projects and Brief Novels*. Peace Project 14 starts:

> constructed of large stones
>   features drawn together
> as our scape
>   measured   they are together but once
>   stood here <u>drawn</u> <u>arcs</u>   <u>horizon</u> <u>shape</u>
>   ellipsis   the sky flight egg

> drawn from position
> without front or back
> sight's arcs known to surround
> inside no place on which to pivot
> routeless holds
> without exit or entrance
> centreless in these ellipses
> the heights distanced so that star movement
>   (from 'Megalithic')

The first four words explain what 'megalithic' means. The poem moves on to the idea that stone circles were used in astronomy, and into the geometrical principles behind the design of the megalithic arrays. It may be a write-up of material from a book about megaliths or it may be material drawn from a source and simply re-arranged. The scraps do fit together in an argument that is public, I mean that the argument about 'megalithic observatories' was carried out by a number of people; Mottram only has to refer *back* to it. I am not sure if the poem would make sense if you didn't already know those arguments, from Peter Lancaster Brown or wherever. The word 'abstract' does not fit, because a megalith is a concrete object, but the way the arc of the poem interacts with objects and with a time-line is complicated and it is *driven* by ideas. The speaker is connecting to ideas about the stone circles, not to a stage in his life. The connectives can be deleted partly because the solid logical framework is *already* present. I am wondering about the egg. The stones might be arranged in ovals, egg shapes. And an oval could also be an ellipse, which is the course many heavenly bodies follow.

    'Peace Project 21' starts

> have you preserved time
> raced tide paced outpaced the sun
>
> fixed what goes
> not memory but a work
>
> waited for a war to end
> a long voyage home Rangoon west
>
> never ideal conditions but seized
> seizures in what designs brought to slow head

luck from unpredicted bond
penetrated shores valleys rock sides

open seas dark blue terrors
ahead might not come

conditions to destroy a creating hand
mind furrowed by stress

luck from steady crisis
when choices narrowed

Peace Project 14 gave away its theme in the title: megaliths. Who knows how hard that poem might be if Mottram had gone full-on Pound and deleted the word that gives the whole situation away. Peace Project 21 has no title but the theme is memory, and it deals with some of Mottram's personal memories and then with 'footage' from artistic figures he admires. One of these runs

'black rage of poetry – crazy old-age youth'
cold orchard under icy sun

gaze from a white-washed house
salt rimed on walls from ruins

– this passage reads like an Imagist poem and gives a glimpse of a possible truth, that the modern poem is a cluster of Imagist poems that are set together without connectives, and that this *is* the Pound legacy. Lines like 'salt rimed on walls for ruins' are remarkably vivid, sensuous, precise. If you are going to jump to a new theme then you are relying on texture to show the fact that you have jumped – from one year to another, it might be. Pound's method had roots in Imagism, in intense isolated moments. The precision of the new moment shows you that you have jumped. Indeterminacy cannot be prominent where precision and vividness are structurally vital. I think the idea of *Peace Projects* was the fruits of peace: war had its projects, but prevented almost every freedom; peace projects were everything you really wanted to do, just about anything that the war forbade.

At this point it is convenient to mention the phrase 'open field', which is conventionally used to describe poems without syntax or verse lines, which are scattered over the page along with a lot of spaces of uncertain affiliation. 'Black Mountain' is often used as a phrase to describe work related to Olson. It was the name of a tiny college in North Carolina, where Olson taught, and that went bust in 1957. Most probably, 'Black Mountain poetry' means the same as 'open field'. I don't like the phrase *open field* because it is attached to a propaganda work by Charles Olson (1950) that contains all sorts of toxic ideological baggage. Pound's Canto LXIV, for example, includes lines like 'his potatoes', 'Navy Board, Eastern Department', 'wherein deacon (later general) Palmer'. These are supposed to be lines of verse? It was published in 1940. If we scrap most of Olson's wigged-out jive, we can just talk about field poetry. That is to distinguish poetry that uses the page as a unit rather than following a series of brief phonetic instants, which is after all how speech works. Layout is marked by apparently pointless white spaces, which we can call blotches. Where you see blotches, failed lines, and missing connectives, you are probably looking at open-field poetry. This is a new system which may seem like collapse, it means the dominance of the visual over the oral, its potential is unfathomed and may stretch for a long way. No longer serial, it is centreless and diffuse. All the parts of the field can relate to each other. Its lack of forward movement is suited for static data such as a landscape or an existing text which the poet is cutting up. It may even suit the parataxis which was such a feature of the new poetry.

Mottram makes some unexpected comments about megaliths:

> without up
> and down
> inside is said and outside
> azimuths for random places
> no centre to stand on in any weather.

The directionless geometry could be a reminder of open field poetry with its lack of focus and onward direction. The lack of emphasis seems to cooperate with the unvoicing of what is notes rather than finished language – irresolute but perhaps suggestive fragments. It is an achievement to articulate thought, but there are other qualities available to the inarticulate. This kind of murmur has its domain, perhaps akin to chamber music. The conventions in question are all found in Pound's *Cantos*, where the collapse of rhythm is not unrelated to the use of prose texts as sources of material that had no rhythm at all. Why didn't Pound identify the data sources and mark the points where the voice speaking changed? Why didn't he use some identifiers to show where the origin of the words (on the page) changed? If it is a mosaic of quotes why aren't there topic sentences or headings? Other poets followed Pound in this but it may not have been a good idea at the outset. A quick check shows that only one of the 36 poets listed as the British Poetry Revival used 'open field' layout. A second one, Barry MacSweeney, may be an open-field writer, viz. in *Black Torch 1* (1977). But he left this poetry out of his big *Selected Poems*.

There are indications that the unlabelling was moving towards acting as a marker of poemicity, demarcating poetry from prose (to replace other markers no longer custom and practice). This was a corollary of writing poems that were so reliant on source prose. The argument of the prose was deleted and individual high points were acquired – isolated by leaving out the rest. Each era has its signs of poemicity, frame markers or realm boundaries.

Pound's closest model was Robert Browning, and he took great pains to label the source of every stream of language, although he was found obscure by Victorian readers. More recently, it isn't hard to figure out that poems like this annoyed a lot of people and why they didn't calm down enough to move along with them. But with the luxury of retrospect we don't have to prove him wrong, we can just enjoy the poem.

If we describe this as data provided serially around a theme present at the outset we can conveniently say that the mainstream poem could also be described in that way. The differences can be exaggerated, which is why global write-offs of the Underground variant are so irrational. It may be fair to add that Mottram is not highly regarded by other poets and these are hardly classic examples of the Underground style. Everything behaves as if the new poem were based on a more complicated and free shot plan (and vitiated by weak metalanguage to signal changes of topic and standpoint). But the distinctive feature may be less the number of edits than the abandonment of a physical situation for a narrative of ideas that follows an intellectual logic and is not 'someone standing in front of a scene' most of the time.

In the period 1960-1997, a lot of critics disliked modern poetry so much that they didn't want to understand it. They wrote about it to disqualify it. They saw this as their achievement. They waved it around their heads, yelling 'look!'. This was part of a 'finding of winners' process, where someone could be the apex of the system only if other people were definitively losers. A poetry world imprinted by an academic world that was in love with winners and fewness was bound to run this kind of process.

WELL, I'M JUST A MODERN GUY: THE REALM OF THE ALTERNATIVE

Mottram wrote a catalogue for a weekend event at the Polytechnic of Central London in June 1974 that is the original definition of the British Poetry Revival. Something needs revival only if it has died; the implication of a mid-century decline is now widely accepted. Mottram first lists the poets in an existing anthology (by John Matthias): of an older generation, David Jones, Hugh MacDiarmid, Basil Bunting; then Christopher Middleton, Charles Tomlinson, Gael Turnbull, Roy Fisher, Ted Hughes, Ian Hamilton Finlay, Christopher Logue, Matthew Mead, Nathaniel Tarn; and of 'younger poets' Anselm Hollo, Ken Smith, Lee Harwood, Harry Guest, and Tom Raworth. Mottram adds to these the names Tom Pickard, Bob Cobbing, Stuart Montgomery, Jeff Nuttall, Allen Fisher, Dom Silvester Houédard, Jeremy Hilton, Elaine Feinstein, Michael Horovitz, David Chaloner, Andrew Crozier, Peter Redgrove, Barry MacSweeney, Jim Burns, Edwin Morgan, Chris Torrance, John James, Peter Riley, and John Hall.

'A study of the period should start here', he says, *here* being Matthias' well-informed list. Mottram is talking about the important poets of the period; he does talk about the resistance to them of reactionary critics, but he is not setting any entrance exam. (Matthias, in 1971, had included six other poets not mentioned by Mottram: Peter Whigham, John Daniel, John Montague, Gavin Bantock, D.M. Thomas, and George MacBeth. Possibly they failed to meet Mottram's standards.) It would be problematic to describe an entrance exam if it doesn't exist. We have possibly a double boundary wall (*in* are the poets whom Mottram, just a modern guy, likes and admires, simultaneously *in* as ones whom reactionary critics dislike and want to convict of artistic immorality) but both walls work at the level of *gestalt*, overall and unconscious patterns that synthesise dozens of different visible factors, and neither is amenable to definition at the conscious plane – *where it's not happening*. Another possible definition is 'an area reached by breaking out of the coherent restrictions of the centre but not otherwise defined'; points on the perimeter are further away from each other than each is from the centre.

There is a difference between the Underground and the British Poetry Revival. Hughes and Redgrove were not the Underground.

In 1960, there was a nucleus of poets who had identified the poetic of the central poetry as limited by a code and who were willing to publish exposures of that code. This nucleus would include Denise Levertov, Charles Tomlinson, Gael Turnbull, and Roy Fisher. The articulation preceded the composition of a large body of poetry built on a *different* code.

A Various Art, the 1987 anthology edited by Tim Longville and Andrew Crozier, which covered, roughly, the generation born in the 1940s, included: Anthony Barnett, J.H. Prynne, Tim Longville, John James, John Hall, John Temple, John Riley, Veronica Forrest-Thomson, Peter Riley, Andrew Crozier, Doug Oliver, David Chaloner, Roy Fisher, Peter Philpott, Ralph Hawkins, Iain Sinclair, Nick Totton.

Iain Sinclair's ground-breaking anthology of 1996, *Conductors of Chaos*, included the following recent poets: Out To Lunch, Caroline Bergvall, B. Catling, cris cheek, Kelvin Corcoran, Andrew Crozier, Andrew Duncan, Bill Griffiths, Allen Fisher, Alan Halsey, Lee Harwood, Michael Haslam, John James, Grace Lake, Tony Lopez, Barry MacSweeney, Rod Mengham, Drew Milne, Geraldine Monk, Maggie O'Sullivan, Doug Oliver, Ian Patterson, J.H. Prynne, Jeremy Reed, Denise Riley, Peter Riley, Chris Torrance, John Wilkinson, Aaron Williamson, Stewart Home.

The question of continuity from 1974-1996 is difficult. If we describe the two lists as simply what two individuals liked to read at two points in time, that is accurate but may be missing something. At the risk of altering the evidence, I am going to add a further list of poets without whom the Underground could not be imagined: Colin Simms, Peter Finch, Asa Benveniste, Adrian Clarke, Brian Marley, Martin Thom, John Ash, Paul Gogarty, Paul Brown, Gavin Selerie, Nigel Wheale, Philip Jenkins. A brief check suggests that of the 36 people Mottram lists only two had studied at Oxford. What does this mean? I can't give an exact answer but behind it lies a skein of face-to-face contacts, meetings in pubs and classrooms, readings, lengthy conversations, all contributing to a sense of why you're writing and who your reader is going to be. Some of these conversations were precursors to poems. This history is unwritten and unknown to me. In recollection, people may talk more about the scene than about what they were reading.

Is the Underground an organism? I doubt that. An organism naturally has a history and an anatomy. The Underground evaporates on approach, by definition.

THE AMERICAN 1950S

An important topic for the radical British poets at least up to 1974 is the influence of American avant-garde poetry of the 1950s. Thus poets like Frank O'Hara, Charles Olson, Robert Duncan, Jack Spicer, John Wieners, Louis Zukofsky, George Oppen. It was normal to discuss English poets in terms of which US poets they were deriving from. This was the shared vocabulary. (I should add the names of Robert Lowell and Allen Ginsberg, influential on poetry I prefer not to think about. Ted Berrigan and John Ashbery need to be added, without being poets of the 1950s.) It is possible to believe that the American thing was the key difference between the BPR poets and the reactionaries (and thus not creativity, intelligence, innovation, etc). Something often discussed but indefinable was the effect of British speech and personality structures, so that the American model could work only by arduous adaptation processes. This was a competitive shopping experience much like owning a car. The more obscure (and extreme) your pet American poet, the more you had won the game. Just as Jung wrapped up, branded, and streamlined the *symboliste* tradition, so the named poets had, by 1960, somehow wrapped up the modernist line in literature: they were the current showroom models in modernism. But also, they gave the impression of having the power of translating fantasies about how to be a poet into actual poems, and at the time the British team did not seem able to do that. This was intoxicating and the feeling of power is the key thing at every stage. The American thing gave new poets the impression that they had something precious and splendid at a point when they had really written nothing at all. This was a secure feeling in which to learn. The pioneer poets in English cities had a feeling that all they had to do was to repeat a story that had already happened – if you tell the real story it is unwelcome, even today. Writing in the American way was like English musicians, from 1960 on, playing blues and R'n'B: they felt protected inside the existing sounds, the more accurately copied the better. This meant flow but a loss of self-awareness.

Mandragora

As we look at the map of the 1960s it is striking how good the poetry of Hughes and Redgrove is. It is quite apart from the new Underground and from the empirical mainstream. They excel by the amount of poetry they wrote in their lives, by the originality of their stories and characters, by the detail with which they render scenes and by the vigour and variety of their imagery. Some poets may not want to excel in those qualities, but surely most do. Peter Grey, in an essay in the anthology *Mandragora*, discusses Hughes and Redgrove from the occultist point of view. It seems that part of occultism is cultivating the power of mythological fantasy and that by practice one comes to spend hours a day in directed dreamlike improvisation that produces copious new material. I want to suggest that this practice of mythological fantasy is something completely separate from the usual poetic practice of the time and that this cognitive technique explains why both these poets stand aside from the poetry around them and tower above it, in a realm of their own.

This towering can be related to their rejection of empirical knowledge as the source for the information related in poems. This is a whole 'manner of perception and discourse' and we should not look at an empirical bias covering the entire landscape without looking at this anti-empirical group as well. Grey describes these two poets as inspired by Graves, i.e. the processes of inventing the pseudo-antique material written up in *The White Goddess* rather than his poetry. I understand that this process (which gets stronger with many years of practice) is unusual among poets but far from unusual among occultists; in fact the way of life of occultists is based on much time plunged in creative fantasising, and the other apparatus is mainly a way of triggering and protecting this state of mind. The key to the empirical principle of most modern English poets is a heightened sensitivity to this type of fantasy material and a profound dislike of it. This is a reasoned rejection, and the background to it is that in modern Europe this faculty of fantasy has been mainly directed at politics and that its powers have had anti-democratic outcomes. The word ideology describes, in fact, intellectual material that is not based on social observation but on mythological fantasy. It is arguable that what is distinctive about Hughes and Redgrove is the apolitical nature of their fantasy life. To look away for a moment, I suspect that ideology can be seen as productivity – that it is anomalous to have a tier of intellectuals in a society that does not have this power of ideological creativity (and whose education is designed to train it out).

In the poetic world of 1960-1990, Hughes was predominant as a poet and there was no literary theory around that even allowed it to be possible that Hughes' poems could be good. Academics had a pervasive feeling in this period that poetry finally did not belong to them and that the imposing building of their literary knowledge was made of billowing dust. There was an abiding legitimacy problem, as myth is the core of culture. Yet the myths we use come from archaic cultures, from the Bronze Age or even the Neolithic, material that was taken up and recycled in Hellenistic times by poets who could read and write. The power of actually creating myth vanished and was buried from 20th-century consciousness by a geology of inhibitions. Scholars know they can't create myths, and this is a part of the fundamental knowledge of philologers, rarely voiced. At this point we can see that Hughes and Redgrove actually did have this power of creating new myths. It was an intoxicating feeling. This recourse to archaic, alien, fertile (and repetitive) strata was one of the things happening in the 1960s.

Bronze Age myth was collective and 20th-century myth is individual and 'proprietary'. This is a fundamental fact.

JUNGIAN POETRY

Maud Bodkin wrote a vital book about archetypes in literature in 1934. She was close to Jessie L. Weston, author of *From Ritual to Romance*, which influenced *The Waste Land*. Weston was not alien to occultism, which favoured the Grail legends, or to G.R.S. Mead. So Eliot's 1923 poem incorporates that material: it's already there. But this is not Jungian, it's part of the *symboliste*/mythical line that *produced* Jung. The problem with writing about the influence of Carl Gustav Jung on British poetry is that Jung was just one of thousands of people involved in the occult revival and its fall-out, and that despite his academic or medical certification he was not unusual or a great originator. He had ideas about art, in books like *Symbols of Transformation*. One is the idea of a personal spirit who has a link to an individual human being and who can act as a leader for them. This spirit has a voice and the flow of language that becomes poems is seen as coming from this spirit. The verbal flows are real even if the spirit is not. Individuation is a watchword. Intellectual history is normally written about saints or theologians, or about people who fit into the history of science. Jung found a third group, a large share of the surviving past, keepers of esoteric knowledge, mages, sorcerers, or alchemists; their texts included a vast stock of images and narratives, poorly studied and yet endlessly suggestive. When Olson, a devout Jungian, wrote about Apollonius of Tyana, Apollonius was an example of these mages or wonder-workers. Arguably, all indigenous myth-creators are seen as forming part of the mage-sorcerer class.

The acquisitive process does not respect property rights in another direction, I mean that the mythology of all cultures is seen as representing parts of the human mind, and so as belonging to each individual, including Westerners. This is the theory of archetypes. Culture is seen as closely related to recovery from illness, and as this illness is individual the theory of creativity is biased towards the individual. Followers of Jung see his ideas as the rules of art in general and so do not see themselves as following a theory. The idea of eternal symbols is significantly linked to the power of these art ideas to heal people; illness must be temporary, the problem is a route out of it and into a state of health that is normal for humans and so as old and widespread as the species. Believing this is healing for people for whom a key anxiety is that the illness can reproduce itself and not go away.

It is not clear why this process of individuation and being called by a spirit would be of interest to someone else; the artistic drive of this poetry is separate from its fidelity to Jungian models. Jungian poets do not strongly identify with each other. There is no anthology for them. Conversely, the method encourages originality.

External time is not important for them, the state of time within the story and its personal and mythical course is always more important. Dating this material has proved elusive but we can find clear-cut 'archetypal' poems in Edwin Muir's volume *One Foot in Eden* in 1955. Also in the 1950s, Kathleen Raine (1908-2003) was attending Eranos conferences at Ascona and giving papers to an audience that included Jung as well as eminent magi. The style was a marginal thing in the 1950s and shot to prominence in the 1960s.

Jungian poets would include Edwin Muir, Peter Redgrove, Ted Hughes, D.M. Black, Tom Lowenstein, Kathleen Raine, Hilary Llewellyn-Williams, David Wevill, Michael Haslam, Penelope Shuttle, Maggie O'Sullivan, David Barnett, Elisabeth Bletsoe, David Harsent, Sarah Law. This is a staggering list in terms of quality and quantity of output. Naïve art is a theme in art history. Intellectual art is cynical and tired, naïve artists like what they see and like to paint. There is no folklore about naïve poetry. That is because the intact, joyful, life-enhancing forms of creativity began entering poetry a long time ago – precisely through these Jungians.

FOLKSONG

There is a modality of poetry that links to folk songs, a literary model that goes back to the time before the Renaissance and that in principle lacks all the flourishes which were new in Elizabethan times and the ones that have been developed in learnèd poetry ever since. Charles Causley, in many of his poems, makes this link. As it turns out the Renaissance has extremely complex consequences. In the period I am discussing, the folk song was a largely unimportant model for poetry, comprising 2% or maybe 3% of the poetry I cover. Evidently people were surrounded by folk music (on the radio or on record) all the time. George Mackay Brown exploited folk forms but had broken his poems out of the older rhythmical, stanzaic matrix to allow something new. The weakening of something that had been around in the 1950s draws us to speculate that it had evolved, rather than lost energy; becoming in fact the Jungian current. Folk literature had embodied pre-rational components that could be escalated into myth and as myth throve and became New Age and so on the folk current dried up.

Part of the reason for regression to folk forms had been a feeling among Christians that the rise of secularism had begun at the Renaissance and that to recover a wholly Christian landscape it was necessary to find a way back to the Middle Ages. The manner of religiosity that grew in the 1960s, with its eclecticism, was thus in a position to take over from the Folk thing. The Renaissance style models were often Greek and Latin, but also often Italian and Spanish. In Scotland, the 16th century saw the advent of English as the language of poetry, even before the union of crowns in 1603. It followed that anti-English feeling was expressed by using pre-Renaissance models.

A Note on J.H. Layard

J.H. Layard (1891-1974) was an ethnologist and later a psychoanalyst who intersects with the history of poetry in a tantalising way. He was a friend of W.H. Auden in Berlin in the late 1920s. In 1944, Faber published his book *The Lady of the Hare*, a mythical-psychoanalytical book that may be a mediator of Jungian concepts in England. He psychoanalysed Peter Redgrove, a friend of his, in the early 1960s. David Harsent read him as a teenager (so before 1962) and published two groups of poems (one was 'Lepus', in *Marriage*, 2002) based on his hare imagery. Ultimately, Layard is not important in the history of poetry – he just wasn't a strong enough personality. The *Lady* book starts with hare dreams of a patient he was analysing, and goes on to a catalogue of perhaps a hundred different appearances of the hare in folklore around the world. The implication, that world mythology belongs to the deep stratum of one individual's mind, was suggestive. This unbound free grammar of images does seem to be present in modern poets. The idea, that every appearance of the hare in any country is related to all the others, has a weak factual basis. It belongs to an era of comparatism – Layard's book is related to *The Golden Bough*, to Lord Raglan, to A.M. Hocart and Grafton Elliot Smith.

Layard was an outlier, a little world. Few people have heard of him. By discussing individual technical areas, I create patches of information that do not by any means add up to a complete picture of the BPR. No more do these patches apply to all the poets listed by Mottram, or another; there is no constancy across that whole field.

Scrolls of Damaged Language

A reaction where dialogue is failing is to damage the part of language shared with the other person as part of the withdrawal. The damage is then exhibited as a component of the poetic text as an expressive sign of rage. It is a withdrawal of respect; the declaration of low status is analogous to the utterance of high status via high language, which is a well documented function of poetry. It is an utterance at risk, a contentious proposal. The poetry lurks in the very area of damage, the crush zone, and does not bother to repair language. The burnt-out wrecks were strewn by the side of the road; the photographic wreck paths as visual highlights. The carnage of intransigence. There was another idea, in which the role of the reader was to have their attachments severed, and the process of erasing affection, in a general erasure of habit and self-regard, was the clear intent of the poem. This was also because of despising their ideas. The poem was a deconditioning environment for deprogramming. If you combined these two tendencies, the outcome was totally unbearable. The political project could produce some very aggressive art.

Variations on a Time Theme

One version of the last 50 years of cultural history is that it climaxed with the Scottish National Party victory in the election of May 2015. The end of sentiment and kitsch. A boiling off and purgation process. Striking out for cultural creativity and autonomy.

Sprachkrise (speech crisis) is where the decision of which language to write in becomes so fraught that no state of certainty is possible. The subtext is that this crisis promotes the resort to avant-garde language in a fertile way. The oscillation of the avant-garde style may reflect the crisis as a form of energy and self-knowledge. The artificiality of the avant-garde style may 'narrate' the story of a utopian political solution where the stresses that produced the *Sprachkrise* are resolved by the return of equality and autonomy. 'How do you pronounce this word?' could have many answers. The question applies to places where feelings about English are like the feelings of the Croats about Serbo-Croat. Scottish poets are always seen as answers to the questions being set by Scottish thinkers. This may extend to how they approach the poem.

The Now Tense of Folklore

Pauline Stainer belongs in a group with Edwin Muir, Kathleen Raine, and George Mackay Brown. The link between those four is one of the most satisfactory connections in this field. Poets, and especially significant modern ones, do not group easily. Stainer took the possibilities a lot further. Muir published his long poem 'Variations on a Time Theme' in 1934, a strange but brilliant work that explains time in a heraldic way, as stylised characters appear and re-appear throughout history. If we are looking at Stainer's poems of 60 years later as part of the same realm of forms, we have a set of affinities – non-secular, indebted to Symbolism, cyclic and full of symmetries, brushing the occult – which do not fit into any periodisation. If you actually like British poetry you probably have a spot somewhere where books like *The Lady & the Hare*, *Time Theme*, *Fishermen with Ploughs*, and *The Year One* are stored and carefully protected. It's so much easier producing a schema if you don't actually like poetry. It is worth pointing to this link because Stainer fans might want to know a direction they could go in. But it may also be worthwhile taking a longer look at the verbal structures that they share.

Alexander Carmichael collected, over the last 40 years of the 19th century, Gaelic charms and private hymns that he published as *Carmina Gadelica*. I had to look closely at the text of Macleod's 1953 volume *Script from Norway* and finally recognised several passages that were based on the *Carmina*. While these Hebridean charms resemble very early Irish manuscript material and represent mediaeval Gaelic versification, there are didactic elements in their construction that are Catholic rather than Gaelic, so there may be an element of European, even eastern Mediterranean, literary culture in them. Kathleen Raine's *The Year One*, of 1952, contains many poems in spell structures which, on comparison, turn out to be based on the *Carmina*. About half the poems in that book go back to their generative models. This may sound like national pride on my part, but in fact both the poets mentioned had that pride in Scotland as well as that interest in folk literature – before I was born. Muir is the theorist, and Muir wrote of the end of an organic community and its folk creativity in his 1940 book, *The Story and the Fable*, located in the gap between the Orkney of his childhood and the Glasgow where he moved at about 14. He stages folklore as the wonderful thing that we can't have any more, the content of our yearning. He sees a great loss, when the old culture died. This loss cannot be located precisely, but the new culture is highly centralised and in this way includes both the Renaissance and the leisure products of industrial capitalism. For him Scotland had fallen out of the timeless and cyclic into changing time, which is also meaningless. He does not see any way of getting back. His idea of folk culture included the Orkney of the late 19th century, which he experienced as a child, and the Gaelic-speaking areas of Scotland, not so far away, where the folk culture persisted even later. His poetry is not folkloric but he belongs with 'folky poets' because of his prose writing. It is not so surprising if, after a great theorist describes something we can't have, a later generation of poets writes that something. This is what you become a poet in order to do. Ted Hughes was greatly influenced by Muir. It is interesting that Muir proposed the Orkney of his childhood as the land of intact folk sensibility; Mackay Brown never wrote about anything but Orkney, and Stainer went to live there. The other thing about Muir is that he underwent a Jungian analysis in 1919. This raises the question of whether the Jungian current entered British poetry not in the 1960s but much earlier. This is an odd moment. Muir was so rational in many ways – but he had these contacts with deeply irrational and quasi-occultist areas. Jung was an occultist, you can't get away from that. There is a boundary where the folk element borders on archetypal poetry, and we have to consider whether the use of folk was also a stage on a journey towards a new mythology.

The *Carmina* poems are generally based on compounds of two – units come in twos and fours. The verse is made of fulfilments – the binding structure means that every unit starts an arc and almost every unit completes an arc. In fact the lines are a double fulfilment. The structure is like a boat, everything grips everything else. The most famous of the grace poems, for example, deals with the core of substances because the cosmos is evoked in terms of wood, gold, etc.: all objects made of wood are evoked at once. It is based on analogy. There is some analogy between all objects made of wood. (A group of poems are labelled 'graces' as a translation of a Gaelic word *buadh* which can also be translated as excellence or talent. Generically, 'things you wish a child to have'.) This cosmos of essences and analogies exists too in poems by Pauline Stainer, Kathleen Raine, and George Mackay Brown. Muir's idea of personalities repeating across great Time is like the internal time relations in this poem, where everything repeats. Folklore could in fact be used by a 20th-century poet to produce literary objects whose internal time was built of arcs and fulfilments and mirrored a version of human time that was cyclic and not progressive. Where nothing is lost, in fact. The boat cuts the water. The water heals. The boat stays afloat.

A COUNTRY WITH NO GOVERNMENT: FALSE TIME

To follow Muir's thought, we have to look at some other local theories about Time. Murray G.H. Pittock's book, *The Invention of Scotland: The Stuart Myth and the Scottish Identity, 1638 to the Present,* recovers the history of Jacobitism as a lost cause of some cultural weight. Just to recall: James II was deposed in 1688 because he was a Catholic and many people thought he was plotting a Catholic coup in Britain which would have led to the disenfranchisement and persecution of Protestants. He was replaced by his sister, but since succeeding monarchs were not the legitimate heirs there continued to be hold-out supporters of the Stuart dynasty. James is 'Jacobus' in Latin so this party were called Jacobites. Ruskin was a Jacobite. Pittock says, '[b]y 1905, neo-Jacobitism in England was largely a spent force'. Just as well, you may think. He shows that it was still an emotional focus for some people in Scotland in the 1940s.

Pittock describes a salt-glazed Jacobite tea-pot; there is a whole (small) world of Jacobite objects; what had been a government (until 1688) is reduced to a set of knick-knacks. Loyalist families were still pro-Stuart around 1770 – this was not on the scale of 'oppositional politics' but rather of domestic ceremonies and keepsakes. This reduction is a kind of aestheticisation – and points ahead to a merely literary version of politics. It is a forerunner of the pictures on tins of shortbread which are so often mocked as kitsch versions of Scottish history. Yet these lost causes could give rise to intense emotions, just as the Catholics also developed an emotional intensity almost to compensate for the failure of their cause. Because Scotland ceased to be a country, its writers developed a lost time, a displaced terrain where they could speak freely. Sacred objects embodied intact space, expanded at times to chapels. The intense use of symbolic objects may be relevant to our poets. A poem may be words written on a small domestic object that originates in another universe.

When the new Scottish National Party (not yet called that) presented its first parliamentary candidate in 1929, Lewis Spence (1875-1955) was chosen. He also wrote an early statement of their platform: *Freedom for Scotland. The Case for Scottish Self-Government* (1926) and the poems in a revived 16th-century Scots which gave MacDiarmid the stimulus to start writing similar poems – 'complete' Lallans as opposed to a dialect with restricted vocabulary and range of social contexts.

The occultism has nothing to do with Scottish politics. That is why I was perturbed to see Lewis Spence as that first parliamentary candidate – because Spence was an occultist. In 1943 he published *The Occult Causes of the Present War*, which links it back to Atlantis. Of course he wasn't the only occultist in Europe in 1943. Spence (as quoted by Pittock) said that there were two currents of thinking among 'disloyal' Scots: one which rejected the Reformation, so that everything had been wrong since John Knox; and one which rejected the Hanoverians, so that, while the Jacobite risings were OK, everything that had happened since the failure of the last one in 1746 had gone wrong. We have to add another theory: the Scottish language has been losing its sociological grip and range of uses in Scotland since the later 16th century and this is wrong too. The idea of reversing this and writing poetry in a Scots which covers the full range of intellectual possibilities of contemporary culture was what animated MacDiarmid. It incorporates the ideas of reliving the bad past in a good way and of four centuries of cultural failure. MacDiarmid thought the whole course of Scottish culture since 1603 was corrupted by England, and wanted to cut back to a pre-Renaissance stage. Mackay Brown and Fionn MacColla were two writers who believed that Scottish history had gone wrong with John Knox, but as Pittock points out Edwin Muir was also someone who had Jacobite sympathies, although he did not have any expectation that this wrong step would be reversed. There is some kind of relationship between the transformed and frozen time of 'Variations on a Time Theme' and the 'misdirected and lost time' of anti-Reformation or anti-Hanoverian theories of history. The 'damaged time' is recouped in aesthetic form. The idealised 'good time' disappears into a mere idea, which is too small to live in, teapot-sized, but for that reason can be stylised and heightened as a poem. We have to mention Peter Davidson whose *The Palace of Oblivion* recovers a number of partisans of lost causes and is utterly amazing.

GEORGE MACKAY BROWN

Brown (1921-96) stated that his main influences were the Catholic service book, the Norse sagas, and the ballads (text in his Penguin Modern Poets volume), and also that

> [i]t was then [*at the time of the Reformation, AD*] that the old heraldry began to crack, that the idea of 'progress' took root in men's minds. What was broken, irremediably, in the 16th century was the fullness of life in a community, its simple interwoven identity. In earlier times the temporal and the eternal, the story and the fable, were not divorced, as they came to be after Knox: they used the same language and imagery, so that the whole of life was illuminated ... Innocence gave place to a dark brooding awareness ... from that time, too, the old music and poetry died out, because the single vision which is the source of all art had been choked. Poets followed priests into the darkness.
> (from *Memoirs of a Modern Scotland*, ed. Karl Miller).

Mackay Brown also came from Orkney and was Muir's pupil in the 1950s. His idea of time involves repeating and static roles, and is acquired from Edwin Muir's extraordinary 1934 poem; they live in the same special theory. To this he adds a steeping in folk modes – he has disappeared into folk literature. The use by Raine and Macleod of the *Carmina*, in the cultural complex of the 1950s, may shed light on Brown's use of symbols and analogy. To recycle what I have said elsewhere, he uses forms as stylised as if they were in a textile – he writes in a textile mode. The embroideries illustrated in a book of Norwegian art treasures (from an exhibition) I have are a reference point for this comparison. The exhibition catalogue remarks, 'Together with the simple linear and flat-patterned treatment of pictorial elements in the tapestry, their evenly toned and sharply defined panes serve to enhance the decorative effect.' He solved his stylistic problems by an advance into flat images. As part of this reduction to a decorative schema with rules sharply detached from reality, we have to bear in mind that the designs were simplifications of rather grander designs from centres like Flanders and Byzantium – the quality of picking up driftwood, metaphorically, which grew in a forest far away, is significant for Brown. His language has an invisible loom that makes it come out like something from the fifteenth century – he hides inside a folk idiom but at no point reproduces a real folk form, such as a Scots ballad or a Norse tale. Like Spence, he seems to be speaking from another century. He has recovered time by abandoning the present. Much of his work is an astonishingly rich reworking of basically wrong theories about the course of history. Brown's last volume has a poem dealing with his parents' wedding, which included Gaelic-speaking relatives of his mother:

> The bridegroom, he was drowning
>   In a sea of lovely Gaelic;
> And woke, his mouth cold
> With dew of the wild white rose.
>   (from 'Mhari', *Collected Poems*, p.444)

The white rose was a Jacobite emblem. This was about 1910. If the Stuart dynasty fell in 1688, would Highlanders still have been emotionally Jacobite in 1910? Brown is not really interested in chronology. It is a beautiful stanza though. The story about being whirled away in a dance and waking up cold is actually one about being carried away by the fairies; the identification of Celticity with the supernatural is lurking there, beneath the threshold. Brown died in 1996 but the volume published in 2001 seems to be his best. Perhaps I had re-read the earlier ones so often that their power wore out. This late material has his clearest references to Muir, in the poem about him and in 'Uranium', where Brown refers to 'the fable' and 'the story' (after Muir's autobiography) in a poem warning against mining uranium in Orkney. Here he moves the fatal exit from the fable to the atomic age – no longer in the 1540s. This flexibility shows him thinking, which is not what he normally does and is admirable. The poem recapitulates human history but this time does not wheel on either the Reformation or the fall of the Stuarts or industrialisation.

The poem about Muir is unusually explicit about a time theory:

> The labyrinth: an old blind man in the centre of it with a crystal key.
> The labyrinth: towers, vennels, cellars.
> The labyrinth: wilderness of dark doors, with one bright lintel here
>   and there.
>   Bright lock by bright lock he turns the crystal key.
> At every door, a rag of time falls from him.
>   Through ghetto, shambles, graveyard he goes.

The brightness spills out, spills out in front of him.
He brings the poem to the hidden bestiary.
The labyrinth. The labyrinth.
He stands, a young man, at a threshold of unbearable brightness.
(from 'Edwin Muir', *Collected Poems* p. 438)

The style is near Muir (who wrote a book of poems called *The Labyrinth*), it could be Muir rather than Mackay Brown. The sequence whereby an old man becomes a young one is part of an unusual theory of time. Perhaps unconsciously, this poem also tells the tale of Brown replacing Muir as the poet of archetypes – and orkneytypes. The repetition in this passage is related to the refusal of a syntactic organisation that is not possible in folklore. It is like a tapestry preferring flatness to spatial depth.

In Orkney, people traditionally regard themselves as Scandinavians rather than Scots (transfer of control from the Norwegian Crown was in 1469, but only as a pledge against loans of which the canny Scots turned down repayment). Brown rarely left Orkney, but did spend ten years in Edinburgh, where he attended New Battle Abbey College, which was run by Edwin Muir (another Orcadian), There he hung out with other Scottish poets. I have a friend from north-eastern Scotland who reports that among the gay community in that region the presence of Mackay Brown for recreational purposes in certain public lavatories favoured by the fraternity was quite noted a few years ago. As his appearance was so distinctive this presence was unmistakable, especially to a community that valued cultural achievement so much (above all among creative figures from the north-east itself). Sympathy for someone who was so demonstrably one of their own was only very slightly tempered by the duty to gossip and so raise everyone's consciousness, if only gradually. I take this on as a highly probable fact. It is not hard fact.

If Brown was gay, he undoubtedly kept it as quiet as almost everyone else born in 1921 who had the same sexual orientation. The story helps to recognise the inner meaning of his poetry in one way, that the central figure of Saint Magnus as martyr can be interpreted as an emblem of Brown's martyrdom to the morality of his rural community. Magnus' celibacy is an aspect of this. Magnus meant much more to Brown than he ever seems to mean to readers of Brown's work. Symbols can be used to hide things as well as reveal them. There are anecdotes about Brown: first, that – as stated in his obituaries – he only visited England once; he lived in a world whose centre was Orkney. England was meaningless to him. Second, that he had travelled on a sleeper the whole way from Caithness to Edinburgh without discovering the cord which turned the light on. His political dislike of technology was matched by a remarkable lack of grasp of it. Urban life was simply too much for him. Catholicism – he converted in 1960 – would have mandated a celibacy that was easier to defend in Orkney than in a big town full of the temptations of the flesh. If someone is so keen on arrested development, you have to wonder how they apply that to their personal life. Yet his ideas have no connection with politics. Theoretically he could have campaigned for the reversal of the Reformation. But this is an impossible goal – his literary pattern is fundamentally detached from reality.

Brown wrote absolutely no personal poetry. This was pretty rare for someone born when he was. It can easily be attributed to a love of folk poetry and a belief in the importance of the community as a whole. There are other interpretations though. If we suppose that he had a pressing wish to avoid the topic of his personal life, then the creation of a set of patterned and stylised stories, unfolding in a fascinating and highly controlled way and not demanding his participation, was an adequate literary habitat for that. The patterning is notably archaic and decorative, and frozen and repetitive; it was something he could hide inside. The doctrine of timeless and ineluctable roles, adopted from his teacher Edwin Muir, can act as an explanation of being gay; it's as natural as a horse being a horse, then. But the escape into the past can also act as an evasion of the question of becoming what you have to become, by postponing the whole issue, refusing to develop. The present with its fatal decisions, its burning desires, its conflicts with the family or with religion, can be permanently side-lined in an aesthetic labyrinth designed not to have an exit. There is no question of Brown's unrevealed sexual identity damaging the quality of his work. He never pretended to be anything else, to have a set of feelings that he did not truly possess. The intensity of his stylisation (closer to Walter Pater than to a village bard) masks everything but also transforms it, and is robust beyond the point where mere biography could erode it.

His most ambitious poetic work is his 1971 volume, *Fishermen with Ploughs*, much influenced by Muir. It's obvious that he was reaching outside poetry, and he wrote some prose fiction after this. *Fishermen* narrates the story of one village in Orkney, from its settlement in the ninth century by a tribe emigrating from Norway bringing seed corn, through witch trials in the Middle Ages, to nuclear disaster in the modern age, and resettlement by refugees who try to master low-input agriculture enough to survive, and are ruled by a cruel but potent leader from then.

Because the *Collected Poems* includes an index of first lines, you can check where Brown uses numbers to start poems. None of them is a two or a four. If he was using the utterly binary *Carmina* poems, he was reshaping them significantly. He did like count-off forms, where everything is a foretelling or a fulfilment. Brown never literally remakes folk poems. He uses standard English, never dialect, in this most remote area of Anglian speech. Both Orkneys and Shetlands spoke a Scandinavian language (called Norn) until the late 18th century, possibly just early 19th: it was replaced by a dialect of Scots similar to that of Caithness and adjacent areas of the mainland, which had themselves spoken Norn until the 16th century. When Orkney changed language, the complete range of folk literature embodied in language would have disappeared. Tales can be translated but things like songs and poems, where the metre depends on the exact verbal form, would just have vanished. Gaelic is also in steep decline, and districts that have shifted language have lost their folklore. A group of the Ossianic ballads collected in the 19th century had definitely been memorised by people who didn't understand them (fully) because they hadn't learnt the bardic code, the specialised synonyms and word formations, the Irish words. Also the poems were several hundred years old. However, they learnt them because they were the supreme achievement of the old Gaelic society. As for theories of time, it is clear that the Gaelic language was in rapid decay in modern times. You can't apply the chronology of the southern two-thirds of Britain to the north. You have to get things like this in order to get what it means to be Scottish. Brown has always written in English, but the linguistic identity of the Orcadians (who are always his subject) is encoded indirectly. Since Scots reached the islands after the Reformation, it is probable that he would not use it on political grounds. Brown is a major writer because he isn't just recreating an imaginary 15th century, but is drawing on genuine stylistic features of insular speech and daily life. I think a lot of Scandinavian writing, and Northern Scottish writing for that matter, has strong similarities to Brown. He is not a mythomaniac. Brown has occupied a Scandinavian/Old Orcadian identity by using kennings, a living echo of Old Norse.

> 'A dove must fold your seed from dragon flame'.
> That blind rune stabbed the sea tribe.
> Fishermen sought a bird in the mountains.
>
> Their axes kept them that year from the dragon.
> Logs throttled a mountain torrent
> A goatherd gaped on the lumbering tons.
>
> Saws shrieked, sputtered, were sharpened, sang.
> Dunes were pale with strewment of boards.

Seaward a keel was set.
Sprang from that spine, a vibrant cluster of ribs.

Forge and envy begot a host of rivets.
Shavings, blond hair of excited children,
Curled from the combing adzes.
A woodman died of a rotten nail.
(Njal found, near falcons, an urn for his fires)
   (from 'Building the Ship', *Collected Poems*, p.90)

The verbal ornament of this poem, set in perhaps the ninth century, is close to the kenning style of Norse skaldic poetry – it is less common in Anglo-Saxon poetry. Brown used this style to evoke a ninth-century setting.

The static quality of his poetic organization deserves comparison with a folk museum (and related writings), where there is an absence of history because the daily objects don't change very much, often, for hundreds of years. The static feeling also has to do with the enveloping quality of monotonous work and the sacramental quality of objects. Once you decide that you don't look down on fishermen and housewives (even in the guise of 'alienation') you are forced to attribute great virtues to the objects that sustain and occupy daily life. There is a reassurance in monotony – something related is the study of wordfields in the lexical structure of poetry and their possible relation to a social structure. Every text must have a latent lexical lattice of some kind. It is of great interest to understand where these come from and how they organise primary sense data. Brown certainly approves of the elevation of everyday activities (the breaking of bread, but also harvesting and other kinds of work) in Christian liturgy. This aesthetic is the opposite of change and liberation. Interesting is the use of objects that have become half-inner, that is, they are 'objects' but also emblematic of some emotional message, based on their role in everyday life. They are a lot more rich in meaning than literal objects. This method is also close to folk-song.

Brown has described more of Orkney's working reality than almost any other poet has of their district. Certainly no one could write about north London in such clear-cut terms, the social structure is too complex to think about and too much of the work is 'virtualised', it doesn't involve objects. When most poets write about objects, it's despair – and bad faith because they don't believe their own theories about society, the evidence is too difficult: Brown describes objects, made by people, as parts of the human life-world. Brown's poetry is simple because there are only 50,000 people in the society he lives in, and a great deal of the work is physical work and can be described by pictorial methods. Only 80% of the population lives in cities, and I believe that human groups in somewhere like West Dorset, North Wales, or the Orkneys, probably do live like communities.

REACHING THE ATEMPORAL

The discourse around these poets has, correctly, used the word neo-Platonism. I am adding the use of folklore. Is there an arc between neo-Platonism and folklore? This is baffling. The use of substances as symbols, and of analogy as the way symbols work and are combined in verbal constructs, could be a link. The *Carmina* poems are based on hymn forms. Some of the early Christian hymns go back to a Greek intellectual milieu which was still 'freighted' with the beautiful patterns of pagan hymns. Plotinus wrote pagan hymns. Synesius wrote Christian hymns and was a neo-Platonist. This may have left latent links for someone like Raine to exploit.

The grouping of these four poets (Muir, Raine, Brown, Stainer) is very satisfying. The more these poets are bound to each other, the more they share a language of forms (with archaic indigenous sources), the longer the gap between *Time Theme* and *The Ice-Pilot Speaks*, the more they breach the idea of a public culture that changes every ten years and a history of style that includes everyone. (Stainer is an exception, she has not expressed any theory of time so far as I know.) Even more, they challenge the idea that a modern poet has to be an intellectual. For these four poets, time is an element of poetic style, a paint to be applied in intricate motifs by the poet. Naturally they don't fit into my version of time; I offer this essay as a check on my main thesis, an example of artistic cults living in private versions of time. Style-time is convergence but there can be many centres of convergence. Any statement about stylistics and history has to deal with the peculiar excellence of G. M. Brown as a test of its accuracy. The four poets form a discrete group, distinct from the other Jungian poets.

There is a link between these malnourished and largely fantastic causes and Scotland as a people without organs for so many years; more devolution led to better quality political discourse, just as the nationalist argument proposed. Other countries had politics and governments, Scotland had these halfway-visionaries with their aesthetic systems and their total detachment from ordinary people. Now that Scotland has a government it does not need these deviant theories of time based on the nothingness, vacuity, failure of the present. The present is now where we live. Nationalist politics succeeded by throwing out the infantile forms.

Blowing Your Mind:
Immediacy in the Sixties

1960
Ted Hughes, *Lupercal*;
Ian Hamilton Finlay, *The Dancers Inherit the Party*.

1961
Francis Berry, *Morant Bay*;
Peter Redgrove, *The Nature of Cold Weather*;
Roy Fisher, *City*.

1962
Christopher Middleton, *torse 3. Poems 1948-61*.

1963
Rosemary Tonks, *Notes on Cafés and Bedrooms*;
Christopher Logue, *The Arrival of the Poet in the City*;
Adrian Mitchell, *Poems*;
Peter Redgrove, *At the White Monument*.

1964
David Wevill, *Birth of a Shark*.

1965
Kathleen Raine, *The Hollow Hill*;
George Barker, *The True Confession of George Barker* (part 2);
George Mackay Brown, *The Year of the Whale*;
Christopher Middleton, *nonsequences. selfpoems*.

1966
Basil Bunting, *Briggflatts*;
Peter Redgrove, *The Force*;
Francis Berry, *Ghosts of Greenland*;
David Wevill, *A Christ of the Ice-Floes*;
Tom Raworth, *the relation ship*.

1967
Alan Ross, *Poems 1942-67*;
Rosemary Tonks, *Iliad of Broken Sentences*;
John James, *Mmm... ah yes*;
Ken Smith, *The Pity*;

John Riley, *Ancient and Modern*;
Andrew Crozier, *Loved Litter of Time Spent*;
Ted Hughes, *Wodwo*.

1968
J.H. Prynne, *Kitchen Poems*;
Edwin Morgan, *The Second Life*;
Geoffrey Hill, *King Log*;
Tom Raworth, *the big green day*;
Spike Hawkins, *the lost fire brigade*;
Barry MacSweeney, *The Boy From the Green Cabaret Tells of His Mother*.

1969
J.H. Prynne, *The White Stones*;
Roy Fisher, *Collected Poems 1968*;
David Jones, *The Tribune's Visitation*;
Charles Tomlinson, *The Way of a World*;
D.M. Black, *The Educators*;
Christopher Logue, *New Numbers*;
John James, *The Small Henderson Room*;
Christopher Middleton, *Our Flowers and Nice Bones*;
Andrew Crozier, *Walking on Grass*.

The classic anthology is Edward Lucie-Smith's *British Poetry Since 1945*, first published in 1970; later editions are of no value. *Contemporary Scottish Verse 1959-69* (1970), ed. Norman MacCaig and Alexander Scott; *The Lilting House* (1969), ed. Meic Stephens, John Stuart Williams (Welsh); for the non-traditional poetry of the decade, John Matthias' anthology in *TriQuarterly* #21 (1971), *Contemporary British Poetry*, remains classic; *A Group Anthology*, ed. Edward Lucie-Smith and Philip Hobsbaum (1963); *Love Love Love*, ed. Pete Roche (1967).

POLITICS IN THE 1960S

The government dedicated itself to the economic indices (exchange rate, growth of GNP, interest rates, growth of income, inflation) in the expectation that a favourable combination of all these could be obtained. Prices and Income Policy was the sacred ring: where shared sacrifice gave rise to economic virtue. The frustrations and theatricals attendant on this pointed to its alternative: naked market forces.

The Wilson government was dominated by sterling exchange rate crises from start to finish, and any other act of policy was waved through without the full attention of the Cabinet. The temptation for the historian must be to take the whole period, 1945-79, of governments striving to manage the economy in detail, draw a line round it, and scrub out all the details inside it. A variant on this is to identify, as Keith Middlemas has done, the First World War as the origin of a power-sharing triangle of capital, unions, and government (the 'Three Kingdoms' era), accepting a limited share of unions in affairs of state in order to end the labour militancy of the 1911-12 wave that a wartime boom in profits and output had accelerated; and to identify 1979 as the end of this accommodation. The Labour Party guaranteed high government spending and continuity of employment in return for throttling back strikes; but could only deliver the co-operation of employers and of the middle-class voters so long as the barely-chained demon of all-out universal strikes remained convincing. High unemployment, engineered in the slump of 1979-81, simultaneously did away with labour militancy and made the costs of any full-employment scheme so forbidding as to drive middle-class voters away from Labour.

Perhaps the hardest thing to recover today is the dominance of the Old Left: Wilson's Labour government from 1964 to 1970, the trade unions protecting the workers in about half of the economy from redundancy and exploitation, the welfare state. The date of 1964 suggests a better division of time than decades: the 1960s of popular imagination arguably didn't begin until 1965, and then didn't close until perhaps 1975. The climate of opinion was so collectivist that it reacted to images of bad housing as collective shame, proof that government intervention was needed. Even deviant behaviour – crime, unhappiness, madness – was seen as a failure of inclusion that was a summons to collective virtue. The delicacy of the system produced poets who surrendered individuality, seeing it as a form of sacrifice to the collective, and are indignant about self-expression as some kind of semi-criminal, self-indulgent breach of government guidelines. This total vision led to a degree of complexity that soon gave rise to infinite quantities, or other paradoxes and insoluble equations. However, the arrival of more processing power, better theories, or new means of capturing data, was likely to push out the limits of the tractable. New ideas were there to animate poems, exanimated by old ideas.

Modernisation was put on the agenda around 1963 by both major political parties, in one of those consensual redefinitions of reality that are so important in British life and so hard to locate in retrospect. The cult of the new that marked the 1960s and has never perceptibly decreased made it unacceptable for any artist or art consumer to see themselves as not new;

this has quite crippled the awareness of stylistic change, since everything is always claimed as new willy-nilly. This defective awareness makes it quite hard for eager young poets to realise that they are 30 years out of date.

The Labour Party was very deeply split between the Left and the Right. Wilson's genius was expended in conjuring tricks to keep the two in the same party; this is allegedly why he resigned, fed up, in 1976. It was because Wilson's men were marching in two different directions that he always led them in circles. If ideas are what threatens to sink the ship, the sailors start to resent ideas and see them as selfish and short-sighted, while the official lack of ideas is so humiliating that mention of it becomes obscene and anyone with ideas seems radiantly attractive by comparison. The demand for structural reform in poetry is a vent for the frustration with the government's inability to carry out structural reforms, while immersed in price/incomes/sterling rate crises. The managed system brought affluence, which allowed personal experimentation and innovation to take place, relatively unhindered by poverty and anxiety. The culture of ideas that animated poetry was outside both the Labour Party and the Communist Party. The radicalism of the time produced its clean slate for sketching on by ignoring the triangle of powers and the problems of price-and-incomes policy. Did this decision guarantee failure? What the New Left gave up on in theory, the New Right gave up on in practice from 1979.

Perhaps the lines 'high loyalty' and 'high theoretical activity' never intersect, for the following reason: intense theoretical activity relies on a highly unexpected landscape. Political success starves it of new problems to solve. It also relies on unoccupied and untreated ideas; a close cluster of theorists uses up the ideas. By the time you have a policy old enough to be understood by the whole party and by the electorate, it's not new enough to be theoretically interesting. An arrangement that is luxurious in the intellectual stimulation it provides may be useless in practical political results. However, this wealth of ideas also provided a psychological landscape of the unfamiliar, the fundamental, and the radical, for poetry to work on. It is conventional to distinguish between the Old Left and the New Left, although the distinction may not be recognised by the people it supposedly describes. In general parlance, the opposition includes these poles:

Old	New
unions	women, ethnic groups, gays, non-unionised labour

Labour Party, Communist Party	
working class, esp. in	middle-class university graduates
manufacturing industry	
industrial regions (South Wales,	London
the North, Birmingham, etc).	
the money economy	leisure and the household semiotics; the politics of representation in the media
elections	grassroots community organisations
action through professional bureaucrats, legislation	changes of attitude brought about by propaganda
agreements with employers	
continuity	spontaneity
pragmatism	
delegation of power via election	demos, meetings, the media
institutions	the individual
economics	sociology

There are differences of style and vocabulary too subtle to lay out. Perhaps the best definition of the New Left is their willingness to give up trying to find a solution to the managerial equations. This area just wasn't interesting enough. The Old Left actually used to win strikes and elections, and subsequently transfer purchasing power, in the form of wages, benefits, and subsidies, from the rich to the poor. Nobody could accuse the New Left of doing any of this. The revolt of the New Left was either going to push the sharing mechanism into higher gear, with abolition of wealth and poverty, or damage the triangular accommodation so laboriously sustained by the Old Left to the point where it collapsed, a New Right took over, and the electorate acquiesced in a system without mercy. One of the things the New Left shed was the idea of sacrifice: in a strike, everyone went through anxiety and deprivation, trusting only in each other, to achieve a political goal. Today, people go through anxiety and deprivation on the dole, but it's not buying them anything; and you're not part of anything, you're on your own. The concern with revolt that marked the era stemmed partly from the prominence on the news of strikes, official or unofficial, breaking government guidelines. There were too many government guide-lines. The glamour of revolt was seized on the high seas in the 1980s by young entrepreneurs, whose swinish greed was presented by the media as unconventional and dynamic. Their business tricks were presented as new thought. A social system that cannot contain its own youth is over-specified and too delicate. It cannot redesign itself quickly enough to adjust to changes in the outside world. The system has not been smashed, but is functioning at a lower capacity; one result of this cutback is youth unemployment.

The natural alliance was of the New Left theorists with the militant shop stewards and the non-unionised elements of the workforce; this probably would have overthrown the whole system, but contacts were only realised for a few days, even a few minutes. The New Left couldn't offer the shop stewards what they needed.

Engineering systems can never stay within the beautiful perfection of machine design. Today, they are being extended to include problems with the stock of raw materials and the disposal and eventual fate of waste products; back then the problem was with the influence on them of social systems, fluctuating demand (to be solved by advertising), and the wishes of the workforce. The machine might work for one cycle, but what if it goes through a million cycles? If its parts evolve, are they likely to degrade? An interest in cybernetics derives from the social machine, so generally expected to produce full employment and high output. The metaphor was illusory, since after all the machine parts were human beings with local intelligence. The recognition that problems of prices-and-income policy came only from the unwillingness of different interests to co-operate led to an interest in spontaneous mass decisions, a dream that the rival groups would abandon polarisation in favour of enthusiasm, like consumers suddenly embracing a new product. New mass media were seen as mediating a new togetherness and openness. The artlessness of poetry without structures was seen as a trailer for this new experience.

The Empire was effectively scrapped in the first half of the decade, (independence of Nigeria and Cyprus in 1960; Tanzania in 1961; Jamaica, Trinidad and Tobago, and Uganda in 1962; Kenya and Malaysia in 1963; Zambia in 1964; Barbados in 1966; Aden in 1967), nearly completing a process begun in 1947 (India, Pakistan, Sri Lanka), 1922 (the Irish Free State), or even 1901 (Australian Federation). The 1960s mainly affected APC countries (Africa, Pacific, Caribbean); these were not very profitable territories, and the results of relinquishing them weren't especially tangible. A shift towards European markets meant the rise of the south-east, and east-coast ports, as a manufacturing and shipping centres. The decline of the Atlantic trade meant a decline of the west-coast ports and their hinterland; Canada, Australia, and South America were no longer such good customers for British manufactures. The UK economy began to break apart on a geographical basis. This regional decline was hardly influenced by the wave of decolonisation. The EEC policy of agricultural subsidies ended the dependence of Europe on African foodstuffs, which had provoked the continuation of African empires beyond their natural end in the 1940s. Britain's fortunes were tied to the other OECD countries, which meant she had to compete with them or go down. The British retail sector, and consumer market, were prominently not chained to the triangular accommodation. The unexpected rise of Welsh and Scottish nationalism was due to the inspiring example of nationalism in decolonising countries; the analogy of colonization became plausible to people in the outlying parts of the United Kingdom in a way it was not in the 1950s.

A NEW SOUND; OR, BANALITY AS IDEOLOGY

The *Penguin Book of Poetry Since 1945* (ed. Robert Crawford and Simon Armitage, 1999) has an Introduction that attempts to describe the history of poetry during the period. It describes the whole era since 1945 as the triumph of the democratic voice. If you assert your unique identity, or if you assert pluralism and inconsistency, you are counted as part of the democratic voice. This is meaningless; I can't see how it analyses anything if it has no boundaries. It seems more like a cultural field than anything existing in the works of any single poet. The division between post-1945 and pre-1945 is said to be the domination of the 1930s by an educated coterie ('mandarin'), and of the later period by the democratic voice. The idea that the reading audience of the 1930s, the *ancien régime*, were intellectual, is charming but absurd. The English middle class disliked ideas, as any social history will point out; they were up to 40 times as likely to read Robert Bridges or Vita Sackville-West as W.H. Auden. Auden dominates the 1930s only in a retro-selective perspective set up by Oxford poets and critics and now accepted by Crawford. The overall shape in the 1930s shows an advanced, 'difficult', minority taste, and a comfortable, undemanding, safe majority taste, and this shape has not changed. This anthology eliminates 'low' work by authors who matured before about 1966, and 'high' work by writers who emerged since that date. This identifies, rather accurately, a 30-year lag in the dissemination of cultural attitudes. It gives the bizarre impression that, the more hundreds of thousands of graduates there were in the population, the less intelligent poetry became. Why would an increase in the scale of national education produce a decrease in the intelligence of poetry? I don't follow this, but one reading is 'because I am going to deny the existence of intelligent modern poetry in order to peddle the pop/mainstream merger'. I think the memorable poetry of the time was quite outside this current. I would add that the more ambitious poetry of the era was not at all animated by anti-democratic political ideas. In the anthology, we get experimental (or: linguistically radical) poems by Ian Hamilton Finlay (1925-2006) and Edwin Morgan (1920-2010), both of them pacifists during the Second World War; younger radical poets don't get a look in. One version could be: someone conservative couldn't believe they were important or significant or important because they weren't displaying the traditional signs of authority. The pacifist stance was extremely unpopular in the war; could it be the fact that we are still reading their work today, and not that of their contemporaries, is related to their political extremism? And that Crawford's band of conformists will also vanish like snow in Las Vegas when a few years have gone by?

The claim of the rise of a colloquial and plain manner is too true to be in dispute. However, additions need however to be made to Crawford's model. First, more exact dating. I agree that there was a new poetry that scrapped the past and used very simple language. Where I would amend this thesis is, first, that I think this boundless spread of the colloquial and personal came with the advent of singer-songwriters and happened after 1964. Secondly, the idea of dominance. There was light verse, and brainless lyric verse, aplenty before 1945. It is hard to remember but so is most of the colloquial verse that Crawford likes. Most of the artistically valid poetry has been more ambitious linguistically, and it is unreasonable to describe the weakest sector of the field as dominant. The use of the word 'democratic' (like the parallel usage of *accessible*) is dubious; the plain poetry has limited variation, limited information, and limited ability to deal with ideas. These are not features of the speech of good citizens in a democracy. Moreover, it is apparent that Nazi Germany or Soviet Russia had a special line in simplistic and plain poetry without being in any way democratic. I am afraid that the defence of democracy lies with the dissenters, those who have detailed issues with the acts of the powerful and who develop a complex language to deal with the realm beyond cliché and conformism. Profound originality of language and critique is the sign of a belief that political power is actually with the people. Low-tone poetry is the voice of the ruled.

His definition of the democratic voice, then, is interchangeable with 'dumbing down'. As a description of the cultural field, it is a screen behind which the issues of market preferences, the division of the market, the clash of classes represented by different educational levels, and the process of making taste, are hidden. Crawford has no interest in educating public taste; some critics or editors want to help the reader to deal with complex, dense, and innovative poetry, but not this one. If he does not engage with a 30-year lag between public taste and the practice of poets, it may be because he personally is 30 years behind (at 'time now' 1999). This is not a crime, but he fares badly from a comparison with Iain Sinclair or Ken Edwards, as an anthologist. Much modern poetry is critical of conventional poetics and of the dominant social order. Crawford finds this shocking and unpleasant – and therefore unaesthetic and not part of real poetry. The chronology within the volume reveals that age brings legitimacy and authority: he is able to stomach senior rebels but not ones under 70. Someone who enforces order is not going to be happy about critique or dissidence.

The account of history offered reproduces what Crawford says in his specialist works on territory and decentralisation. It has limited salience for the English poetry included. As a treatment of time or sociology, it's a failure. He does not attempt to differentiate between the 1970s, 1980s, and 1990s. Disagreement is retro-edited out; and the offensive of a restorative and aggressive new middle class after 1979 does not get mentioned, neither in the introduction nor in any of the poems in the book. He is a low-conflict type chap: good observation spots differences, but social unity is favoured by suppressing them. Strange things happen to language when social conflict surfaces in it. The denial of change denies the conscious activity of cultural managers; by making it invisible, their work is made uncontroversial. The only real power is invisible power. Suppose what is defined as common sense is actually a set of frail, tendentious, factional, and non-consultative guesses? Suppose what you are conforming to, to avoid conflict, is something this tendentious?

Claiming the advance to 'democracy' as starting in 1944 elides the foreground stylistic feature of the 1950s, the advance of academic and neo-metaphysical poetry based in the universities and in the New Criticism. The leading new poets from the 1950s as printed here are Geoffrey Hill, Roy Fisher, and Charles Tomlinson, not usually regarded as chatty, cheeky, and cheerful. The new style in poetry was serious and ambitious because that is what the working-class teenagers who got into university were like. Meanwhile, it was John Betjeman who enjoyed the mass sales, and it was his comforting and amusing family sentimentality that became mandatory for non-high poets over the next 40 years. He had spotted the mass middle-class market: it was Auden who assimilated to him, not vice versa. Underneath this old middle-class security, competitive, critical, and class-conscious working-class youth created a revolutionary art in the 1960s and 1970s. After 1979, a lot of retrospective repression and effacing had to be done, and qualified staff emerged to do it.

Homberger defines the end of formalism as taking place in the early 1960s – he says it was out of date by 1964.

THE HISTORY OF BANALITY

Clearly the poetry written by most amateur poets today owes little to the past of English poetry. If we look at Wordsworth, Shakespeare, Donne, Keats, Tennyson, they are high and most poetry is low. The problem is not a positive legacy of norms and of textual machines for the pre-20th century past, but of inhibitions about exploring the possibilities of language; conservatism in a different sense. Certainly someone writing colloquial, free verse, protest poetry, connecting to what they see in the news, in 1970, is able to claim that what they are doing is a radical innovation with respect to the norms of 1955. It is obviously indebted to the singer-songwriter movement, to Elektra Records, and not to the *Oxford Book of English Verse*. It is arguable that this was the mainstream of modernisation and that the experimentalism of the British Poetry Revival was merely marginal.

The most widespread change in the era is the rise of a poetry of great simplicity, with a high empathy quotient but a quite stultified use of language, written by huge numbers of people. Its tricky combination of egoism, empathy, and bareness is tied, probably rather precisely, to the spread of the singer-songwriter current in popular music. We would hardly expect the significant poetry of the time to come from this sector. But if thousands of people write it, it becomes significant. I suspect that this style was not there in the 1950s, reached a large number of people in the 1960s, and has remained stable over the entire period since. It is tied up with ideas of authenticity and the deceptive powers of ornate language in ways we do not have room to explore. To write poetry in this way means that you entrust your feelings entirely to language but that you think language as a project does not work and must be resisted. The great majority of poetry written in this country since 1965 belongs to this type. Few people want to read it. The content of 'domestic anecdote' is not quite all, because there is an element of protest poetry, and this was reinforced by the expectations of the singer-songwriter world.

Feminist poetry, when it arrived in the 1970s, frequently accepted the dominant norms of protest poetry and of domestic anecdote and of lack of rhetoric. There was a kind of poem written by hundreds of poets which was deeply familiar, even though the poets that we tend to remember wrote in a much more original and 'high' way. The functional, reality-based feminist line produced great poetry when it was genuinely culturally critical. That's the twist with the singer-songwriter thing – those protest songs were great (and there is a reason why far more people listen to singer-songwriters than read new poetry).

My feeling about poetry since 1980 is that it represents a fusion between the old pop poem and the old Movement poem. This leaves space for a few dozen poets of exceptional talent to explore the possibilities of new social constellations. But, of maybe 8,000 or 10,000 poets working and able to get books out, that is the general truth. If we look at the pop line and the academic mainstream, they are *both* dead set on getting rid of rhetoric. The textbooks by which close reading was taught never attacked rhetoric. The poems printed in *The Well Wrought Urn* are full of rhetoric and these are the ones being consecrated. It is a mystery why people, in the growing academic world of English Literature, taking up ever more years of everyone's life, developed an allergy for rhetoric. Maybe it was an effect of reading poems at the wrong speed: too slowly. Rhetoric is at home in the oral world, and the classic, favoured texts of such classes were close to orality: Shakespeare in the theatre and Donne in his sermons. Every figure of language that makes a poem interesting has been found obnoxious by modern poets and has been discarded from the poem of plainness to expose something quite unmemorable. This cannot be to do with orality, it may be an agonising and belated exit from the oral world into the world of print.

Herbert Read wrote 'Ode Without Rhetoric' already in 1940. The idea in that poem was to assert the truth of what Read was saying, its exit from the fallible status of language into the solidity of an object. You can't quite date a poem by its thinness of rhetoric. And there are striking differences between the pop poem and the Movement poem. The dislike of rhetoric, though, is pervasive. Periodising banality is a thankless task. After all, banality is part of the linguistic environment. You don't need to go to a library to find it.

To return to what we were saying just now about the high 1950s poem, the early statements of The Movement mentioned poets like Donne and Empson as the models. If this idea had persisted – and for some writers it did – the loathing of the 1950s (and the Movement) would not be so widespread, and the national poetry would not be undisguised banality. The idea of professors struggling with Metaphysical poets in the classroom by day and writing Metaphysical poetry by night, like someone reviving stanzaic folk songs, is quite exciting.

When Bob Dylan sang 'Blowin' in the Wind' the lyrics were an example of deep rhetoric. The personalisation of the answer, the answer that is blowing in the wind, is a rhetorical figure. The other lyrics are one whole string of rhetorical questions. You can't have a great lyric without rhetoric. Folk songs are soaked in rhetorical figures, even if they are different ones from those in Shakespeare's sonnets.

There is a great question as to whether modern banality represents a continuation of the Movement. This is something I said in the first edition that has been challenged. My vision was of the Movement reaching cultural power, imposing a poverty of expectations, imprinting everyone in school, and devising a situation in which people broke out of convention after 1983 but were crippled by it at a deeper level, so that they only broke out into a sort of cellar with no windows, a cellar of the Movement house. Some positions are:

(1) The Movement created a funnel effect whereby people socialised into the dominant English line and conforming to its imperatives had such a restricted view of art that they wrote banal poetry and took tiny deviations from the norms as signs of wonderful originality amounting to modernism.

(2) The restricted nature of banal English poetry came from other sources and the Movement was just a decaying carcass carried on a stream of much deeper and more indigenous banality.

(3) The banality came from accepting the singer-songwriter style, with its ideal of bareness, as the model for poetry.

(4) The mainstream of 1980-2010 was not paralysed by banality any more.

(5) Post-modernism represented a dent in the norms (but was not able to become a new dominant element because it was too difficult to carry off).

Because of the disagreement about (1) I am retreating from a definitive statement of truth. I notice that banal poets have a vested interest in portraying themselves as radical and modernist. I would vote for statements (1) and (5).

A colleague wrote to me

maybe the need for something different [...] was displaced onto European and US poets, of whom I read a great number [...] (Tranströmer, Herbert, Holub, Bienek, Bobrowski, Celan, Montale, Ritsos, Dorn). The PEP [Penguin European Poets] series in that sense paradoxically abetted the lack of knowledge and curiosity about an English poetry that wasn't in the neo-Larkinian mould. Poetic modernism is something that Europeans do, not us.

This was in discussing why he had written mainstream poetry before conversion to writing 'alternative poetry' rather late in life. The date of all this reading is roughly the 1980s. Why is it you admire ambitious, expressive, philosophically nourished, art poetry and yet write poetry in a neo-Movement style? This is the Gap of Dread. Why did thousands of people waste their lives writing dull poetry in numbing quantities? Is this banality based in English personality structures? The shopping list with its 300 titles is included as an extended refutation of that idea. Not everybody bought into Movement inhibitions. I am fantasising about a camera which captures the structure of inhibitions to write the history of the gap between reading great European poetry and feeling obliged to write banal poetry in the first person. I suspect that the authorisation of codes by the cultural centre is more to blame; Robert Conquest, an Oxford don with links to British Intelligence, wrote an essay saying that nobody wants ambitious or interesting poetry any more, and the organs of cultural assimilation process that as a policy document. We didn't go out and ask 100 mainstream poets, 'tell me why your poetry didn't include innovations or ideas'. I doubt that would have gone well. Is there a name for that traumatic gap between reading Penguin European Poets and writing banal sub-Dylan poems yourself? It has a history. If you press on the bruise the memory comes back.

If you set out to get rid of figures of language, you can end up querying the value of metaphor, categorisation, and so on, and end up with non-representational texts. Concrete poetry has none of the compromises of language. It does not represent anything, it stands for itself. Every cultural task has a possible over-fulfilment. There was an avant-garde stream that just went on taking language apart. This was a development from being taught close reading at school.

Pop Poetry

There is a little question of dates. 1963 saw an interesting anthology named *Jazz Poems*, edited by Anselm Hollo. Contributors were Dannie Abse, David Ball, Alan Brownjohn, Ian Hamilton Finlay, Roy Fisher, Piero Heliczer, Anselm Hollo, Michael Horovitz, Bernard Kops, Christopher Logue, Adrian Mitchell, Iris Orton, Jeremy Robson, Michael Shayer, Jon Silkin, and Gael Turnbull. Confusingly, this poetry has little to do with jazz, but the book is so named because of the series of *Poetry and Jazz* readings, which started in 1958 (with Christopher Logue). The title is misleading in another way, because these evenings were not simple socials but in fact protest poetry, with the idea of reaching a new audience for radical ideas. The introduction claims the first poetry-jazz shows (in Britain) were put on by Lindsay Anderson at the Royal Court Theatre, which just emphasises the Leftist affiliations of the movement. Jon Silkin had edited an earlier book in the same series called *Living Voices*, linked to live readings.

First, the live poetry thing was associated with jazz before the folk thing. Poetry was almost wholly taken over by the singer-songwriter wave but simple poetry for live reading was happening in parallel with the origins of the song-writing thing in Greenwich Village. I don't think that the songwriters were really visible, on television for example, until 1965, and that is when poetry began to copy them. Secondly, the history of the protest poem. Edwyn Collins' famous song jibes at the lack of protest songs and people who began with protest poems developed into writing very simple poems that no longer had any protest element. A slide to the Right, towards writing egocentrically, is absolutely pervasive. But the two anthologies mentioned clearly include protest poems. *Living Voices* includes Ewart Milne's (1903-87) great poem, 'Elegy for a Lost Submarine', which was originally published in 1951. This is a protest poem and sums up Cold War fear (although in 1951 there were no nuclear submarines). This date and Milne's whole political history open up a different perspective: the protest poem is just a version of the whole left-wing poetic tradition. 'Elegy' surely continues the Marxist poetry Milne was writing in the 1930s, even if it is a great improvement. The penalisation of *solitary* writing or reading of poetry and belief in *collective* live events, or in the music of the people, was a Stalinist doctrine and was articulated by George Thomson (*Marxism and Poetry*, 1945).

Live events as the annihilation of personal consciousness do in fact parallel the philosophical proposal that individual awareness is wrong; the elimination of stylistic choice in favour of rule-bound folk forms follows from this proposal. First poetry is simplified to get over important and urgent ideas; then the ideas too are eliminated in favour of presenting the self. Poetry and jazz is a relation of the leftist political cabarets of the Weimar era; a pale imitation of mass culture in the dance-halls, it may also be a pale imitation of intellectual culture. The style involves, crucially, direct address; simplified structures; the replacement of argument by an assumed trust in the poet's character, on the lines of a product endorsement; less frequently, an apocalyptic view of world affairs, reminiscent of a religious sect, and the claim that political decisions are utterly simple and that the authorities who make things complicated are simply deluded. This style led directly on to feminist poetry, 15 years later (as in the anthology *Purple and Green*). Mixed in with the dewy-eyed reductionism are some serious poems; it is a real problem to explain how the nascent avant-garde like Roy Fisher and Michael Shayer came to be intertwined with the nascent simplified-vocabulary soporifics. The link is partly through jazz, which in the heat of the moment could conflate the avant-garde and the barrelhouse foot-stomping. Some poets were prepared to rebuild a new complexity and some just wanted the admiration of the audience. Silkin doesn't use the liberal theological terms *commitment* and *dialogue* and *relevance*. Still, he says that reading live to an audience is 'a means of testing the accuracy and validity of his intuitions and convictions'. He talks about having something to say, and the importance of the poet's voice in 'working on an entirely new prosody'; the reading session as *ecclesia*. Silkin seems much closer to socially concerned theology than to the Left, and this is presumably part of the management of the events: coming out of the church because it is empty.

This new common style of the 1960s allowed broad similarities between pop song lyrics and the avant-garde. It is the fore-stage of psychedelia: 'and in the palace I danced with the Great Bear / while the stars rained down in colours like balloons' (Dave Ball). The element of surrealism, already visible in *Jazz Poems* in the work of Pete Brown, was much more prominent in the work of Adrian Henri, who took his cue from the poems from Jacques Prévert, which he encountered as an art student in Paris. Prévert, Henri recalled, used to write poems on tablecloths in cafés: so spontaneous. Even Prévert was a second-generation Surrealist, and a populariser of the technique; it is a little embarrassing to see how the drop-dead modernity of 1960s England was an astute repackaging of the avant-garde of the 1920s for a new mass market. In a sense, that is what art-school trained people to do.

NIL HYSTERESIS AND THE ALLOVER EFFECT

'We are in the preliminary stages of an enormous revival of oral tradition. Everyone knows that.' –Hamish Henderson, 1964

'Time was telescoped, memory was lost. The picture, a semi-abstract, had no perspective, existing only in the single plane of the Present.' –Harry Hopkins, *The Look*, 1963

Hysteresis is literally the influence of the past, the persistence of past states in the future states of a system; it is retardation. Features of the 1960s are: immediacy, hedonism, simultaneity, immersion, spontaneity, montage, direct address. The source of this new immediacy could be:

(1) The influence of the camera, which has no memory and moves in a continuous present with a glut of data.
(2) Distrust of the past and its social semantics, as discussed in the previous chapter.
(3) The cult of modernity, so that the past is devalued and existing poetic concepts don't help to explain a new world.

These hypotheses must remain open. We could add (4), *existentialism*, and (5), *jazz* and its belief in improvisation. The new direct address demanded that the 'continuous present' possess the complexity formerly offered by hoarded stores of knowledge. Variants on (1–5) include the desire to create an autonomous artistic world not based on existing knowledge, an *imitatio creatoris*, as part of an anti-authoritarian project, in which the 'past' of the system consists only of its inner rules; the belief that only immersion in the passing moment, oblivious to the past, is real happiness and being completely given; the Cartesian project, with the exclusion of existing knowledge, perhaps updated in the manner of Merleau-Ponty or Heidegger; and the new significance of live events. In a bizarre way, it laid more stress on the poet's personality.

A number of features of the 1960s are foreshadowed in the typical public avant-garde of the 1950s. According to Martin Esslin,

> [a]s the Theatre of the Absurd is not concerned with conveying information or presenting the problems or destinies of characters who exist outside the author's inner world, as it does not expound a thesis or debate ideological propositions, it is not concerned with the representation of events, the narration of the fate or the adventures of characters, but instead with the presentation of one individual's basic situation. It is theatre of situation as against a theatre of events in sequence, and therefore it uses a language based on patterns of concrete images rather than argument and discursive speech. And since it is trying to present a sense of being, it can neither investigate nor solve problems of conduct or morals.

He also evokes the beginnings of the style based on parataxis:

> Seen from this angle [of Zen] the dethronement of language and logic forms part of an essentially mystical attitude towards the basis of reality as being too complex and at the same time too unified, too much of one piece, to be validly expressed by the analytical means of orderly syntax and conceptual thought.

The whole issue of sequence of ideas, which led to the replacement of narrative by montage, is anticipated by Esslin:

> In the Theatre of the Absurd, the audience is confronted with actions that lack apparent motivation, characters that are in constant flux, and often happenings that are clearly outside the realm of rational experience. (…) While the play with a linear plot describes a development in time, in a dramatic form that presents a concretised poetic image the play's extension in time is purely incidental. Expressing an intuition in depth, it should ideally be apprehended in a single moment, and only because it is physically impossible to present so complex an image in an instant does it have to be spread over a period of time. The formal structure of such a play is, therefore, merely a device to express a complex total image by unfolding it in a sequence of interacting elements.
> (Esslin, *Theatre of the Absurd*, 1961)

The new poetry didn't come from nowhere, its linguistic space was being drawn and built in the 1950s, but outside the estate walls of British poetry. Montage came directly from the Theatre of the Absurd, from Ionesco, Beckett, Adamov, Arrabal, Artmann, Grass, and so on. Most of these texts were published by Calder and Boyars in the early 1960s. As a literary device it follows the paradox so dear to 18th-century aphorists and moralistes and anticipates the structural metaphors unmasked as axioms of which deconstruction was to make such play in the 1970s. In 1950, it probably seemed merely an on-stage version of Surrealism. Because the notion of being up to date was valued at the time, one has to ask how pioneering the 'advanced' figures of 1960s poetry were, or how far they were conforming to a marginal norm.

The early 1960s were fascinated by the three static matrices of the absurd, structuralism, and the immanent personality; bringing a crisis of sequence that is still with us. The word became something of a fetish in Germany after Gottfried Benn's *Statische Gedichte* (1948), where the static quality is linked to much older impulses of European art to create a form lifted out of the destroying flux of time. The shape-making force that fights this heroic struggle is the personality; the theme of Benn's poetry could either be a personality or a set of consciously chosen rules, lifted out of and above the flux of biology. The intent was to deny emotions; this is the link between Benn and static systems that followed in his wake, such as Gomringer's *constellations*, (1953), the foundation of concrete poetry.

The non-sequitur, produced by montage, was a dominant device:

in the morning there is opera, faïencerie
dance dance to break off the filter

singing songs he could not play on his teeth

edge edge dance dance
in the morning to opera along the cliff road

his teeth were the filter and filled
with gold
(Tom Raworth, from 'Provence 1', *Collected Poems*, p.56)

In this lyric translation of the dramatic absurd, there is a invisible splice at each line-break. The lines do not explain the foregoing ones; the semantic complex of the poem does not represent a physical scene, or perhaps anything outside itself. One version of this disconnectedness is that it represents human freedom, the uniqueness of each new arriving second, revealing the bonds of the past as perpetually recreated only by inertia and vested interests. The uniqueness subverts organised knowledge and Christian morality, implying that it is talent that counts, not tradition and position. Another explanation for the apparent lack of content of the works of Lee Harwood and Tom Raworth, the developing emptiness, is that it has made way for a personality cult; the unconnected details are actually a signal of domesticity, and the overwhelming content of that domesticity is the poet himself. Just as foreign towns only exist in order to maintain the poet as tourist, so also overt subject matter has been sacrificed because it would compete with the poet's desire for total presence. A detailed description of anything at all would reduce the tone of intimacy, the fictive closeness. This tendency was already apparent in the Surrealists of the 1920s: they wrote empty works but promoted themselves as personalities. The suspension of reason generally leads to the attempt to dominate people by force of personality; or vice versa.

The dominant genres of the time are the photograph (as domestic snap-shot), the interview, and the advertisement. Every work of art is pressed by these hegemonic forces, which correspond in importance to Christian art in (say) the 13th century. All three are: domestic; (super-) realistic; and dominated by the Personality to the exclusion of other signifieds. I would argue that the 'high' art of the 1960s and 1970s was taken over by these genres. The public wanted 'total intimacy' with the stars and actually regarded art as an obstacle blocking the personality from total visibility.

The equation [blown-up personality = emptied technique] neatly sums up the Liverpool poets (Patten, McGough, Henri); at an inconceivably lower level, they were in fact using the same methods as the poets published by Trigram. The use of irony is necessary to tone down the insistent presence of the poet's ego, which has squeezed out all the subject matter. A comparison is the 1960s belief in divinatory systems: the cosmos outside is reduced to a series of signs depicting the Self and Its ways. Everything Means Me. Because the trigrams are total representations of your personality however they fall, you no longer have to write, but only to be: to throw signs on the paper. Every poem becomes a Snapshot. Verbal effort ceases.

The presentation of the personality as the universal background logically corresponds to the sound features that are parts of that illusion of 'presence' which records give and printed poems fail to. The construction of a 'voice' on the page apparently implies the exclusion of 'speech' in favour of 'voice characteristics'.

The poet of the 1960s was trying to occupy the dominant genres (of interviews, snapshots, advertisements) by draining the poem of content. This occupation is rigorously comparable to 'pop art' in the field of painting, where the theft of imagery from the 'mega-visual' tradition went hand in hand with the explosion of the artist's 'personality' so that the signature, the interview, the personal appearance, outweighed the emptied and derivative visual surface.

These diverse explanations emphasise that the non-sequitur, or montage, is indefinable, because too empty and polyvalent. Perhaps, each non-sequitur is unique. In the work of Asa Benveniste (1925-90), the containing conceptual structure is determinism, of the holy will fore-encoded in Scripture, but on a scale so complex that the world of the senses is durably mysterious:

> surmounted by butterflies sleeping asses
> and thick rainwear assigning tickets
> to aragonese boxes where visitors
> familiar in deep religious fat tango
> to the music of gematria
> this is where it all fails.
> (from 'Mute Leaders' in *Throw out the Life Line*, 1983, p. 81)

The point of gematria (number divination) is that everything yields meaning (and, to a certain extent, everything is prefigured in the Bible); and Benveniste's poetry has this thorough structure. But he is using a heterodox Jewish divinatory system... within which the 'scatter' of individual sensory data is a way of glorifying the complexity of the universe impinging on the senses. The rapidity of flow of Benveniste's ideas is the idiom of someone quick-witted and easily bored, and this is why his poetry appeals. Every detail of its fabrication is expressive; the details bear out the intellectual message. Unintelligent people grasp ideas as if they were objects: if you are laborious, ideas lose their life and become part of an authority situation. Ideas in poetry can only be intelligent if they are fluent and transient, mere analogues. His technique reflects a way of talking, it is the expression of a personality, an idiom; the 'break of sequence' is actorly, almost an impersonation. This is why his poetry is confined inside it. So: even though the 'non-sequitur' is typical of an era, we have to analyse its specific function afresh in every poet.

Montage is the flickering disappearance of the text; the recognition of the limits of a single set of generation rules. This moment of complexity breaking in can also be seen as a critique of the rules of genre by the poet. Montaged poems can't be allocated to a genre. The poet is either operating a critique of conventional poems, and of the poet's self encapsulated in those poems, as self-seeking, manipulative, grabbing at protective formal security; or being more ambitious about adorning and projecting the self. Montage can act like the conscious artificiality in Brechtian plays, anti-realistic gaits and gestures, which makes us conscious of the rules of genre, directing attention away from the poet and towards the way social institutions and symbolism are constructed. Inconsistency can become controllable, flaws in the circuit can be used as switches, perhaps switching an illusion on and off, introducing new layers of complexity into the poem, winding out new microstructures. In the post-montage text, the edit rate is pulsing away like the beat of a piece of club music, a clock resetting every other process.

The wish for hyper-association follows the severance of existing rules of association. The goal is to destabilise existing patterns of ideas, including their sequence. Cutting in cinema is often from one camera to another, allowing multiple points of view; which in a poem would be those of different people, or, therefore, of different hypotheses about what the world is like and what should be done. The poet is faced with a mass of readers, or non-readers, who dislike the poet; whose world-hypothesis is peculiarly fragile. The adoption of multiple viewpoints is perhaps an escape from sheer intransigence and rage ('everyone who dislikes my poetry is wrong') into accepting that subjectivity is not going to become stable or solid. The idea of the artist as a tower of strength, who held to certain values doggedly and with heroic will, being therefore simpler and more monotonous than the shifts of time and society, dissolved in the 1960s, with poets (less so than cineastes) lifting the sluice-gates on the valueless surges of unorganised data, and trying to create a verbal order that was like a floating ship, not like a fortress.

The impact of learning on modern poetry was to add new series of analogies, drawn for example from psychology, anthropology, and history; this responsible line of ideas-linking passed through an irresponsible stage, as the existing, set, analogies had to be shaken loose. There is a close connection between the daft links of a certain 1960s style, Spike Hawkins for example, and the erudite links of a Nathaniel Tarn; Tarn is an anthropologist by profession, and his poems jump very freely between different societies to set up comparisons.

The urge to broaden the range of available associations could, again, be purely aesthetic, and akin to the hyper-association of drug experiences, or could be didactic and serious. In either case we have to deal, in the 1960s, with a complete refounding of the laws of the sequence of ideas in a poem. The point of going outside the fixed collocations of ideas seems to be to experience learning, as if the forming of new associations throws the brain into a chemically different state that is inherently desirable, rejuvenating, and unpredictable in its consequences. Indeed, playing the old sequences is giving people information they already have.

Before the indeterminable, we can name three forms of determinism. The first type is repetition: that is, regular metre, regular stanzas, but also regularized vocabulary and established personalities, stock types that do not need to be re-invented afresh in every poem. The second type is the sign-referent chain: language is built from experience, and this imitation is deterministic. The third type has to do with the construction of behaviour (reaction, motivation, etc.) within the poem. In an old-fashioned narrative, everything is motivated by the narrative itself, which continually throws the characters into jeopardy (captivity, enchantment, a Moorish invasion, etc). Their reactions have an imperative external motivation; and are therefore determined.

Poetry like Raworth's jettisons all three types. Consequence is suppressed. We are saturated in the logical chains that say, 'you are irrational because you are unhappy because you are poor, because you can't work out what employers want, because you aren't very rational', and tend to disappear inside this bourgeois teleology. The aim is no less than to challenge the whole apparatus of bourgeois knowledge, in which human beings are judged by their exam results and their Social Security files, and financial soundness is the main index of character. Leaving the telltale signs of power and status inexplicit is a way of suggesting new and urgent possibilities in the situation. It's right for culture to pass over certain things; because the alternative is for the imagination to reproduce the most brutal and humiliating features of reality *ad nauseam*. Fantasy heals by denying reality. The narcissistic focus on personal volition follows from a robust distrust of the external rules of the social system. An important statement of the arbitrariness of social rules, from a sociological point of view, was *The Social Construction of Reality*, by Peter Berger and Thomas Luckmann (1966). A social micro-system began to be seen as a matrix in which every value could be reset. Berger and Luckmann speak of nihilation as the negation by any closed system of events that it does not wish to acknowledge. A language, for example, might define 30 sound envelopes as phonemes and define any phonations outside those envelopes as bad sounds. No world-model describes everything in the real world; but it is clear that in the 1960s attention was directed steadily at the incomprehensible as a fabulous wilderness and the source of the new. A conventional taste subjected irregular form to nihilation; so that what lacks decorum, or rhyme, is not proper language.

Look at this poem by Asa Benveniste:

> in the distance
> where you have defined heaped ashtrays
> with dotted cries of the flag
> russian warships bear down upon
> disparate wife and her vestal
> charges in smoke and byzantium
> o camel-faced companion of the stove
> blind stitcher they imagine also
> that I tamp meaningless sequences
> (from 'OM', from *Throw Out the Life Line Lay Out the Corse*)

The rejection of consequence is conspicuous: the rhetorical pivot is the 'interruption of ideas', the 'cut' from one sequence to the next. This is like 'divisionism': the relation between contour and object has been reversed, so that the contours of the verbal idea are dominant over the idea itself. Just as the line break (but also the caesura and 'end of foot') were hard-worked devices in the classical metre, so the 'break' had by 1966 become the 'dominant' on which verse was constructed. In Raworth the line break has also become the phonetic event *par excellence*.

The insistence with which poets used the *non-sequitur* suggests that it was taking the place of rhyme as the device that marked the end of the line and so scanned the sonic mass into formal units. In this context of absolute regularity, the inhibition towards writing an idea that lasted for longer than a line or two became rigid. The idea vanishes to admit the idea. The space between lines became as essential to the technique of the poem as the difference between hard-edged lines and blurred-edge lines in an American minimalist painting. Montage was the locus of mystery that for other eras had been the supernatural, the revelation of the past, the influence of sensibility on 'objective' sensation, typology and interpretation. It is the verbal mark of hyper-association, reliably induced by LSD but posited and achieved both by poets and by pop musicians well before LSD was around.

It was a decade of plenty following the constraints of the 1950s. The phrase, 'you've never had it so good' is owed to Macmillan in 1957 ('most of our people have never had it so good'). Material plenty went along with new polymer technology in dyes and plastics allowing a variety of colour and texture that made the domestic and everyday more delightful. People looked more beautiful than in the previous decade. Ornament as the basic aesthetic urge was outdistancing the Christian gloom of the previous 13 centuries. The narcissistic drive of the photograph, a static allover simultaneity, presenting with striking clarity whatever beauty, energy, and life the subject possessed, ruthlessly illuminating their unhappiness, indifference, and fatigue, redefined the poem as a presentation of the self.

The 1960s were a decade of hedonism where it was common to seek gratification, talk about it, invite to it; you attract people because you feel good, which is what they want; the project of satisfying this want brings up all the obstacles, and these cast up the need for politics. But above all hedonism makes you want to avoid people who don't feel good, because they aren't the place to be looking. 1960s poets were trying to live, not to explain why earthly life is flawed. Dithyrambic immersion is the coveted state. Not giving yourself over to the continuous present and the people you're with lets them down and therefore makes sure you can't really be happy. The inadequacy theory of the 1950s devalues the experience in the poems, and therefore the poems themselves. It embodies a closed version of character, fixed in childhood, or by the events of the Bible, or by the definition of English culture, and never to be unfixed and rewritten. Simultaneity is valued because a single track of data allows too great control, is too predictable, and allows the artist to withdraw emotionally and manipulate the art object. It is there to avoid the terror of absence. In fact, it's the alienation of a specialised society brought to light in poetry. The preoccupation with presence arrived because too many books were full of absence. The stress on immediacy makes self the biggest part of the signal and highlights coordination, like a singer on camera. This made people open and uninhibited, even if they were also competitive and terrified of boredom. Being switched off is a sign of boredom or unhappiness and so poetry in which you are switched off, blank, at a loss, is a giveaway that where you are is not where a good time is to be found.

Jon Silkin remarked in the introduction to a 1960 anthology of the new poetry, *Living Voices*, 'the poem expresses a social problem, or situation, in which the poet as a voice is frequently, even explicitly, at the centre.' The unstated horror is of the attenuation of the poet and poem as merely a remote spectator processing other texts – newspapers, books of poetry, etc. – and the desired writing of the observer into the scene observed could come as much from a theological desire to witness as from a phenomenological belief in the importance of the perceiver to any perception, noticeable especially in the work of Andrew Crozier, J.H. Prynne, and Denise Riley. Unwavering attention on the observing self may have 'aggrandised' this figure by giving up much of the pictorial field to it, but also attenuated it by showing it to be full of inconsistencies, specular imitations, irrational rushes of mimesis. The plot of the film entrained the dissolution of the camera. The rule of direct address implied that all information in the text was as unreliable as the self uttering it. The lability implied by the local attention to fortune telling and trigrams encapsulated, unseen, the forthcoming feminist attack on the act of writing as one of self-adornment and exhibition of trophies.

Simultaneity demands integration, much as the TV camera demanded that singers be well-dressed, mobile of face, and finally that they dance as they perform; failing in any one of these hugely reduced the appeal to the audience, which also wanted them to be good-looking. A primal unity of the different levels of human faculty seemed to burst upon the performers, a totality of meaning-bearing surfaces that engulfed both singer and onlooker in a high that left no room for anything else. This simultaneity is a form of complexity; it made the split between past and present unbearable and so gave rise to the present without hysteresis; it was an all-over effect craved by poetry; it foreshadowed a typical concern with multi-media events – light-shows, dance, music coming from all around the room. The continuous present imposes the complete giving up of the artist to the people then present, whether in the audience or in the poem; to retreat into memory would indicate unhappiness, reserve, indifference, not being immersed in the concrete situation. This is close to the ideal of autogestion, spontaneous political decisions without hierarchy, and all power being given to the people currently within any group, so favoured in the 1960s. We will have to ask about the status of those reservations, because the success or failure of 1960s poetry depends upon them. The theme of place, still exoticisms in the 1960s, came into its own in the following decade.

Esslin remarks:

> (T)he Theatre of the Absurd makes no pretence at explaining the ways of God to man. It can merely present, in anxiety or with derision, an individual human being's intuition of the ultimate realities as he experiences them; the fruit of one man's descent into the depths of his personality, his dreams, fantasies, and nightmares.
> (from *The Theatre of the Absurd*, p.340)

The change from the malnourished pessimism of the absurd to the hedonism and affluence of the 1960s rewrote the nature of this intimacy. The discrediting of ideology (a static rule-based system) brought a vacuum that could only be filled by the personality.

Hyper-association takes the reader further inside the poet's associative processes than before; replacing observable reality; another immersion. The separation between the structure of the world and the rules of the text is collapsed. The writer's eye, unable to perceive large structures, perceives instead structures that are small-scale because they vanish so quickly. Mimesis, the direct imitation by suggestion of someone else's feelings, is intensified: in the monumental intimacy of hoardings (now coloured), the nuances of voice recorded by close microphones, the ever more brilliant and unmodulated images of sex. Person-to-person relations bring us into the world of pinups, stars, romantic ego-identifications.

Association was one of the devices under strain in the period. Montage and hyper-association were two symptoms of a rejection of the unconscious rules accepted in the previous period. Subjective association makes the person the semantic frame in which events are collected. It evokes a less formal and more intimate relationship to the reader. This persuasiveness somehow related to the wish to go beyond prices-and-incomes policy as a form of national unity. The utopian project of the 1970s was a wished-for restoration of a primal integrity of feeling and experience made visible by simultaneity.

The single unique complex of experience of the world that Esslin describes was replaced in the 1960s by serial unique moments, each different and each involving a new hypothesis about the world. It was these constant transitions that led to the deification of fashion, as a sovereign dissolver and resetter of rules, and to the preoccupation with the sequence of ideas in a poem.

Imagine a text file that consists of instructions read either by a screen builder or a printer compiler. Suppose the software for a particular font is

100 kilobytes, while a single character is about 1 byte. The absolute size of a file 100 characters long could be 10,000 kilobytes (about ten megabytes) if we store, or load, the whole font along with each character; or it could be only one kilobyte if we leave the fonts out.

If a single word implies a social context, and therefore a set of behavioural rules, it is like the single character that pulls a whole font program with it. If you string together a dozen characters in a dozen different fonts, the font becomes foregrounded and the literal value of the literal sinks into the background. Let's say 200 characters, for a little song. But you can also consider it as containing the whole historical milieu around it, all the interpretative rules with which you read 11th-century poems; so how much information does that little character string contain? If you read a comprehensive anthology like Lucie-Smith's, there are a dozen different literary systems contained inside it; if you jump from one poem to another, you change your internal state, reconfigure your reading faculty, at huge speed; it's already a psychedelic experience, a freak-out.

As the text itself is reduced to a serial Raworthian intermittence, coherence migrates to subsystems, parts bound to each other by structural resistance, and embodying interpretative regimes. If you start to make the application of interpretative rules, and the encapsulated triggers that tell the reader which rule set to apply, consciously, you can start writing to the rule sets rather than just generating sentences that obey the rules of one or other of them. All writing is specifying a situation; the writer can specify also how to read. Structure becomes narrative.

The subject really at stake in the disengagement of rule sets is the class system, and the rules which decide what your status is and how other people behave towards you. This is only one step beyond lexical registers and any closely pursued thought about language will reach it. The value of a human is a symbolic object in the way that an utterance or a sum of money is. After a certain point, the social hierarchy is not arbitrary, and important people have to be talented; but where exactly is that point?

Although there are the 12 discrete rule sets which I mentioned, post-1960s poets have probably not internalised any of those sets, and poetry is no longer a folk art; the poet does a *bricolage*, implementing code switching and creating provisional syntheses. (This does not apply to poets who are completely unaware of style, or to the Mainstream.)

The camera sucked in an excess of data, making everyone more sophisticated in their awareness of context as a variable. There are rules specific to each cognitive frame. Attention to context reveals these, like ridges on the bottom of a drained lake. The typical 1960s feel is when two frames are superimposed, or the rules of one frame are applied within the bounds of another. Artistic identity is necessarily withdrawn from the overt content of the piece, which is reduced to a form of dressing-up, a bright thing snatched as for a scrap-book, and re-sited in the nature of the junctures the poet makes, for example the overall rate of cuts: identity as blink rate. The dissolution of overall sets of behavioural rules, revealed as merely inherent to a world-hypothesis floating among thousands of others, leaves local rules as the only guides to behaviour; these are like buildings, deposits of labour and design, but the proximity of other local rule-sets, made pungent by montage, confines each one to a single nick on a spatial or temporal grid. This attachment is turned into information, and therefore a form of wealth: genre rules and figures are used to evoke a period or a mentality.

This much serves as a basic commentary on the styles of J.H. Prynne, Tom Raworth, Asa Benveniste, George MacBeth, Edwin Morgan, Rosemary Tonks, Ken Smith, John James, and Andrew Crozier. Other up-to-date poets were Lee Harwood, Nathaniel Tarn, Gael Turnbull, Jeff Nuttall, and Anselm Hollo. The special issue of the *Times Literary Supplement* of 6 August 1964 on the avant-garde, to which the reader is recommended, lists as catchwords: 'semantics, structuralism, alienation, programming, eroticism, kinetics, and do-it-yourself'. Clearly there were more enthusiasms of the time than my account can contain.

THE MASTIFF; DEFENCE OF TERRITORY

We can assume that the basic model for poetry, as for all language, is the argument, which is something common to small children and adults, found in all human societies, essential in education, politics, and business. People are engaged in constant arguments with parents, teachers, employers, pupils, sexual partners, house-mates, customers, political opponents, intellectual rivals; with, actually, everyone they are socially bound to. The basic aim of using language is then to assert claims.

There is an emotional figure like a mastiff, obsessed by territorial boundaries and by the need to prevent other people from crossing them: a poet (or critic) purple in the face and outraged, lurking beneath fruit-trees with a shotgun to mow down nimble children who constantly raid the trees for fruit. My assumption, of course, is that the fruit is there for the children, and the concept of property is a result of the malevolence and wish to control of the irascible spoilsports.

It is interesting how many of the professions have to do with demarcating and defending property. The 'manager' in general is someone delegated to look after an absent owner's property, a descendant of the estate bailiff. There is an analogy between the archaic rural 'organised knowledge' of ownership and boundaries, guarded by lawyers and bailiffs, and the topography that is central to traditional English poetry. The poet describes and defines place, and the poem defines a symbolic 'place' where everyone behaves in an appropriate way or is rebuked for breaking the bounds. The classic form of this is regular metre, that can be described as thousands of rules that the reader is the keeper of and that the poet must observe. Religion is like regular metre in that it defines virtually everything you do or want to do as sin, and is administered by venerable, puce-faced authority figures. The doctrine of fidelity to reality is a punishment schema, which allows authority to chastise poets for everything they imagine; it is a projection of the virtues of lawyers, bailiffs, and accountants into the realms of art. Printed poetry is largely read by social groups descended, historically, from the bourgeois professions, the literate servants of the rich.

The key area is not, however, metre, but association of ideas. The point of modern art is its freedom of association of ideas, to gain which it overset the artistic machines of the 19th century; and that the aesthetic payoff for this is subjectivity, hyper-association, freedom. We can easily associate this with the linguistic freedom of classical Latin, Welsh, and Norse poetry. Poetry uses the linguistic code but also strains it as if pursuing a goal quite outside it. But very many of the literary audience do not subscribe to the idea that the imagination should be free.

Conservatives present frozen and congealed realities because those are the qualities that make them happy. The slightest thermal eddy would bring about a new configuration in which their status would be lesser. The various display behaviours of the young are all re-defined as threatening behaviour; an interesting watershed. Is display of strength a threat? Rock music is certainly to do with power and exhibitionism and defiance. A certain segment of the population hates rock music because it makes them afraid. So what they want is for the young to be afraid. Rules, repression, psychological intimidation, heavy policing, withdrawal of privileges for disobedience, constant surveillance, make them feel safer. So one can speak of a constituency in favour of repression. This is the atmosphere of certain literary reviews: prissy, immobile, disgusted, scared. The dissolution of a power order does not after all benefit everybody; some people will be worse off in a state of unconstrained spontaneity.

The act of reading is to decode abstract symbols using a set of memories and a set of conventional codes of meaning, which hopefully match up with each other. These are both performances, subject to failure. So to strain both of them is to risk failure. Freedom is in this sense elitist. The point of modern poetry is to reorganise memory, which is only retrievable because of its organisation. Modern poetry sets out to overthrow the set of categories and associations that are the only map we have for using words to bring up stored knowledge. These boundaries are another place where the fat, shouting, puce men wait with their clubs. The possibility of multiple interpretations of the past and of policy gives the opportunity to pick the one that optimised the distribution of resources; and is therefore a threat to the system already optimised for the benefit of a minority. Not all knowledge is tightly coupled to the distribution of power, but the knowledge we argue over clearly is. The rules most fought over in modern times have to do with individual potential and defining the personality: because what kind of person you are decides what kind of work you do and which rewards you get, one has to ask who decides what kind of person you are.

Freedom penalises people who have personality blocks. There was a stock figure in 1960s mythology of the authoritarian curmudgeon who never has any fun and makes life a misery for the youthful heroes and heroines. Serious poetry has been associated with this figure by astute propaganda from sub-pop poets. Donald Davie and C.H. Sisson did their best to incarnate this figure in their punitive ideological stance. It does seem important to remember that art is a form of pleasure, the artist's claim to credibility is to have reached that point of psychological liberation where they can understand pleasure. The modern tendency to identify art with the lifestyle it embodies is to that extent justified, and in tune with classical European ideals. This 'villainous authority figure' specifically resisted young people because he saw them as a threat: he was the teacher who hated talent rather than liking it; he competed unfairly with the young because he controlled institutional power and used it against them to the extent that the institutions themselves were corrupt and had to be called to account, as indeed happened in the 1960s. Some people felt that the phrase 'respecting tradition' could be translated as 'respecting the wishes of old people whom nobody likes'.

We need to imagine figures in social couples to explain the process by which they came to have what now seems a character of inner origin. Surely it is the bellowing of puce tipstaffs that gives rise to colourless conformist poetry from people who want acceptance from the miserly, where self-castration is the precondition of success. Feminist critique has uncovered in the utterances of authority, beside the overt information, covert imperatives about the behaviour it wishes its charges to adopt; someone, whether male or female, who complies with these imperatives becomes unable to achieve emotional integration, self-confidence, or poetic style. They become suited to the role of a servant. There is a drama going on in the cultural world that is either unrecorded in texts, or invisible in their smooth, benign surface. Any ideal is punitive for someone who internalises it and fails to live up to it; if the literature of the past solemnly elevates ideals, much of modern literature is about vomiting them out, choking on the discourse of damaged and authoritarian relationships. It is impossible to assess the poetry of our period without supplying the authority figure, gurning and chiding, dogging the poet, defining every move except imitation as defiance. It does seem anomalous that people who are too miserable to enjoy anything should be administratively in control of poetry, which is supposed to be a form of pleasure.

The accounts of modern English poetry that I have identified as 'para-noid-Christian' are carrying out an act of symbolic exclusion from space, in order to cleanse the territory.

ADDITION 2016. How deep an urge I feel to moderate this, to strike 'sleazy old fascists' and insert 'venerable old fascists and their place in national life'. And, in general, how little attempt I have made to explain all that went wrong and why the best poetry was so carefully hidden from view. This is a makeweight to distract people from how bad it all was.

SCOTTISH POETRY IN THE 1960S

The beginning of the decade saw three spectacular literary rows, the form that aesthetic debate takes in tiny artistic communities where the indifference of the outside world, mindless solidarity, and national loyalty inhibit the give and take of criticism and endeavour. All aimed at deposing a literary monarch whose nationalist and communist caparisons did not conceal his jealousy and ambition. The first was the row between Maurice Lindsay and Hugh MacDiarmid. Lindsay, formerly a disciple of MacDiarmid and his programme of abolishing Scottish poetry in English, recanted spectacularly (in the introduction to his volume, *Snow Warning*, 1962) and attacked the project as arbitrary and remote from Scottish reality. Lindsay was right; the main reason being that English is the spoken language of the Scottish middle class, who make up the bulk of the (admittedly slight) audience for Scottish poetry. The solemn assertion that this audience was damned, as linguistic traitors and members of the international bourgeoisie, was balefully persuasive but led in the long run to rebellion and disillusion.

The second row was the one between Ian Hamilton Finlay and MacDiarmid, who struck an obscurantist and obstructive stance towards Finlay's concrete poetry, not merely disliking it but actively agitating to prevent it from being published in the *Oxford Book of Scottish Verse*. He also published a pamphlet against concrete poetry, *The Ugly Birds with No Wings* (1962). It was wrong for a man of his eminence to lay such a cannonade on a group of young poets who were virtually invisible. Finlay, a former admirer of the overbearing antisyzygist, responded, with his co-editor Jessie McGuffie, in the form of a letter to *The Scotsman* (19/5/62) attacking the 'Rose Street group', accusing MacDiarmid of Stalinism and repressing younger poets. The third row involved attacks on MacDiarmid in *Scottish Field*, February 1962, by Tom Wright and Hugh Rae.

D.M. Black, in his survey of the period in *Akros* 28, cites 'pop, op, public, concrete, psychedelic, Marshall MacLuhan, cybernetic, semiotic, Vietnam, commitment, pot, bells, flowers, or Scottish renaissance', and further 'extravagance of self-assertion... mounting affluence... ardent revolutionary opinion... ideology and occultism... new oral culture... relaxation and increasing individuality.' He remarks that it became much easier to get published, and that this reduced the aggressiveness of Scottish literary life.

If one looks at the list of new poets emerging during the decade – Stewart Conn, Alastair Mackie, Alan Jackson, Kenneth White, D.M. Black, Stephen Mulrine, Robin Fulton, Flora Garry, Tom Leonard, Tom McGrath, Alastair Maclean, Alan Bold, Tom Buchan, Duncan Glen – one is impressed by their number. The sociological basis of poetry was broadening. But in retrospect the new imaginative world was not properly assimilated; most of these poets have had very disappointing careers. Meanwhile, the older poets continued to disappoint. More important was the blossoming of Edwin Morgan and Ian Hamilton Finlay, both of them old enough to have taken part in the war (both as conscious objectors in non-military roles), but hardly visible until the early 1960s. The stereotype of the linguistic realist as evoking, after a lapse of several decades and from the security of a comfortable urban middle-class position, the characters and seasons of the rural community of the writer's childhood, instils a fearful ennui. Flora Garry is just that, but is also an excellent poet. Her poems, published in a single volume as *Bennygoak and other poems* (1974), are both realistic and moving. Part of this may be the 'deep' nature of her rural Buchan dialect: it's quite moving for me to hear (on the Scotstoun cassette) the readers pronounce (as 'v') the 'w' in 'write'. The extreme distance between rural north-eastern Scots and English may have helped her preserve the Buchan part of her memory as completely unaffected by

English speech patterns. Garry was born in 1900 and, while I believe she wrote most of her Buchan poems during the 1960s, they refer to a time long gone, and show a number of themes familiar in Scottish poetry of the 1920s. Her poems about the time after she left Buchan are in English. The north-east is one of the 'deepest' regions of folklore in Western Europe; an alternative pole of attraction to (English or French) literary highness. (Garry has also translated Baudelaire into Buchan dialect.) Information on this living folklore can be found in David Buchan's magnificent *The Ballad and the Folk*, a study of the ballads in Gavin Greig and James Duncan's collection in the context of the north-eastern region's history and sociology. Garry's poetry draws on a north-eastern tradition of popular poetry, typically shrewd character sketches, exemplified by Charles Murray (1864-1941) and David Rorie (1867-1946). These, when they work, are nothing to do with songs, but draw on the photographic detail and biological sharpness of observation of the 19th century. Garry's accounts of rural poverty draw on this as well as Baudelaire.

David Black's second account of the period refers to American poetry being seen as a way of breaking into the 20th century without compromising on English poetic ideas. Confusingly, this included oriental religion, copied from the U.S.A. (rather than from MacDiarmid's 'Diamond Body'), as well as direct address, frank autobiography and open forms. The concrete project of Ian Hamilton Finlay, and his magazine *Poor.Old.Tired.Horse.* defined the page as a symbolic space to be populated by procedural rules; confusingly, this entrance into space and non-temporal allover relation sets also served to let back in landscape, or maritime pastoral, a brilliant way of reconciling bristling Scottish traditionalists. Kenneth White (1936–) had brilliant ideas for poems, mixing Zen flashes of enlightenment, the sense of immersing space, and a sense of planetary geography; his technique is so sloppy-poppy and 'immediate' and apodictic that little bears looking at.

> And the hills then, red fern entang-
> lements and thorn and wild rose and
> holy-red holly among the snow and
> the trees stark hung with water-
> walking there over blue-ice paths the
> streams rushing air driving sharp
> and that light crazy-clear that
> savage angelic and cosmo-demential light
> that shows up the world in its nakedness
> swift-changing darkly-bright realness
>   (from 'The Western Gateway', in *The Most Difficult Area*, 1968;
>   see also *The Cold Wind Before Dawn*, 1966).

More effective is a moment, in the same book, from 'Theory':

> Rough shape, clifted, that kwartz
> chaos-given, ashored, tide-washed and
> in the good space gazed-at.

where the packing of adjectives is like Gaelic poetry. The image of
moments of peak awareness as jewels implies that awareness is static, a
denial of process that reminds one of Edwin Muir (as well as of the Tibetan
'diamond body'). The KLF, in their more pastoral moments, also remind
me of Finlay; see 'Build a Fire', from the album *The White Room*.

Mike Hart recalls that in Glasgow around 1967 the first pop poets
read their poems in Liverpool accents because that was the model and they
thought that was how it was done. Robin Hamilton (quoted, yet again,
from *Akros*) recalls Glasgow University from 1965-69:

> 'there were at least four active poets on the staff for most of that
> time – Alexander Scott, Edwin Morgan, Ken White [...] and
> Philip Hobsbaum[.] As a student, I overlapped with [...] Stephen
> Mulrine, Tom Leonard, Angus Nicholson, and Alan Spence. It all
> seemed terribly natural, at the time, that any university should
> have about five magazines publishing poetry. [...] Despite the
> magazines and writers, Glasgow poetry in the late sixties and later
> simply wouldn't have been the same without Philip Hobsbaum.
> [...] One thing which was common to us all was an interest in
> American poetry, particularly the line of Ezra Pound.'

ENGLISH POETS

Christopher Middleton (1926-2015) was a colloquial writer in the sense
that he was close to conversation all the time. His confidence in talking
in a difficult manner points to the self-inflicted problems of callowness
and embarrassment that most English poets have about introducing the
fruits of culture into poetry. He knew he could pitch his talk at a high
level, he knew he was amusing, he knew he was attractive; he seemed to
owe more loyalty to a virtual audience of quick-witted people than to his
own reactions. I suppose social awkwardness is a concomitant of overrating
your inner life. In an oblique way, he embodied a community (a kind
of cosmopolitan café society), and his appeal depended on the appeal of
that milieu. If you hate talking about art, you will hate Middleton. It is

erroneous to say that his style comes from his academic background as a Germanist (a background that I share, incidentally), although it is afloat on a dégagé self-confidence and curiosity about the world that languages and travel are supposed to bring.

Although Middleton's *Selected Writings* (Carcanet) started with *torse 3*, which came out in 1962 and is subtitled *poems 1949-61*, his first publications were in 1944. His absence in the 1950s is significant – he was a casualty of the reaction against the 1940s poets. *Torse*, he explains in a note, is '[a] developable surface; a surface generated by a moving straight line which at every instant is turning, in some plane or other through it, about some point or other in its length.' It may imply a constantly moving but still rule-bound point of view: 'Imagination, precisely because it is deceptive and demonic, needs artifice, needs the pressure of craft, the pleasure of artistry, for a dialectical counterpart.' His career combined precocity and late development, both products of intelligence. Middleton reached technical fluency very early (and rushed into print in 1944, as chronicled by A. T. Tolley, in a fervid New Romantic style) but reached his mature style late (he recorded a pause of seven or eight years, from about 1948, as he worked things out) because it took a long time to integrate all the parts of his sensibility. His career structure was quite similar to Edwin Morgan's; the 1940s were a blind alley from which it took years to recover, the 1950s were a career disaster that made them invisible, but they had the resilience to grow and take on new procedures. I think public opinion underrates the time needed for a modern poet to reach artistic maturity; there are no supporting structures for someone undertaking such a long trajectory and, indeed, all the funds are concentrated on people who are writing something showy (but generally very bad) when barely out of their teens. Actually Middleton's achievement (to produce a first book of real excellence at the age of 36) is much more typical; it's regrettable that institutional pressures, dying fashions, and brutal theories of 'talent' force most poets to give up by the time they're 25.

One of the keynotes of his mature style is the avoidance of emotion; his perpetual cool is not unrelated to the lush excesses of the 1940s, to which it was an antidote. The mythic and geographic eclecticism of his poetry is a direct continuation of the 1940s:

> Swat a fly, scratch the wall
> Of an ear with a toothpick: four, suddenly,
> The grouped figurines
> Loom huge from the desk angle,

And glow, clay Chupicuaro, bronze
Krishna, the wooden African –

As gods. To construct them
Ancestors broke through their skins,
Getting this far at least: the rock
Crystal coyote, stud him
With turquoise, let the orange fire
Be a tail like a beacon;

For the unseen escapes...
    (from 'The Turquoise', in
    Two Horse Wagon Going By, 1986, p.140).

It is typical of Middleton's cunning to use concrete objects to (apparently) ground his visionary ideas, instead of acting like a visionary staring out into space and mumbling metrical sooths. He thus indulges a non-realist view of the world without getting blamed for it.

A central technique for him is the unfolding of the meaning across time, made possible by the withholding of information (*ostranenie*, see 'Unit Structures'). This produces a 'strangeness' in the opening stages: we are in a state where data arrive that are novel and astonishing and take us away from what we know, and this state is what every primate wants. He started from the careful cutting out of the set linguistic frames that have been destroyed by entropy because their whole course is predictable from the moment they start. His effort as a poet is therefore one of analysis of situations back into their real nature, before conventional cognitive frames and verbalisation, so that he reaches the existential freedom to present a verbal pattern that represents reality. This operation is akin to that of a modern painter, trying to paint something – a hill, a bunch of flowers, a table decked with objects – in such a way that it is striking, and the real characteristics of the subject emerge from under layers of habituation and teleology. This method is no doubt specific to the West and to the period since about 1870; it's relevant to Middleton that it was furiously resisted by English artists until well into the 20th century. Modernism is not simply 'foreignness', rather it belongs to a small stratum of intelligent people, who are just as much a minority in Germany and France as in England, Spain, or Ireland.

Like every other poet of a certain maturity, he condemned both the concrete/experimental and the confessional/egomaniac modes that stood for 'liberation' in the 1950s. One is reminded of Helmut Heissenbüttel's remark that,

> [t]he original notion of experimental literature as an avant-garde movement parallel to abstract visual art loses its general validity at the moment when this literary vanguardism was reduced to typographic and sound poems. The true counter-movement to conventional, descriptive, discursive use of language is based rather on the discovery that one can move in language as if in another world, without having still to cling to connections, objective facts, and events, as navigating in the so-called real world compels us to. What remains of it in the linguistic realm of relations is, seen from the understanding of reality, in which we can't help living, not replaced, distorted, deformed, organized in quite different perspectives.
>
> (quoted from Hermann Glaser, *Kulturgeschichte der Bundesrepublik Deutschland*, Vol. 2, 1949-1967, 1990, p.281).

Heissenbüttel was of course the most distinguished German experimental poet. The question remains how this autonomous world can acquire the resistance and durability to protect it from collapse. Middleton has said, in his essay, 'Reflections on a Viking Prow':

> Lace, icons, handblown glass, handstruck Greek coins, bone implements, masks, figurines, old books, paintings, carts, and bedspreads and ploughs – such handmade things are real, did become real, because they were brought to life by currents of formalized energy, desire crystallizing as it passed from imagination to skilled hands, through to treasured materials, and back again in a circuit never broken. Some artefacts were charged with a 'spirit' which, as in Kwakiutl masks, formalized itself while the skill of the artificer conducted it, like lightning, and crystallized it into socially significant objects [...] the artificer fashions a group wisdom in the thing which speaks for itself. [...] Thinking about artifice of this kind [...] one comes to have doubts about poems which conform to the scripts of subjective expression; doubts also about anecdotal or confessional poems, poems that catalogue impressions additively, and so forth.
>
> (Christopher Middleton, 'Reflections on a Viking Prow', in *The Pursuit of the Kingfisher*, 1983, pp.80-1)

He lists a series of 'artificer' writers, and

Their cities, landscapes, and rooms are not photographically literal. Never frontal reportage about apparent localities, their writings are formal creations which enshrine and radiate poetic space. A particular time/space axis, as 'world of appearance', may be recognized, certainly, in the words and the imagination words embody. But that embodiment includes a crucial moment of change. Nothing is neutral any more, all is transvalued and animated by the rhythms of a unique formal vision grounded in an original sensibility.

(ibid, p.84)

So he was a leading theorist of social space and defined its difference from literal space. He correctly draws attention to the possible strain at the line of juncture where individual subjective space becomes social. He nearly espoused a work ethic in this essay: the life of the intellect disappears unless one does intellectual work, for example learning a language, reading anthropology or philosophy, writing, reading difficult poetry. If you reduce culture to a leisure activity, effortless, your brain atrophies and you will be unable to participate in a 'life of the intellect' beyond TV, a newspaper, and the pub. Once the intellect ceases to offer rewards, it also rapidly loses its attractions. The majority of published English poets have certainly reached this state. Reward is always proportional to effort – I must admit, though, that some people's effort is in vain.

If you want to live with people who think about life and argue about issues, then you need to have access to a huge range of examples in order to sustain the discussion; culture is just a source of these examples. Poetry that confines itself to examples from one person's experience is artificially crippled. Middleton's 'allusions' sustain belief because we can sense that they are part of the life-world of his group of friends, not part of some isolated, starved, remoteness. Objects are the 'literal space' and people's minds are the 'symbolic space'. Regrettably, most English poets aren't thinking people and don't talk about ideas with their friends. This is why they write about frogs, toasters, and old churches all the time. Symbolic experience isn't just a 'fantasy', it allows people to share subjective experience, and emotional closeness can be reached in no other way. We have a straight choice between reaching 'harmony' by making disagreement illegal, both politically and in the family and the workplace, or reaching harmony by dialogue and emotional openness.

§

The legend about Rosemary Tonks (1928-2014) is that she got religion and renounced all her previous work (as immoral, erotic, the work of the Devil, etc.) and went on to write a religious epic. She then burnt this as well. All this happened in about 1976. I have no means of confirming the story, but her disappearance from the literary scene has been uniquely thorough. References in her novels to the heroines leaving a private school at 15 and having to do office work, and working in the electronic sound workshop of the BBC, may be quite irrelevant to the author's career. (The ending of her first novel, *Emir* – itself removed from all subsequent lists of her works – has the poet-heroine facing her lover condemning her works precisely because they include amorous thoughts.) It's a little regrettable that the one really first-rate English female poet of the 1960s (*Notes on Cafés and Bedrooms*, 1963; *Iliad of Broken Sentences*, 1967) should have been erased from history in this way. It's tragic that Christianity, which had paralysed the efforts of so many female poets over the centuries, should strike down one who had seemed to be morally free.

The key word here is narcissism, and the poems have the exact shape of the heroine, smouldering, scornful, and swishing slightly. Throwing away personally dear theories, I admire the way that every line is alive, saturated with character and wit. Perhaps most self-centred poets fail because they have such boring personalities. Live-wire narcissism implies quick thinking, instinctive grace, attention to detail, heightened awareness of pleasure, keenness of the senses. She writes like a brilliant conversationalist. One thinks of Colette and Apollinaire. There is nothing weighty, yet every possible idea is taken on and played with exactly as it hits the sensibility.

> I have lived it, and lived it,
> My nervous, luxury civilization,
> My sugar-loving nerves have battered me to pieces.
>
> …Their idea of literature is hopeless.
> Make them drink their own poetry!
> Let them eat their own gross novel, full of mud.

One sees how unnecessary and lumpish most heavy things are. The flâneur is easily bored and consequently lives life at an accelerated rate, idle, voracious and quick-witted. Reading Tonks made it clear how many English poets were fantastically boring yet covered this up by astute manipulation of guilt so that to admit boredom seemed heartless. Tonks reminds you that intelligence is the capacity to be bored, that is almost its first quality, it is a set of aesthetic reactions to the quality of ideas, people, food, and places;

an intelligent person is exciting just by the way they move, their irritability is a reassurance that they will never be boring.

> No, I... go to the cinema,
>   I particularly like it when the fog is thick, the street
>   Is like a hole in an old coat, and the light is brown as laudanum,
>   ...the fogs! the fogs! the cinemas
>   Where the criminal shadow-literature flickers over our faces,
>   The screen is spread out like a thundercloud – that bangs
>   And splashes you with acid... or lies derelict, with lighted waters
>   in it,
>   And in the silence, drips and crackles – taciturn, luxurious.
>   ...The drugged and battered Philistines
>   Are all around you in the auditorium...
> (both quotes from 'The Sofas, Fogs, and Cinemas',
> *Iliad of Broken Sentences*, 1967, pp7-8)

Tonks arouses doubts about the appeal of radical ideas – did one adopt them out of selflessness, or simply because being conventional made thought impossible?

Tonks' novels are full of destructive comments about the fashionable, but her work is purely of the 1960s because it happens in a continuous present, shows always an individual's point of view, and never a moralising voice, is hedonistic, and is written in *vers libre* of an intensely personal rhythm. Although anti-political and by no means feminist (she worked for the *Daily Telegraph* at one point), her poems dwell on the inadequacies of male companions with a kind of anguished and infuriated detailing that scarcely fits in with the women's magazine romance of the period.

When I first read John Ash it struck me that he had exactly caught the tone of Rosemary Tonks. Yet he doesn't know who she is. There must have been a specific conversational manner aimed at by vain and glamorous young females in the late 1950s, and adopted by gay men in the 1960s. The archaeology of this manner could perhaps be reconstructed by studying actresses of the era, on film, or old copies of smart women's magazines.

Tonks' two books of poetry are classics. However, the novels seldom get beyond a 'Five put on perfume and go to the opera' tone, satisfied with demonstrating how pretty and vivacious and witty the heroine narrator is. It was predictable that whoever wrote them would make a radical break on reaching middle age.

The first volume from Peter Redgrove (1932-2003), *The Collector and Other Poems*, is dated 1959, although a slip informs us that it didn't come out until 1960; it is an anomaly in 1959, an anticipation not so much of the 1960s as of the 1980s. Redgrove's influence only became visible in the second half of the 1980s, with poets such as Norman Jope, Elisabeth Bletsoe, Andrew Jordan, and Vittoria Vaughan. In 1959, the visible antecedents were Robert Graves, in his Jungian robes, and Alex Comfort, for his interest in science, sex, and witchcraft.

His inventiveness, measured in the number of his poems, the density of the imagery contained in them, the sensuous detailing of the effects, the ability of the images to take on a life of their own and grow, the fluency of the handling, is far in excess of any other contemporary poet. His inner world buds and fruits with greater fertility than other people's. The only poet who compares with him, in the sheer density and scope of linguistic figures, is John Wilkinson. The loss of inhibitions is not simply perfection in art; having an intense inner world, and realising it in language, is not the end of artistic achievement. Relations between people must be respected on both sides, and the effect of the artist's power on the reader's inner world must be examined. Redgrove becomes unbearable when he sees himself as a spiritual authority who can tell other people what to do, who interprets their inner lives and even, by the persuasive power of his images, floods and controls those lives. He proclaims that the rules of his fantasies are the rules of biology. Inconsistently, it is only when we feel that his imagery does describe part of the outer world that we share that his art really has a hold on us. Perhaps it was inevitable that the anti-daemon of the 1950s should bear out the edicts of that decade by showing excessive lack of restraint.

His external career involved traumatic experiences in the army, where he was diagnosed (incorrectly, he states) as schizophrenic and put through many insulin shocks, an alleged cure also favoured as a treatment for Soviet dissidents. A science degree at Cambridge in the mid 1950s was followed by a Gregory Award and a first volume of poetry. He worked as a science writer before becoming resident poet at Falmouth College of Art from 1966 until the late 1990s.

Redgrove became very popular after his selected poems (*Sons of My Skin*) generated critical acclaim in 1975, and he capitalised on this by presenting a commercial image as New Age priest/feminist/psychotherapist and a long series of promotional readings. Being aligned with a social current outside poetry also means you can vanish into thin air when people tire of the fad.

Redgrove looked at a large number of English poets who were too diffident to recount their inner lives, couldn't develop another kind of poetry, and ended up with a complete lack of material; he has worked very hard to stay in the race, and has a fearless attitude about what to include in poems. He has internalised all parts of his work. One feels, reading him, that the objects and scenes that other poets use exist for them only as the wares on a grocer's shelves, rational, counted, dead, without imaginative commitment. He produced seven volumes of poetry up to *Sons of My Skin*. A book-jacket note of the 1990s announces 'between 800 and 900 published poems'. But daily work on confidence has produced physical damage. Willpower isn't a linear quality that you can just step up without any side-effects. No, action and reaction are equal and opposite. If you work every day to silence doubt then the 'reaction' is that you become humourless, repetitive, domineering, and boring. If you try hard enough you can wipe out every trace of understanding of other consciousnesses, who might disagree with you. If you treat your ego like a muscle it winds up starving your brain. Redgrove evidently makes systematic use of his dreams, although he can clearly produce the same kind of material when awake. Most of these dreams involve sex. Combined with Redgrove's blade-of-grass-counting description, what you end up with is suspiciously close to 'the vital cultural patrimony you have to acquire is the knowledge of how good I am at sex'. Combined with the medical subtext of his artistic apparatus, it ends up like 'you're ill and unhappy because you refuse to recognise how good I am at sex and spend a few years studying me in proper detail'. Maybe if you have to use the force of your personality on hundreds of students expecting you to be an 'artist' (and also sceptical about authority figures) then you end up either completely drained and compliant or with a hypertrophied 'creative personality' like a politician's smile.

He has an impressive list of virtues. A broad view of mental behaviour, allowing all kinds of phenomenon to become visible. Drive, pursuing possibilities to their logical culmination, and never flagging in rhythm or invention. Vision, going beyond the limits of consciousness and rationality; grasp of detail, binding the vision in tenacious, rippling verbal webs. Attentiveness to Nature, no doubt more than any contemporary poet's; his projection of human feelings into the animal and plant world finds hundreds of equivalents and gives a convincing symbolic account of how our mind-body connection works. He isn't just interested in big infantile emotions, but in every part of our life. The aim of transformation, without which any art is dreary and deterministic. The use of gratification, so unusual in modern poetry, giving his work its urgent quality and its weight as a philosophy of life. The absence of the usual teleologies. His fertility, the unfailing quality of the energies he draws on.

One weak point is the absence of class and social relations. His people are driven by internal stored programs, influenced by the weather but not really by human relations. Another weak point in his work is the crossing point between observing the outside world and observing himself. In *The Apple Broadcast* we have a man who turns to gold:

> He found his golden sister of the work
> Moving about the room quickly, tidying up
> Laughing between gold teeth at the sheer pleasure
>
> Of being gold. [...]
> 'Still, we've got plenty to live on', pointing to the floor,
> 'Yes, and you've got a penis suitable for gold girls'.
>
> 'I wish my brain were gold like yours'; 'When I whisper
> Thoughts to you, your brain glows gold
> Like coals in the fire; do not ask
>
> To be dead' said the golden shade.
> (from 'The Midas Variation')

This is a mere fantasy; whereas some of his poems apply the same manic detail to the outside world; and are more interesting. The pure fantasy poems are flat and have no interpretative tension. They weigh the volume down. Their self-referential quality takes the goodness out of the air.

I think Redgrove is a major poet. But I deplore the attitude that starts from the poverty and low status of poets and moves out into 'art therapy' and 'self-confidence training' because the hourly wage for them is appreciably higher. Amplified introspection is usually simply hypochondria. Redgrove's close observation is analogous to Greek and Chinese medicine, where a great many phenomena are accurately observed so as to bring their occurrence into relation; a *souci du soi*, continued I suppose by a Proust, which offers the possibility of explaining our moods and why they vary. Perhaps this is the real aim of literature. He imagines the human subject on more levels than most writers, tracing neglected behaviour patterns that are mysterious as well as embarrassing; he accepts mental phenomena as genuine and is beyond the objective-subjective split and its attendant guilt. Today zoo-keepers observe complex animals very closely to see what makes them happy or irritable, and this lucid and unprejudiced observation, applied to humans, is not far from Redgrove's project.

George MacBeth (1932-1992) was a flâneur with none of the virtues the English audience looks for, although the cover of his first book bemusingly claims the Scottish virtues for him: '[h]is work is in the tradition of Hogg and Stevenson, a mixture of sober nostalgia, Calvinist gloom and Byronic wit.' Other comments on the dust jacket of his first *Collected Poems* (1958-70) sum it up: 'extraordinary gifts arrogantly wasted' (*Times Literary Supplement*) and 'One would love George much more if he decided to pack it in, or if he would simply state that he did not wish his verses to be considered as literary, thus sparing reviewers some embarrassment'. (Martin Seymour-Smith). I owe him a debt partly because his anthology of *Poetry 1900-65* was the book that converted me to poetry, in 1973 (in a remedial English class for scientists), partly because of the sheer heroism of someone with so many speech defects giving a poetry reading to cynical and articulate schoolboys ('Pwoust got wushes tortuwing wats in a cage' sticks in the mind, after 20 years), partly because he did write some good poems, obscured by his career. He sums up a good deal of the 1960s predicament, where media people desperately seeking novelty because they haven't got enough talent for anything except knowing about the latest big thing, resemble modernists, throwing away the past in favour of aleatory and exclusive procedures. Both are driven by boredom and contempt for 'provincials'. Both occasionally show an ability to function in completely new social landscapes. The good poems are 'The World of the Oboe', 'The Bamboo Owl', 'Land Mine', 'The God of Love' and a few others. There are four volumes of poems (*A War Quartet, Lusus, The Cleaver Garden, Anatomy of a Divorce*) not reprised in the second *Collected Poems* (1958-82; published in 1989), which was followed by *Trespassing* and *The Patient*.

A decisive phase of MacBeth's life (this is narrated in 'Land Mine') was the experience of anxiety during the bombing in the Second World War, in which his father was killed by a defective shell. This gave him his two principal themes: that of animals (the contact with warm fur is a recapitulation allowing him to project his dissatisfied childish feelings onto small affectionate creatures), and of war, especially nuclear war. He was perhaps unlucky that these areas were crowded (war protest being the theme of millions of poems since Hiroshima, and animal poems being a commercial minor genre). The animals/war thematic made him a natural lesser copy of Hughes, something he recognised when he parodied *Crow* by a myth-epic about a cat (*The Orlando Poems*). The sight of beloved cats killing other animals mixed his two themes and threatened his whole poetic system; he returned to this crossing again and again.

MacBeth claimed in an interview that he saw himself 'as a Scottish and European poet', speaking also of violence, masks, the preservation of decorum, the avoidance of sentimentality. 'I think I write more than almost anybody else who is writing', he said: an obsession with seizing the transient moment derived from an awareness of historical style so keen that he could scarcely believe in the reality of the present except as a hallucinatory configuration to be exploited as much as possible before turning into a period style for connoisseur antiquarians. His wardrobe of transformations resembles those of the cat Orlando, as well as the decadent time-warrior Jerry Cornelius. This dandy-trophy collector's approach allowed him to bring off extraordinary effects:

> [o]utside the snow falls in a mindless blank
> where the downward turn
> is all the hand can feel. If she lifts
>
> her face (the girl in the glass cage) she is old
> enough to be tasting
> the dipped salt on her tongue. The forgotten sea
>
> drips into the grained skin that is ready
> for it. So many crystals
> of grey light in the sugar-sifter of
>
> steel sponges! The nose hurts, it is
> pressurized by the freezing-point
> of anonymous water. Come in, Mercy, no
>
> other name in the black roll of
> the Norse winter
> challenges the moment your head rests in.
> (from 'The World of the Oboe', a synaesthetic *Symboliste*
> evocation of the sounds an oboe makes, from ca. 1966).

MacBeth entered the fickle, high-velocity, nil-hysteresis world of the 1960s more than anyone else, burning up everything that distracted from the present minute even at the cost of reducing the poems of the past to clothes that one buys in junk-shops for dressing up in. He took on the insatiable, memoryless ability of photographic media (film, TV, magazines) to glut on and spew out images, and rode it, without a hangover. He understood the unbiddable nature of the timeline to the point of being reduced by it to a mere quivering in the shared sensorium. He leads naturally on to the analytical fragmentation of the conscious subject that arrives in later decades. (The super-prolific poets who scored well over a thousand published poems are Peter Redgrove, Jeremy Reed and Colin Simms along with MacBeth. But nothing else seems to link them. There is also someone called Colin Nixon.)

Ken Smith (1938-2003) is distinguished among British poets for his extremely humble origins: his father was a farm labourer (in various parts of Yorkshire). Smith has given an excellent account of his career up until the mid-1970s in an interview with Eric Mottram in *Poetry Information* no. 18. He took an English degree, went on to teach poetry at Exeter College of Art, was very heavily involved in the 1968 political revolt there, and in the heady ensuing mobility quit the service and decided at 30 to become a full-time poet. Some of the uproar may be obliquely described in 'Apocrypha from the Western Kingdom':

> Schism, rebellion, grumblings
> over coffee, strange alliances,
> manifestoes, knives in the dark,
> religious upheavals, slander,
> fanatics under arms, chance,
> palace coups, gossip, non-
> aggression treaties, cults,
> independence movements, the wind
> weaving through the wheat,
> client kingdoms, petty republics,
> nods to the blind man, winks,
> signs under the table, flags,
> beasts, bureaucrats, piles,
> foreign syndicalist ideas, –
> all these bother the emperor.
>   (from *The Poet Reclining. Selected Poems 1962-1980*,
>   1982, pp.114-123)

Smith's work is characterized by its lack of abstraction, immersed instead in the spatial position at a moment in time of a living being in a 'perpetual present', in a set of spatial relations (at least as complex as those in abstract thought), experiencing life somatically, aware of the future in terms of scents and anxieties rather than conscious planning, with senses heightened by bodies moving around him and by imminent danger. He is at one extreme of the 'physical: abstract' axis, and no doubt one could relate this to class origins and his late start in formal education. His poetry is kinetic – it moves forward because the protagonist is moving through a landscape and does not have sufficient knowledge to form a conceptual map which would be static, and relate his movement to a stable set of (spatial) relations; instead the relations shift constantly, as he shifts, and the whole poem rushes forward. Most extremely in *Fox Running*, Smith thinks like a film-maker, a camera following a protagonist who is himself chasing or being chased. Smith has explained this long poem as describing someone wondering whether to commit a major robbery in order to overcome desperate poverty; and in the meantime wandering round London fighting off problems on the most basic material level of existence. Fox's detachment from any stable set (at the level of food and a lair) is the source of the poem's high uncertainty, but is also an analogue to Thatcherite Britain, with social and material security (and the knowledge of the world it made possible) radically dissolved.

In *The Poet Reclining* (selected poems 1962-80) I find virtually no hypotaxis at all. There are no causal analyses, either; Smith constantly presents us with facts, almost like a series of photographs, and also states of mind; but no explanations. This is an effective way of presenting human relations; we can work out the connections for ourselves once given the essential facts. After all there is never an abstract moment in a relationship; one moves through successive real (somatic and emotional) states and even reflection only has to represent those states. Maybe picking ideas out of books of psychology, biology, and anthropology cannot be integrated with life experience. Maybe there is no 'privileged place' from which universal laws become apparent. This would also liberate us from predictability.

It's natural that Smith should have picked on the subject of Tristan (*Tristan Crazy*, 1978), because the later part of the story, when Tristan is living rough in the forest, represents that loss of mediation between the body and the elements that is central to whatever Smith does. This theme of a murderer amongst green things is close to *Fox Running*, with its hero on the run in a city scanned only in terms of shelter and hostility. A book has been published identifying all the places appearing in Beroul's 12th-century account of the tale, in Cornwall; this was bound to appeal to Smith (who used to live in Exeter, in Devon but not too far away), as locating the mythical in the unimaginably complex spatial relations of real places. The 'crazy' of the title reflects the key anxiety of Smith's work, namely that the hero will have to live outdoors (forfeiting the benefits of four walls and a fire) because he has been unable to integrate emotions and the drive for freedom with the code of civilisation, which allows the houses to come about. The same theme inspires poems such as 'Remembering when he was a wolf'. At some level, this conflict is also the political to-do at Exeter College of Art. A lot of poets in the 1960s wanted to avoid working in an office all their lives, but Smith actually took the idea seriously enough to give it existential density, not just a weekend off. The title, from the fragmentary Anglo-Norman poem 'La folie Tristan', closely resembles *Buile Suibhne Geilt*, i.e. 'Sweeny crazy'. This is a *scela*, prose with poems interspersed, in which the hero goes mad and lives in the tops of trees, as Merlin also does in the *Vita Merlini*; it was a classic theme of early Celtic poetry such as the lost proto-Tristan saga presumably was. The whole thematic is close to Barry MacSweeney in poems like 'Ranter'.

The problem is to explain why, when poets who talk about concrete things are so tedious and limited, Smith can be constantly interesting without ever leaving the concrete. Two reasons would be: first, he defines space by moving through it, rather than implying the static nullness of a bourgeois kitchen, the objects appearing at speed and as parts of navigation; second, he made a crucial progression from talking about place-as-myself to talking about the protagonist from the outside, allowing the eye to track motion rather than simply take part in it. I suspect he worked out his technique by writing rather than by studying other writers, based on emotional states rather than on theorizing.

Smith exhibits to perfection a number of characteristics of 1960s poetry. The 'memoryless' diction, immediate and mobile as a camera, is quite systematic. Anyone who is puzzled about the removal of organised knowledge and of organised syntax should study him. Features such as the interest in animals (creatures dominated by the immediate situation) and the revival of mediaeval narrative poems, skipping anything intermediate, are also typical. At present he is acceptable both to the Mottramite avant-garde and to the suspicious anti-intellectualism of Bloodaxe Books.

THEY CAN'T TAKE THAT AWAY FROM ME:
review of Dreaming Flesh *by John James (1939-)*

My conception of John James has always been as someone impossibly romantic and optimistic, miraculously avoiding gloom and didacticism to achieve a continuously surprising and euphoric surface. A poetry, in fact, like the big, fruity, colour-drenched, abstracts that some English painters have brought off. *Dreaming Flesh* follows the same affirmative line as the classic *Berlin Return*. Reviewing it gives an opportunity to tinker with these beautiful creations, and in particular to ask why they are never annoying.

(1) FOUND TEXTS
On page 27 we find pastiches of David Bowie and 'Lead kindly light' within four lines. In the extended 'Poem for Bruce McLean' we see 'the way

you stroke your nose/ the way you swing off key'. This hits off a Gershwin song, for me specially in the 1937 Billie Holiday version:

> The way you wear your hat, the way you sip your tea
> The memory of all that
> No, no they can't take that away from me.
> The way your smile just gleams
> The way you sing off key
> The way you haunt my dreams
> No, no they can't take that away from me.

This is a sad song, about a lost love; an ambiguity (if one reads the James version as full of optimism and hilarity), but let's note how deftly that snatch sums up intimacy, those sequences of another person's behaviour which make up so much of what we know in this life. Human beings recognise these tiny traits, so as to disengage inner changes of mood from even slighter variations within them. The details are there as traces of intimacy: two people close in space; the typical space of these poems. The signs emitted don't have to carry very far, just that short distance. Perhaps poems are strings of behaviour. Most of the lines in *Dreaming Flesh* describe flakes of behaviour seen in just this physiognomic light:

> we live so much by the eye
> but the ear's an organ too
> which sticks out neatly from the side of your head
> & carries an earnest of desire in the ring that dangles there.

One step on from these traits is a method of the 'minimal recognizable' for objects: a single classical window frame evokes a classical house, so just draw the window. Genres and symbols can be manipulated as 'minimal recognisables' – the supplies you need if you're going to evoke an idea instantly and then change course. Not far away, either, is the style of popular song: James is always close to song (the direct lifts never jar), just that he goes round a corner every two lines.

(2) KINETICS

James' art is carefully based in kinetics, in kinaesthetics (the location of the body in space and its relation to other bodies) and in physiognomy (in the broad sense of noting human movements as well as faces). This explains its differences from art based in abstraction and in static organised knowledge.

Kinetics is the plane in which events are presented: every line is an instant from a series moving against a moving background, consequently unique and in a unique configuration, which it would be pointless to describe in detail because of its transience. One difference between paintings and poems is that paintings are allover while poems are serial. Static poems are a disaster. Poems can move through landscape, but regrettably modern paintings do this too, the static observer and its perspective have been eaten by the trees.

There is an opposition between poems of a transient conjuncture and generalising poems, which can sum up the results of experiences as knowledge but can't be kinetic or immediate. There is a point of view that the actual world (of places, faces, of the poet as a body moving through a space full of other bodies) is banal, just because the world is like that. Knowledge as power is quite other, for example theology, law, stock exchange prices, examinable knowledge. You could only write poems about big central truths if there were big central things. For James, the centre of the world is explicitly the space around two people.

(3)

Are you now or have you ever been in The Baron of Beef? Recent good resolutions have made me renounce the 'Cambridge experimental axis' as an analytical tool. Formal analysis suggests that there is no resemblance between the usual suspects. Market makers are now more interested in the far more elusive Essex School. Andrew Crozier, Denise Riley, Anthony Barnett can all be accused of writing poetry that is not crypto-philosophy and that centres on the personal; brief reflection tells us that virtually all contemporary poetry in England has these two characteristics. So we've learned nothing. To locate James, it would be better to read Apollinaire, or to look closely at the painters whose shows he has curated from time to time (Richard Long, Bruce McLean, Tom Phillips, Howard Hodgkin) or to look at his own *prises de position*.

(4) BEAUTIFUL SUNSETS ENDURING CAPITALISM

An oblique approach is to ask why contemporary taste rejects beautiful and optimistic poetry. Well, it does and it doesn't. It's accidental (read: catastrophic) that poetry is dominated by oppositional intellectuals, resentful of happiness because it seems to justify the power structure, anti-sensuous because of the abstract nature of their daily work. A lot of art of the 1970s felt, subjectively, like being in an Army sensory deprivation room.

Does romantic, social, optimistic poetry really represent compromise with the power structure? Does withholding data provoke or empty artistic experience? Are gloom and rage the best propaganda? James' calm on this topic perhaps derives from a securely contestatory politics:

> you can rest on the bench near the bowling green
> & later go back by the old orphans' home
> & drink from the glass the hammer and the sickle
> so carefully chased Jim Peck made that for me
>   ('On Romsey Rec', in *Collected Poems*, 2002, p.308)

These symbols are not accidentally present.

(5) WORK AND PLEASURE

Evidently James' ability to respond to experience at the speed at which it unfolds is related to his classic simplicity of line; evidently thought, as slow reacting, suspends contact with sensuous reality. And with social reality: other people aren't going to wait around for you to cogitate. Conversation is improvisation. Learned poetry, I suppose, is ponderous and one-sided. And I suppose that much poetry fails because of the work ethic, it does things because they are difficult and is unnatural and laboured.

Escaping the work ethic, why don't I rip off someone else's ideas. Only way to go. Let's do it.

> 'In the late '50s Hodgkin embarked on a series of portraits which were to absorb him for the next twenty years – friends, very often fellow artists, presented in their own interiors, and very often incorporating invented pastiches of their work.' [...] 'The luminous blobs of *In Alexander Street* again suggest a box-like perspective, but the image seems to drift in and out of register, coalescing into legibility, swimming into euphoric reverie.'(...) 'The exact placing of colour creates spaces of poignant mystery'.
>   (from Teresa Gleadowe's article on back of a poster of 'The
>   Bay of Naples', handed out at the Venice Biennale, 1984.)

This all sounds very John James-like to me. Pastiche is close to physiognomy. One reason why James is never annoying is the economy of means: you don't get acres of paint, you get tiny stripes, plus incredible care given to the placement of signs. This reminds me of abstract painters of the 1960s applying the paint with a roller: to prevent the finicky, highly-trained craft work of brush strokes getting in the way of mood. What remains of James is the euphoria, as what remains of Hodgkin is the abandon and daze of colour; but, at a technical level, the effect is achieved partly by near-ironical restraint, partly by a very subtle manipulation of the authorial presence to make the image a reverie about the Bay of Naples, not a mere copy of it. James gives amazingly few details.

Hodgkin makes paintings that look like cassata ice-cream. That's nothing; the really elusive question is how he signals a lush, sloppy, lolly mood to go with them. The Mediterranean is two slices of colour. One recalls a series of photos of Bruce McLean, possibly entitled 'Pose Works for Plinths': I think he was mocking some fashionable sculptors, but the message (you can take everything out of art except the artist) is memorable. James only pulls off his effects because his control of the intention-signalling, gestural and mood aspects is so rigorous. He evokes a dégagé mood in a dégagé style – unlike most writers, who would work hard to do it and wonder why it wouldn't work. Oh I know, let's make a rule that paintings have to be full of grey sludge. Let's make a rule that the poet has to be grim and clenched up.

(6) Ambiguity

After deciding that the flavour of James' poetry was lyric optimism, it became clear that the symbols point in several different directions: it is just as possible to read them as humorous, melancholic, or sceptical. Consider the Celtic landscapes which sprinkle *Dreaming Flesh*: does anyone Welsh go up Eryri without thinking bad thoughts about the English? In this context of snatches of song, do we really see:

> it's spring & a child in red smocking
> walks unsteadily near the byre
> her name is Roisin
> (from 'Local', in *Collected Poems*, 2002, p.291)

without thinking of 'Roisin dubh'? As for 'Stacking':

> A little benzedrine to clear the airways
> night gathers itself towards the dawn
> the stars zap through my room again
>
> the head was of some importance in all this
> though sometimes I think I'm just another little piece of
> River Avon driftwood well who isn't?
>
> You are called Michael who is like God
> A big sulking bruiser like yourself
> o dark lovely phantom we wake again in our separate nations
> (from 'Stacking', in *Collected Poems*, 2002, p.312)

The poet, kept awake by asthma, has his vigil rewarded by a visit from Michael Collins; a dead hero, fleeting in flickering light, as in thousands of Irish rebel songs. The paintings the encounter is based on are of Catholic saints and martyrs, ennobled by death, lit by just such a nimbus as dawn arriving; Michael (literal meaning as James gives it) is the warrior angel, seen smiting down Satan and the rebel angels in a Battle-of-Britain type aerial situation. I haven't the faintest idea what the middle stanza's opposition of decision and drift means, although having heard *Kinderlieder* read I guess that a childhood migration from Cardiff to Bristol is the scenery. Nor do I know what 'Stacking' is (delays to wraiths landing? Airways? Waiting to come down from the chest fever?). So: three stanzas, three planes. Point of view rotating like a waltzer; nothing could be more quick-witted, more nimble. Overt simplicity becomes complex as soon as we start to ask how the planes and contact zones compose with each other. But it all makes me feel euphoric.

(7) The history of what was taken away
Pursuing this ambiguity, one finds that the first two poems are remarkably explicit about the writer's intentions:

> this great volcanic frame of things in all
> the revolutionary hope & practices
> of women & of men does not remain unchanged
> it too has its faults through which an exile voice can sing.
> (from 'The Conversation', in *Collected Poems*, 2002, p.296)

Joy and physiognomy reappear in the guise of hope and memory. Finally, writing about happiness reproaches the power order just as much as writing about unhappiness. 'The Conversation' is more like Wordsworth than Apollinaire – note it is still physiognomic, the soaring idealism based in the extra oxygenation attendant on climbing mountains. James is critical of consciousness: 'the inviolable &/ imaginary self', a dialectic phrase readable equally as disillusion and triumph of illusion. Solitude and integrity are opposite things: defence mechanisms cut you off from existence. '[I]f there is always memory in working-class life/ it is because things are always being taken away [...] & love's the chief the drug'. Compare this to '[a] blank erotic mouth sings the history of lack'. (This line is not from any of the poems in *Dreaming Flesh*. Descriptions of mouths occur throughout the book. You can tell from someone's mouth if they're happy or unhappy.) Folk song is always made up of 'minimal recognisables'. The blankness has to do with unlearning *protagonismo*; the poem can only be a potential space for the audience's dreams if the writer somehow vacates it. The bit about 'the history of lack' is more depressing: it's not just any old blues as sex dirge, but maybe a prison song, even the 'chiliastic serenity' of a Gospel song. Minimal but durable. The memory of not being alone is a skill that allows us to reconstruct intimacy. Compare further with 'hanging by unseen fissures in the grey and slippery rock': here the 'fissures' are another mouth, 'faults' precisely, through which a completely alien discourse of liberation is seeping from across, and in whose clasp the living climber hangs.

(*The above was written in 1991, and originally published in Parataxis, 1993*).

Postscript

I can't bear to tinker with this review, but it seems fair to mention that James' best single book is 1983's *Berlin Return*, while his work was collected in 2002. The first poem I know that shows the modern James is in *Resuscitator*, the magazine he and Nick Wayte ran in Bristol, in 1964. He is perhaps the best reader of poetry I have ever heard, and all his poems work best in that format: everything which is not immediate is discarded, while the line of the poem jumps to something new, with daring montage logic, at every turn. His work would have been unthinkable in the 1950s. Reading James, and his associates in *A Various Art*, reminds one that the opposition between live poetry and intellectual poetry was dissolved at that time (in Cambridge, 1966), as the directness and hedonism of the 1960s style also applied to ideas, which became pleasurable as soon as people dedicated to the punitive element are removed from the scene.

The poets discussed here were all born in the 1930s. However, poets born in the 1940s were also living in the 1960s, and were arguably much more affected by the shared imaginary of the decade. It is also arguable that the technical advances of the poets discussed were taken a vertiginous step further in the years of chaos and experiment that followed 1968, and that the self-limiting lightness and elegance that characterised 1960s poetry, like the 1960s pop song, were replaced by something that presented rivals to the real world, at once impossibly elaborate and comprehensive in their design and impossibly loose, porous, and hypothetical in their detailed fabric.

MAINSTREAM POETRY

Of course writing about artistic ideologies like immediacy must have the effect of pushing offstage everyone who was happy in some other configuration of ideals. I have explored the total present at length because that is productive in understanding the decision processes of certain poets. I don't have room to do this for other cultural patterns – but of course they were present. A longer treatment would explore more patterns and have less of a marginalising effect. I can see from the publication record that the Christian poets of the 1950s – Hill, Levi, and Thwaite – were being productive. The immediacy thing did not sweep them away. It is useful to read their poems in order to see what the conservative critics were defending. Naturally, defending something good is a genuine position that does not validate allied attacks on something you haven't even read. Alan Ross, George Barker, or Kathleen Raine stood for other sectors of the field, hardly subverted even if not so well accepted by academic gate-keepers. John Holloway's *The Landfallers* (1962) represents possibly the end of formalism. If you scrap the British Poetry Revival you still have a literary history with its triumphs and its frustrations. The image of poetry continuing the 1950s may have been distorted on all sides by the business always promoting poets of very limited ability. It is evident that the majority of people who bought a book of poetry in 1967 were not besotted with modernity. This other part of the industry also deserves to be in the picture.

There is a mass of poetry that is non-direct, i.e. generalised, impersonal, relating the past, but it is clearly *passé* and neo-traditionalist in the climate of 1964. If I look at *For the Unfallen*, the 1959 volume by Geoffrey Hill, I don't find any positive moments, any direct self-revelation by the author, any beautiful textures, any situations I would wish to project myself into (one moment on the beach is not a poster of golden sands!), any joy in the intellect even. It is not pretty poetry, yet I find it vivid and compelling. Prettiness would be a distraction from its moral concerns. The author's personality comes across in the style. I would absolutely not be without this kind of poetry. But the conservative counterblast – that immediate poetry cannot be intelligent or beautiful – is a snare and a delusion. Poetry that is indirect, that is 'on' the whole time, might be concealing a grand design in stealth, or could be attenuated only. To silence the self in a poem might empty a space for more exciting information but I am afraid this self-effacement is usually the pretext for something drab, dowdy, absent-minded, flat, tired, imitative, old, and conventional. Our minds are clearly involved in steering selves about the world and so can get more excited and alert about incoming self-information than about, say, the geography of Greenland. The constant directness calls for strong personalities; but who thinks poetry can be written by someone weak? The personality grows strong if you stop starving it; traditionalism takes away the choices that you would have the energy to make if you allowed yourself to. Was this crisis or liberation?

My impression is that the 1950s were discouraging and inhibiting even for poets associated with the 1950s style, and that the 1960s brought new enthusiasm and daring to poets like John Wain and Anthony Thwaite, as well as to young poets listening to rock music. Thwaite's 1967 sequence of poems temporally cuts between himself, living in Libya, and Synesius, living in late fourth-century Cyrene. He described this in his book about Libya:

> Within the same patch of featureless and stony Libyan ground you might pick up a Neolithic flint, a scrap of Greek pottery, a spent Italian cartridge, and an empty tin left by some oil-prospector who passed that way last year.
> (from *Deserts of the Hesperides: An Experience of Libya*, 1969, p.162)

The letters 'use Synesius not so much as a consistent persona but as a running commentary, or chorus, on the conflicts, apprehensions, anomalies, strains, stresses, and [...] epiphanies I found in Libya and in myself.' Hill's expansion from highly-wrought lyrics into the long form of *Mercian Hymns*, with its montage of different times, is an example of new possibilities being realised, not merely in fantasy. Someone told me that *Crow* was the product of Ted Hughes taking acid; surely not, but it reproduces the structure of an acid trip, hyper-associating, freed from temporal constraints, and experiencing revelations of being. Hughes made a fundamental shift into the new technology: the stakes had been raised and all attempts to regress since have been a play-acting kind of Bourbon restoration.

Earthly and Lying Tales:
the History of Data Processing

There is a classic definition that runs *program* = *data* + *procedures*. This would also work as a definition of a poem. The data of which the poem is made is not autonomous, rather it seems that the question of where that data comes from and how it is validated has been urgent, and that changes in the economics of information in a wider world of data acquisition and storage technology have affected how a poem can be written or read.

The Collapse of Authority

A basic question is why poetry is not aligned with the Cold War and with capitalism. It would resolve so many problems if poetry reproduced the dominant reality structures.

In about 1943, the literary world essentially was aligned with Britain as a war polity. (The main poetic current of the 1940s couldn't even manage that.) Modern poetry starts with a void left by the clearance of a pre-existing means for ordering texts. At a certain moment – perhaps too ideal ever to actually exist, of the 1950s, a poet could combine Cold War ideology and Christianity and literary creativity and write exalted poems in which the social order was successfully defended and the literary act reached perfect fruition. People pretended this was happening, but more visible was disenchantment. The effort of writing propaganda for a common cause during the era of ideological mobilisation, roughly 1933-56, had produced a state of deep dislike of propaganda. That was enough, people didn't want to do that any more. This left a void. The poetic world, abidingly, longs for art committed to social ideals and to the high ideas of art, but has an overdeveloped ability to unstitch and rip out propaganda intent.

We can illustrate the new problem of credibility by a single case. Christian literature is notably monotonous. A Christian poet is actively trying to reproduce patterns laid down in preserved texts dating from the later first millennium BC up to about 300 AD. The repetitious quality of Christian texts is seen as authenticity by an insider. They confirm each other because they present the laws of the cosmos. If you stop being an insider, their repetitive quality seems just like imitation. They represent a learning exercise that leads away from real life; endless reinforcement of simple schemas. Real life starts to seem like something mysterious and far more diverse than Christianity allows for. Christian writing stops being credible because it is just an endless series of repetitions of an original moment.

Suppose you look at a writer and find that their work repeats the same patterns, numerously. Is this a sign of authenticity or simply of artificiality and indifference to the very diverse patterns of the cosmos? Is the idea of a pattern found everywhere in the cosmos flawed because finding patterns is a gratification and the brain can give up reality functions in favour of gratification? The absurd saw individuals trapped in a subjective and personal world that was full of angst. The shift in the 1960s was to dissolve the angst and fill that world with a hedonistic principle, with gratification as imperative.

This sensitisation to propaganda meant a deep suspicion of the literary telltales that were the trace of propaganda composition. One example was the use of schemas. The exploration of these was productive. Naturally the impulse of poets is to know what defines something as being not-propaganda so that they can write their own poems in that fashion. This sensitivity discovered schemas as omnipresent, not just in Christian poetry, but in poetry in general. In fact, this gave a new definition of the realm of poetry, as the site of authenticity demonstrated by being wholly non-schematic. The more the personality of the poet came to be the central matter of poetry, the more the critique of narcissism came to be integral to reading, and the more it looked as if any poet's claims to wisdom resembled the claims of priests to wisdom.

Schemas have a delicate relationship to power. The schema does not exist only in literature or music, it represents a module of the imagination itself and the social fabric is the imagination of certain mighty individuals. Where their imagination of tasks and duties relies on schemas, it is oppressive for those trapped inside these schemas. Where ideology took over an entire society, for example in the Third Reich or Soviet Russia, the fantasy element of the conceptual grid proved to be oppressive for the citizen. The image of women in recent stages of British society was idealised and oppressive at the same time. The two things were concomitant. What they don't include is the imagination of the people being represented. Everyone knows that folklore is based on formulae, repeated again and again with whatever variations. They express the limits of memory. It is possible that official thought has also relied on formulae visible as schemas, also expressing the limits of memory as it is available in continuous discourse. Greater availability of information, and perhaps also larger numbers of educated people, have progressively been finding the outlines of these schemas and exposing them. Perhaps we are seeing a slow revolution where the schemas are replaced by the far greater variability of fact. The relationship between power and public language, however, has not changed in the same way and still requires discourse to lead back to legitimation.

The implication of cheap and abundant data is really that the authority of the data in poetry collapses. The decline of belief in Christian priests and their sacrosanct founding texts is merely central, it runs side by side with the decline of the believers in Marx and Freud. Finally the presentation of the book of poems as a pattern centring on a set of special insights, a revelation, attained by the poet, is damaged by the same process. The issue of data abundance thus turns out to be a problem in authenticity theory. The authority of the text runs out due to a lack of people who accept authority. The search for authenticity cannot be resolved theoretically, partly because a thousand subjects locate it in so many different places and there is no basis for disqualifying any of them and, partly, because authenticity is present everywhere, in a dappled pattern. Its topology does not lend itself to compression.

People who read poetry have as their main strength empathy. They find it easy to identify with poets and find authenticity in many places. The demolition of literary patterns is not something they are fond of. This exclusion line of course outlines the limits of the poetic market.

COLD WAR PROPAGANDA

The Cold War produced a fascination with conditioning – both sides proclaiming that the population governed by the other side was conditioned into submission. Fairly obviously brainwashing is a heightened form of propaganda and advertising is propaganda for a commodity. The transition to a consumer economy from the middle 1950s onwards meant a shift of energy from patriotic propaganda into advertising. If I look at the pilot for *Hawaii Five-O* from 1967, it is apparent now that the whole thing is an advertisement for masculinity. The lead character is filmed as if he were the model in an advertisement for shirts. A whole series of technical objects act as props for him. He is mostly seen running, it is a brand image. He has an amazing Billy Fury-style quiff, and much of the interest of the pilot episode comes from watching him immersed in a swimming pool for purposes of sensory deprivation-driven brainwashing by the utterly evil Red Chinese and wondering how the quiff is going to survive the watery principle. If today we realise that the whole set of events and *mise en scène* is planned as an advertisement, and actually one promoting the male characters, (while the female characters are present as their escorts), this is the impact of feminism. *Book 'em Danno – patriarchy one.* It is very hard to get back to a cultural atmosphere where that kind of rewrite never happened. Although the staging asks us to believe that the sensory deprivation torture is something that marks the Red Chinese as wicked and deserving ruin, the scriptwriter has lots of detail about it (neatly served up in gruff yet glib techno-talk by the macho lead characters) evidently because the CIA had poured money into developing it, via contracts with Donald Hebb among others, and details of it were available in popularisations for fans of Intelligence.

Some of the research into cognitive psychology (and psychoto-mimetic drugs) had been funded by the Cold War defence establishments. It was the wish to reduce the control of 'hearts and minds' to a technology that could be mass-produced and enjoy economies of scale. Belief spread in a world-generating machine, generating patterns of irresistible persuasiveness, betrayed only by privileged moments when a seam, or suppressed real data, becomes visible. Both Moscow and Washington were certainly spending billions on such a project. The myth of brainwashing, so central to radical critics of Western governments in this era, was a paranoid projection of the Cold Warriors themselves, always eager to believe in a secret weapon in the hands of their enemy. If you believe in this brain-weapon (allegedly tried out on British and American POWs in Manchuria during the Korean War), you obviously research into cognitive psychology, animated at the time by paranoid theories about 'control' and 'there is a reality other than the one we see'; on acid, you could see three or four of them.

'Cocoon', the *Hawaii Five-O* pilot, also has someone explaining that in sensory deprivation you recite everything that ever happened to you. Also, you become completely compliant to the controller, ready for re-programming. It was inevitable in an age of gadgets that people would want to acquire a domestic version of these conditioning machines. Privatisation means you own your own conditioning machine. So the idea of feminist culture was of gradual re-learning of a (non-patriarchal) truth. The purpose of reliving of childhood and adolescent experiences in many poems was to undo the behavioural learning that had accompanied them. This too provided a project for poetry. It would be logical for McGarrett to go through the fiendish brainwashing and then emerge in episode two as a dedicated Communist. That would have been a lot more interesting. But no, he resists it by prior hypnosis, as does his quiff. This 'I can submerge in your conditioning and come out intact' riff was big at the time. If you lined up 2,000 poets and asked each of them, 'have you resisted lifelong conditioning and produced authentic consciousness which is now the very substance of your poetry', 2,000 of them would say yes. Suppose someone said no. 'My poetry is the substance of the inauthentic, sprawling pleasurably in every downhill direction. I am the deceived and I recite my deceit.' That would be interesting. The culture of the time believed in hard-won authenticity, strips of intact being recovered by steadfastness from the billowing films of deception, home-made, badly co-ordinated, evanescent, patterns dimly present because they had never been mega'd and hyped, noise and signal almost equal to each other, yet containing all things...

The track of sense data is so unimportant, compared to the abstract constructs and acts of identification, in the make-up of experience. There is that subliminal symmetry of the water of the sensory deprivation tank and the inner biochemicals: the inner and outer waters. Both immersive and psychoactive, both representing a fundamental withdrawal from consensual reality. The cocoon irresistibly brings to mind the idea of a worm that spins itself, and the red colour of the immersion suit suggests an insect concentrating psychoactive chemicals, a cocoon that can be swallowed. The popularity of Cold War imagery made it inevitable that one would see the text as a conditioning engine and that society would be seen as a pattern of behaviour modules that were being learnt and taught all the time. It was a didactic era in literature.

There is a latent scene in all this hi-tech conditioning in which the self, instead of being a master above and outside the behaviour patterns spinning away as they map from one web to another, drowns in them and turns out to be no more than a cluster of behaviour patterns itself. The idea of changing society implies a separation between the agents of change and the subjects undergoing change, a distinction that is unlikely to survive a few weeks of real change, as new conditions dissolve the integrity of the would-be masters of time. So we also have to explore the problem of the self dissolving.

If there is a command centre of Cold War ideology that distributes instructions to all citizens as auxiliary services for the war effort, then you can reverse the centre-locality relationship and by seizing the instructions available locally decode the imperatives of the central command and attack them. The Cold War is everywhere; if you take the back off your transistor radio you can find out about transistors and other components, and equally if you take the back off your brain you can find out about Cold War conditioning. It does seem strange that a TV programme that was pumping Cold War propaganda should also be enjoyable. The Cold War was running out in the late 1980s, with perestroika, but our whole period up to then was the culture of the Cold War; a large proportion of poets were convinced that if they disassembled the domestic structures of language, property, and law they would get to the throne-room of the modern era. Your transistor radio is connected to the grand hall of secrets.

There are problems in periodising the changes in data. The changes have been continuous, however radical they are. It is glaringly obvious that the ideas complex of the Cold War dominated literary ideas for a long time. What is more difficult is to date the stages of its decline. During the Cold War, the impact of the times may have been a huge overrating of the political power of artists, which is not going to come back. Reducing political geography to two possibilities made a single choice crucial; if the 'ideas market' perceives a million possibilities, no choice of one idea or by one individual has any great importance.

Completely getting rid of schemas may be too much. This is one of the variables in modern poetry. The schemas may have a protective value, and the interest in the pre-modern schemas of folklore and myth is very noticeable. You can ask too much of the reader.

COMPLEXITY: THE ERA OF CHEAP AND ABUNDANT INFORMATION

The economics of information change with easier availability of books, cheaper high-fidelity electronics, better reprographic and camera technology; more access to and more refined apprehension of the world's cultures, more university graduates, more scholars in the world refining knowledge and argument. The effect of more information on the recipient consumer is not merely additive, but affects the grammar of perception, making it, at the least, more critical about the process of illusion, more aware of style, less inclined to recognise moral authority, less inhibited about symbolic gratification, and perhaps more passive and craving. The general timetable of the impact of cheap information is:

1960s
the freak-out. psychedelia. montage
dispersion of inherited knowledge structures
anti-authoritarianism
decline of middle class culture, rise of working-class media stars
confutation of Christianity, Freudism, Marxism
concern with immediacy and simultaneity
rejection of authority and poetic tradition
narcissism and finicky study of rules of dress
interest in linguistics, information theory, rule-bound systems
drugs

1970s

conceptual reconfiguration. the project of rebuilding the world from scratch
preoccupation with social rules
foregrounding of rules of art and language
fashion for multi-media artworks
search for origins of social forms
attempt to devise a new society
concern with reorganisation of knowledge, new overall metaphors
attention to context and genre framework
radical politics: Marxism, nationalism, personal politics, feminism

1980s

awareness of complexity
conflict of propaganda and fidelity within the text
feminism
New Age ethos; art as ritual and therapy; suspension of realism
preoccupation with sampling and with designing the points of juncture
popularity of 'World Music' and poetic equivalents
return of psychedelic drugs
privatisation of experimental experience

1990s

parodic knowledge
Informationism
evasion of commitment and definite statement
return of fast cuts and inconsequentiality
retreat into incoherence

Strands of change in data processing:
montage
data capture
image enhancements
increasing specialisation of knowledge
finer time-sense
data manipulation (post-processing)
freakout/repacking of stored data as basic assumptions or the classification
rules are upset
distinction between rules of format and the data itself
awareness/displacement of structural rules
critique of personal awareness
conflicts of authority

dissolution of objects into temporal series
dissolution of the 'natural and inevitable' by comparisons; undermining
of all norms

The discovery of multiple interpretations of the world is also the
discovery that each one of them is fictional or bounded: the value of the
contents of consciousness shrinks even as the possible variations expand
to an uncountable wealth. A cline leads either to the humiliation of the
individual mind, the exploration of how its intellectual investments are
projections of socioeconomic interests; or to the irresponsible gaiety and
goggling contemplation of psychedelic overflow.

THE ATTACK ON ORGANISED KNOWLEDGE IN THE 1960S

The links between data complexity and novelty and aesthetic reward became
so clear as to make it appear that something had gone fundamentally
wrong with the aesthetic sense in poetry in the previous decade. Perhaps
the wish to have a set morality had induced people to simplify the data in
their world-models, including poems, to the point where it didn't burst the
bounds of the morality's founding fables. Perhaps the new data flooding
in – from cameras, science labs, the global communications network, the
hugely increased number of researchers – reached a critical mass which
destroyed moral orthodoxies – Christian, Freudian, Marxist – and changed
their apparent nature to paranoid authoritarian systems, based on sacred
texts, closed to new data and ideas, generating power for a minority of
leaders, protecting themselves against disproof and explosion by concealed
barriers in the form of self-referential logical traps. That is, they appeared as
self-stabilising data machines rather than as sets of hypotheses in a sincere
project of understanding the world. This is perhaps why the 1950s seem
like a different world; the engulfing wave of complexity is already breaking
on the horizon in 1961. Absurdity in the guise of unpredictability turns
into Complexity. The defiance of logic is the explosion of a model of
defined characteristics, a triumph of the unknown over the world-model
which guarantees consciousness new intrigue and new model-making.

However, complexity is something that is fragile and temporary,
judging by the efforts to which 1960s poets went to make it stick around.
The density of writers still using the 1950s style in the 1990s was quite
formidable. The great terror is of life slowing down or sinking into a
groove of repetition. These bad states can be satisfactorily described
by information theory and point to a unification of data richness with

aesthetic pleasure, labelling curiosity as the drive above all others. How is the gratification seeking mind to seek richness in unpredictability when all control, including the furnishing of unpredictability, relies on predictability? The decade sought to attract and capture diversity within two frames: the narrating personality and the place, both chosen to provide an allover simultaneity of diverse stimuli that were yet associated by the frame; which evades the set collocations of existing bodies of knowledge, sequences of images, and aesthetic conventions, without fragmenting into meaninglessness and disconnection. Pattern is pursued to the point where it threatens to break down into disorder.

THE 1980s

The poem is made of information and the new economics of information affected both how the poet acquires information and how the poem was read. The idea of complexity or chaos in the 1980s redefined experiences of overload and lost access to conscious control observed in a previous decade. Some of the shared imagery has been redecorated over time. We can see an identity of result between the themes I have rather artificially separated for three decades: if the awareness of the relativising effects of change themed for the 1960s was based on a new plenty of cheap information, and the struggle over the future themed for the 1970s was founded on an insecurising awareness of the rate of change of social forms, mediated again by cheap access to recorded evidence, then the themes starred for the 1980s (the awareness of information as a product and commodity, the search for power) are products of the same incessantly effective data abundancy, and are representations therefore appearing, not as solid, but as the products of human willpower and linked in a temporal series in which time inexorably washes away each link. The idea of loss of self is key. If you accept that the human mind is a kind of vapour, it follows that coherence and rigidity are products of purpose: the vapour acquires pattern as part of a goal. The era after 1968 had a shared goal, of ending inequality and oppression and even monotony. The goal produced very intense patterning. Conversely, the loss of that shared goal – which turned to vapour, and indeed evaporated – meant the loss of pattern. A sense of incoherence stole over people. Poems could not exhibit a link between political events and emotional events when that link was not there. Conversely, the vapour turned out to be capable of almost infinite patterns. This is what ludic poetry exploited. The patterns could not bind people together and had no grip on the outside world, the one where banks, manufactures, and governments lived.

My chosen image for the 1980s is a villain in an issue of the Indiana Jones spin-off Marvel comic-book. Entirely dedicated to aesthetic sensation, he lives in a secret underground chamber beneath the Australian desert, which he has filled with looted *objets d'art* from all the world's cultures: African, Oceanian, Egyptian, Chinese, European, Byzantine, avant-garde, Palaeolithic. An externalised, impossibly vivid and ornate, replacement for memory offers the frozen experience of what was once alive and being lived by someone else. A dozen different kinds of spirit and demon gesture to each other, in effigy. Of course, since they're all stolen, the sinister Symbolist aesthete who has accumulated these treasures cannot publicly enjoy them: he is stuck in his desert bunker, a sensory deprivation cum overload chamber; it's like the treasure-room of a Pyramid, you have to die to enter into possession. But everyone today lives in such a pyramid, piled high with videos, cassettes, CDs, personal computers, televisions and books; decadence in the High Street. And what of the poet? Raised to an object of covetousness, reduced to a consumable item, appropriated and recontextualised in the larder-bank vault of the 1980s consumer's stash of precious objects. The poem as artificial environment, recording perhaps a time-section of a real environment, is sucked in and subsumed into the buyer's personalised suite of montages and indulgences. The poem has to appease the reader's satiation and ravenous boredom.

The gap between artist and consumer was narrowed by the practice of making private tapes, where you could control juxtaposition and so context yourself, and by remix DJs, acquiring ever new devices to re-animate and rebuild pop records after the artist had left them. This privileging of montage over creation brought dance culture to understand what poetry had been involved with around 1965: from Raworth to Cold Cut. Context is not quite the set of all juxtapositions, there is also an interpretative structure that is substantially unspecified within the work itself, rules of identification, genre, plausibility, etc. What montage casts into question is the demarcation between the creator's self and the rule set governing the consumption of artworks. Montage could make the rule sets the hero and make their static, folded structure the path along which attention flowed. Structure as narrative. Experimental artists had spent years in the 1970s doing just that; but most of the techniques of the avant-garde had by now become familiar in the music consumer's living room. As music deprivileges the singer vis-à-vis the producer, poetry replaces 'voice' with 'procedures'. Declining to mention the word deconstruction, we nonetheless see that the vast popularity of works of art that have no artist-centre, no originary experience, no realism, no unity, no hand-on-heart, no heart, sell millions of copies and inspire thousands of imitations, has un-bottomed what were taken to be The Rules twenty years ago. D-word or no d-word, a poet who didn't understand appropriation, fast editing, the customisation of genre expectations, and juxtaposition, wasn't going to be any big thrill. As authenticity turned out to be something like a guitar track that you could fade out – and fade in? – the similarity between the reader's appropriation and the poet's made the link between appetite and deep internal structures seem tenuous.

The decade saw consciousness increasing its definition to take on many fine-grain objects rather than a few large ones: data objects in computers; the many agents of the market taking over from governments; historians abandoning the history of governments for that of the family, of classes for individuals; coming to look at fine details of representation, no longer at crude features; breaking time down into finer segments. PCs replaced mainframes. Local radio stations took much of the market from the BBC's national ones. Theories of consciousness explained it as an emerging function of complexity, as a swarm intelligence – originally decentralised – that had to fight to create a slow and stumbling central co-ordination unit to stop the subsystems, where all the programme complexity resided, from moving in two directions at once. In the labour-capital struggle, the myth of individual progress replaced national strikes, as management struggled to replace flat block increases with individually negotiated merit increases. Industry began to shy away from mass production and look longingly towards one-by-one assembly where goods were very finely differentiated or even made up singly to the specifications of a single customer. Some of the change was due to systematic attacks on collective institutions by the government, trying to get its enemies to waste their time fighting each other. However, a splendid and apocalyptic view of the Future as the cessation of the Past at one go and the mass attainment of happiness also became less fashionable, as everyone's understanding both of society and of psychological processes became more differentiated. The same processes that cracked apart and dispersed the homogeneous power order of the 18th-century monarchies were by now cracking apart the homogeneous libertarian order of the imagined post-revolutionary society.

Because of psychoactive chemicals, self-administered or prescribed, unhappiness stops being seen as an energy leading to social disaffection and the overthrow of a social order, and starts to be seen as a personal, individual, imbalance, possibly of chemical origin. Time is internalised and seen as a chemical (perhaps melanotonin); experience is seen as a selection from an ambient plethora of strands or data channels that the person selects by affinity, like someone tuning a radio. Anxious people have anxious experiences. The temperament that differentiates a thousand poets from one other is seen as a foreground, not a sort of tinge; an instability in the material substructure of all experience. This decision raises the spectre of a power order that defines itself as perfect without contradiction; but, in an era of overweening and frightening aggrandisement and repression by right-wing government and corporations, it conversely offered the prospect of some alleviation of personal misery to make you stronger before moving out to destroy a superior enemy.

The need for revolution ebbed because more happiness had accumulated in the present day. People were less tired out by work, had more spending money, more leisure, fewer constraints on their behaviour and economic progress, were more fulfilled by things like sex, drugs, and in-home entertainment. The blissful psychedelic experience of the freak-out had become so interwoven in the structure of mass leisure as to seem ordinary; the revolution had nothing better to offer, and art that didn't offer this dazing, shimmering complexity came to seem ridiculous. Leisure, especially art, was one of the factors differentiating society away from a collective similar enough to act as one; happiness became, I suppose, more competitive.

The shift away from a single revolutionary change was not the abandonment of the project, but a shift from the large to the small. The pursuit of excellence in poetry, a specialised form of the search for happiness, always tends to locate itself in the infinitely small rather than the large-scale decision. The increased differentiation affecting industrial goods could only be beneficial to poetry, which has always been low on kilos, high on design man-hours.

The new complexity in physics is a frontier of knowledge to add to the frontier of the small (particle physics) and of the large (cosmology). It appeared that traditional physics had imagined the world in discrete boxes small enough to be dealt with by the powers of mathematics (*scil.* data processing in general) then available: the defects were covered up in real-world applications (engineering) by practical experience or by restraints, built into the machines or installations, which restricted interactions. Engineering thus had a series of protective limits analogous to those of physical science. Cheap processing power in the form of computers now made a new physics possible. Engineering too was becoming less interested in very large heavy objects and more interested in tiny things like integrated circuits. The human sciences, and the data-content of literature, changed too: not because humanists read *Scientific American* but because data had become cheaper there too – not only through better cameras and electronics but also because of the larger number of writers and the number and range of books available. This destabilising could take two forms: the dizziness of looking into the abyss of not-self, loose from supports; and the self-aggrandising, uncritical, fantasy of being what you want, erasing other people's awareness as an infraction of this autonomy. Self-deception plugged into the new big processing power.

The former socialist propaganda had been based on a vision of society as a whole. Reducing its scope to the individual, or three or four individuals in a household, brought it into the zone of capitalist propaganda, or advertising; and naturally enough the new personal politics adopted the ethical standards and formal conventions of advertising. The new artist was an ad for a certain social fraction, changing an 'image' that the consumer could share in by virtue of allegiance to the same faction, thus also setting up a home market for the artist. In Britain this kind of promotion mixed with the views of the Tourist Board to form a kind of feudal tapestry of intellectually stunted, xenophobic, fiefs. Does the concentration on small units resemble the 'old science' reduction of intractable complexity to boxes with (imaginary) uncrossable borders? 'I am whatever I say I am and if you disagree you are being oppressive'. Thus the two era principles of cheap labour and cheap information combined in the semi-military assumption that other people's awareness was groundless and simply there to be controlled. The north-west European tradition of painstaking truth-telling was under threat; the new technology made it easier to do a million things to the data after it had been collected, and the value of fidelity became obscured.

One of the typical reading experiences of the era was to plunge into a text that didn't hold water, where the accounts of events seemed thin and simplistic, the genre rules were too obvious and weighted everything down as if burying it under tons of collapsed masonry, and the author's explanation of events was swept aside by more telling versions of events even in situations he had invented. The complexity that a writer has to deal with is that of the reader's psyche, always threatening to abandon attention and move on to something else more interesting. Here is the source of leaks through which the text escapes and dissipates. (Note that a text in breaking up may become more complex, anomalies letting additional patterns leak in.)

As the market grows more sophisticated, so does the writer; problems only arise if you cling to outmoded methods and tricks, to comic and antiquarian effect. It's still possible to fascinate, delight, move, and impress, and indeed the reader is looking for just those experiences. The activity of all those students picking open the weak spots of set texts and utterances of authority, to expose the rhetoric with which they were held together, could hardly leave contemporary literature intact. The incredulous audience has to be matched with a super-credible text, or else give up. The artist may be perfectly happy to cut up pictorial space into quadrilaterals, to match the frames they go inside, but if the viewer homes in on the line of juncture between the picture and the frame and says, 'this is an illusion and I can see the edge of it', it's not good enough for the artist to be astonished and indignant and wave the rule-book, no, an adequate response has to be found. This has hardly got worse in the past thirty years; it was just as possible for a reader to be bored and unimpressed in 1930 as it is today. The hitch is when a writer deliberately switches off his or her intelligence, thinking 'Ah! intelligence is fatal to art. We must regress to a pre-thought stage where there is no criticism, and especially not criticism of me.' Writers who don't think about each poem are bound to be outgunned by readers who do. Keeping this attention seems to call for stable, coherent, forms, even if predictability and repetition also lose the reader if they edge up beyond a certain critical notch on the meter. For example, tune in music is a form of predictability, riding over the chaos of uncoordinated sound. Organisation is predictability. The perceptual world we live in and make decisions on is necessarily stabilised and made to cohere.

The age of leisure and education demands complex poetry. This cannot mean more and more facts serially enumerated. Logical complexity can only be achieved by tampering with the unit structures of language. If the reader is quicker at spotting patterns (i.e. rules, i.e. to some extent the elements of the artistic work that are artificial and do not correspond to something in the outside world), then the writer can signal the framing regularities much more economically and lightly, leaving more room for the unpredictable variation that generates complexity. The conscious artist can profit from this.

If deceit and projection are constant unconscious human activities, and the very fact that a message emanates from a human suggests that those features are part of its burden, how can a poem acquire any higher logical status than that of self-aggrandising, doubtful, and suspended? Surely indicating disbelief in the message one is sending makes the problem more acute, not less. The answer might be to define the primary data of consciousness as a set of hypotheses, concentrate on the action of testing hypotheses against past moments of consciousness, telltale signs in the outside world, and the utterances, verbal or other, of other people. If this process is undertaken constantly, the whole fabric of the poem takes on a much stronger, tested, albeit scarred, texture. Where one deceives, there one is deceived.

THE FIRST POSSIBLE DISCONTINUITY:
THE ENGLISH INTELLIGENCER AND ITS OFFSHOOTS

J.H. Prynne (1936-) published some relatively traditional poems in *Force of Circumstance* (1962), his first volume, which the poet excluded from the first collected volume, *Poems* (1982). He was aged 26 at that time; evidence is missing to assess Prynne as a 1950s poet, but there are affinities with his friend Charles Tomlinson (1927-2015). Tomlinson's unwillingness to write about people, or write beautifully, was presumably in its origins a distaste for cheap and dubious emotions, both in life and literature. This distaste could be imagined, if amplified and speeded up, to be Prynne's typical scorn. Tomlinson's aesthetic was, at the outset, one of dryness and precision: he never became drier or more precise after that, but one way of imagining Prynne is as someone who began by concentrating on the details of language and on tearing out large and imprecise metaphorical structures, and pursued this goal with increasing speed. Even the cultivation of a narrow tract is a feature of Tomlinson's career, he seems to have set out to write a thousand poems of the same dimensions and in the same set of tones. This may have encouraged Prynne's irritable questioning and subversion of his own writing practices, increasingly vexing and breaking up the verbal texture. Although a poet of the 1960s, he is decidedly un-1960s in working inside an implied moral schema, rather than a hedonistic one; the hedonism, personal and intellectual, of other people, is grist to his mill, and is fitted into a grid that mercilessly reveals its errors and anisotropies. The hypothesis is that he is really a continuator of the limit-obsessed poets of the 1950s, when what passed for political astuteness was scepticism and careful textual analysis. This is why you have *Stand* magazine titling itself 'the magazine of the committed individual' when in fact they never ever publish committed work, and what they are pledged to is strictly 'not being committed to anything'.

After the era of rather hysterical commitment in the 1930s, and paid propaganda work (better than killing people, I suppose) in the first half of the 1940s, and the Cold War hysteria over the following 15 years, there was a bad aftertaste. Rejecting general concepts as inaccurate, and dealing with events in the order they happened, without preconceptions, was summed up by a line in Arthur Miller's script for *The Misfits*: '[m]aybe all there is is the next thing that happens'. The fallout of dismantling large-scale artistic structures of intentionality and destiny has continued; the kicking away, as a preconception, of the ruled future course of the text, may have led on to the 'incongruous montage' so typical of the 1960s.

When Prynne writes, 'The pitch is first sung over a drone, then laid out/ in expensive copper', it looks like a trick montage, but actually it's about a field trip recording ethnic music (on wire), possibly somewhere on the steppe frontiers of China ('The limit/ of combat between spools lies at the capstan/ north & west of Kalat, two miles out of Kendal') if not, in fact, in the Lake District. *The White Stones* is the perfect product of the New Thing of the 1960s; always melodic even when the twining of melodies makes them too complex to hear, always a delight to the ear, composed to flow from start to finish, promising moral and intellectual breakthrough even while mocking such a possibility, an organization that transcends without subverting itself:

> Again he is
> watchful, the dream slides right up to the
> true Adam and he keeps silent among the
> branches. The approach, here, of streamy recall
> seems like the touch of Europe, an invert logic
> brought in with too vivid a pastoral sense,
> too certain for Alsace, the double eagle or the
> Gulf of Lions. He is a dark outline, already
>> struck by sacred
>> emptiness. He goes
>> slowly, her body
>> fades into reason,
>> the memory ever-
>> green and planted,
>> like the lost child.
> And so slowly, still, draining gradually into
> the Rhine, the huge barges freeze in the heat
> of trade. How much power, the machine gun in
> a Polish scenario, black and white fade into those
> passionless excursions of childhood. The small
> copse, water rusted in, an adventure! With which
> the flimsy self pivots in wilful envy and lusts
> after its strange body, its limbs gorged & inert.
> (from 'Chemins de Fer', *The White Stones*, p.93)

The sceptical absence of ideas and ideals was also the Movement's formula. Prynne and Donald Davie were friends when he was a postgraduate at Caius in the late 1950s. The cult of Prynne, already a presence in 1966, is due to his uncannily fine sense of divisions of time and tone, and his ruthless purging of any micro-gestures, or sub-syllabic weights, which offend that microscopic, impassioned, quivering instrument. If the difference between Geoffrey Hill and his contemporary Adrian Mitchell is Hill's far superior refinement, the same gap of delicacy and eschewing of effect again separates Prynne from Hill.

His moral disgust at the gross processes pulsing around him took the form of Marxism. Prynne studied at Caius after National Service (which, for some inexplicable reason, was with a Polish tank regiment. When I mentioned T-34s in a poem, I was startled to find Prynne reminiscing about what they felt like to drive in. Presumably the vehicles in question had been captured by the Wehrmacht in the war, and made booty in 1945). He was a friend of R.F. Langley and, slightly later, of John Riley, Tim Longville, and Michael Grant. He has since pursued an academic career at Caius. Concrete evidence of Prynne's early attitudes is lacking, although he did write for a magazine called *Prospect* around 1961, which included a philosophical essay of his called 'Resistance and Difficulty':

> the concept of resistance may provide an alternative criterion of intelligibility; one which does not undermine the 'presence, actuality, and existence' of an object or person, but which makes accessible the fact of its existence without impairing its status as a substantial, independent entity. And hence the reality of the external world may be constituted (7) on the basis of the world's perceived existence, the resistance that it offers to our awareness.'

Further, he quotes Abelard: '[w]here is the battle if the antagonist is away? For a contest, an opponent is needed, not one who simply submits'. This reminds me of the Mongolian ritual wrestling that Prynne's ethnomusicologist friend collected on a field trip in the 1950s. Merleau-Ponty was certainly important to Prynne's development, and the belief that pain proves a set of processes are not merely a fantasy (which would only be gratifying) may come from him. This vanity-pricking concept of resistance can be the underpinning of his style; F. R. Leavis and William Empson were popular (in different ways) in the Cambridge English School in the 1950s, a cult of strenuousness and acuity that were somehow equated with moral seriousness. By unfailing vigilance, it is alleged, we can avoid distorting other people in our relations with them. Art is to be redeemed from the licentiousness of gratification fantasies and propaganda by difficulty: 'the tensions between metre and rhythm [...] the stringencies of artifice and discipline generally which constitute the dimensions within which the imagination is realised [...] embody both the process and its difficulties.' This is the opposite of poets who believe in the subjective reality of the imagination; these might include Iain Sinclair and Peter Redgrove. The figure of Kotope in Sinclair's *Suicide Bridge* is in fact a mythic transformation of Prynne.

The supreme fantasy is a political transformation. One of Prynne's permanent themes is how system limits induce finitude and form on any utopian project, and there is a moral obligation on political reformers to refine their scheme in order to avoid deception and disaster emanating from what was left out of account in simplification. He is someone living in the midst of the radicals of 1968, who moved into academic or literary life around Cambridge; and adolescent radicals, supplied in endless waves by the university system; he is perpetually trying to criticise and refine their ideas, with an even scabrous tone. The residue of utopian vision is the totality of his aesthetic project, its view of the whole range of human knowledge, its expectation that the reader can handle the most complex ideas and the most rapid movement; the phantom of the ideal reader, a constituent ideal relationship with which to found the whole set of perfected relationships.

THE ENGLISH INTELLIGENCER

It was the period of 1962-4, with the Olson correspondence, which wiped out his sub-Tomlinson style and led on to the fully-fledged Prynne. I believe the key link to Olson, then at Buffalo, was through letters; it was all about letters and this was the revolutionary new technique for getting through the gaps. There is a shocking contrast between *Force of Circumstance* (1962) and *Kitchen Poems* (1968); a personal revolution even if ownership of the means of production was not transferred. A book on *The English Intelligencer* (TEI) (*Certain Prose of the English Intelligencer*) has allowed some historical understanding of the 20 years of poetry that followed this project. The original series of this magazine, actually a large set of shared letters, ran from 1966-8, and the people involved in it produced an associated body of poetry that was anthologised 20 years later in *A Various Art*. That poetry seems today to be the most important of its time. *TEI* was a solution, or at least a high-end research establishment testing out a solution. We can say that the problem was of finding a tenor of language that was not swallowed up by the functionality of everyday speech or by the queasy boundlessness of the poetic language of the past. The participants saw the problem, more specifically, as how to become like the Americans (*viz.* the avant-garde of the 1950s) and to stop being 'English'. This was a mistake, because being

English wasn't really the problem, and the solution was much more original and difficult than becoming 'American'. But the idea that the solution was waiting for you was luxurious and encouraging.

The idea of *TEI* was that participants would write poems and these would be criticised by other people and the whole would be duplicated and distributed free to the interested. It was a kind of research project. Because it was not a product, it was free to become a process. It was written by the people who read it. Quite rapidly they turned into primary readers and even primary writers for each other. The arguments created a verbal tenor that evolved directly into a language in which poetry could be written; they were a safe transitional space. One quote:

> 'Poetry is currency too but life is barter. And I'm not a bit concerned with the state of the nation or its religion, because nation only makes sense as the land we inhabit, the conditions we find around us, liable or not to change, impressionable or not to our influences. The concern is ourselves isn't it. Olson in his Gloucester. Which is exactly why men find it easier to talk about a city than a nation. The city is radial to them as a nation can only be axial to the course of a man's movement through it. Nation moves in on you as a legal structure & what we can love is land[.]'
> (John Hall)

(That is Charles Olson.) There was a 'hidden syllabus' with the project – very roughly a discussion of the problems with preparation for writing Olsonesque long poems, on the lines of *Maximus*, about the 'deep time' of Britain, or parts of Britain. There was the stifling presence of English clichés about what was 'eternal' or 'abiding' or 'English identity', regarding the village and the ploughman or rural craftsman. Writers had knowledge to knit up into texts but it was acquired by virtue of staying in one place for a long time, and it reproduced that immobility. Perception was so much based on where you were; it was class-based perception that reproduced legacy structures (inert and immobile again). The self was the fund on which poems drew, but the self seemed to come back down to 'where', and so the poet had to dissolve the 'where' of who they were to reach the poem. In order to clear this stuff away, new archaeological data was being gathered. It was supposed to define 'the relationship of man to the earth'; to understand the behaviour-controlling forces of British geography was to understand the failure of British poetry (in the years running up to 1966) and to bring that to an end by funding a batch of post-Olson geosophical epics. The research into what life was like in Britain since the end of the last Ice Age was supposed both to dissolve the 'where' into the unfamiliar or the *conceptual* and to supply subject matter.

I don't think any of these long poems ever got written, but the research in *TEI* is goal-directed. To descend to detail, the legacy hang-up about the village and being static incited Prynne to write here about how the Mesolithic lasted much longer than the Neolithic and was fundamentally *nomadic*: the village was a late invention. Thus movement and flight pre-existed over the dry North Sea grounds and the European Plain before it degenerated into cycles and settlement and pattern. This chimes with Allen Fisher's extensive writing about pathways and roads in *Place* but I think that is coincidence. The shift to mobility is expressed as writing about ideas rather than about the sociologically inevitable, and exhausted. All the prose seems to be about geography plus archaeology – Olson was easy to argue about, but the vital influence of the New York School on the group of poets concerned doesn't get voiced.

Certain Prose represents the transition from poets channelling Olson to poets channelling Prynne. It is irritatingly incomplete and yet tosses you into the middle of a revolution. It is part of a knowledge process: it seems to open with episode 58 and to stop (at episode 99) before the stories you most want to know about. The project led on to work by Prynne, John James, John Hall, Andrew Crozier. Meanwhile Tim Longville and John Riley founded the *Grosseteste Review*, which ran from 1967 to 1984 and had similar interests to the *TEI*.

MYTH TERRITORY LANDSCAPE

Eric Mottram's second area-defining essay for the old Polytechnic of Central London was 'Inheritance Landscape Location' (1977), about writing on human geography. This was also about the influence of Olson. Mysteriously, Mottram left out the *Intelligencer* group, who would seem to be 90% of the Olson downstream terrain. It seems worthwhile to list the poets influenced by Olson and interested in writing about geography. The *Maximus* work, which ran to several hundred pages, was begun in 1950, with publication of the collected first volume in 1960. It is a sequel to *The Cantos* and Maximus of Tyre, in poem one, is a hark back to the figure of Odysseus in the first Canto. It is also a sequel to William Carlos Williams' *Paterson*, a book about the life of a small town. The documentary plus woozy theories about history manner is essentially mediating the Pound influence. Much of *Maximus* is fishing stories resembling *Captains Courageous*, by Rudyard Kipling. It is baffling how paranoids in different towns get to know each other, but there is a scrap of evidence in an English magazine called *Nine*, which around 1950 was the flag bearer for right-wing modernism and paranoia. Issue four (1950) carries an advertisement for the essay 'Projective Verse', just published in a New York magazine. The avant-garde likes genealogy, the passing of legitimacy in secret and face-to-face meetings. An aura that has wings and flies from one eye to another.

Prynne and Langley went to the lectures by Donald Davie, in Cambridge in the late 1950s, which introduced listeners to the legacy of Ezra Pound and to Olson as a station of it. Prynne later wrote to Olson and became his friend. Mottram wrote under the influence of Olson, notably in *Tunis* (1977). Davie, a junk bond of poetic reputations, definitely wrote under Olson's influence. We have mentioned the *TEI* group, but not yet Peter Riley. Colin Simms is a naturalist from Yorkshire who wrote a series of great poems about North American biogeography in the 1970s, now collected as *The American Poems,* and clearly in the wake of Olson. What Mottram says about Allen Fisher in 1977 is '*Place* is a major ongoing set of complex definitions of location and inheritance. The basis is South London [...] *Paxton's Beacon* radiates from the meanings of the Crystal Palace and its designer.'

Fisher's *Place* project lasted from 1971-80, although the publication record did not quite keep up. His points of departure were Olson, and Jung's synchronicity principle. Iain Sinclair wrote a response to Olson, in an essay in *Suicide Bridge*, another radical extension of Olsonian principles. This must be a reaction to *TEI* and, like that, is part of a conversation about what place is. Sinclair took it in the direction of defining places in terms of myth. When Chris Torrance moved to the Neath Valley in 1970, he brought the whole *TEI* package of 'landscape geography myth' with him and when he began teaching creative writing he transmitted it to his students in Cardiff. Torrance was never in the top flight of poets but he was clearly a good teacher. Poets writing about landscape in South Wales include Graham Hartill, whose work is collected in the large volume *Cennau's Bell,* and Elisabeth Bletsoe, whose best work is available as *Landscape from a Dream.* This was the third generation after Olson. Martin Thom was enthusiastic about Olson and found him an antidote to the distrust of the narrated past found in English social anthropology. Gavin Selerie spent ten years writing his long work *Azimuth* (1984), strongly oriented towards Olson.

Prynne's *The White Stones* is probably the most significant single volume of the 1960s. Prynne sums up the span of the decade, with a poetic facies which seems like a roll-out of instrumental and mathematical knowledge and simultaneously could come from inside the shimmering, hyper-associative, helical logic of an acid trip. Contact with the delusions and disillusions of 1968 was hardly likely to dilute Prynne's natural acerbity. The other Caius English don, for decades, was John Casey, a legendary right-winger; while Cambridge poets were conversing in Prynne's rooms, the Conservative Philosophy Group was meeting elsewhere in the same building. Acerbity could well be applied to those ideological adventurers. I feel that Prynne's dominant theme is his resistance to political idealism. His most positive affect is rage against examples of idealism – located in various forms, e.g. heroism, polarisation, moralistic division into good and evil, craving quick solutions, simplification of the facts to supply stories with heroes and happy endings. I say 'anti-idealistic' because I find this scepticism and scorn one-sided; it is very scorching and verbally impressive, but it lacks dialectic. The difficulty with forming symbols is close to a generalised withdrawal; it seems to me that happiness and normal functioning is impossible unless one has hope, love, trust, and ambitions, all of which involve idealism of some kind.

STOP. At this distance the idea of a dominant seems to reflect an emotional need for my essay to get somewhere before reaching its word limit. Hindenburg said that an offensive without a *Schwerpunkt* is like a man without a character. The corollary is that we want a man to have a character so that we can drive towards it and bring the campaign to an end. In 2016 I incline more to say that pursuing the evanescent complexity of the immediate moment is vital to Prynne's creation, all along the line, and the perception of scepticism was just the contact surface of my youthful idealism coming into contact with an adult. In fact Prynne is probably the most committed and uncompromised anti-capitalist poet there is.

Prynne launched the cult of shamanism, already in the mid-1960s identifying certain practices of the steppe realm described by Herodotus with the ones described by Eliade. The results were codified in 'Aristeas: in Seven Years', perhaps the finest poem in *The White Stones*. This is not quite separable from the cult of nomadism, a glamorised version of pastoralism, alluded to in *The Oval Window*, a hut used by wandering shepherds in Cumbria (locally known as a 'shoale'), and raised to the level of myth in 'Aristeas'. This predates *Mille Plateaux*, but not Giacomo Leopardi's 'Canto notturno di un pastor errante dell'Asia'. The simplicity of the hut also has strong associations with Daoism, a wisdom cult practised in rustic retreats.

This influence came from the Master of Caius. Joseph Needham had been posted to the Burma border area of China in the Second World War, to use his knowledge of infections – he was an organic chemist – for practical help to the Chinese. Needham returned to England and Caius fired with enthusiasm for, and practical knowledge of, China. He spent fifty years writing a *magnum opus* on *Science and Civilisation in China*. As a result, Caius was full of Chinese researchers, his collaborators. Needham (undoubtedly of broad Maoist sympathies) was also a Daoist; it was unusual for members of a Cambridge college to be exposed to Daoist, rather than Anglican, addresses and sermons from the Master. The simplicity of Prynne's work after the 1980s has undoubtedly been influenced by Daoist poetry. He has sought in this a detachment from organisationally bound forms of knowledge, moving towards something less mediated and more graspable in an individual life.

Another strand has been the exilic mood of Daoism, as the attitude of graduates and distinguished men who know that public affairs are out of tune with the cosmic harmony, and must therefore be avoided, although their inevitable collapse cannot be accelerated; a kind of 'chiliastic serenity'. Mao Zedong prepared the peasantry in remote base areas for 20 years before coming out to strike the Kuomintang's death-blow. Prynne has told me (reporting Needham's words) that Daoism is not an alternative principle to the hierarchy and totalitarian homogeneity latent in Chinese cultural ideals, since in fact it has most tenets in common with Confucianism; its anti-establishment flavour is illusory, since it is the politics of a displaced group of the graduate and land-owning ruling class, not of the peasantry. The only democratic moment in pre-modern Chinese art is (rare) depictions of peasants working together in a group; Daoist art shows solitary individuals communing with nature in contemplative manner; the economic basis for this is owning estates worked by other people and the political philosophy behind it is more elitism, the State run by the wise literate man while the peasants stay in the fields doing the work.

Even if he didn't tell me this exclusively to annoy me, the pessimism (even within the postulated 'ideal state') is typical. The implied comment about the elitism of the ruling group reproducing itself in the elitist salvation theology of the revolutionary conspirators is, in a town filled with cadres of '68, unanswerable and (almost) social satire. Prynne's pessimism closely resembles the position of many people who committed themselves to a revolution in 1968, and later found themselves unemployed at every level of life. His central anti-idealism may be part of a daily tactical conflict, within a 'subversive' faction, between realism (in pursuit of short-term survival and gains) and idealism (the long-term end). An example might be the need for military discipline within the Red Army at a time when the comrades expected the issue of the struggle to be a society without offices. This shift of attention between long timescales and short is important for Prynne; much of his work can be seen as an intricate mapping of conventional wisdom onto a finer grid, where every part of it is untrue, so that there is a temporary bankruptcy of ideas, and a seething mass of aporias. We can at least learn from this that the margin of error is one of the defining characteristics of every system of knowledge, and that Prynne is inordinately interested in the aporial gaps where the edges of surveyed grid squares don't quite meet.

Another question is: is complete political despair revolutionary or anti-revolutionary? The confinement to the immediate and concrete brings an appalling narrowing of the field of view, so that the poet pours into a couple of square metres all the energy that formerly irrigated a whole cosmos and the whole of imagined history. There are two elements that contradict this. The first is Prynne's concern with almost infinite geological and geographical sweeps. He associated with Charles Olson, who, although far from the most brilliant poet on the block, had ideas that stimulated the torpid and politically intimidated American literary scene of the time. Olson was trying to be like a European in accepting the length of history, and the importance of local conditions, as factors in social life. The second is a suspicion that the escape into the microscopic (a door opened by due attention to aporias) is like Needham's biochemistry, and that such tininess culminates in knowledge of medicine, which abolishes disease, and of plant breeding, which abolishes hunger. This particular exile into impotence changes history in a way that 'an exchange of elites' could never do. The retirement of the Daoists to their estates and to cultivating their bodies had such results, as Needham documents, suiting Prynne's sense of microscopic verbal time. Any consideration of navigational means or vehicle design will confirm that precision is the prerequisite of long intellectual journeys, not their opposite.

Somewhere in the prehistory of these poems is an English fondness for plants and stones, observed on long discursive walks. It's not just the Chinese who are fond of nature poetry. A historian named Bernard DeVoto wrote

> The Appalachian system then, though a decelerant, implied neither economic nor political discontinuity.' 'Precisely here the acceleration of time had become decisive. Industrial development was the final centripetal force in American expansion: it enabled the single system [...] to absorb the ellipses and fill out the continuum.
>
> (from *The Course of Empire*, 1998 [1952] p.406)

I feel that sentences like these are the precursors of sentences in *The White Stones*, which is a book about geography more than anything else. It deals with the effect of settlement on political patterns, with the effect of climate on national character and so on the states of mind that poetry captures. From whatever Marxist staging point, which sweeps aside centuries of mere emotional solidarity, it moves into the language of system theory, and model formation, to explain how a society came about and what constraints there are on its self-development. The rapid and recent nature of North American settlement made the geography–sociology link easy to view, a preparation for the more stratified and sheared British or European surfaces. On these the full glaciation was however a kind of null state of origin:

> The striations are part of the heart's
> desire, the parkland of what is coast
> *inwards from which*, rather than the reverse.
> And as the caps melted, the eustatic rise
> in the sea-level curls round the clay, the
> basal rise, what we hope to call 'land'.
>
> And the curving spine of the cretaceous
> ridge, masked as it is by the drift, is
> wedged up to the thrust: the ice fronting
> the earlier marine, so that the sentiment
> of 'cliffs' is the weathered stump of a feeling
> into the worst climate of all.
>   Or if that's
> too violent, then it's the closest balance that
> holds the tilt: land/sea to icecap from
> parkland, not more than 2°–3° F.
>   (from 'The Glacial Question, Unsolved', in
>   *The White Stones*, p.37).

The description is of the rollback of the glaciers that led to the emergence of potential farmland and so the material conditions for a farming society: the invention of the village. From white to green. The conformation of stones suggests vast geological epochs, the spatial distribution of plants suggests the match of physiological pattern to the incidences of the planet's surface and of solar radiation. In line with systems theory, Prynne identifies the switch band: two or three degrees in air temperature is the difference between ice coverage and Northern European farmland. The surfacing of ice-free humus is itself the switch which permits the surfacing of Britain and British people. It is not clear to me that our poet pursued this geographical project beyond *The White Stones*. Still, DeVoto was writing a Prynnean language: 'Here however there was latent the first possible discontinuity or aberration.'

The books since *Poems* (1982) have little of the melodious and bel-canto quality of *White Stones*. Take *Word Order*, for example. Repeatedly, I find myself harking back to Richard Cook's 1985 evaluation (in *The Wire*) of the soprano sax player, Steve Lacy:

> If he sounds primitive, sneering and squawking down the sop-rano's pinched tube, we are always conscious of the ruthless and exacting mind behind that peculiar sound. ... I used to call Lacy's music song-like, but that's wrong: he uses scraps, bits of doggerel, long threads of sound, rhymes, any effects he can get out of that twist of metal. But he doesn't play songs.

Lacy (1934-2004) was about Prynne's age; the *art informel* concern with interrupted objects has an obvious reflex in the practice of spontaneous improvisation – of which Lacy is a master – apparently closer to the human voice than a score or anything rehearsed: the bare landscape left by the demolition of inherited artistic structures. Look at this:

> Cut and blow dry as
> we shall have snow
> art so unkind
>
> Pinkepinke invincible
> who has so much
> a rush of wind
>
> invasive, ground cover
> fire down below
> vinca alkaloids

Phrases (cut and blow dry, fire down below), are grabbed in from the outside to be reduced to objects without the attempt to 'possess' them; a sardonic parody of the 'discourse of authenticity', just as the weird verbal tune (PINKe- VINCible- VINCa) is a Lacy-like exploration of a theme too simple to be noble. 'Pinkepinke' is a slang term (Berlin, I think) for money, so 'pinkepinke invincible' is a pidgin proverb. (Pinke might be a West Slavonic decomposition of *pennige*, pennies.) Squawking and sneering? 'Fire down below' is actually a sea-shanty, rather obstinately rooted in West Indian folksong, just as line two comes from a weather rhyme ('The North wind doth blow. And we shall have snow'); Prynne makes a frottage of rags and tags of language, 'bits of doggerel' quoted not in homage but in derision.

This reminds me of the 'frottage' of certain French artists of the 1950s, such as Niki de Saint-Phalle, taking rubbings of walls where several layers of torn posters were superimposed, tattered and rubbed, shreds of popular mythology posthumously caught up in the work of art, with the dead glow of minerals. In Britain similar works were made by Liliane Lijn and Gwyther Irwin. The whole book concerns an attempt to say something beautiful, noble, consoling, and true, to guide unhappy adolescents: the printed text is a kind of tormented defacement of an irrecoverable lyric exaltation. I can point to two powerful tides of the 1950s: one of removing the social from language, to unleash various monologues or babble; one of academicism, i.e. of removing the personal from the work of verbal art. Both of these follow a withdrawal from existing literary norms; and, perhaps, a loss of confidence in the figure of the Writer. Both reveal a far more complex order of phenomena: 'the real world towards/ which we travel in purity and in truth'. All love songs (let's say) say the same things, the human essence is repetitive; a thousand writers writing about psychological events (or natural events) without Emotions will hardly even overlap with each other. So, although I think sometimes of Beckett, Robert Pinget, Claude Simon, Saint-Phalle, or Henri Pichette, when reading Prynne's works, I also think he is quite unlike any other writer.

If nature is so disordered, one cannot be reassured about the future or about another person's love for you. This is not a message the world much wants to hear. One poem of *Word Order* (p.8) runs:

> As you knew why
> you took me for
> just as well you knew
>
> you I took, as you
> could hardly, with
> me if you offer
>
> taken for anything
> as I knew, you as
> can lay on nature

> deceived your friends.

Look at this sentence: not syntactic or paratactic, but actually sporadic, not speech but a collage of speech fragments turned into objects. Prynne's verbal tic is a ceaseless sarcastic interruption of his own voice, a strobe shutter cutting the image perhaps dozens of times a page. The analogy with *art informel* draftsmanship is near: the vagaries of the self are revealed in the discontinuity of the strokes, the object is badly rendered because ultimately it is not part of the self. Organised poetry is infidelity, because the self is composed of warring and fleeting impulses. If imitation is the bane of mankind, which is monkey kind, then art might cease to be imitative to lay bare the human essence – which is, no doubt, to imitate.

Word Order is completely lacking in the tours of detailed and practical knowledge heard in some of Prynne's other books. It is written in extremely difficult colloquial language, as difficult as Russian folk particles or as certain folk songs. Prynne now seems to believe that knowledge clouds the senses, satisfyingly numbs the psyche to the true intermittent and dissonant flow of the human group. Archaic impulses to reassure and to sing have taken over; a condition to which erudition leads (and one thinks of the fragrant winds of Caius Daoism here). This tendency was always there, beside the didactic details; once again from *Word Order*, for example:

> We inserted our names would we sing
>   out on sight and give in full
> the free the offer repeatedly, hit as he lay on
>   the ground stroked no struck to put
> words into the mouth the truth the life
>   and take the ethereal vapour
>   like a chance
> crossing the street.
> (from *Word Order*, p.7)

In this lust for risk and anguish about singing, one recalls the poet's daily job: of lecturing to adolescents with an imposed formalism (which he can't demolish), knowing they desperately need reassurance, endlessly wanting to say 'yes, everything's going to be all right, no don't believe anything anybody says or I say'.

Cook again: 'He is so rigorous, even when juggling note values small enough for bop, that he seems to speak only in proverbs. Why, then, is his music so bitter on the ears, such a cold bath for the romantic?' The interest in exchanges conditioned the earlier passion for economics; now it becomes clear that the elements of Prynne's verbal style also derive from a never satiable search for fidelity in exchange. Social life is an exchange whose cessation would cause the end of the self, yet which cannot show a clear advantage; or even a clear difference between one legal person and the other, or between before and after. The reader can no more immerse and relax in this discourse than any rhythmic sequence can be expected to repeat itself. Looked at from the point of view of social interaction, the style can seem to be a merciless shredding of position and personality, so that all that is left is the interaction itself; like someone drawing the area of contact of two objects while effacing both of the objects. The elimination of the poet's voice creates an acoustic gap in which something disquiet and inconstant becomes audible: human interaction, perhaps, language in its natural state.

The *Intelligencer* group evolved with great force but this is a story I cannot tell at this time. I am aware that telling this story leaves out lots of other underground poets, but this has been one story.

From the Counter-Culture
to Personal Politics:
Speculation and Experiment, 1967-75

The Counter-Culture

David Caute has helpfully summed up the 'counter-culture' (which only began in 1965, or even in 1967) as

> a term which embraces a plethora of disparate motions: drop-out hippies, obscene language, acid trips, underground newspapers and films, 'alternative theatre' with attendant 'happenings', anti-universities, surrealist street politics, communal self-help, folk and rock music alien to ears attuned to Beethoven or the Palm Court Orchestra, mystical cults, aggressive sexuality, flamboyant clothing, ecological awareness, rejection of ambition and careerism.

However intact the institutions were afterwards, British poetry was irrevocably split by this desired and imagined break. The resulting struggle for legitimacy has never ended.

The counter-culture touched perhaps half a million people on campuses and in the big cities; but it was only an experimental projection of changes in moral standards and consumption patterns that affected the majority in the long run. The 1960s saw a social revolution, which was however not a radical break from behavioural and consumer trends of the 1950s and even the 1930s; a glance at its manifestations – swinging London, hedonism, pop, psychedelia, the New Left of 1968 – suggests that the revolutionary break was the advance in electronic media and reproduction of graphics, their means of realisation, exploitation, and consumer penetration. The media were changed much faster than actual social patterns, which certainly did shift towards hedonism and prosperity. So the new things existed in the media before being real; but one has to allow for a long delay before they permeate poetry – partly because everyone who was capable of immediate response was involved in genres, from television to street riots, which rewarded such immediacy, and partly because the new ideas stemmed, in their artistic manifestation, from genres other than – and incompatible with – poetry, and it took a long time to work out how to express them in poetic terms.

Dom Sylvester Houédard, the concrete poet, writing in the *Times Literary Supplement* of 06.08.64 (the special avant-garde number), asks that the poem should no longer be a *creationis imitatio* but an *imitatio creatoris*: not an imitation of part of the created world, but of the act of the creator in devising the cosmos. This integrality works even at the level of an advertisement: where the advertiser creates a social scene which appeals to the viewer as a whole, with the commodity being only an object within it. The poet too creates a situation, which has to appeal to the reader, in however diverse ways, or it will not be read. Because the reader perceives the text on every level at once, the poet has to examine every detail; able to select and modify so as to make it a true *imitatio creatoris*. The world-hypothesis as adornment.

The Utopian Project, or, The Regiment of a Faint Star

J.H. Prynne wrote, in 'In Cimmerian Darkness':

> When the faint star does take
> us into the deeper parts
> of the night there *is*
> that sudden dip
> and we swing across into
> some other version of this
> present age, where any curving
> trust is set into
> the nature of man, the green raw and fabulous
> love of it, where every star that shines,
> as he said, exists
> in love, the *brother*
> dipping into the equal limit,
> help as the ready art...
> (from *The White Stones*, p.46)

The bringing together of the small distances of walking and the far distances of the stars brings about paradox and the sublime, evoking the utopian space within which the largest proportion of the art of that time (the pamphlet *Aristeas* was published in 1968) carried out its evolutions. Beside the principle of self-help proposed by the anarchist prince Kropotkin (help as the ready art), and the common Romantic idealism caught in set phrases (starry-eyed, reach for the stars, star-gazing), he draws in more far-fetched references to the boundless spaces wandered over by the nomadic Cimmerians: where the land is owned by nobody, and where, as in 'Aristeas: In Seven Years', from the same pamphlet, the shepherd-peoples cover endless distances, practising shamanism and, as in Giacomo Leopardi's poem, transported by the rhythms of their songs. Could this be a reference to Russia, not the real place of Leninist death-camps, but the workers' paradise imagined by so many people even at that late date, and foreseen by Kropotkin from his exile? In any case, the unbounded space, the thousand steppes, of the Cimmerians, with their Iranian language and fire-worshipping religion, is a kind of playground where that other version of the present age can be held down and refined.

Faced with two phrases, the poet chooses the more beautiful one. This choice is not so open as one might wish: if the poet is using a realist principle, this constrains the poem. Faced with two poems, the reader chooses the more beautiful of them; the poet is faced with demands for beauty that are more basic than the businesslike demand for realism. The point at which the regime of aesthetic choice gives way to the regime of accepting what is ugly but true cannot be fixed in any particular place. The situation is part of the rules of the poem; the reader's aesthetic choice reduces situation to its index of attractiveness despite any attempts to lift realness into a separate and superordinate domain. The appetite for symbolic experience is governed by rules of which some are visible. Any real human situation, with its blocks and conflicts, offers limits that feed the practical intelligence only by stimulating it to find solutions; these represent the return of choice of the beautiful in a different form. Suffering without solution offends the laws of perception. The quality of allowing planning of multiple behavioural strategies, and of letting these become complex, testable, and well-formed, is the situational part of the beauty of the poem: the appearance of freedom, which mysteriously echoes the original choice the reader possesses by nature, of devolving awareness into this poem or a thousand others. The realistic poem asks us both to take its representations for a reality and to accept that the social institutions by which the predicament came about have the solidity of natural law. The idealistic poem offers a double attack whereby the reader is simultaneously asked to imagine a situation, and to imagine the changes to social institutions that would provide a solution to the predicament it enmeshes its people in. Exposure to such works of art stimulated curiosity about the socialisation process by which infants come to internalise social laws, since a conscious and adult form of that process was what could give rise to a new society. The remarkable number of teachers in the real new society of the 1960s spread the insight that a new-born child could be socialised into any society it was born into, Turkish, Eskimo, Russian, English, Mennonite, and this behavioural 'before' was as exciting as space travel, which was also the chasing of 'the faint star'. Once there was a realm defined and held steady in which the creation of social systems took place, the poet was moved by the natural affect of envy to imitate the shape of that space, its linguistic regimes, rhetorically closing the distance between the lesser creativity of the poem and the greater of the 'culture hero' or of the all-absorbing infant. Pure aesthetic choice will select the place more full of potential over other spaces; the poet's choice of radical politics benefits the poet. Vacuity is necessary for any growth and play to take place, yet finished vacuity is what discourages any play or pattern forming and matching from taking place.

The themes of navigation and uncertainty are anticipated in Christopher Logue's long poem 'Wand and Quadrant' (1953). The title refers to a navigational device: a vertical is needed to get a positional fix with the quadrant, using the sun (or perhaps a faint star), but the text is much about divination, and the object of this searching for a way is the Western Paradise, Avalon or the Hesperides, other figures of Utopia. The edges of the classical world are favourite sites for utopian scenes: Western for Logue (and Homer), Northern for Prynne (and Hesiod). The abandonment of territorial boundaries for a steppe or maritime landscape moves the relation of the observer to the observed to the centre of the question 'where are we', and so a transition from a navigational fix to fortune-telling and the question 'where can I be happy?'. Both poets are saying where you are is decided by the conceptual rules you carry about with you. Underlying Prynne's poem is the unspoken saw, 'when you wish upon a star'; given the generally Inner Asian locale of that 1968 pamphlet, it may be fair to cite an invocation in Heissig's *Die Religionen der Mongolei* that does the same, addressing the star Urukini, 'who makes a single cow to a hundred red cattle', taking us into a world of astral magic.

The primary utopian impulse is the belief that another poetry is possible than the 1950s poem; the reformed society that the poet revealed could be socialist, libertarian, feminist, or peripheral nationalist. The figure of utopia is the large fiction within whose domain all smaller fictions unfold their wings and fly. Any close examination of the 1950s shows a world different from the one we live in; it is likely that the changes are due to changes in the governance of behaviour and communication. So the project fell short of, for example, abolishing private property, but did bring about rather numerous fragments of utopia; of which certain volumes of poetry are some. But even these days or years of happiness would have been impossible without an overall vision as the horizon that surrounds them and also seals them off. Their fragments display the geometry of the whole.

FEMINISM

'In the autumn of 1968 vague rumours of the women's movement in America and Germany reached Britain' (from the feminist historian Sheila Rowbotham's 'The Beginning of Women's Liberation in Britain', in Wandor, ed., *Once a Feminist, Stories of a Generation*, 1990).

The first Women's Conference took place at Ruskin College, Oxford, in February 1970, and is often taken as the start of modern feminism in Britain, as an offshoot of the radical socialist movement. The transformed future seemed so close, so vivid, that it was necessary to move immediately to alter the comrades' vision of it, so that it wouldn't be oppressive to women, and the women issue wouldn't be packed up in the knapsack, as before, to be unpacked untold decades later when the long march had ended:

> 'It was agreed that one of the themes of the next issue of *Black Dwarf* should be women. One of the men was appointed to do the women's issue, because he was a proper theoretical comrade. He knew about Reich and therefore he was meant to know all about women and sex. But because I made so much noise and wouldn't shut up, I was allowed to be his helper.'
> –Sheila Rowbotham (Trotskyite newspaper;
>   the women's issue was published in January 1969)

At a History Workshop session in November 1969, Sheila Rowbotham issued an invitation to other people working on women's history to attend a meeting on the subject –

> She gave out a time and a place for anyone interested to meet, but before she could get to that practical point there was a great guffaw from the floor. Ruskin is a trade-union college, and in 1969 it was male-dominated and had some very traditional men. Clearly, it seemed funny to them that women's history could be seen as needing separate attention, or that there'd be any point in our getting together.
> –Anna Davin (interview in *Once a Feminist*, p.56).

When I went to Sussex, I had a very bad experience politically, because Sussex already in 1963 was dominated by Militant [*a Trotskyist organisation*, AD]. It was awful. I had two other women friends at Sussex – in fact, that must have been the beginnings of

the stirrings of my feminist conscience, because we were so badly treated by the men. The Militant men there basically thought they should get us to bed, and then we would shut up and stop going on about CND. When we didn't shut up, then they just started denouncing us as petty bourgeois agitators. They were very hard line, and very nasty. So left politics became extremely difficult for me at that period.'
–Catherine Hall (interview in *Once a Feminist*, p.171-80)

This event in the world of political intellectuals corresponded to a shift in the economy towards women working for wages; the abstract ideas helped to guide a mass demographic movement in its aspirations and plans for advance. The convergence can be seen in the world of women's magazines: the high circulation weeklies like *Woman's Own*, which in 1968 were all about home and family and vexed the political writers by representing a 'voice of women' that was different from theirs, had by 1979 adopted a wide range of the attitudes and images floated by the radicals. This reversal of alliances shows how an idea first nurtured by a couple of dozen people specialised in ideas can spread to reach tens of millions; its eventual fate being determined, I suppose, by the quality built into it during the original research and speculation.

Feminists were not initially separate from the counter-culture as a whole, and the basis of feminism remains a set of utopian ideas about how daily life should work. The initial flaw – which widened and led to a later geography – was an aspect of any utopia: that the utopia from one person's egoistic point of view involves other people acting in highly specified ways that are non-utopian from their personal perspective. The more utopian the scenery, the more constraints on the behaviour of the people who are the decisive components of that scene. This utopian dream was not a strong sound before 1968. Feminism is the one current of the idealistic tide of 1968 that has become mainstream, which probably indicates deep tactical and strategic flaws in all the other currents.

Pressing the cultural legacy revealed it as largely composed of fantasy material in which inflated figures designed to project onto went through exalted acts immune to the laws of physics or anatomy. Objects, far from adding elements of realism, become effectively projections of the ego. So it was that the earliest impact of feminism was as an erasure of assets: the male subject felt them as 'you're demolishing the narratives I love, demolishing the heroes I identify with, tearing to bits the poets I look up to, reducing beautiful and uplifting scenes to squalor'. There was a tension between building utopia and demolishing the strips of utopia that could be seen on TV each evening. As a question of history, the proposition that kinetic and elaborately decorated idealisations were the substance of normal culture seemed quite likely; all I can say is that the attack on one estate of ego-investments was very productive, even if a culture that simply had no fantasy element was a very unlikely outcome.

(There was indeed the possibility of crushing all idealisations and producing art from within that formal and psychological position – this was pretty much what punk rock was delivering. The punk movement cited a nebula of proto-punk art.) If you set out from the idea that falling in love was very bad for you, as forfeiting reason, and further that it was an invention that had been launched during the Romantic era (and not during the era of Provençal lyrics?), and further that the Romantic poets had been complicit in inventing it, then to attack the style and material of the Romantic poets was a logical step. This was unlikely to make the literary world happy. The further step was of guessing that the counter-culture was a large-scale collaboration of charismatic but self-idealising individuals to wind up people in the role of starry-eyed followers in an exercise that would never go beyond rituals of personal stardom. This is not up my street but someone must have pushed that idea.

Society did seem like an irrigation network, which took its human flow and channelled it down a great series of switch-gates where each time male and female were divided and poured at ever greater speed down different pipes. Resisting this pattern was difficult but understanding it offered hours of fascination. For example, why was it there? Was there a mighty centre that had imposed it on passively willing local but dependent groups, or was it something flourishing everywhere which was passively reproduced by the centre? Where was the centre of society, for example in television, Westminster, Whitehall, the middle class, the school system, the language? Was there really a gap of understanding between individuals and the way society worked? What was the history of this network, for example? If you went back 2,000 years would you find only parts of it? How had its changes been developed and spread? Would geographical inequalities show where sub-patterns had originated and spread over only part of the available field? Were there differences between England and adjacent societies, for example Scotland or France? What happened if you said no to it? People's ideas of the 'centre' were influenced by their wish to change the system, for which a control box would be necessary. Because society only continued by conditioning people to apply its distinctions, every moment of social being could reveal the principle of conditioning. Poetically, quite simple situations could give glimpses of the social structure, a sort of blueprint with a million fascinating details that became visible if you breached a pattern. Imagining how society worked was a grand project, a sustaining plan of which individual poems gave exciting modules. It was a part work.

This very book appears in the story. As, almost the first step of feminism was to reject narratives of fact written by men. The idea was offered that the inner state of the spectator could completely alter the value of the work of art – so that there was no valid account of a work, or therefore of any period of art history. How can I write a history of subjective states that is also an objective account? The acts of judgement of other people's behaviour, which were basic to the act of writing were revealed as a huge, archaic, ruinous, opaque or hidden, structure.

The heading says '1975' and there was very little feminist poetry by that time. A process of self-education was taking place, as individuals first acquired a state of political dissidence and then developed ideas of feminism within that more encompassing radicalism.

> The last Women's Liberation conference was in Birmingham in 1978. It was a very unhappy experience. [...] It just turned into the most hideous argument between socialist feminists and radical feminists. In the end it was so bitter and the recognition of differences so deep, that there hasn't been a national conference since. The conflict was around sexuality, but it wasn't just lesbian-ism versus socialism.
>
> (*ibid.*)

No-one would have given up the intellectual excitement of self-determination in return for the absence of conflict.

A NOTE ON PSYCHEDELIA

First, a couple of quotes to refresh your minds.

> (*spoken*) Tangerine music turns purple for Julie.
> (*sung*) Mexican clowns are all dancing for Julie
> With green bells on their ankles that peal out hello
> Strawberry monkeys are smiling for Julie
> With bell-button eyes that reflect velvet clouds
> Can you hear them smiling, etc.
> Purple drops upwards and comes down for Julie
> While spotlight is dancing and drinking rose wine
> Can you hear them dancing, etc.

In your dream?
Treacle-tight thimbles and silver for Julie
The clocks are all dead so the living is fine
Can you hear them living, etc.
　　(from Edmund Plumer and Peter James Daltrey,
　　　　'Dream for Julie', for Kaleidoscope)

Dynamic explosions in my brain
Shatter me to drops of rain
Falling from a yellow sky
Orange faces through an opened eye
　　(from Arthur Brown's 'Nightmare', for
　　　　The Crazy World of Arthur Brown)

George MacBeth's 'The World of the Oboe' is the purest psychedelia, but also firmly placed in various morphological series of European literature. The interest in the brain as a kind of cybernetic machine, and in various cybernetic toys, goes back to Edwin Morgan's *The Whittrick* (1961), where he introduces the brain scientist W. Grey Walter (*The Living Brain*, 1953), and an early world-interaction robot (*machina docilis*, a teachable machine). The malfunctions brought about by drugs made a generation aware that the brain was like a machine, its performance dependent on the stable condition of the material substrate, of neurone cells, blood, and hormones, which it was staged in. This material-symbolic nature is at once the paradox that motivates the absurd and the reliability that, in an atmosphere of unlimited technical progress, allows artists to dream of unrestrained and designed illusion. Psychedelia is important as an atmosphere which everyone noticed, even if they didn't inhale it; but it was a popular modification of devices already switched on in high culture. In its full-fledged form, the psychedelic song is a modern classic in the same way that the protest song is.

Dissolving realism so that the poet's irrational linking of images brings mimetic intimacy and makes the reader hyper-suggestible reached a peak in psychedelia. The psychedelic style was growing in 1966, became almost unavoidable in 1967, and continued, with various mutations, until perhaps 1974, when it had become something else (progressive rock). The lascivious redefinition of the brain as a pleasure appliance turns sensation, no longer an orienting device, into a kind of library, where we seek maximum diversity and novelty, repeating sensations merely in order to absorb them, playing with the world like a kitten with a ball of wool, interacting without purpose in order to elicit patterns we can't foresee. This we find in 'The World of the Oboe', a dizzying flow of textures suspended from any economic activity.

What is the value of these quotes? Partly to make the point that having neural sluices flooded is a total condition. Partly perhaps to say that the conscious brain assimilates data very quickly and that catalogues of information do not have the impact of destabilising the recipient and bringing about hyper-association. Partly also to say that there was a new lyricism here, even if brief in duration. Partly just out of nostalgia. The poetry of the time was aiming to reach a specific state of hyper-association, loss of bearings, even enchantment. This was not brought about by cycling through ingrained processes such as relativising, categorising, detachment, rationalising. These in many ways bureaucratic processes carried disenchantment and conservatism with them – the new poetry marched with the new pop song in moving towards a starry-eyed condition.

Psychedelia resembles the absurd, its equivalent in a previous decade. The advance into complete subjectivity, with vivid sensory images providing fields of focus – could leave angst behind and advance into hedonism, free association drifting towards what is desirable. The mind wished for what it wished. Art became cyclic, rotating back towards dominant images, if drifting gradually towards a state of origin. This advance of hedonism was the quality of a whole era – a dream often identified as coming to an end in the political strife of the mid-1970s.

Herbert Read's books of the 1930s, where the photo sequences go from the Stone Age to the *dernier cri*, drawing analogies all the way, as if 40,000 years could be consumed by a single gazing subject without the subject breaking up and without cognitive barriers arising between the eye and the picture so passively laid out to be possessed, are already psychedelic. Montage was never more extreme. A kind of reflux of this is the view of all world culture as a colour supplement, a kind of infinite cut-out and paste book. The ideology of sampling, new in 1987, is already present in montage. Art-school students were being taught to pick up and recombine elements from past styles. Edoardo Paolozzi had already in 1949 pioneered the collage-images that were to become Pop Art by 1956; a heady, eclectic, free helping-yourself to stocked-up imagery.

Record companies liked to put logograms on record labels which behaved oddly when they rotated: Op Art into psychedelia. The forerunner of psychedelic patterns was Op Art, an example of an experimental, cold, art form, rooted in mathematics and cognitive psychology, turning into something warmly subjective and acceptable to the mass market. We can in fact recognise Constructivist wire nets of tangents, as on the cover of Christopher Middleton's *torse 3*, as a sort of underlay in psychedelics.

Visual art has had roots in mathematics and the theory of illusion (proto-cognitive psychology) since the Renaissance at least. Op Art ambiguously possessed the material-symbolic ambiguity that we have already discussed, as illusory pictorial space shimmering between existence and non-existence in its fluorescing patterns.

If the absurd hands over to psychedelia, the latter hands over to data complexity. At some level, hyper-association is basic to all poetry. It is hard to reduce to a clear statement. The question is how to field large cognitive implications without simply writing at great length – catalogues. Many of the successful devices of poetry have as their goal the state of data overload. I get frustrated with poets who don't take the time to make something beautiful because they're too busy winning some argument or displaying some asset. I remain convinced that there is a poetic equivalent to *Dear Mr Fantasy, Axis: Bold as Love*, and *Sergeant Pepper's*. Also, that every song lyric is a poem and that the history of poetry finally has to consider songs and poems in one widescreen view. However, the poetry world is averse to such comparisons. Also, the fusion of words and music in any successful song means that extracting the words produces an artificial object that yields false results. All the same works like *The Apple Broadcast, The Bloodshed the Shaking House, Continual Song, Springtime in the Rockies, Suicide Bridge*, and *All the Year Round* can be viewed in this light.

The typical 1960s phenomenon was the freak-out, a conversion experience where an unfamiliar set of values and theories about living rapidly became more credible than the set you'd been living by and knew about. This atmosphere of radical criticality and dazed innocent suggestibility was ideal for art and just put more at stake than existing forms had ever been able to offer.

RECITAL FROM THE FIELD OF REEDS

I can hardly get away without a statement on *Brass* and *Place*, as the texts which overtower the 1970s scene, although I ducked this issue in the first edition. A certain trepidation, and apprehension that I didn't understand those texts, held me back. You can't get with the 1970s as a decade without having read those two works, extremist and monumental.

Brass occupies about 37 pages of the collected *Poems* and was published as a book in 1971. I don't feel able to make uncategorical statements about it. But I feel that the dissolution of schemas is a key to it, perhaps. Take 'The Bee Target on his Shoulder' as an example of natural language. The details of the poem are all about TV and a garden, a domestic scene, probably where a family is spending a day together. If we go back to the original idea of open field, it said that the poem should be an improvisation. This was related to the 'spatial thinking' whereby the poet should not take up a position – and not sit on an investment, something owned as the territory that the poem delimits. This may be a clue to how *Brass* was written – as utterly anti-schematic. 'Bee Target' is a poem about a suburban garden because the poet spent a day in such a garden. It is not making the garden into a token in some elaborate symbolic statement. The flow of meaning is much more evanescent, more immediate, than that. It doesn't give the critic a bone to carry in his mouth – look, I've understood the poem. But it contains much more potential for the transformation of daily life, for that reason. It is intimately related to the home movie line of underground cinema, Brakhage for example, where the data of daily life are captured without the overlay of illusionist structures that would make them 'significant'. Flowers are designed as targets for bees (or other pollinators), often having concentric bands emphasising a centre in the way that targets are painted. The bee-target is therefore a flower and the character has a flower on his shoulder. Why? Well, not everything has a reason. Maybe it just fell off a bush. Maybe he's wearing a flowered shirt. My guess is that the weird flow of the poems in *Brass* is due to a very high level of spontaneity, a form of orality – the flight into the evanescent present is a way of avoiding political and literary schemas, among other things. Prynne strikes me as someone willing to improvise, to ride the waves of emptiness and uncertainty which that implies, to feel serene about the intractable unsolid realms that would make someone else anxious. It is the anxiety that makes us fall back on schemas. Freezing, always. The theme of the poem may be the use of leisure, something that was important in sociological discussion of the time – leisure implying an uncontrolled flow of associations of ideas which was directed towards pleasure and yet constitutively undirected. Where unpredictability meets gratification.

Brass seems to me overgrown in the sense of a garden where every plant is expending its energies and geometrical order is not being imposed by poison and blade. Its sequences are not chopped off and presented as a flat and elegant surface. Grass runs to seed, climbing up into feathery stalks, tall, with paler colours and seed-heads. It sees consciousness as a strip like the wrack line – only there for five minutes, offering wonderful things from the deeps. We see acephalous information flows not converging on an ego function. Dissipative structures falling into new forms. *Brass* is coherent only in the way a suburb is random and realistic. It jumps tracks between data channels but without schema. It has that eerie vividness, like a photograph taken with much finer registration than usual, trapping ephemeral patterns, monumentalising the ephemeral. A hyperrealist photograph of a summer garden, precisely. Static but dissolving into a million micro-events. Where improvisation normally involves running off a new copy from structural models that are public and pre-existing, *Brass* may be showing a *structural* improvisation, where the activity generates a new pattern. This was something important in the jazz of the time, no longer playing variations and elaborations of pop tunes. One of the themes of *The White Stones* was nomadism – perhaps *Brass* follows that up by having the poetic art abandon its familiar and secure grounds. Prynne has that irrational profusion of ideas, like television or supermarkets, it is unable to stop. To deliver a critique of suburban leisure hours would be conventional – I don't think 'Bee Target' is even doing that, I don't see the critique. Some of Prynne's poems are sarcastic, but most of them aren't, and 'Bee Target' is not so easily reduced to a fixed quantity. The fixed quantities are made out and get bombed to death very quickly. Mobility recommends itself. The poems in *Brass* may fit together in the way that all the stories in a newspaper do: the idea is variety, each story is different. There may be unity at the level of composition but there is no *theme*.

The transition through the critique of immediate consciousness does not express itself through laborious descriptions of illusions and acts of smoothing out awkward details to create coherence. Is it there at all? I think it shows up as a tone of voice. The poet avoids a certain range of statements or feelings. Certain emphases are missed out; a reader who found those reassuring may experience an emptiness. The action is proceeding without accompanying music to reduce its level of ambiguity. Is this like the end of rhetoric?

No-Place

The new thing presents itself as a breakdown; actually, the aftermath of a breakdown. What is breaking down is the old authoritative self. The poet sees a breach with the old life – followed by a phase of collapse, actually a labyrinth through which the poet moves to an exit. Then the debouching into a new life – which we have referred to as the field of reeds (an Egyptian figure for the land of the dead). This is no longer secular life, but a realm where everything is coming into being for the first time. This is thus both a creation myth and a 'ground' for epistemology, where the origins of objects of knowledge are visible. It often takes the form of a historical sequence narrating origins. The transit had as an essential feature the effect of redemption; thus it begins with emptiness when the count of minutes after the new life has started is zero. Then as the number of minutes increases to 100, 200, etc., the emptiness is gradually replenished. The recital of the objects of knowledge simultaneously brings them into being and fits them into a new pattern, the city of redemption. In this place there is no distinction between code and data. The poem is the unpredisposed site where behavioural improvisation takes place. It is a testing ground for the act of redefining oneself.

This pattern was described by the anthropologist Victor Turner, who found it more generally in many societies and different ritual forms. He describes it as starting with a conflict bringing withdrawal. This was a very prominent feature of the 1970s political scene. The breach that these poets suffered can be related to the following key anxieties:

– Supporting the ruling order and the ambient Cold War culture, complicity as denounced by John Berger.

– Compulsiveness, inability to control drives, an area just beginning to be called sexism.

– Meaninglessness, writing poetry that interested no-one because after the ruin of collective symbolic orders it was merely individualism.

– Fragmentation, the inconstancy of the self described by J.A.C. Brown that made any poetic statement only partially true.

– Deadness as opposed to spontaneity.

It is not obviously true that the breach got rid of these problems but it was the *feeling* that counted. This is the core and this is why some poets of the 1970s had discovered a new landscape. The doubts are, probably, not invented by the poet, but reflections of feelings that the primary readers of poetry have. Turner described the area outside the normal world as a liminal place, from the Latin for threshold – he set out from the description of *rites de passage* and the passage was the crossing of a threshold.

PLACE

Allen Fisher's *Place* was written between 1971-80 although published 1974-1981. The collected version (2005) is 400 pages long and makes the design visible and definite. The status of work in progress was important, the commitment drew the reader in. The work is about learning exercises and hope. A key supposition is that the recital of knowledge works as if new, even though the information is available in other forms. It is as if preceded by an act of oblivion under which everything was forgotten and so everything from the start line on is new. The writer appears in the picture as someone with revolutionary hopes and deeply troubled by what he sees. The work is, before anything else, multi-themed, but one strand is a narrative about routes. Thus Book III, *Stane*, is named after Stane Street, the Roman road from Chichester to London Bridge that is envisaged as the access core that brought about the settlement of Lambeth – which is the unifying subject of the book. Stane Street may originally have led from the Roman port and supply depot at Fishbourne, a base for military stores carried from Gaul and used by troops marching, in AD 43, on London and the realm of the Catuvellauni but preceding the founding of Chichester. The book consists of a hundred or so sections, each including numerous elements – not bound by syntactic markers. The elements join horizontally in themes, of which paths are possibly number one. The nub here is that an originally featureless plain acquires a path that then channels walking because it is clear of obstacles. That means, to a reader steeped in post-1968 radicalism, that there was a time before paths, that Mesolithic man could have trodden-in those paths somewhere else, and that there was an arbitrary power open to us (us?) then and that we can recover this power as soon as we become conscious of it. The routes are a metaphor for routines – the brain was originally featureless and acquired habits that became an anatomy of neural pathways (where each repetition deepens the path and makes it more able to compete with other pathways). The disposition of cities (and land values) follows the course of paths.

When I wrote the first edition of this book, I was unable to summarise *Place*, because although I had read many of the instalments in which it was published, and all them had been published in some form by that time, I had never glimpsed the overall structure. The collected version allowed me to see that shape. Incidentally, the definitive issue excludes numerous sections that had already been published. I can say now that it involves an assemblage of data about Lambeth, a London borough, through the ages, but that it is all about ideas and procedures. The appeal of the work is partly the revolutionary intent and partly the pleasure of completion as its multiple themes recur and mutate. It has thoroughly said farewell to sounding like a song, with lines and so on, and its structure is at a much higher level – architectonic. It is unlike any known topographical work and more resembles anthropological notebooks – to be more exact, a secondary set of notebooks in which the primary notes are grouped together under themes. It is inscribed on a virtual object of complex design, and part of the text results from a (virtual) crushing of that object. It is also like a set of photographs of pre-existing data objects, rather than something that imitates the voice of an egocentric subject. Much of its pleasure emerges from reading the sources which it draws on. Because the story of Lambeth has no real edges, the work has none either. It has multiple symmetries, but no edges. Where the sources include information of which Fisher was unaware, which I believe to be true of the early history of Stane Street, recovered by excavations by Barry Cunliffe during the 1960s, the aura of the work continues into that new information.

Place is not a fragile product of sensibility that needs to be protected from outside impact; it is continuous with reality and easily absorbs new material. Parts 81 to 45 of Book III are a mirror image of parts 1 to 37. One sequence is rising and one is falling. The reflection that relates the two series is of an abstruse and indeed conceptual nature: recovering it is an intricate process. I have the serials F-H of *Unpolished Mirrors* which were excluded from the collected edition, and one of these includes at the back a diagram of *Place*, a rotation in what looks like an expanding spiral, described verbally as points on a moving sphere. Fisher relies on procedures to an unusual extent. The process is one of replacing intuitive processes with conscious ones, an imitation that exposes the nature of subjectivity, something archaic and repetitive yet fascinating to think about. Somehow this replacement is related to the replacement of inherited behaviour patterns by more modern egalitarian, liberating ones. The back cover of the original issue of *Stane* shows a street map of part of south London, partly overlaid by a diagrammatic view of a texture; a note informs us 'includes photos and drawings of environments given way under stresses it was assumed they could bear'. They seem to be structural materials now showing rips. A small image on the front cover shows a map of Greater London. That is, we are being shown something at three different scales. Much of the text inside deals with the Captain Swing riots during the agricultural depression of the 1820s, marked by rick-burnings that are also seen as examples of a structure yielding under strain. This interest in transformable or scalable structures may come from René Thom's catastrophe theory, rather than from more mainstream 'general systems theory'.

There is a moment in *Place* where Fisher has three lines, 'of lifting decisive moments / searching out cunnen/ of Structure, time and Place', where *cunnen* is a form of an Anglo-Saxon verb meaning 'to know or be able', modern *can* and *cunning*. On the lower half of the page is a passage about rabbits who by digging disturb the historiography of archaeological deposits ('in Neolithic kitchens') so that time sequences get confused. The juxtaposition is surely because *cunnen* looks like forms of coney (rhymes with *money*), meaning *rabbit*. This is an example of Fisher working through the compositional processes of *Place* but using spontaneous alignments or jokes in order to be free on a particular day. Another passage takes a whole page to recite the boundaries of the old parish of St Mary in Lambeth. There is evidently a link between paths and boundaries. Beneath both lies the pristine territory, the mere realm of the unknowable that will yield to any skein of paths. This has a meaning for me because of early exposure to Anglo-Saxon Readers that had charters, including very similar lists of boundaries. They both represent a recapture of the ingrained life-knowledge of ancestors who rarely left their own parish, and how the substance of knowledge is property – we memorise an arbitrary set of limits, the outer edges of what we don't have. Fisher is interested in knowledge structures, the high-level patterns that change everything when they change.

In around 2002 I wrote an essay on 'Long Poems of the 1970s' which is now available on the Web. I listed 50 long poems. Then I worked through six of them and at a certain point noticed that three of them mentioned the invention of coinage and four of them discussed the Anglo-Saxon settlements. Clearly the recital is going back to origins in order to find a clear space. The breach is a tiny hole through which a universe can flow drop by drop. Comparison with older narratives of the development of English society quickly shows that the new poems do not have heroes, do not recount victories, and have a bias towards equality and solidarity. The post-breach state is so distinctive – but even counter-cultural figures had to live in the workaday world of supermarkets, landlords and, after a while, Conservative government. The beautiful state dissolved back into real life.

I am not sure that the liminal quality is typical of the new poetry of the 1970s. On the contrary, I think the poetry has diffused out over a broad range of possibilities. The patterns classically described by Turner are a handhold, a way of talking about something puzzling and fluid.

WILDERNESS

The 'front line' for poetry over many years does seem to be to push people into a state where they forget how society actually is so they have to re-imagine it. I find it hard to describe this imagination for want of a notation. Elements of longing, autobiography, idealisation, narrative, make it what it is. There is no description of the social fabric in modern poetry, the method is always to destabilise the version of the social order that the reader already possesses and trigger a state of uncertainty and speculation in which the order of business is essentially decided by the reader. Poets see a wilderness that represents the unused possibilities of our society, which is adjacent to the inhabited world; which can be reached by a journey that starts as soon as one departs from the knowledge that holds a social order in static being. It is essentially empty. This is an interesting way of spending your time and the problem of modern poetry is abidingly how to trip people into this state when the obvious techniques for doing it have been used so many times that they have lost their edge. My feeling is that no-one really knows how society works, it is far too complicated and the fabric of organised knowledge is a battery of ridiculous schemas and limiting defence mechanisms. That is personal, you don't have to agree with me. Of course, a lot of poetry reproduces these defence mechanisms, their appeal is its appeal. There is an abiding rift between poets who think that the recital of concrete experiences is the path to destabilising investments in social normality, and poets who think that an attack on the productive symbolic matrix on which images of power and conformism are based is more effective. It is a fight worth watching.

WALES IN THE 1960S

Tony Conran (1931-2013) describes the group around the magazine *Wales*, roughly 1939-45, as the 'first flowering'. The unstated presence looming over this group of writers is guilt about not writing in Welsh, and the presence of writers who do. An excessive conformance to models was the consequence of a fear of not being Welsh enough. Certainly anything English had to be avoided (as the English language was not being avoided). The writers did not have the expertise to adapt Welsh models into their work (there are exceptions). Actually, a major influence was Irish literature, which had influenced the first group of Anglo-Welsh writing in the late 1930s, when the Free State was seen as an exciting political model. This was great writing using the living speech of a realm of a non-standard English, and Anglo-Welsh poetry wanted to be close to English as spoken in Wales.

'The period 1948-65 still strikes me [...] as especially dolorous' (Roland Mathias); there was a dip during which Mathias and Glyn Jones provided the artistic continuity. The Anglo-Welsh tradition had largely been created in England, as a check on the residence of its major figures indicates; Tony Conran identified 1963 as the moment when the centre of gravity of Anglo-Welsh poetry shifted from London to Cardiff. The expansion of higher education in the 1960s created many more opportunities on the spot for Welsh graduates, some of whom were also poets. The new or expanded institutions also created critical masses of thinking Welsh people, a natural audience to address in poetry, and a hotbed of nationalism. The decision to so expand was made, naturally, in Westminster. Conran describes the poets of the 1960s as the 'second flowering'; this would include Conran, Brenda Chamberlain, Raymond Garlick, T. Harri Jones, Harri Webb, John Tripp, Gwyn Williams, and eventually Emyr Humphreys. *The Lilting House* (1969) collects their memorable poems.

Meic Stephens (1938–) says, 'We were very few in number who had any interest in what we called Anglo-Welsh literature in 1962, and there was no English-language 'publishing scene' in Wales.' The Arts Council decided in 1967 to devolve funds to a new separate Welsh Arts Council, and this started putting money into literature, appointing Stephens, a nationalist and editor of *Poetry Wales* since 1965, as Literature Director. The reason for excluding literature before was the excellence and high outlay of the public library system. This money started the flow of poetry books, notably from Seren and Gwasg Gomer. According to Jeremy Hooker, a literary upturn followed: *The Dragon Has Two Tongues*, a history of Anglo-Welsh literature by Glyn Jones (1968); Ned Thomas' *The Welsh Extremist* (1971); the anthologies *Welsh Voices* (1967), *This World of Wales* (1968), and *The Lilting House* (1969), and the launch of *Planet* (1970). More decisive were the poetry of R.S. Thomas and Conran's translations from Welsh in his *Penguin Book of Welsh Verse* (1967). The 1960s were an era of reform rather than achievement, and the poets wrote their significant works in the 1970s. I am omitting R.S. Thomas and Vernon Watkins, survivors of the 1940s, whose work I find antipathetic, for different reasons.

> During the sixties and seventies, when I was living in Wales, there was quite a lot of very self-conscious poetry: 'I'm proving myself to be Welsh', or on the other hand, 'I'm a wretch who is unworthy to claim to be Welsh.' At the same time there was lots of anti-English rhetoric, at a rather superficial level antagonistic to tourism. There were recognizable kinds of poems...
>
> (Jeremy Hooker interviewed by David T. Lloyd, in *Writing on the Edge: Interviews with Writers and Editors of Wales,* 1997, p.43).

The philosophy of small-nation nationalism has almost nothing in common with the militarist expansion of countries like France, Russia, and Germany. Both Welsh and Scottish parties have something in common with the Liberal Democrats, formerly the Liberals, in their espousal of a community politics, in which government is not run by professionals but by 'local people' without qualifications, and no decisions are made outside the village that affect the village. This theory was radical insofar as it was latently against the corporation. It also bears a puzzling resemblance to the contemporary anarchist ideas of autogestion, dissolving all authority outside the immediate group. The local philosopher J.R. Jones made the case for the small and local in his book *Bychanfyd* (Microcosm). It became possible to say, for example, that no-one should make an (administrative) decision for someone they didn't know personally. The stress was on alienation, and on tightening the microstructure of society so that individuals couldn't fall out of the social net. You look after others, and get looked after. Wendy Davies has hypothesised that early mediæval Wales had few roads, no markets, no towns, no money, and almost no specialised craftsmen. The picture Davies draws is of a patchwork of aristocratic estates, the original *bychanfyds*, but the Plaid's vision is more of distribution of work and goods within the family, with capitalism disappearing. Saunders Lewis' ideas hark back to the late Empire, when the aristocratic villas strove to be self-sufficient, when the Catholic Church took its historic form, and when King Arthur was alive and smiting the Saxon. Clearly, if there are no roads, people will go on speaking Welsh. I suppose we have to call this vision of society radical. Other adjectives spring to mind. Lewis' vision of a nationalist Wales is then a kind of social memory, but by 1900 there was a huge South Welsh mine-factory-port economy founded entirely on exports.

Nationalism has been largely the theory of why South Wales isn't really Welsh enough and can be made to go away, perhaps; but the Plaid needs the electoral support of those reviled and fervently leftist southerners. Nationalism became very popular among students and literati in the 1960s, popular eventually among the electorate, mainly in the Welsh-speaking North, winning a first seat in Parliament in 1966, climaxing with about 11% of votes cast. The transition from aesthetics to politics has arguably never been made. The timing of the nationalist revival was influenced partly by the example of decolonisation, seen on the TV news so much in the early 1960s; the metaphor of imperialism, never used before to describe English-Welsh relations, penetrated public awareness.

The doctrine that 'small is beautiful' bears an alarming resemblance to one of the unconscious rules of modern poetry, namely that significance can be read into the experience of one individual, or better of a small group of people. If I deride the idea of concentration on the local, how can I also defend the segment of modern poetry that describes events in the bedroom, the kitchen, or the living-room, or the poet wandering alone in the hills? This structural coincidence suggests that the rules of the poem are being projected onto political discourse. If you don't see the realm of ideas as vast, and subsuming the small space of the little human group, you see it as a head-tangle of one of the members of the group, a kind of peculiarity of character; therefore within the group and much smaller than it. This degradation of thought invites the poet to ossify all difficult ideas as complicit assumptions, so that the reader from outside sees only narrowing of the verbal area. Instead of exploring ideas, the regional poet defines them as values and loyalty tests.

This kit of picturesque local characters, particularism, belief in community, home-made poetry, dislike of regulations, business, government and preservation of rural services, is familiar in England but is not close to power. The English immigrants Jeremy Hooker and Peter Abbs absorbed this ethos easily, and even expounded it more convincingly than their Welsh confrères. In describing Welsh rootedness and small-mindedness we also describe a vast swathe of English poetry. The ancestry of localism includes the Christian Socialists, William Morris, John Ruskin, the arts and crafts movement, E. F. Schumacher, Georgian poetry, Cecil Sharp, besides the continental Catholic social thought read by Ambrose Bebb and Saunders Lewis.

The exception is Conran, whose adoption of Welsh social, commemorative, and encomiastic mediaeval genres of greetings, thanks for gifts, epithalamia, birthday congratulations, etc., is distinctively un-English. His early volumes are enormously influenced by Robert Graves, but towards the pre-modern European poetry that Graves commends. I feel that Conran's ventures into the past, although patriotic, have been decisive in the failure of this extraordinarily gifted poet and great translator to quite reach excellence of his own. If only he'd explored the future, not the past!

To master a foreign culture is perhaps to learn and adopt the attitudes of its native members, so that the successful study of Welsh culture climaxes with acquiring Welsh attitudes, including their taste in poetry. In this sense, I have failed; the idea of reading 24 volumes of R.S. Thomas makes me go pale with horror. I can point to an amateur interest in the Welsh language, beginning some 20 years ago with reading the *Mabinogion* and the *cywyddwyr* as part of the Anglo-Saxon, Norse and Celtic Tripos at Cambridge. [ADDITION 2016. That is now 40 years ago. All I can say is that Welsh is a lot easier than Gaelic.]

Shrinking the scale of analysis bears an odd resemblance to the precept that the personal is political. However, peripheral nationalism, and Liberalism, defined the small-scale as perfect *per se*, and really wasn't up for any criticism of the family, which was possibly the most intellectually productive area in the 1970s. The area of close attention of the anti-metropolitan tradition is really zero: while the large scale is abolished, the small-scale is viewed uncritically, as a frozen, hazy, spot of beauty. The community becomes a big family and the family becomes a thing where there is no conflict. So what then if someone refuses to conform? It must be due to their wickedness. The projected society comes to look very much like the Methodist congregation of so many small Welsh towns, the real social order which was disaggregated in the 1920s or 1930s. It was the areas where the clergy had retained their authority and prestige which eventually came to vote Plaid Cymru.

Conran criticised the *Anglo-Welsh Review* (AWR), as edited by Mathias (1915-2007) from 1961-76, for not being nationalist enough, but AWR engaged with all aspects of the Welsh past in an intellectually serious way. Abused or not, Mathias (1915-2007; *Break in Harvest*, 1946; *Roses of Tretower*, 1952; *The Flooded Valley*, 1960; *Absalom in the Tree*, 1971; *Snipe's Castle*, 1979) was the best of the Anglo-Welsh poets in the 1960s and 1970s, and his seriousness utters itself as a massive scepticism about factional claims to define what the past means or what kind of place Wales is. Mathias' poetry occupies the sentimental *topoi* of Welsh mythology only to unmask and undermine them in his dialectically profound, if unsentimental and unconsoling, staging of history. Patriotism craves to document the national past, documentation like AWR's demolishes shallow and partial views of the Welsh past, which is unfortunate for poets who had bought into them. Do wrong ideas amount to subjectivity and authenticity?

The behaviour patterns of nationalist students in 1967 or so resembled those of radical students at other universities. If we recall the *new nationality* of students in the 1960s, a people in 80 different countries, among their new customs was being destabilised by ideas and being politically radical. The mass condition meant that being top student was a prize worth winning; being more radical than all the others was an obvious way of competing. This radicalisation involved a complete rethink of the distribution of power, wealth, and social roles, an intellectual journey affecting who you were. This journey was in many ways similar for feminists, Marxists, hippies, and peripheral nationalists. The poetry boom of the same era was largely an offshoot of this new student nation, and the initially coherent group of ex-students which it developed into.

Separating this deluge of activity into distinct tracks is efficient but misleading. Texts may be assigned to different zones but the psychological differences were not important. It would also be efficient if all this radicalism and idealism stopped at a point in history. Of course that is not true either. But the wave broke. Politics might become, for example, more realistic and closer to academic research – or more stuck into stubborn resistance to New Right advances. A classic point made about 1968 is the contrast between the exciting and radical strike of students at Haringey Art College and the choice of Haringey voters (then still called Haringay) in favour of the Conservatives at local elections in the same year. Defeat in elections does not signify that the counter-culture was wrong or that their ideas would evaporate on contact with reality.

SCOTTISH POETRY IN THE 1970S

The decade saw the disintegration of the centre of the Scottish polity, as both major British parties adopted devolution as their policy. This made the centre of political imagination, if anything, the mysterious and unknown status of independence and self-government. Jim Bulpitt (1937-1999) explained the time as one of the periodic dips in the prestige of the centre; a state of disaffection that left a profound mark on the poetry of the period. The legislation creating new centres of power is related to poets, in their rooms, throwing away the authority of inherited decisions and making up their own rules. The story of this policy is roughly as follows. Labour presented their rather weak Devolution Bill in the autumn of 1977, failed to allocate it enough parliamentary time, finally got it passed in July 1978, with the critical amendment that 40% of the electorate had to vote in favour in a subsequent referendum. This took place in February 1979, and failed to get the numbers; in Wales, a majority voted against. The low turnout in Scotland was probably due to boredom. The apathy, fickleness, and inefficiency of the British politicians in managing this event crucial to the future of Scotland disproved for ever their ability to govern the affairs of Scotland. In 1979 a fanatically Unionist Prime Minister was elected; Labour retained the devolution policy but was out of power.

I am impressed by the stability of the poetic scene in Scotland in this decade of radical uncertainty. Established poets became more eminent, Morgan emerged as the flower of them all, but there was no overthrow of existing values and no party of 'underground' poets emerged to plot the inheritance from the established crew, whose techniques remained static and prolific. The deaths of Hugh MacDiarmid, Sydney Goodsir Smith, and Douglas Young altered the landscape and virtually wiped out the original first and second waves of the Lallans movement. The early retirement of both Norman MacCaig and Iain Crichton Smith enabled them to become full-time writers, with more literary scope, and raised the spectre of a sociologically likely development into a poetic world dominated by the retired, both as writers and readers. Some of the most notable publications were collected works by writers over 60 who had been obscure up until then. It is a Scottish publishing practice to wait until late in life and publish a catch-all collected poems. If the new poets of the 1960s were still waiting for a position at high table to become free, the new poets of the 1970s generally couldn't get books out. We can note first volumes by Roderick Watson (1943–), Alastair Fowler (1930–), Walter Perrie (1949–) and Flora Garry (1900-2000), who was 74 at the time. Some of the poems in Fowler's *Catacomb Suburb* are spectacularly brilliant:

> Suppose some
> Skyskin Picts not far from beasts hunted
>
> To rest at this cascade. Was it mere thirst
> Drew them down to look? Or paradise pools
> Disturbed? (…)
>
> We see the clearest, the most rarely
>
> Used stream's conglomerate face through our own
> Complete reflections, and babble of mirrors, the mind's
> Brooking of consciousness. But that flows
>
> At focal depth. Beneath, beneath the mirror's
> Melting surface, unengendered features
> Lour at the sky, ungendered form of a mind's
>
> Insistence.
> (from 'The Landscaping of Badon Mosach')

Brand's book on nationalism stresses the importance of song in the collective activity of the nationalists. The appeal of these folk-song forms (often written by the folklorist Hamish Henderson), recognisable to all Scots, was a fatal diversion for Scottish poets, fighting with *Sprachkrise* and a lack of tradition. Modern English poetry is dominated by the generation which was born in the 1940s and shaped by the radicalism of the 1960s. In both Wales and Scotland, nationalism drained off the enthusiasm of the young, and the poetry it inspired looked backwards. A fearful combination of mediaevalism and populism prevented an avant-garde from emerging; the folksong impersonated and captured the immediacy of the new sound. So there is a profound asymmetry between England on one side, and Wales with Scotland on the other. Innovative poetry embraced Edwin Morgan, increasingly the most important figure but hardly a new arrival; flawed attempts by Walter Perrie; and a streak of minimalist poetry that embodied the *Sprachkrise* rather than transcending it. Ian Hamilton Finlay was by now publishing objects rather than books, but still incarnated the idea of a politicised avant-garde. The poetry readership in Scotland was still very small, and the lists of poets waiting to get a first book out, drawn up in magazines like *Aynd* issue 17 and *Akros*, make depressing reading; sheer invisibility probably stopped many careers.

David Craig (1932–) has published *Latest News* (1977), *Homing* (1980), *Against Looting* (1987), and *The Grasshopper's Burden* (1992). There are several good poems in the last-named, but the volume as a whole is disappointing. The backbone is of stern political diatribes, with an odd flavour of Surrealism. A promising mixture, but the Surrealism is reduced to Pop and the political ideas are starved of the space of information and argument, the most exciting bits are neatly left out of the poem, and what is left in is vehement and one-sided. Where moral values are so black and white, they deny the possibility of speculation; how can you propose political alternatives in a tone that says there is no alternative? One poem goes back to childhood memories of radio news about the war in Spain, while others warn of ecological disaster in the future. The crag-hero image of Marxism transmutes to mountain climbing, geology, and so to the ecological poem, whose apocalyptic imagery and moral wrath recycle the unit structures of the Stalinist poem. A consistent pattern, then. The attempt to include vast stretches of time takes us back to the 19th-century sublime. The technique is amateurish, over-heated, hasty – although Craig was born in 1932. 'Hullo Mormond Hill' is a geographical poem with an anti–American forces in Scotland burden, mentioning whaling out of Dundee and the Greenland waters, linked to ecology and great distances. Craig, a professor at Lancaster, also wrote *Scottish Literature and the Scottish People*, a classic Marxist interpretation. Some of the poems are imaginative, which quite violates current conventions of unflinching, wooden-headed, empiricism. Predictably, this unconventional gesture is underdeveloped just because it is unsupported; it needs to be much more refined, much more interworked with the durable structures of reality. The didactic load is too much aforethought and too inflexible.

Christopher Salvesen (1935-2015) announces in a foreword that his two books (*Floodsheaf*, 1974; *Among the Goths*, 1986) are a history in two volumes of a single parish, Kirkmahoe in Dumfriesshire. I think there are about six really excellent poems in the books, buried however beneath a good deal of idle mainstream fencing with words. Salvesen, an Oxford graduate and later an academic at Reading, is rather good at this sort of thing; his profession predisposes him to literary anecdotes. The weakness of most of the poems, attractive in their way, is obliquity, a lack of engagement, which is also the strength of the good ones, where he evokes the fullness of life in a backwater. He writes excellently, in Scots, about Ninian Winyet, a Catholic propagandist against the Reformation, remote therefore from political success, ageing in geographical remoteness in a college in Salzburg. It seems to me that Salvesen should have taken his subject, of parish history, more seriously, and engaged in material structures as well as anecdotes. Declination away from the totality, as a Romantic error, leads one, in the absence of despair, to a progressive reduction in scale, representing an increase in accuracy. The bounded paradise can be represented by an institution (instead of a society), a text (somehow preserved from dissipation by watertight partitions), a personality (a pseudo-society, lying world), or a locality. Salvesen's method is too close to parochialism, a Scottish vice in which all possibilities of history or literature are buried in quaint topography and unthinking solidarity, not close enough to a radically empirical, anti-nationalist, scholarly approach that would embrace all phenomena within a rigorous partition, a small totality. Salvesen is too interested by the Romans and the Church, i.e. by the things that are easy to evoke because they came from outside and we know all about them already. His poems are also too bounded and too civilised. Galloway was a region where ethnographic originality and deviancy reached a maximum. Sociologically and even linguistically, its history is full of surprises; there is a depth to be uncovered here, if Salvesen would adopt the methods, developed for such needs, in the 1970s, by such as Allen Fisher.

Alison Fell (1944–) took part in the exploration of new poetic and political possibilities as a radical feminist, although in London. Her talent as a poet has remained neglected, with a few strong poems in the collections *Kisses for Mayakovsky* (1984) and *The Crystal Owl* (1988), presumably because of her involvement in political work.

Perrie is familiar as editor of *Chapman*, *Littack*, and *Margin*: an impressive record. *By Moon and Sun* (Canongate, 1980) is an interesting specimen because it adopts the spatial composition, with lines scattered over the page and not hewing to the left-hand margin, which became a hallmark and recognition sign for post-Poundian writers in England. The presuppositions are also modernist, with remarkably inexplicit links between juxtaposed elements, which are themselves far-flung: the oppression of the Palestinians, the breaking of the clans after the revolt of 1745, David and Jonathan (an apparent homoerotic pathos here) re-sited in contemporary Edinburgh, MacDiarmid and Sorley MacLean invoked as revolutionaries and great poets. Perrie has rejected the limits that Salvesen regards as tests of sense. But the juxtapositions somehow don't give the impression of mighty concepts being wrenched out of darkness into light; perhaps because the furniture of the poem includes too much old-fashioned sentiment, about love, regret at the ethnic damage done to the Highlanders, and the need for solidarity. The modernity is decoration; the poetry is full, nearly fulsome, doesn't contain any mysterious space. *Lamentation for the Children* (Canongate, 1977), despite the sonorous Biblical archaism of the title (the name of a piece of pipe music), is better. It is about coal-mining, and about the poet's family of Fife miners. There is a towering evocation of darkness, disease, and geological forces in the mines, Mannerist I suppose, but adequate to the backdrop. This is in a mixture of Scots and English. Again, there is a problem in the associational grammar of the poem, with very loose juxtapositions shaping a rather vague set of co-ordinates above the familiar set of defence of the workers, denunciation of the power order, etc. An initial uncertainty about criticising social authority (English authority BAD, stone-carved Scottish moralists GOOD) has leaked across into his account of parts of history and biology, removing important parts of the poem from conceptual criticism and thus from the poem's range of view.

Apart from the books discussed, the decade saw notable volumes by Norman MacCaig and George Mackay Brown, and especially Edwin Morgan, as well as the republication of MacDiarmid's classic past. The anthology *Twelve Modern Scottish Poets* (edited by Charles King) was informative, although reaching back deep in time; it was followed by *Twelve More Modern Scottish Poets* (1986).

T. S. Law (1916-97) collected *Referendum* in 1989, but the poems, some of the most politically committed of our time, were written in the disturbed years before the referendum of 1979, and sold directly to nationalist crowds. This bristling polemic is written in a Scots as wuthering as a day on the Fife coast and as reeky as a kipper. While the idea of someone so polarised running a government is deeply frightening, Law's diction is like someone running their head against an oak door, hundreds of times and with eventual success. It reminds me of some coarse marketplace sermon of the 16th century, that pure century before the union with England, perhaps the Reformation polemics of Thomas Murner and Niklaus Manuel, or indeed of John Knox and Andrew Melville; later intellectual structures have been shaken off. His first book came out in 1948, from the communist milieu of the Clyde Group, and most of his work remains unprinted. His grasp of gutter invective may possibly come from a youth in the Communist Party. Fife miners are not the 'Scottish picturesque', and the Cold War may have inclined the cultural managers away from him. [Addition 2016: Most of it is still unprinted so far as I can check.]

The Gaelic poet from Raasay, MacLean, published translations of his poems into English, and a new, or a reworked and previously unpublished, long poem, 'The Cuilinns'; the most significant work of the period.

OUR LOST LIMBS RETURNED
Stepping Space (1990) by Ulli Freer (1947–)

Recent outbreaks of 'rave culture' have led to a burst of psychedelic poetry, inducing perhaps a backward look at the 1960s. Any revolution has to be judged by its long-term achievements. Looking at this retrospective of someone indisputably of the generation of '68, one has a glimmering awareness that some writers of the 1960s reached a set of cognitive procedures so evolved that the critic as paper-keeper has yet to assimilate them.

I suppose I ought, facing a retrospective volume, to trace phases within Freer's work. I feel unable to do this. The tentative work (if any) is not visible. An early printed work is the astounding 'Bone Songs' (1968, published 1973), already completely mature. As a reviewer, I am surprised that reviewers at that time did not hail this as a great work. Early legends show Ulli starting to write while at school, where he was taught English by Jeff Nuttall, and studying art at Hornsey Art College. Later sightings show him in performance art in the 1960s. One suspects that the negative rules of 'performance' (no text, no plot, no realist logic) at least coincided with some of Freer's private rules: reaching Presence by throwing away status and organised knowledge. Improvisation trusted the 'here and now', favouring opportunities of time and place over the stale commodified tricks of personality. Known pen-names include Lox, Lane, Flamme, and McCarthy.

> reproduction of counter
> beneath counters
> duplicating amounts
> pyramids in the mirror
> rattle of stiff fingers
> snow ministers office
> fossilized veins
> administers flakes
> feeding silent wing
> track a mixture

called

passage of peine.
(from: 'Trophies', in *Stepping Space*)

Like this excerpt, any page of *Stepping Space* strikes immediately more by what it omits. The rigorous absence of certain linguistic features figures emotional and political resistance to regimens associated with organised knowledge and administration. *Stepping Space*, a retrospective sample of work from 1979-85, allows for the first time (I believe) a sufficient extent of Freer's work to permit his rigour and radicalism to spread their wings, while also raising an urgent need for collection of his work of the 1970s, and since 1985. Eight works are included, three in excerpt.

One has to make a journey in order to reach such poetry; arriving there, we are faced by the mismatch between memory and perception, as what seemed to be identity was merely a kind of daily task. The new place is specifically the place in which the mind can grow again. That feeling in the head as one's ingrained habits become inoperative is the experience of change: you can't become the new thing without ceasing to be the old one. A rehearsal for change, just as photo romances are a rehearsal for 'going out'. The most obvious handhold in this elusive poetry is the recurrence of horrified depictions of interrogation, classification, measurement, and control. This is a clue to the motives of structural decisions, specifying a unique syntax and method of representation. Certainly, the phantoms of liberty are near, phantoms of a society without hierarchy and where roles are allocated afresh each day, as the day commends. The standpoint is perhaps not too far away from a piece of Daoism:

> By taking a particular standpoint and thus becoming polarized, one loses one's originally well-balanced nature. [...] Nothing external can be added to one's own nature. [...] There is nothing to achieve and nothing to sacrifice, for all truth is here and now.

Language, however, is built up from polarisations and oppositions.

Every poem sets the reader a task: some kind of mimicry of the poet's state of mind is needed just to follow the track. Many modern poems reward the reader for complex logical thought, or for knowledge of literary history, or of recent academic fashions, or for a methodical ability to pick up slight clues and use them to puzzle out structures. They so mimic the assessment of working ability and intelligence; part of the working routines of the graduate or professional class. These procedures can be treated as systematic alienation:

> though knives yield distinctively
> every feature to a siphoned point
> reflections in steel white
>   from decomposed closed hoods
>   bled during the wear
>   so that men lived
>   full moon a frozen plant
>   nothing opens
> stores files climate to scan
> a section can
> pigeons pierce holes
>   into central lifeless collapse.
> (from 'Sun Broke', in *Stepping Space*)

It is the privilege of formally radical art that it can bury its inclinations in the deepest procedures: structure as statement. I take it this loss of whole-body awareness, due to pigeonholing, submission to authority, etc., is the insight most important to Freer's poetry. Consequently, he has rigorously eliminated all that distracts from the basic acts of intuition and identification and sharing.

It's normal to express emotions, intangible by their nature, by physical objects: a heart of stone. As if, we find the senses' world more reliable and more shareable than the inner world. This points to a certain strain between painting and poetry. There is a school of poets who have taken over from certain painters a secure and satisfying attitude to space. One resolves the polarisation between the 'ideal space' and 'facticity', not by the archaic withdrawal into fantasy and frustration, but by finding an authentic way of moving and feeling. Whereas abstract painting has striven to free individual expression at all costs, poetry has generally stabilised external space by recognising that the personality is a limit, a cognitive block.

One could call *Stepping Space* a gesture of utopian sensuousness:

> floor quakes & the more city sinks
> in response   to the sirens
> yet we feel each other
>   ourselves
> giant of origin & weaned off all dimension
> menschen in exteriors that spread no doors

> sinking city
> where the law snakes domination
> sweats blue fists circling around necks
>   (from 'Floor Quakes', in *Stepping Space*)

Number and property disintegrate space that must be healed by the poet's effacing of separations. To put this in (crudely) rational terms:

– Because knowledge encodes rules that infringe and break up primary social space with a series of polarisations and assumptions of authority that prevent people from authentic emotional contact, it is a burden the poet jettisons in order to achieve presence.

– Social hierarchy is deeply rooted in knowledge, a story that is already over, a fraction of the power stores of bureaucracy. This set of rules competes with the movements of humans, which it uses punishment to control. One must observe human behaviour to find out who they are, not insert them into sets of Rules excluding most of the possibilities of the real situation.

– The artist seizes power within art through a series of technical tricks. It's wrong for the poet to decide how the reader must react. This compromises the poem in a thousand ways. The claim to insight as elitist expertise, cutting dialogue and flow out of the situation. Art is a 'work practice' of ingrained purpose and known finality, which competes with perception.

– Because emotion so often involves denial (e.g. rage, jealousy), it limits one's contact with sensuous reality. Our passive knowledge is far broader than our emotional level of awareness: we know A is so and as agents deny it and fight against it. Freer's poetry has accepted the problem of moving on from desire of what is not to desire of what is. Clearly, description of what is not can never be genuinely sensuous; its high affect goes along with vagueness, and gives rise to blemishes of proportion. A true concern for pattern must partake of the real or starve.

– Emotion is founded on the individual's drive for power. An emotion is when you want to make someone else do what you want. Political ideas that scale this up to 'everybody doing what I want' are an illusory liberation. Art too can be authoritarian.

Such poetry is a tangible part of the 'good place' not because it shows palaces of glass, orchards laden with fruit, etc., but because it shows the unity of the mind with the ambient space. We don't live in a world of objects. We live rather in a world of sequences of motions and cognitive frames based on the body image. Evoking objects does not evoke human experience. Mail-order catalogues are not sensuous. For this reason, the greatest pleasure of sensuous poetry, including Freer's, is not laborious descriptions of flowers and recipes, but its evocation of social and physical space. The organisation is in flakes:

> a plague doctors costume
> crystal eyes a beak filled with perfumes
> pecking pecking
> at our string pearl hearts
> splitting precious knots

–slight and flexible enough to pick out the contours of the real. Space is compelled by depolarising and overall stressing to reveal its very grounds. The effacing of the rationalist boundary between inner and outer experience sites emotions (of horror, revolt, integration and hope) within the single event-space given tension and depth by the disciplined and even flow of local markings, acting like a light source.

The least effective method of describing landscape is by cataloguing all the things in it. Language is successive and contrastive, space is simultaneous and without emphasis. (Precisely this problem with emphasis is why the personality is a hindrance to poetry that handles spatial frames; natural space has no focuses.) A method of rendering landscape, which is huge, not by huge paintings, but by minimal signs distributed around a suggested shape. A negative rendering. A few dabs of paint making a fundamental structure visible. Carefully breaking down the successive feature of language structure, so that A does not disappear when we move onto B. Using a few dabs in the knowledge that the stability of nature will supply the underlying massive reality:

> undulations of marginal capital
> & the deep repose of this arm
> thickly strewn pulse pervades
> & erroneously decorates breath
> gorse & crow
> archipelago
> allows discharge

sweeping ditches
more mouthe drainage
(from 'Rushlight', a recent poem).

The reliable structures alluded to are not only those of hills and forests but also those of human behaviour and emotions. This method allows the artist to stay with what is familiar and common: a stable and exterior space, then. Neither landscape nor personality are aesthetic objects, all things considered, yet they are the durable subjects of art.

I wonder if the existence of tense could be described as a kind of alienation. Real experience is all in a present; a picture has no tense. The concept 'I was' invokes a kind of split. Possibly the removal of tense, throughout *Stepping Space*, equates to the removal of recession, in modern painting: the canvas, no longer expressing distance, achieves immersion, filling the horizon. A kind of planar simultaneity animates these poems, distribution unbroken by emphatic peaks and syntactic contrasts. There is only the here and now. Emphases (although implied by line-breaks and by the spoken language) would perhaps create marginal areas, a kind of relationship of centre and margin unacceptable within a planar poem.

Freer's publication of a pamphlet by Tom Raworth in the Micro-brigade series allows comparison with *Stepping Space*. But what a difference of tone: Raworth bright, mocking, sceptical; Freer subjective, effusive at times, never clear-cut. There is an affinity between the two: in the 'breaking up' of syntax in search of simultaneity and motion. 'Fragmented syntax' is not a fragment unless 'ordered' syntax is a norm which the 'broken' parts long for. A tradition opens with Greek oratory in the fifth century BC. Some of their prized texts were courtroom speeches, which is why many of these (e.g. those of Antiphon) have been preserved. Reason has, ever since, imitated the courtroom model of polarised appeals to authority. This education trains you to look after the property of rich men, and apply regulations. Every move asserts rights, and undermines someone else. Later, even theology was conducted by polemics, by competitive dispute. Politics also has revolved around legislation and party strife. They invented our syntax, or at least the syntax of formal and rational discourse. We write bad poetry because we're taught how to write essays, and it takes. That data topology (branchy, full of fine oppositions defining categories ever more narrowly, contrastive, emphatic, demonstrative) conceals an allegiance to a written law code; something authoritarian and fixed. Verbal conformance runs against human intuition. Syntax generated a series of sites in which contrast, achieved by symmetry, made successively finer boundaries. Yet our sensory experience is non-oppositional, continuous, without sharp edges.

Space is homogeneous, not dissected. Clearly a pre- or non-Athenian way of writing is both difficult and natural. We reach the world by looking, not by logic.

Poetry has imitated this courtroom rhetoric, pleading the cause of the self. The recent spate of naïve poetic autobiography creates, with its poster-level self-assertion, an authoritarian version of other people- reduced to reflections of the ego in the form of 'you did me wrong' or 'I'm cleverer than you' trophies. A polarised and contentious model is there called liberation. Freer has always been aware that such self-centredness is a betrayal of the self. We know something more than our own emotions know. The line drawn between the self and the rest of the world is a polarisation no less tendentious than others. The self is not property, even of itself. Emotional liberation (another utopian project) seems to demand depolarisation: forsaking positions and effacing boundaries to free shared space and make unconstrained movement possible.

ADDITION 2016.
I can see this poetry wasn't written in the 1970s. There is a story. In 1991, I lived in the next street to Ulli Freer; I used to see him all the time, even before we were on friendly terms. I found him alien but I could also see that he embodied a complex of hippie beliefs that you would be accurate in summing up as counter-cultural. It emerged also that by empathising with him I could get to know a lot about those beliefs, not by direct instruction. This empathy led up to the review reproduced above, my first successful attempt at writing about modern poetry. I am certain that the poems in *Stepping Space* are part of the counter-culture, even if literally they were written in the 1980s. Dates don't apply to someone who has abiding values.

The Gothic Strain in 1970s Poetry

We are going to start with a review that I wrote in 1993.

The Long Shrine of Hunger: Written Rooms and Pencilled Crimes, selected poems 1969-88, by Brian Catling, in: Allen Fisher, Bill Griffiths, Brian Catling, *Re/Active anthology No. 1: future exiles; 3 london poets* (1992)

Four and a half years after John Muckle first broached the topic to me, here is the first Paladin triple-header: 150 pages per poet. At that time, I was supposed to be in volume 1; but I guess we both mistook the wall for more road. Two more (Crozier/Davie/Sisson and Thomas A. Clark/ MacSweeney/Torrance) wait in the wings, but Iain Sinclair admits to having planned a series of 30. This makes him the Grand Sorcerer of poetic gorging, the dream orchestrator of world-historical greed: pandering to a flock of phantoms, wings wetted down, tumescent enough to satisfy the queasiest of aesthetes. It would have made the world almost unrecognisable; and, like the planned MC5/Stooges/ Flamin' Groovies world tour of 1973, the industry could not allow it to happen. Not enough has been said about the poem as lust object, and the only problem with modern poetry being that I want it more/harder/faster/louder/bigger/now/incessantly. I believe in the policy of large doses. Fifteen thousand pages would fix my habit for a whole weekend.

These three poets don't belong together (oh, torment of the bewildered reviewer), but commonly evoke the landscape of the late 1960s; if that had been 'one' landscape. There is (so far as I know) no psychedelic poetry of any value, but the three carried on certain preoccupations of that era with a patience and fidelity at odds with the era's native giddiness and lack of connection. Let's just mention (as one doesn't) the topic of drugs. The irritation of tissue (the brain) made it call out for more numerous, diverse, complex, and novel data. The abuse of the body made it sprout ever more queasy, refined, unnerving, and jaded cravings. New data sources, new creators, satiated these yammering primeval cries. The orthogonal code of repression, surveillance, and resignation slipped and warped. The power order failed at the level of its bars striating the ego, as the latter juddered in spasms of nausea and hallucination. Sweating unrecognizable fluids. Maimed organs sent bolts of pulse modulated white light through archaic and closed parts of the nervous system before going off the air for ever. Reptile landscapes fanned out during the palsies and outages of more modern faculties. The Artaudian formula of 'hallucination, ecstasy, and fear' stalked and diced young reason. But we know that hallucination is part of a phase more primary than reason. Art, religion, emotion, dreams – none of these need industrial chemicals.

Most writers have too much guilt and not enough crime. Brian Catling (1948–) reverses this relationship, a parity mirror catching either side in a singular, binding lattice. A stiff, binary rhythm.

Poetry after 1968 followed two related courses: politics as the transcendence of the body in the direction of its connectivity; and social representation, answerable to Gothic violation of body image at the level of skin and insides. The middle term is the self-image; stressed perhaps by the new massive availability of representations. The notion of 'sexism' relates to Gothic mutilation simply as recto and verso of the same card, idealisation and distortion. Class society was shifted (a few inches) off its axis by the logic of the body, physical vigour replacing (in spectacle) the signs of wealth, office, and background. The poem, roughly a hundred thousand times less important than the pin-up, adopted some of the logic of this hegemonic genre. Jeremy Reed's and Brian Catling's poems used a fantastic, hyperbolic body as the substance in which their signs were worked. Some of the charge of their work was actually a livid, turncoat kind of sexuality. Fastidious, jaded, and imperious.

Sculpture has mostly chosen a body, animal or human, as its ostensible subject. Suppose this public body, mutated and mutilated, were the liturgical figure of the shared imaginary. Didier Anzieu has suggested that 'the group's imaginary space is the projection of the mother's body'. The sculptor has given birth, by an act of violence and incision, to a Golem body, more compliant than the first: exteriorised but purely interior, a sheer sign. Idealization and distortion in one twisted body plan. Drugs bring a new understanding of the body as the universal substrate and fund of operant symbols. As acid starts fast-playback and recoding of the body ego, the brain appears as a store of organ representations. As body images ripple and reverberate around the room, new violations and new idealisations, realized in new substances, become tangible.

As pioneer avengers, these creators began reversing out 2,000 years of Christian murder of the body, of *asomatoi* – bodiless, pure, obedient creatures. The early Christian imagery of *lorica* (breastplate) and *castrum* (armed camp) revealed a fatal anxiety about the body, threatened by demonic forces from within and from an otherworld. Bodies without desire or organs were depicted as models to emulate; a frozen body image. This curious equation of the inside of the body with a plane of cunning monsters will recur. I equate, of course, religion with psychosis; and with the effects of psychotomimetics.

Eugen Bleuler defined the negative hallucination as the perceptual block. An intercept, segmenting the real like a pastry-cutter. A film of surface-making, pink candy forms, at visible speed, to skin over the dense zone of denial. According to Peter Fuller (1947-1990):

> I also believe that the famous flat or linear aspect of British art in part arises because the flattened forms characteristic of feudalism (e.g. in stained glass windows, altar pieces, and manuscript illumination) were never thoroughly challenged and overthrown by an indigenous bourgeois realism which emphasized the tangibility and three-dimensional materiality of things. The rise of the bourgeoisie in Britain culminated in Burne-Jones's angels, and the flat ethereality of Pre-Raphaelitism.

Further:

> the peculiar ataraxy of the bourgeois aesthetic in nineteenth century England goes far beyond subject matter; after Constable the attempt to find visual equivalents for 'moments of becoming' in the natural and social worlds simply freezes. The Victorian world view, as expressed through Victorian paintings, is simply one of stasis.
> (from 'Fine Art after Modernism', in *New Left Review* I/119, 1980)

The concept of change, in English art, is caught up in the taboo, the speech block, of inherited wealth, whose sly ideological frontage is 'heritage' and 'cultural capital'. For 'Victorian paintings' read 'contemporary mainstream poetry'; an achieved stasis. Catling's art and poetry, in contrast, is: somatic; kinetic; physiognomic; rapid; with a geometry of moving bodies; time-based; metabolic; appetite driven; involves violence and damage of the body image; involves triumph and the end of the self.

My nephew, aged 15 months, was observed recently getting very upset because he wasn't allowed to take the vacuum cleaner from the closet and clean the floor with it. Through such minimal vocabulary elements in a material cinema we acquire our behaviour patterns and models of other people's likely reactions. The ritual of the Mass is, as Robertson Smith very astutely observed, a version of the central act of every household, that of breaking bread and eating together. The decor of our fantasies is not painted flats but the human body. For Catling, every space is the terrain of a new childhood under controlled conditions: 'Another deserted room, its history functional, economic, and unquestionably material. Its details undisturbed: peeled paint, chipped plaster, uneven constant usage: a room where people have worked, aged and dented all the angles of respect and time.' The family repossessed and re-enacted in respect of its Home and its rituals. Out of LSD or Trotskyism, usually, the key theme of the 1960s was that of conditioning and the means of seizing and recoding it, and led naturally onto the design of rituals.

> The arteries from the house wind out
> curling their sinews of incident; coil
> the loophole in identity. [...]

> Through the gap the dark can drain
> sucking light motors in, their
> magnetic weight screening the trivial
> domestic triggers.
> (from 'The arteries from the house wind out', in *future exiles*, p.361)

If the hand-kneaded Golems of Catling's poems are the infant body starting from pure primary process, the frequent recording devices are the 'behaviour camera' that allows the infant to store and reproduce familial behaviour; a toxin cured by massive doses of itself. Forget about derivative rituals, conspiracies of priests against the people, comperes of dungeons-and-dragons-style ancient wisdom. The only sort which counts is designing your own rituals from scratch, which is what Catling does. Religion was a failure of the human race accidentally revealing the faculties we can now begin to use.

Several of the poems here are from a part of *Tulpa Index* dealing with a smart dinosaur, *Deinonychus*. The day before, I had read a Ted Hughes poem about a shark (*Megalon karcharodon* in fact) –

> The long Shrine of hunger. Window spectra
> Breaks on the retina. It is the hunger
> Humbles the eye-beam.

> The slime's Great Orme. Stranded, immense Mollusk!
> A carapace of stone, cruciform,
> Sculpted, as are all God's creatures, by hunger.

> Gill-arches high and dry –
> It filters
> The breath off the water's face, the salt airs.
> ('Us He Devours', in *Wolfwatching; Collected Poems* p.774-5)

This suggested that Iain Sinclair, Hughes, Catling, and Reed were not only central poets of the 1970s but also very closely linked by the themes of 'horror' and the 'Gothic'. Hughes [1930-1988] is of course the greatest living English-language poet, I measure Catling's stature by the way something like *Pleiades in Nine* holds up against *Crow* or *Remains of Elmet*. Let's note that the last spurt of the Sinclair reign at Harper Collins was *Red Headed Android*, by Jeremy Reed, in 1992. Catling writes:

> He tried the gas-cylinder walk
> that led him into the fur-nailed
> history.
> In coma
> the instrumentation of legend
> ticked & flickered
> wildly. [...] With his hand he broke
> the neck of the wind.
>   (from 'He tried the gas cylinder walk' from *future exiles*, p. 359)

Surely this could be the classic Reed of *Saints and Psychotics* or *Walk on Through*?

The Gothic precept is that the chase is quite meaningless unless motivated by fear; J.E. Harrison points out that the Greeks explained decay in the grave as the dental spoor of a feeding demon, a Ker or 'blue-black Euronymus'. Necrosis in life lends itself to a similar zoology of fear. The monsters caused the hallucinatory flights of anxiety of the decadent artist – actually vice versa. For Hughes the forms bodies have are the fruit of endless cycles of hunger, tearing at captive body images to appropriate and annihilate their fine dead organs. Perhaps the start point for all four writers was the primacy of art, a mirror process of appropriation and self-annihilation.

Given Catling's main career as a sculptor, it's curious to look at the early sculpture in the British Museum. The technical perfection (implying laws that are real prisons because everyone consents to them) of classical sculpture, in say the fifth century BC, was never excelled and remained a dominant and castrating influence into the 19th century. Some of the Assyrian sculptures (I follow Ekrem Akurgal here) have muscles indicated by curved bands of colour, a stage before the articulation of muscles and folds of robes by the Greeks. Some Assyrian steles, closely related, show a lion pouncing in successive images: a narrative strip. The attempt to make physiology visible through the skin, in the form of exaggerated muscles, is a failure: the inside of the body can only be apprehended through motion, the visible exchange of energy. The choice of 'frozen frame', single-point, images by the Greeks points to the exit line from their marginalising classical splendour: through time-based sculpture. In fact it was cinema which liberated Catling's sculpture; and perhaps, in particular, the cine-ballistics of Peckinpah and Lucien Ballard. And how many scary monsters the Western Asiatics made; dinosaurs touched the public because they were applying for a job, a niche in cosmological space, which already existed.

You give the creature muscles, at once you've got to give it space to move through (or against) and a reason to move. We rely, in frozen static art, on expression and body plan. But body plan is illusory, behaviour can only be apprehended in sequences, in cellular flux rhythmically destroying shape and state. The claws of *Deinonychus* are only meaningful in relation to the flesh they tear and Hughes' wolf's paws are only self-narrating over distance, and in pursuit or evasion: the dangling of a single body in a gallery void is not enough. A quasi-*asomatos*. The solution was to develop systems for marking space, and for depicting time-lapses, known today as performance art. The realisation that the body does not have a 'zero metabolism' but is percoursed by fleeting energies leads to a perception of these energies as autonomous beings and an obsession with naming them and trapping the heat trails of their motions. The classic Catling theme is stalking; delicately, in a hush; as anxiety and hunger spiral out of control on either side. The empty room is a sparse clear path for the energy creature to alight in; the Golem body is the empty flesh that gives it substance. Precisely who is caught and who is the hunter? That is the question.

One of the Gothic themes extrapolated by Reed was the moment of possession by a dead artist, a self-organising spore or spectre lurking in hallowed spaces.

> The haloes first started to appear at the end of an acrid summer, which cooked stains and scars deep into the pavements of the city. Human, vegetable and animal fluids boiled fast to the insomniac grit screen of streets.
> [...]
> Children and derelicts found them first; the panic and laughter drew pilgrims to the backstreets, waste lots and previously ignored penetralia of the city.
> [...]
> Fear hit when the transient spinning dust was identified [...] Each halo composed of a single drug, each in its own orbit of poison
> [...]

[...] They knew these traces, vivacious in their guilt, would outlive
them and their home[.]
(Brian Catling, 'Written Rooms and Pencilled Crimes', xxxii,
in *future exiles*, p.452-3).

The energy demons are perhaps part of the fundamental structure of space,
as their hunger is vacuity itself. Pattern swallows all substance impartially.
The borders of the body are insecure; trance and working of supra-temporal
form permit certain crossings. In Catling, the arrival of the anxiety monster
is also the descent of the God who indwells Romanesque sculpture; as the
sculptor seizes a series of bodies. Possession was of course a figure for the
experience of art itself, a convulsive bout realised by the two puzzles or
dies, worked to narrow tolerances, of the poem-effigy and the audient body
(tooled along certain axes of symmetries and variations) ordered as to state
and shape by its command sequences.

(Further on Catling: articles by Iain Sinclair in *Torn: curtains*, 1973, and
Modern Painters, 1991. Interview in *Parataxis* 6. *Soundings* (1991) describes
his performances. This review first published in *Angel Exhaust* 11, 1995.)

§

David Harsent (1942–) first came to the public eye in the late 1960s in
the company of Ian Hamilton's crew of cultured but faint young men in
The New Review, concerned with 'shy references to personal problems'.
Through resilience and grace, he was able to survive among so much tasteful
distress without being rumbled as someone violent and expressionist. His
public breakthrough – and his artistic self-realisation – came with *Mister
Punch* (1984), which had itself come out of an opera libretto he wrote for
the composer Harrison Birtwhistle. This was the second time Birtwhistle
had set texts about Punch to music, so presumably he chose the theme.
Mister Punch is the total male, his phallus externalised as a huge nose and
the truncheon with which he beats his wife; he is all lies, greed, and rage.
Harsent used this subhuman figure as a tool to prise open sexual relations
and shed a weird but bright light on (precisely) lust, greed, and rage. He
is the first male post-feminist poet; since any number of poets eager to
be loved had responded to feminism by saying, 'I'm lovable and sensitive
and I do the washing-up and love me', but no-one before had accepted
feminist accusations in a forthright way. Harsent certainly isn't providing
any answers, his only task as an artist is to crank up the contradictions to
the point of destabilising the audience. He shows a situation that demands
change.

Moving on to his *Selected Poems*, 'The Windhound' is about a debauched woman, the 'windhound', who is sitting, presumably waiting to pick someone up, in a bar where obscene dialogue is heard.

> The bar-room cirrus is volatile.
> She sifts the odours: Scotch,
> jet-fuel, and something hot
> like camphor.

(Jet fuel is some inadvisable mixture of spirits and beer.) The dialogue is divisive, able to annoy almost everybody; like rock music in this way. It also reminds me of 'You can't always get what you want', by Jagger and Richard: 'I saw her today at the reception, at her feet was a bleeding man; I knew she was going to meet her connection, I could tell by her bloodstained hands.' She, like 'Milady' in a poem from *Dreams of the Dead*, is trying to lead the fast life, among sexual adventurers high on risk and direly afraid of anything less than designer clothes and Olympic-level physical passion.

> The room is a dish of light.
> She goes from hand to hand,
> a rind of canapé
> stuck to her teeth like smegma.
> Now and then she startles herself:
> tipped to the edge of a run
> by the soft white scut
> of a dropped glove
> [...]
> She wants to be a blueprint
> for the well-bred, a skin-flick
> for the pot-valiant.
> (both quotes from 'The Windhound',
>   in *Selected Poems*, 1989, pp92-3)

The phrases are divisive because they put libido in its barest form, and society is based on controlling and even denying that libido. Moral integration is a process that cannot be interesting if it works all the time. Harsent is interested in animal part-selves, agents which are much simpler than real people but also less ambiguous. Compare the poem 'The Analysand', also in *Selected Poems*, where the female speaker dreams she is a hare. I suppose he learned this from Hughes, and the objections to Harsent are largely those also made against Hughes, rock'n'roll, and magazines talking about sex. An artist should walk on fragile ground. No-one is ever going to write an interesting poem about two lovers being nice to each other all the time. Gratification is the most widely shared goal of our consumer society, we have sought liberation from an older social order in its name, but this goal is able to destroy the society nurturing it – by ecological disaster, by breaking up the social compact, by breaking up marriages. Even if sexual repression is necessary to society, sexual repression is being blown apart anyway. Perhaps we have a unique chance now to integrate the various selves in poetry, the several appetites, fantasies, and anxieties, and if poetry fails to do that it will seem Victorian and obsolete.

Punch may have originated as an animus, the 'pure male' figure in Jung's theories, less heard about than the gentle *anima*. Harsent is courageous to field these ideas, since such violent gratification might well scupper the more elusive thrills of poetry. The 'virtualisation' that allows us to enjoy symbols is related to the 'withdrawal' that means we don't fight for cocaine and sex with strangers. If poetry isn't better than cocaine, why bother with it? He uses engorged sex entities as a way of writing about disgust and frustration. His grotesques shed light on statues with their idealized proportions and missing genitalia. Poetry relates to more sensuous art forms as a loss of primary gratifications and their replacement by more intellectual ones. Displacement is a key issue: social integration requires one to displace the desire for sex and money, the problem is to replace them with bonds of loyalty and affection rather than simple repression.

Both 'The Windhound' and 'Milady' are quite long narrative poems. *News from the Front* is a volume-length narrative, although treated as a series of intense, staccato, short exposures. As for writing about sexual behaviour, Harsent doesn't have a moral message which solves all our problems, but he has an exceptional ability to dramatize contentious issues.

§

Jeremy Reed (born 1951, in the Channel Islands) debuted with stunning assurance in 1972; he had, then or shortly later, a regime of writing a poem every day, which led him to complete artistic maturity at the latest in 1973-4, when he composed the poems of *The Isthmus of Samuel Greenberg*. The poet's world view was extreme:

> the metamorphosis is slow [...]
> the victim weightless as a child's shadow
> balanced on an orange ball,
> a displacement;

> and against the night-wall,
> savagely pink with a hare's hind
> legs, pursued with the city's velleities
> is locked in the mirror
> unalterably stooped over a cat's saucer.
>
> (from: 'Infesting', in *Saints and Psychotics, Poems 1973-74,* 1979)

For ten years, he pursued this creative voracity, through half a dozen pamphlets and as many books; invisible, in a literary underground, where the other 'radicals' had wives and jobs; Reed has never had a job except poetry. In about 1982, Reed was subject to a glamorous makeover: exchanging programmatic stylisation for tourist-class bird and flower poems. *Bleecker Street* was the last blast of a long uprising. All trace of conflict or dissonance disappeared from his work; it fluttered away into an affluent world of good taste. What he achieved during the 1970s is permanent and unforgettable. There were many uncollected poems from the earlier, more authentic, phase, a part of which I arranged to be published as *Black Russian Out-takes* (2010).

I don't believe that these exotic words (tabid, telaesthetic, syntonic, etc.) are used because they are the most precise and efficient. The point of using rare or made-up words was to make communication between poet and reader more difficult, making the line shake with a terrible vibration; stressing the uniqueness of the sensations, denying that a fund of shared sensations exists enough to make shared words a reasonable proposal. The exotic words are the dynamic peaks of the poem, screaming with arrogance and alienation. The denatured words vibrate between meaning and blocked autonomy, language almost crumbling under the imagined stress of the reader's moral contempt. They almost offer the poet the desired transformation into a butterfly: the sloughing of the ugly skin of truth, the emergence of a glorious creature, soaked in colour and popularity. 'Malversation of language' is emotional denial of the opinions of other humans. How could the pressure of flight and self-revelation be resolved without breaking the linguistic surface up altogether? The unstated premise of this stylistic rule was a characterological one: that someone shrill and disordered was unreliable. It was possible, for a poet with intuition and determination, to invert this rule and use an unnatural, gaudy, style as a way of expressing painful sensitivity and disorder. Rules of taste, it became apparent, had a hidden sociological component – marginalising a certain sector of the population as 'unsound'; effacing their message before it arrived. Voices were heard at the time condemning Reed for being louche, tawdry, hysterical, gaudy, overbright, shrill, sordid, etc. Today we realise that these qualities are the basis of his appeal.

You may well ask, is it legitimate for a poet to be obscure? Usually, such a self-serving procedure implies vanity, lack of respect for the reader, and, indeed, lack of an interesting message. So often, lack of clarity is a sign of disdain, competing with the reader in an absurd attempt to establish superiority; an opaque code overlaid over a basic apathy and indifference and vacuity. With Reed, this finally does not apply: partly because the stylistic distortions directly signal character and also because of the intensely emotive and explicit nature of the poems, once seen for what they are. In retrospect, it's remarkable how few other male poets of that time were writing about their own emotional lives; the stress on myths and process elaborately deflected attention to quite another sphere.

Hypersensitivity implies inaccurate perceptions, as consciousness is flooded by unbalanced data, and loses data by building barriers against flooding. Moreover, hypersensitivity is, probably, caused by a sense of vulnerability, rather than by abnormally keen perceptual equipment. Such a person would have a resistance to other people's perceptions, so perceiving less. Such a posture always had the potential for advancing into vacuous classicism, as the defence mechanisms became more and more efficient. The resort to 'psychic' messages is an elaborate device of invalidation: any-one who resists your ego-myth is not confronted, but simply dismissed as someone without psychic gifts. A special needs case.

A similar doctrine underlies the re-inhabitation of other writers' works. The official version of this is 'psychic oneness', a special cloak of office of the gifted mind; a coverall against a ruder interpretation, that the poet spends his leisure hours reading biographies of other poets. The presiding spirit is Francis Bacon: a cold eye gazing on human decay, in an odd mixture of documentary and distortion. Reed's character studies reveal the core of the being, not superficial and unmotivated choices of ideas and leisure activities.

To my surprise, a re-reading revealed some traits common with other writers of the 1970s: the preoccupation with mutilation, animals, disturbing attacks on the body image, and re-enactment of the lives of past writers as 'myths' inherent in places, are now oddly close to Sinclair and B. Catling. Looking at Reed's obsessive relating of human experience to the species characteristics of human physiology, illustrated at every step by animals, we notice a resemblance to Ted Hughes. All four writers are close to the horror genre: whether we can sign this off as representing the whole body of unfiltered human experience outside the lit circle of repressive, bourgeois consciousness, or whether we ought to posit some more historically conditioned over-reaction of undermined patriarchy to threats to its body-image and military power, I do not know. 'Murder and mutilation' are acts of punishment, pointing to who knows what line of defence of a power order against transgression. Certainly, this Gothic strand in English poetry of the 1970s (and 1980s) demands assessment. Reed is close to the staples of 'Gothic':

> Where are we going to? I see a hole
> and in it blackened roots of a tree bole
> and staring from that pit a blood-stained owl.
>
> Where are we going to? I do not know.
> The scapegoat sacrificed to Azazel
> left footprints here, the reek of animal.
>
> ... Why did we come here? To divine the dead
> who are unquiet, and would walk the road
> and commit necromancy in a wood.
>
> And should we follow? That is why we're here
> to follow that on every wind we fear
> and dance with iron hooves around the fire.
>
> And you'll not even leave me? Yes I will.
> I see all nations gather at a hill
> and gathered have no reason why they're there.
>   (from 'Riddle of the Oak', in *Straight Lines* 5, 1980)

I was much struck by David Punter's review – in James Lasdun's magazine *Straight Lines* no. 5, which is also where the above poem was printed –of *Bleecker Street*, which I will quote *in extenso*:

> There is a great deal of imagery of light, but its effect is not cheering: typically we see veins and arteries lighting up, showing the lines of inner pain and [...] enabling the viciousness of the world to home in more accurately on its unfortunate victims. Dying fugitives are pursued across endless beaches, their story told in advance: mouths remain perpetually open in the jagged shapes of fear. [...] Reed's gift seems to me to have to do with stasis, with catching the frozen moment and concentrating on it until we hear a slight snap, and the scene has been dislocated from the flux of life, become an icon, often one of deadly portent.

The icons take the form of *objets d'art*, for example a 'Chinese terra cotta snuff bottle'. Punter quotes 'Three Devils Reef':

> I heard him bunched down chattering
> to the ebb-tide, on clinical parole.
> The sea steaming west of Three Devils Reef –
>
> a white alliterative damnation.
> Both sea and sky suddenly moving left;
> the right a black impenetrable wall
>
> that follows his simian agility
> (from *Bleecker Street*, 1980)

and goes on: 'Perhaps the numerous fears which assail Reed's figures are simply manifestations of perceptual shift: as one moves one's eyes, one is perpetually pursued by the 'darkness' of that which is no longer within one's field of vision or control. Thus stasis becomes salvation: but only if not examined for too long. Reed demonstrates for us a maddening geometry: maddening because it denies motion and mind.'

Analysis of Reed's specialised lexicon reveals the following areas of special stress and discolouration:

(1) ARTIFICIAL PARTS OF THE BODY
Transformation. Exchange of one body for another. In saints' lives, the exchange of an earthly corrupt body for a 'glorious body'. In Romantic poetry, the exchange of the poet's sordid life for pure and ethereal works of art. The exchange of a caterpillar form for a butterfly's. The exchange of a man's body for a woman's, by means of attire, makeup, perfume; a message replacing the merely physical. A witch's exchange of human form for an animal's. Half a dozen Reed poems refer to 'incomplete transformations': half hare, half human. The exchange of a style that tells the truth for one that, by marvellous disguise, conceals it.

(2) POISONS
(interpreted as parodic or over-specialized projections of normal biochemicals). 'An optic fissure/ discloses who, left in the mirror/ steamed off acid with toxaemia'. Toxaemia is blood poisoning; more precisely, another organism nourishing itself on your blood. Possible equation of metabolism with illness (as death with pure order).

(3) Distortion; colour as an emanation of the personality
Communication presupposes not only that the two persons share a vocabulary of sensations, but also that enough mutual esteem exists to make the exchange possible. The fantasy of transformation sets out from the weary sensation of rejection. Superstition is a trope for despair of reality: a belief in the impossible.

(3b) Telepathy
communication secret from outsiders, messages not restricted by hegemonic codes. Reading poetry is a special way of communicating with the dead; the figures of Samuel Greenberg, Hart Crane, Kit Marlowe, etc., appear frequently as ideal social partners, in a way which almost denies the authenticity of contact between the living. Being possessed by the thoughts of an admired Poet is close to rejecting the body one lives in, in favour of another.

(4) Externalisation
Typically, emotions are expressed, not as states of mind, but as actual physical changes. This prevents the reader from dismissing them as unimportant and immature. Animals are a form of this physical change. The fabulous interior of the body visualized as mythical and exciting animals. Emotions presented as a neo-zoology. One form of message. Death, of course, is the most extreme example of this.

The *elimination of choice* is a basic tenet of this poetry. Temperament as genetic makeup. The possibility that emotions are due to interactions or imitation is scrupulously effaced. Yet, envy is the driving force behind the butterfly myth.

(5) Inorganic
The purposeful behaviour of dead things, or the feigned death of living things; a basic figure in Reed's work. Hysteria (a quality of saints and psychotics) perhaps causes this violence of nature, while the human is numb in shock or trance. Further, the state of becoming a poem is equated with death. The poet apparently longs to become simply a pattern, something static and incorruptible by dint of the information contained in every fibre. Suicide is the ultimate externalisation, turning the Poet's life into an object or text.

As death is equated with integrity, so the most alive things are often disgusting and teeming: 'Yellow thumb stains/ disfigure the wallpaper and a basin/ swims with maggotal food'.

Reed is obviously the most gifted poet of his generation. Reed's own biography is a difficult myth to publicise, since his decision, after he had perfected the most extreme and affecting of styles, to give it all up because he couldn't stand the isolation any more. The apparent self-revelation of his numerous volumes of the 1980s was perhaps the offering of a star personality to a numerous audience. Acceptance of the projective role of star meant that he moved out of the mainstream into a more disturbing, perverse, and totally Reedian universe.

§

ADDITION 2016

The insertion of this piece on Gothic writers was not meant to say that the whole of British poetry became Gothic at that time, as malicious reviewers pretended to think. The Gothic thing gets us away from the mainstream: underground opposition, as Harsent was clearly a mainstream poet in terms of where he published and who he associated with. At the same time, the Gothic style in its entirety was a breach with the 'standard poem', and even presents the 'night' side, the aspects of desire or physiology normally repressed. It is and was a minority thing in which excessively personal material, the stuff of delusions, was allowed to seize the stage. The energy of Gothic at a certain moment represents the intensity of repression in the conventional world and is a necessary comment on suavity. The artistic success of poets like Hughes, Peter Redgrove, or Harsent does not persuade us that the mainstream is desirable: rather it underlines how you had to break the rules in order to achieve anything real.

What is the effect on the individual awareness of excess availability of information on the bases of behaviour and awareness? Narcissism can fly off into a malaise of preoccupation with the grotesque, sick and misshapen; the flawed shape in the mirror may be the origin of the 1970s Gothic style. If dwelling on one feature destroys its proportion to the others, this may be the origin of the anatomical distortion of monsters; as excess concentration on the individual, outside the social texture, produces a moral monster, the Gothic dandy. Advances in optics, making mirrors more powerful and seductive, make distortion more fluent and appalling.

Our period did produce a return to narrative, as the allure of high uncertainty, and of the new cinematography, or cine-ballistics, produced a new wave of Gothic violence. Narratives or near-narratives appear in books, of around 1970 to 1985, by D.M. Black, Barry MacSweeney, David Harsent, and Ken Smith. Indeterminacy manifests itself at the level of the body image, subjected to monstrous alterations, perforations, and translations. The tendency is to write a static narrative in which there is no succession of events but only the revelation of the existential situation of an individual. This is close to a sculpture, as in Catling's work, where the drama is an anatomy, and raises urgent questions about narrative and internalisation.

The 1970s:
Fragmentation of the Grounds of Debate

Some good books of the 1970s:

1970
W.S. Graham, *Malcolm Mooney's Land*;
Emyr Humphreys, *Ancestor Worship*;
Ted Hughes, *Crow*;
John Riley, *What Reason Was*.

1971
Norman MacCaig, *Selected Poems*;
George Mackay Brown, *Fishermen with Ploughs*;
Geoffrey Hill, *Mercian Hymns*;
Roy Fisher, *Matrix, The Cut Pages*;
J.H. Prynne, *Brass*;
Paul Evans, *February*;
Barry MacSweeney, *Our Mutual Scarlet Boulevard*.

1972
Ken Smith, *Work, Distances. Poems*;
Paul Gogarty, *Snap Box*.

1973
Adrian Stokes, *Selected Poems* (in a Penguin Modern Poets);
Anthony Thwaite, *Inscriptions*;
Gerard Casey, *South Wales Echo*;
Edwin Morgan, *From Glasgow to Saturn, The Whittrick*;
Peter Redgrove and Penelope Shuttle, *The Hermaphrodite Album*;
J.P. Ward, *From Alphabet to Logos*;
David Chaloner, *Chocolate Sauce*;
David Wevill, *Where the Arrow Falls*.

1974
David Jones, *The Sleeping Lord*;
Flora Garry, *Bennygoak and Other Poems*;
Anthony Thwaite, *New Confessions*;
J.H. Prynne, *Wound Response*;
Allen Fisher, *Place* (four volumes, published 1974-81).

1975
Glyn Jones, *Selected Poems*;
F.T. Prince, *Drypoints of the Hasidim*;
Peter Redgrove, *Sons of My Skin* (selected poems 1954-74);
John James, *Striking the Pavilion of Zero*;
Allen Fisher, *long shout to kernewek*;
Anthony Barnett, *Blood Flow*;
Iain Sinclair, *Lud Heat*;
Ulli Freer, *Rooms* (1975-82; never collected in volume form).

1976
George Mackay Brown, *Winterfold*;
Peter Levi, *Collected Poems 1955-75*;
Colin Simms, *No Northwestern Passage*;
Brian Catling, *Pleiades in Nine*;
Jeremy Reed, *The Isthmus of Samuel Greenberg*.

1977
W.S. Graham, *Implements in Their Places*;
Edwin Morgan, *The New Divan*;
Ted Hughes, *Gaudete*;
Judith Kazantzis, *Minefield*;
Anthony Barnett, *Fear and Misadventure / Mud Settles*;
Martin Thom, *The Bloodshed the Shaking House*.

1978
Geoffrey Hill, *Tenebrae*;
Ted Hughes, *Cave Birds*;
Roy Fisher, *The Thing About Joe Sullivan*;
Ken Smith, *Fox Running*;
Peter Abbs, *For Man and Islands*;
Philip Jenkins, *On the Beach with Eugène Boudin*;
Andrew Crozier, *High Zero*;
Alexander Hutchison, *Deep Tap Tree*;
Jeffrey Wainwright, *Heart's Desire*;
Barry MacSweeney, *Black Torch, (part 1)*, *Odes*;
Tom Lowenstein, *Filibustering in Samsara*;
Paul Brown, *Meetings and Pursuits*;
John Ash, *Casino*;
Tony Lopez, *The English Disease*; *Change*;
Brian Marley, *Springtime in the Rockies*.

1979
W.S. Graham, *Collected Poems 1942-77*;
George Mackay Brown, *Wreck of the Archangel*;
Ted Hughes, *Remains of Elmet, Moortown*;
Iain Sinclair, *Suicide Bridge*;
Paul Evans, *The Manual for the Perfect Organization of Tourneys*;
Paul Gogarty, *The Accident Adventure*;
Jeremy Reed, *Saints and Psychotics*.

The absence of *any* anthologies of any worth is striking, and symptomatic of the cultural disillusionment and violence that gave the decade its face.

THE COLLAPSE OF CONSENSUS

Politically, the decade saw a breakdown of the liberal consensus, that recognition of immanent class conflict and the institutional containment of it which had endured since the wage-productivity deals of the First World War. The apocalypse of the first Thatcher administration was only the climax of the 1970s. The tradition of 'bourgeois guardianship' (in the words of Roy Fisher, 'What I resist […] is the connotation of what is for me bourgeois – the social democratic outlook of bourgeois guardianship… I'm deeply sceptical about that point of view and about that view of social structure.') had expressed itself in poetry as a featureless *parlando* tone, devoid of artistic interest but reassuring in its firm rejection of the individual's emotions and desires. Harold Wilson and Edward Heath's problems in getting capital and labour to sign up to a deal were paralleled by the constant collapse of any poetic centre that was neither marginalised nor banal. Since the victims of boundless struggle were bound to be the weak, it is surprising to find the weak as prominent attackers of the social contract. There was ever less consensus for the non-critical poet to be the spokesman of.

The 1970s have now emerged as the classic period of modern British poetry: when the breakthrough paid off in finished poems rather than wild glimpses of an imaginary freedom, before the hangover set in, before the growth of the media made slickness and inauthenticity universal. This revolutionary-classic era was the fallout from the explosion of 1968; productive of neo-religious sects as well as intelligent radicalism; the contrast between the New Left and the post-rationalist, consumerist, drug-oriented faction was a rift right from the start. A radical expansion of the sensory possibilities open to the imagination blew up the boundaries of poetry, poets only needed obstinacy and truth to themselves to permit expanded consciousness. The initial velocity was very great, and as each poet travelled a great way they became distant from each other, as well as far from their point of origin. Reviewing failed to keep up. In this post-explosive geography, almost all serious poetry is uncelebrated. An extraordinary number of good poets came from the generation born in the 1940s – or, more tellingly, the generation formed by the climaxing 1960s.

Heath was the first Conservative Prime Minister to invite the unions to discuss prices and incomes policy; James Callaghan was the last Prime Minister to do so. But how could you solve disputes between such polarised and intractable factions as labour and capital, feminism and traditional, without extending the debate to issues that were so primary and so complex that they were outside the terms of the deadlocked negotiations? Visual art and poetry of the period attacked basic cognitive assumptions because the ones in force had brought about a deadlock, like trench warfare. Maybe that was the only point of the modernist poetry of the 1970s. Maybe that was the only point of expanding consciousness. That was the chance, right there. Once it was lost then things were bound to get on to 'There is no such thing as society' and solving wage disputes by deploying battalions of police. Where debate is the mediator of sovereignty, it is peculiarly subject to overload, seizure, and disruption. Social war broke out because people wanted to suppress the link between their social power and their assumptions about psychology.

Both Heath and Wilson believed that modernisation would solve the class tensions by increasing the size of the national wealth that was there to be fought over. Both of them, probably, knew that it would have to be the other way around. The term 'modernisation', in the poetics of the time, is a token defined by national political debate. The new language of 1968 was aimed at solving the problem that debate about legislation, social and economic policy was couched, because of its complexity, in terms that most of the population couldn't follow. New media made information cheap and offered the phantom of a true popular sovereignty. It's ironic that this impulse eventually made poetry so complex that most of the population couldn't follow it. As we know, what happened in the U.K. was sub-modernisation.

As for poetry, two editorials from the flagship *Poetry Review* read: 'In British poetry today there is no mainstream middle-of-the-road established kind of taste, except in the murderous dreams of censors and government financial controllers.' (Eric Mottram, 66.1, 1975) and

Charm and heavyweight gentility roamed the galleries of art. [...]
It was death. Nothing. Zero. Visions of the half-mind, Advanced
Fool Farms, Unvarying Twitter [...] I came away realising that
contemporary art of any kind must inevitably be offensive to the
majority of otherwise intelligent citizens. The kind of poetry I
like is one which takes this offensiveness seriously and tries to
understand it.
(Douglas Dunn, 68.1, 1978)

THE END OF THE 1960s DREAM

1968 had, by 1978, disappeared from view, unable to influence the
course of events; a traumatic event for a wave that had thrown away every
possession except the future. Accounts of the waves of disenchantment
and regression to personal preoccupations in books on Italian history (*il
riflusso*, dated to 1976) and German (*der deutsche Herbst*, of 1976) and
French (the ebbing of revolutionary ardour dated to 1975) suggest that the
comedown was common to all the democracies of Europe. The decline of
the counterculture began before 1977, even if only a short while before.
Both Martin Booth, in his book on modern poetry, and Barry MacSweeney,
in an interview of December 1974 with Eric Mottram, state that there was
a very sharp decrease of attendance at readings in about 1974: 'Audiences
now are just miniscule compared to what they were [...] Now you're lucky
to get twelve people in a poetry reading even at a university'.

These seem to have been shrinking in scope ever since I began reading
poetry. Booth dates the collapse to the winter of 1975-6. Note that this
decline preceded the traditionalist coup at the Poetry Society. No doubt
MacSweeney's interpretation is the right one, that in the second half of the
1960s the youth market identified poetry with rock music, as part of a big
communal feeling, which would in time take over Society; when poetry
proved not to partake of those reservoirs of wholeness and dullness, the
audience stayed away. There was a fearful dip in the number of magazines,
and probably of readers too; Booth mentions the steep rise in the price of
paper (starting in the commodities boom of 1972 and continuing with
the post-1973 inflation) as a lethal factor; it was most lethal from 1976
to 1981. The demise of the publishers Trigram, Rapp and Whiting, Cape
Goliard, and Fulcrum simplified and emptied the landscape. A hostile critic
would interpret the 'Mottramite' group at the Poetry Society as occupying
the institutions once the mass support has evaporated. The poets on the
Council, or represented by those members, were in any case evolving a

much more complex kind of poetry, which would have provoked a sharp disjunction with the audience.

But MacSweeney says further,

> There were hundreds of magazines in the late Sixties, weren't there, and most of them have died for one reason and another – the dream is over, and most of them went bankrupt – but what was left was good, because it was the hard core of people who really wanted to do it, who were doing it well, who were really interested and wanted to keep in touch. So that's why it's healthier now [1974] than it ever really was.

The 1960s were an era of conversion experiences and so infantility, inchoate fertility that during the 1970s matured into permanent artistic achievements. One sensitive area is simplicity. MacSweeney possibly felt that the simplicity of his early poetry, in his first best-selling book, was an anti–middle-class protest. But, in other poets, simplicity has been soft and queasy, a grab at commerciality; giving way, of course, to the wishes of bourgeois editors and publishers. It suits everyone if working-class writers come over as gormless and ignorant, and you can make much more money out of them like that. So that the complexity of MacSweeney's later work, some of which has classic status, is also a protest. This is what he explains in the interview, that when he was 22 he grew up artistically and the audience vanished.

BELIEVE NAEBODIE BUT OORSELS

The feeling of being overwhelmed by the pressure of new art ideas was diagnostic. No-one was an expert on the scene – the screens were not responding. There may be a simple physical and volumetric basis to this. *Poet's Yearbook* for the year ending June 1978 lists 908 titles by 627 different poets. No way were the organs of the poetry industry set up to process this kind of volume. I think you have a stratum of experts producing expert talk which is completely based on bad conscience. I don't think there were any tough cultural critics on the underground who really knew what was going on – they didn't know either. More adequate was the response, 'Gosh. Wow. That's really amazing.' I have spent a lot of time sifting through the prose of the time and I'm really sure that no-one knew what was going on. Forty years have gone by and it is now possible to look back and say 'Gosh. Wow. That was really amazing.' If a lot of the action of the time was on the lines of 'my subjectivity is being repressed and your view of me is subjective and inadequate', there is an economic basis for this.

Nixon's mishandling of wartime budget deficits led to a commodities boom which was the signal for an oil-price hike. UK inflation reached 25% a year. The employers were really happy to fix this by freezing pay and effectively reducing workers' pay by 25%, and politicians were happy about it too. If you accept that kind of cut you know you have given a signal that they can cut your pay by 25% again the following year. So the papers were full of stories about strikes and inflation every day, and these slid sideways into questions of dignity, as: we are worth 35 pounds a week because of our value to the community. This theme was just everywhere. It was the prose basis for cultural talk in which my subjective value is more than you want to give me.

I don't think any debate was taking place about poetry, at least not in the printed record. I don't think the official critics were reading the radical poetry at all. Maybe they attacked it by proxy, but really the debate and assimilation of the new poetry had not yet happened. As the jibes of the Left about compromise angered the Right and made them vindictive in their denial of the new, the division between these two groups became too clear in the 1970s, and produced group solidarity and hostility. Due to the collapse of a common taste and standards of prose discourse, the prose part of the poetry world, in reviews and theorising, became remarkably ineffective as a map or record of artistic activity.

A number of books and articles claiming that the radical poetics of the 1970s was not happening irritated people and provoked the turn into investigating the fabric of language itself, looking for the naked grounds untouched beneath the stratum of deceit and misrepresentation. The experience of being described by your enemies became familiar, bringing an emotional withdrawal from shared discourse. The poet T.S. Law said, slightly later, '[i]t's aboot tyme we began to believe naebodie but oorsels.' The language world of bourgeois guardianship collapsed: although the deposed bishops went on saying, 'We can give objective descriptions of you but of course you can't give objective descriptions of us because you are subjective and partial and marginal. We understand you. We are impartial. We are the authorised version.' This collapse went *pari passu* with the crisis of the prices and incomes policy, and of shared standards and terms of reference in academic life. The foundations of humanism were shaken.

We now see the regime of the dual optic: objective and unsympathetic for the enemies, warm and glamorising for the in-group. Does anyone here have a unified optic? Since I began voting, publishing poetry, etc., in the 1970s, it would be fruitless to claim that I can judge modern poetry objectively; as no-one can. It remains to crack out the structures of subjectivity.

ANGLO-WELSH POETRY IN THE 1970S

The decade saw the arrival of Emyr Humphreys (1919–) as a poet, the best poems of Raymond Garlick (1926-2011), fine work by Roland Mathias (1915-2007), a prolific flow from Anthony Conran (1931-2013), and even the return of Glyn Jones (1905-95). Recall that all these poets except Jones, like Saunders Lewis, David Jones, and the Welsh-language poet Bobi Jones, were ardent Christians (four of them Catholic); their intellectual milieu was liberal Protestant theology (or Jacques Maritain) and mediæval Welsh poetry, not structuralism and critical theory. Both Humphreys and Mathias were part of an age-group of students of ardent nationalist and Christian beliefs formed in the late 1930s, as a response to the Depression. The younger poets mentioned, who were by 1976 approaching 50, were the generation that absorbed, in the 1950s, beliefs in irony, self-restraint, moral sobriety, rigour and clarity of style, and Christianity, which were obligatory in England and America at that time. Their poetry possessed those virtues, out of time with the world. What is missing in Wales is the formal breakout of the 1960s: the distributional fact that peripheral nationalism was incompatible with formal innovation, as badgers are incompatible with hedgehogs, suggests that they were competing for resources, this because they were similar and wanted the same things. The exceptional concrete poets Peter Finch and John Powell Ward were indignantly rejected by reviewers for not being Welsh enough. (I heard a terrific lecture by Matthew Jarvis in 2012 where he described a whole school of Welsh concrete poets in around 1974.) Celtic nationalists were as revolutionary as anybody else when they were being anti-capitalist and against the government or any authority which promoted the existing power order, but by deifying the national past also overrated and elevated above criticism living members of the national past, whose ideas and poetic values could be narrow, ineffective, and stultifying. This drama of past and future may explain why there are so few poets born in Wales since 1940 who can write good poems.

What were the shafts that articulated poetry to political principles? Linden Peach refers to 'continuity, ancestry, culture and identity'. Hooker states 'Time and again [...] we find intimations of an order encompassing self and community, living and dead, man and nature, man and God.' Some of the founding metaphors of the Anglo-Welsh poem are rootedness, rocks, the *bro*, the corrupt capital city, the hermit, and the apocalyptic end of society. Some of the staple gestures are piety towards the ancestors, acts of respect to the life of someone of low prestige, preserving lost or undesirable knowledge, defying the Centre. What these ritual acts seem like to an outsider is anxiety, explained by the wrath shown by figures vested with patriarchal authority. Anxiety about saying the wrong thing has expelled the aesthetic.

Hooker cites Conran's line, 'A third person poetry can no longer enact a civilization' – from 'Ars Poetica', in the book *Spirit Level*. The ancestry of this is Martin Buber's *Dialogic Principle*; Buber (1878-1965) was Jewish, but wrote in German, and his ideas formulated about 1910-20 (*I and You*, 1923; *Dialogue*, 1932; *The Dialogic Principle* collected 1953) were absorbed into the mainstream of Protestant theology. This reduction of the world to the first and second persons is a parallel to the 1960s radical attack on organised knowledge and the discourse of the State. I-You resembles direct address; the camera shows incessant presence and has no third person: either you're there or you aren't. The rejection of all government institutions seems to mean the death of abstraction, as a correlate.

Humphreys' sequence *Ancestor Worship* (published as a separate volume in 1970 but also available in Penguin Modern Poets 27) makes positive statements of nationalist ideals, implies another unstated layer, but tilts the overall message so far towards pessimism and irresolution that no reassurance can be found. He is almost modern in the dissonance that the poems, if we try to project a single shape behind them, reveal. In poem one, 'Ancestor Worship', the dead are motionless, their words are still alive; they are ghosts in words; grandparents divided fields and bequeathed the land as property, but towns disturb these sacrosanct boundaries. Vikings, or perhaps Saxons, arrive; ancestors 'carved metrical systems out of their own flesh'. (I can't assign a meaning to this line.) The air still speaks their language, which calls out to be spoken. This is 'blood and soil', more or less. Poems three, four, and nine recite the hermit trope, not just as the prophecy for a Wales in which people abandon the old ways, but also a sick and pessimistic understanding of history, as the pure man withdraws from society into the wilds; this is the last projection of the cult of smallness. The beautiful poem eighteen, 'Master Plan', describes the bloodless reconquest of the whole island by the Welsh, reversing the events of the 5th century that gave rise to the hermit trope, with Gildas. Humphreys mocks his own fantasy by giving it to a figure half derelict half demiurge. He lays down his rage, sliding his demands into the merely aesthetic. Humphreys delicately fails quite to occupy either the position of a detached artist drawing a character who takes impossible fantasies for politics, or of a firebrand who, speaking for himself, shouts out unrealistic and enraged wishes; he oscillates between the two, twisting but trapped.

In this poetry as a whole, social control is throttling the other functions of formal speech. It was the role played by the clergy, which was skirmished over in the early decades of the 20th century, and that literature finds intractable and irresistible. The population has migrated out into affluence and secularism. The failure of Anglo-Welsh poetry is intertwined with an excessive regard to duty and moral injunctions, and insufficient self-expression, playfulness, or beauty; the clerical inheritance. All the same, it would be callow to assert that literature must avoid imposing any type of social control; since adultery, alcoholism, breaking promises, drug abuse, and not working hard, will create devastation however much they are the result of freedom. Poetry is caught between Saturday night and Sunday morning. People deserve some pleasure between two weeks of hard work; poetry will cease to exist if it becomes just a bleak call to duty. Somehow the Christians and conservatives seem to have redefined self-expression and formal experiment as selfish and narcissistic; poets who have accepted this have just wasted their lives; I hope that when pointing this out I don't just seem like a stern voice of social control.

There is a scene in Daniel Owen's great Methodist novel *Hunan-gofiant Rhys Lewis* where the hero is in the study of his teacher at the (Nonconformist) Theological College at Bangor, the core of the modern university, looking at the venerable man's splendid library of theology. The striking thing is that the great figures are all 16th-century; Welsh nonconformism looked back towards that era as the time of classics and heroes. A craving for the identifiably Welsh draws you towards folk art, the aristocratic praise poetry of the *cywyddau*, Protestant theology, and hymns. All of these point us towards the sixteenth century. All structures rich in calories, if you like, which offer resistance and have ornamental logic. Pastiche and ornamentalism are the disaster looming over nationalist Welsh writers, who have to struggle to reach the 20th century, or to persuade their readers that this is a good idea.

If you read books about modern theology, it is striking how original thought never seems to come from England, which produces excellent textbooks, editions of texts, histories, syntheses of religion with social work and politics; anything that involves hard work and selflessness. All the stars are German, sometimes Swiss-German or even German-American. This is so much like the human sciences, where the English stand philosophically in awe of the French and the Germans, and the prestige of import goods is sky-high. The inability with abstract thought applies as much to the Welsh, Irish, and Scots; perhaps just slightly less to the Scots. Wales is on the periphery of a radiant Protestant world, but there is no Welsh contribution to theology; they are too pious. Scottish theology is a kind of substitute warfare. The various Protestant churches of Britain may resemble each other more than they would care to admit. I am too ignorant to explain the origin of this role distribution, but there it is. The rise of speculation in the 1960s broke very deep-seated rules, and people have cooperated to hush it up afterwards. I would question whether you can write modern poetry without fluency in the world of ideas. The term rootedness seems to offer us the denial of conscious choice, provoking the speculation that the reality offered to our senses is ambiguous, and thought consists of the construction and exploration of possibilities. This ambiguity is 'fixed' by perceptual blocks. Perhaps abstract thought, alienation, and modern art are found in the same locations, where social control breaks down; Anglo-Welsh literature is the rejection of these. But as soon as two ideas are competing, life becomes gay and interesting. The stone, as gravestones, megaliths, rocks in the sea, crags, castles, geology, is a favourite image. Adjectives suitable for stones are often applied to venerated wrathful patriarch figures. The stone resists inscription. In symbolic terms, this asserts 'I'm not going to pay any attention to your arguments. You are the wrong sort of person.' It is perhaps not a rough block but a perceptual block. If the arguments for nationalism were unambiguous, the other 88% of the Welsh electorate wouldn't lend their voices to other political ideals; if 'region, culture, history, and identity' were taken as hypotheses demanding proof, they could give rise to interesting poetry. R.S. Thomas has an extraordinary sense of doubt, but the movement of argument and rhythm in his poetry is extraordinarily dull; if this highly intelligent man had had someone else intelligent to argue with, he could have been a great poet. Instead, we have someone glowering, steadfast, execrating.

Garlick's important poems are in *Collected Poems 1946-86*; Mathias's *Selected Poems 1944-79* came out in 1983; Emyr Humphreys' poem-cycle *Ancestor Worship* came out in 1970, *Landscape* in 1976, *The Kingdom of Brân* in 1979. Hooker's essays on Welsh poetry are collected in *The Presence of the Past* and Conran's book is *The Cost of Strangeness*. Reference is made to these throughout.

English Poets

'I wish that this heart/Might stare into water/And love what it sees'. Jeffrey Wainwright (1944–) born into a working-class family in the Potteries, was educated thanks to the 1944 Education Act and the expansion of the Universities, and has followed an academic career in EngLit. He has published cautiously; the *Selected Poems* (1985) adds half a dozen precious poems to *Heart's Desire* (1978), but it was not until 1993 that we saw a new book, *The Red Haired Pupil*. Characteristic in Wainwright is a combination of melodrama and absence of interpretation. When he writes about the Battle of Jutland or a little mill-girl drowned in a mill-stream, the subject could be drawn from Victorian prints. When he writes about the Battle of Mousehole Heath and the Thomas Müntzer-led peasant revolt of 1523-4, these events have a latent teleology even though Wainwright chooses not to lay it out (or is even unable to, within his peculiar verse movement). When you watch poorly armed peasants being mowed down in their tens of thousands by professional and heavily-armed soldiers, there is only one way you can react. Even Norman Tebbit would be a socialist if he looked at these pictures. Wainwright is certainly interested in this pathos, and not in 'laying bare cognitive processes' in the way that John Ash or Roy Fisher might be. He isn't showing a 'revisionist view' of ruling-class brutality and the resistance of the masses; what view would that be? He writes about emotive events (which include crises) with a curious stillness, which is his kind of soulfulness:

> The trees in grief
> Their hearts display
> Grand winter takes
> With every hand
> Deep in the love
>
> Of his own demand
> Arrogant thief
> Arrogant thief
> The winter rouses
> All my grief
>   (from 'Five Winter Songs')

I use the word soulful; Wainwright uses language like a song, accumulating intensity by repetition and by scantness of images; not like poetry, which moves and defines itself through new information. His object-choices are like those of folksongs; they are always inner and outer at the same time. We can speak of a pictorial method, of how his syntax (which never moves forward but aims at steady contemplation) has the problem of lacking process, of dissolving the 'picture' so as to represent the experience of change.

It's possible to think that history and class relations – his chosen field – are not his destined subject; he seems more drawn to a boundless suspended feeling. This unconscious resolution almost made more poetry impossible. It's very striking that he devotes nine pages (of his *Selected Poems*) to the experience of being in water; this weightlessness oddly coincides with the stillness of his most tragic poetry, as if being wrapped in depression (as a protection against grief) had led on to being immersed. This relates somehow to the drowning sailors of 'Three Poems on the Battle of Jutland 1916':

> He dies screaming
> In broad fathoms among
> Coal shovels and scalded stokers
> Suddenly washed of their dust.
>
> The scrupulous historian tells
> Of six survivors. One thousand
> And twenty-one went
> Scrambling down.

Of the 19 poems (by the count of the contents pages) in *Selected Poems*, two are about swimming and the sea, three are about drowning, and another has two mentions of swimming. Even in 'Thomas Müntzer', we find the epigraph 'Doubt is the Water, the movement to good and evil. Who swims on the water without a saviour is between life and death': and the odd detail:

> In the pond the cold thick water clothes me.
> I live with the timorous snipe, beetles
> And skaters, the pike smiles and moves with me.

Only Wainwright could treat Müntzer from the point of view of him living in a pond. I am inclined to suspect that the water imagery has to do with the link between the fluids in the body and the fluids outside it; compare

> [...] the purity
> Of metal – the beauty of blood falling.
> Spilt it is refreshed, it freshens also
>
> The soil which when we turn it will become
> Paradise

with 'They poison wells/ And throw fire down the holes where people hide',
a couple of pages later. The moment of bursting and liquids overstepping
their bounds seems important to Wainwright:

> The blossom I caught
> In a yellow jug,
> But that then slipped my hand –
> Upon the flag below
> A single sound.
> Pearls and red drops
> From all the fragments flow.

His imagery works at the unconscious level, so that it is naturally close to
poetry of religion, love, and revolution, which draws on the same stratum.
The state of being 'suspended' is reminiscent of the term 'schweben' (hover,
i.e. in a weightless state), important in 17th-century German mysticism.
Alterations in the position of the body, and in its relationship to referents
such as gravity and ground, shift the experiential basis that holds the ego
and the sense of self. He reminds me of Welsh prophetic verse and of
hymns, as well as of 'The Pentecost Castle', by Geoffrey Hill.

Penelope Shuttle's (1947–) interesting work is found in two volumes:
The Hermaphrodite Album (1973) and *The Orchard Upstairs* (1980). The
former was co-written with Peter Redgrove and one can't separate their
contributions. The composite identity of the hermaphrodite author acts
to undermine excessive notions of the authorial personality, because the
book forms one seamless whole. One could try and work out who wrote
what, but I think this would be artistic vandalism. Shuttle was excluded
both from *British Poetry Since 1945* and *the new british poetry*, alarmingly,
since she is a difficult and worthwhile poet. The first step is the quality of
dreams:

> *What have I been?*
>
> The portrait of a lady said to be queen
> Spectral days between January and March
> An estampie dance in the frost
> Movements of a Jerusalem puppet
> A ship's bestiary
> My mother's needlework
> One orange tree in the forest
> A stalactic shell

A nun's abacus
A cage of small barbaric birds
   (from 'Ashtaroth')

(*Estampie* is a 13th-14th century musical form based on dance rhythms).
Again:

What do you want?
Do you want a wax candle?
Do you want water?
Do you want clothes and shoes?
Do your sisters want any needles and threads?
Do the windows hurt you?
Will you shoot ghost-crabs with your silver gun?
(from 'The Ice Yacht')

It is impossible for me to discuss this rationally in prose. Actually I
suspect that step two or three is a New Age farrago of tendentious systems
interpreting and abusing the unconscious. Shuttle may actually have got
into print in 1967, but she has to be counted as part of the Women's
Liberation Movement which began in 1970, and all her poetry can be
interpreted either through feminist ideas or through Jungian and New Age
ideas which blossomed at much the same time (and much to the disgust
of the Marxist cadres of the Movement). The probable reason why Shuttle
isn't a major poet is that the primary dream material isn't organised by the
will, and the rational, volitional, strata that administer it later in the cycle
are not of her devising or steering, but taken from the prose textbooks. The
poems come from the dreams of the night but recycle the evening class
that preceded it.

The endless parataxis of these poems is worrying. It evokes either
someone gazing in wonder at a dream landscape and identifying primary
things about it, or else a complete block about thinking which reflects itself
in a primitive syntactic and rhythmic organisation.

Shuttle is a pioneer in writing about domestic space as something
dreamlike, mythical, and disturbing; in describing family life in genuinely
imaginative terms rather than in awkward paraphrases of sociological tracts.
The stress is on removing rational repression, and what comes out vindi-
cates the imagination as an inseparable human faculty, a process inevitable
wherever there are human dwellings. The problem comes in relating
the various dream-objects to real events; some of them are illuminating
of what the character really wants, and trap and make visible emotional

atmospheres, but others are not, and then the evasion of reason seems like a way of hiding what is going on and reducing literature to a fairy-tale without a plot.

The Orchard Upstairs is entirely about menstruation. This was worth doing. The contradiction between dream material and programmatic rational intent leaves the middle ground razed, evacuated. At the same time the obstinate treatment of the mental equivalents of a physiological event (one of some complexity) calls into question the physiological bases of the 'shared' symbolic world of literature. Drunkenness, for example, is one of the classic subjects of poetry. Symbols are in part the discourse of the unconscious, and consequently of the body. Pushing back the barriers of silence in this area, and asserting one's right to be ill, reduces inequality within the household. It is progressive because it reduces stress and guilt. Migraines coinciding with menstruation may not be mechanically due to disturbances of blood pressure, but to the ambiguity of a powerful 'pressure' to do housework and look after children, with an equally overwhelming need to lie down and do nothing. Such ambiguity in the individual is the projection of an equivocation by the whole family. The household can cure this stress illness just by altering its rules. The verbal realm exists to treat such questions.

EARL'S COURT

The 1976 affair at the Poetry Society is a murky one, in which the several discrepant versions can never be integrated (although Peter Barry's *Poetry Wars: The Battle of Earl's Court* has shed light on many aspects). Roughly, it goes like this. The Poetry Society, with its 1,200 members, was financially dependent on the Arts Council, constitutionally dependent on its membership. It owned *Poetry Review*, which fee-paying members received free, and a building in Earl's Court. Members liked to think that membership allowed them to be published in the magazine. While in the 1950s the *Review* had been genteel, reactionary, anti-intellectual, and even anti-art, from about 1964 it modernised drastically under the editorship of Derek Parker. This connected with a modern party that included some of the members and, by 1971, most of the committee.

From 1971 Eric Mottram, a lecturer in American Studies at King's College, London, edited the *Review* and published largely English modernist poetry. This provoked the formation of a small, perhaps tiny, Reform Group, who were opposed to anything except rhymed regular verse; their aim was to eliminate Mottram (and the other modern voices of the

Council of 21, elected by the members) and make the modern age shut up and go away. A third group, of mainstream poets, also launched a protest, essentially about not being published in *Poetry Review*. The Arts Council was unhappy at funding a client that was noisily split, was alerted to problems with financial records and other things, and set up two inquiries into the activities of the Poetry Society (not the Reform Group). Because their funding was so high, quite small noises from the Arts Council could induce stress or even terror. The elections of June 1976 saw a loss of some seats held by Mottramites on the 21-strong Council, but not a success for the Reform Group. In March, 1977, the 14 modernist members of the Council all resigned, in protest against the Arts Council's pressure on them. Subsequently, Mottram's contract as editor expired.

The significance of the events is the decline of authority, or of deference. It was hardly likely that 1,200 people would like the same poem. What was specific to the 1970s, with the dissent caused by the breakdown of the prices and income structure due to the oil price hike, was the willingness of dissenters to protest and to demand the overthrow of editors and panel members. What we see is the vexed conservatives being much more subversive and irreconcilable and damaging than the stylistic rebels. This was also a sign of the times. In a way it is unfair that later editors could produce terribly bad issues of *Poetry Review* without anyone protesting and publishing pamphlets. Protest went out of fashion after 1979. Mottram was a victim of democracy and political activism, as well as being a great editor.

The idea that the Arts Council had artistic reasons for threatening to withdraw its grant (thus going beyond its remit) does not seem to have any basis; they voiced misgivings about pumping public money into an organisation whose business management was so shaky and whose membership were so vocally split. Of this they had all the evidence they needed. Price inflation in the 1970s, up to 25% a year, meant an inflation of language and also, for example, vituperation, where the value of a real person was as degraded as the price of paper was inflated. People attribute motives to the Arts Council, conservative critics attribute terrorist motives to the 'avant' poets, theorists talk about poetry which shows no signs of ever getting written – it's a morass of group-think and viscous slurs which I can't turn into history.

A key question is whether the modernist line alienated the bulk of the readers. It has been claimed that sales (including distribution to members of the Society, who got copies of *Poetry Review* as part of their members' rights) were buoyant under Mottram; which would imply that modern-style poetry was just as popular among the culturally interested as pop or the Movement. Yet the Society was facing a financial crisis in 1975. At this point facts sink beneath ideologically motivated turmoil. *Poetry Review* stopped going to a commercial printer and was produced by volunteers at the Society's print shop. Those issues look terrible, a kind of typographical nervous breakdown. It is hard to explain why money wasn't available to do it right if sales were sustained.

There was debate about who was legitimately a good and modern poet, but little of the debate has survived and the several sides were talking past each other. This is not a source for mapping the artistic beliefs of the various groupings. The dispute probably changed nothing. It was a conflict which reveals the contours of a pre-existing field rather than an event that gave rise to a new landscape. Events in poetry are chiefly the publication of books, which would be about 900 titles in 1977. Each book produces a ripple of reception and reaction that changes the field slightly. The polarisation of the poetry 'community' existed before 1976 and even before 1971; it was Mottram's presupposition for editing the way he did.

The people who hung around the print shop and the events at Earl's Court formed a kind of gang. This supplied the damaged labour for the misprinting. They were terribly disappointed by Mottram's departure. However, Mottram printed very few of their poems. This gang later evolved into the London School. The disaffected did not start a major magazine, a new *Poetry Review* for those of modern inclination. The relationship between the *Poetry Society* events and the invisibility of the underground is not easy to explain. Certainly the modernist poets were turned into, and cut out of, history. Their mature works were circulated virtually from hand to hand. But the claim is that Mottram's *Poetry Review* found many buyers. So the unpopularity of the small-press poets is a problem to explain. It may have more to do with not understanding money than with being obscure or remote from the concerns of the culturally aware.

The tale of bookshops and stocking has too many facts to be easily retrievable. If we return to the British Poetry Revival, Mottram's classic formulation names poets like Tomlinson, Logue, Hughes, Redgrove. In the 1980s, they were published by High Street publishers and were undoubtedly stocked by bookshops. This does not extend to 50 or 80 other radical poets. (Actually, Mottram published 200 different poets in six years.) So the limit on everybody being in the High Street may be to do with numbers rather than any right-wing malevolence. The display of books by over 1,000 bookshops is undoubtedly a key component of the history of poetry. It also changed every week. It is a story that can't be told and which contains more twists and turns than any schema. The poetry is the DNA and the bookshop is the organism.

The rollback induced the modernist poets to implode, both in style and in business. The expansiveness of the 1960s was replaced by a siege mentality. Since the Poetry Society now withdrew the self-help printing and production equipment which was in their basement (and which they had paid for), the 'London scene' sulkily responded by years of appallingly produced, sub-mediæval homemade books. This alienated the public and booksellers (and the poetry world outside London) for decades. The siege mentality had three results: fetishisation of the elements of style which signalled 'marginality'; crimped loyalty (so that reviewing and theorisation in the little magazines was cliquey and intellectually dead), and psychological withdrawal from the stage, so that this poetry became invisible to younger poets. The psychological state of an artist who never expects the audience to arrive is complex; of course it selects for fanaticism, as the softer members bale out and find success elsewhere. This can easily mean that the artist abandons the constant fight for clarity, which is the primary virtue of language. Often, the lack of external attention makes the poetry starve and wither: silence is preceded by bouts of what has ceased to be fully language. Often, its natural development is cramped because the artist refuses to broaden his techniques, afraid of character and narrative because they are 'not avant-garde'. Paranoia quite often goes along with not being self-critical. The sense of being abandoned by the local power structures drags with it pitiful loyalty to marginal, foreign, or imaginary authorities, outlaw Popes without artistic attainments except intransigence. My view is that there is a horrible difference between the magazine Mottram edited and the version – bright, bouncy, but without intelligence – that followed in the 1980s. He faced the complexity of a deeply disturbed time without regressing into schemas, dogmas, or dumbing-down.

I am told the Poetry Society production equipment was scrapped. If you regard exclusion as a product, they got the value they wanted. However, it is quite unnecessary to look outside the radical scene for reasons for failure.

I derive my account of the Thermidor of 1977 chiefly from the press cuttings stored at the Poetry Library. These reports by journalists are one and all alarmed at 'squabbling' and welcome a 'moderate pluralist group', but never inquire into the credentials and ideas of the latter. This hatred of extremists is based on a protective model of verbal interaction. If you give up wanting anything you can have what you want. The attacks on 'squabbling': if you propose an idea, you're squabbling. So language isn't a proper way of handling conflicts. If you disagree with someone else, you aren't fit to handle public monies. So 'you're disagreeing with us but we aren't disagreeing with you'. Indifference to poetry as a claim to authority. Mediocrity as financial fidelity.

The flamboyant territorialisation, vituperation, loss of dialogue, grandiosity, and paranoia, now look like a preparation for the ejection of masculine principles from the cultural stage and a kind of clearing the decks before an era where the cultural officials would be women. Who could feel nostalgic for the social interactions of around 1976-7? The disgust with conflict brings us to the question of rollback.

THE MAINSTREAM

The 1970s may have produced no new mainstream poets of any significance. This may be an error of perception or may connect with a national nervous breakdown (in Alexander Walker's memorable phrase) when consensus positions were untenable. Among older poets, we see an expansion by Anthony Thwaite, Geoffrey Hill, Peter Levi and George Mackay Brown into long form; major works by my accounting. One explanation of this is that the high tide of secularism and permissiveness had thrown Christianity into crisis, and this made psychologically necessary a searching and restatement of the basis of something old and traditional. This is part of a wider process, the experimental collapse of the Anglican Church, in which there was a delta of new cultural forms fanning out, as the inherited forms, going back to the 17th century or other times, ceased to be emotionally available. This delta is under-researched. This decade sees cultural crisis bring out the best work of conservatives under pressure. Connoisseurs who want to compare the two sides can put Eric Mottram's poem *Tunis* (1977) alongside Anthony Thwaite's poem-sequence 'Letters of Synesius', which is set further east, in Libya. They are both dealing with similar material – the past and present of North Africa. They are both effective. It would be ridiculous to throw out either of them. This is poetry. The paranoia of conservatives, abusing the new poetry, has to be put into the same camera-shot as the vitality of Christian poets speaking afresh to a secular age.

The Breakdown of Subjectivity

A World in the Individual Mind

Generalisation: 20th-century poetry began with a preoccupation with naval battles involving tens of thousands of tons of steel and Persian oil. Its course has been one of continuous refinement towards fine psychological processes, so that the weight of material in the poem has decreased from tons to kilos. The evaporation of external action has been the line of progress. It has paralleled the development of engine design, so that half a ton of metal in 1780 generated the same amount of horsepower as one kilogram in 1980. The design component has attenuated the material one. The more society has expressed itself in a deluge of material goods, millions of tons of them, the more poetry has retreated into psychology.

Earlier, we saw Martin Esslin's classic definition of the theatre of the absurd as abolishing sequence in favour of an integrated concrete image. We suggested that this described the process of poetry, ever since. *Hamlet* was the play which inspired the whole Absurd. Suppose we go back to the 1942 *Hamlet*, presented at the New Theatre, London, and to Leslie Hurry's great backdrop painting for it. Robert Helpmann saw his whole ballet as 'a nightmare dream in the mind of the dying Prince' with the painting showing the savage creatures that swam in its depths. (We are told that it was a 'mimodrama with dances rather than a ballet', Beaumont.) We are thinking of modern poetry as having moved into that schema: abolishing external action in order to relive thought processes, with the landscape being a handwriting, impulses and fine shakes blown up to gigantic size. The idea of gaps in the nervous system projected as the macrostructure of the entire poetic work: the monumental projection of inherent instability. Style has become the subject.

It can't be that simple. But think of Andrew Young's poem, published in two parts in 1952 and 1958. It starts with the writer's death: he goes on living as a ghost, wandering the tracts of the earth. It is a frozen moment. Time is no longer passing. Eternal processes become visible. The speaker is cut off from the world for 70 pages. The interest in this kind of material is intimately related to the end of narrative and the emergence of fine psychological processes within the poet's brain as the main subject of poetry. The question is whether this space is filled with emotional events or with ideas. One is mainly egocentric, one is factual and in part documentary, being modulated by testing against memories.

The abolition of fact in 1940s poetry really infuriated people but it was a preliminary step to dissolving narrative and dissolving 'sensation' in favour of critique. Virtualisation meant an anticipatory withdrawal from power/fantasy complexes before the feminist artillery barrage comes down. The feminist wave defined (more so then than now) the location of power in society as phallic; reciprocally the male essence was this power and this power supported the position and ego of males. In the U.K. this phallic power was found in the complex of Empire-Navy-Church-Army-history and this is what was being virtualised. This critique is bafflingly offstage for poetry – after all, there was already no poetry which described what a 'great nuclear arsenal of missiles and bombs our government has and how it was bigger than what other countries had'. The feminist critique agreed with a *longue durée* movement in poetry that had evacuated pro-phallic positions. The contrast between the modernist poetry of the 1920s and the position occupied by Newbolt/Noyes/Kipling already shows something very much of this kind happening. This is one reason why an anti-feminist position within contemporary poetry would be very hard to occupy and indeed is very hard to find in print (unless this is selective memory on my part). Another corollary is that the feminist theses made very rapid advances in the poetry world and were rapidly acceptable. Poetry occupies a specific position in the cultural field and that position is not really compatible with investments in fantasies of power. The drug we are on, so to speak, involves empathy and sensitivity.

NARCISSISM AND NARRATIVE

In modern poetry, the dizzy uncertainty of a psychic life in which all the hinges on the frames that provide security and continuity have been unscrewed provides the events. The lyric describes another form of uncertainty. The lyric is generally a banal and short song, awkward when written down and deprived of music. Exceptionally, and in the exclusive realm of cultured poetry, in the sexually and financially charged atmosphere of courts, it becomes extended and dilated to the new form of the sonnet sequence. Here we find, by tradition, desperate insecurity; emotional harmony is not interesting for so long. But we also find two protagonists: the I-figure and the loved object, desired yet capricious. This is another source of uncertainty and indeterminacy. There are lyric poets who write about themselves but make the story interesting. George Barker and Christopher Logue spring to mind here. Being emotionally at risk is simultaneously what makes them interesting and what makes them rascals in the eyes of Christian academic critics. They pose as sexual adventurers, flaring up with carnal excitement, at the same time comic

Harlequin figures, always being chased by shopkeepers or landladies and short of the price of a pound of sausages. Leaving the lyric behind produces a stability that may be excessive. A certain strand of modern English poetry has been the attempt to make writing about married domestic life interesting, and always failing. There is a quadrilateral whose vertices are anecdote-theory-narrative-introspection. The struggle of the poet is to ride along the spectrum between anecdote and theory.

The suggestion that poetry has grown greatly in complexity since 1960 needs some important qualifications. First, the previous and lost state can be taken to be narrative. In narrative, the quality of uncertainty is built-in; the whole appeal is that we don't know what is going to happen next. Narrative is one of the taboos of modern poetry, and there must be a structural reason for this, which can hardly be other than the narrowed focus on the individual mind as the content of the work. The part of ideas has been blown up to fill the whole landscape, which is the equivalent of taking three-minute films and making them last three hours. This already suggests the desperate triviality of most poetry, and the exit into mere anecdote. The ego in the poem is no longer faced with the great, trembling, uncertainties of opera and 19th-century narrative poems. The area of discourse has been moved to the internal plane. The acceleration of uncertainty in other levels of the text is perhaps a conservative measure, to retain levels of indeterminacy at the pre-existing standard. Narrative poems were written in the 1960s by Logue and George MacBeth. Logue's 'The Arrival of the Poet in the City' has no story, but is a commentary for an unmade film, a sequence of documentary images. MacBeth's 'Driving West' and 'The World in Winter' are poems that tell stories. These are in a style influenced by television and cinema. The more they escape into real narrative, the more they travel into a world of images which is common to the people who create television and filmed stories. This world is already there; we prefer the richness of subjectivity, the drama of style. It is unlikely that narrative will remain absent from poetry forever. The best modern narrative poems are probably the ones by D.M. Black.

CRITIQUE OF IDENTIFICATION

The cultural arm of the Cold War involved propaganda that centrally made people identify with its narratives, and trained people to identify as they consumed the narratives; and taught people to disintegrate the narrative of the other side. Any child growing up in this regime was bound at some point to apply the disintegration techniques to the narratives of their own side. As someone did this, they exited from the Cold War, which thus ended head by head, as people withdrew from it to go elsewhere. The huge, cold apparatus of official culture did not make a change of course.

Identification is conditioning. So it became an object of study, however much this founding act resisted analysis. The basis of huge amounts of bad poetry is the assumption that the reader will identify. The Stalinist background of false consciousness theory (i.e. people don't vote Communist because they are deceived) prejudiced people against emotional identification, but as the area evolved it also shed Stalinist assumptions, and also the *parti pris* against participation and optimism. Perhaps in 1953 someone could be so conniving and complicit as to believe all of capitalist art and see all the explanations of communist art as mere tricks (or vice versa), but prolonged exposure broke down this rigorous distribution of credulity and incredulity, and the pattern became more complex. Identification became semi-conscious, and quite obviously part of one's relationship with authority. There cannot have been anyone in 1970 who did not perceive that the same methods used by ideological systems to make their ideas seem noble and sincere and vital were also being used by artists to make their inner lives seem lofty, splendid, large-scale, original, and so forth. The propaganda of the U.S.A. and its allies relied on the admirable figures of men whose rugged integrity proved the attractions of the individualist way. Very similar figures filled the pages of Communist propaganda, featuring the spiritual achievements of Red artists beside the heroic qualities of Red Army tank-drivers and so forth. How did the political illusion differ from the artistic illusion?

Poets in this period had constitutively to persuade people that they were not writing propaganda (for the self, that is), that their artistic devices were not also tricks. This led to durable anxieties, which were not unrelated to the exaltation of anxiety as horror, in the genre of Gothic.

The Attack on Character

The staple of 19th-century art was naturalistic observation of character. This was the burden of the artist's memory, stored up and guarded as a stock in trade or working capital. The realist ethos, under theoretical attack in the 1880s, took an infernally long time to die in the 20th century. Juxtaposition can be claimed to be a new set of rules of sequence, a new start. The displaced can be seen in retrospect to be a naturalist's view of human character, an object of the quest symmetrical to the techniques of the quest, a behaviour-set which was as stable as the character of a duck or a goose. This notion of character was a step away from anatomy, and shadowed the sharp lenses and acute knives of anatomy; observations made in one scene were valid for others years later. The reason for rejecting this in the 1960s, or at other times, was political; rejecting the tragic inevitable theory of character. The exit from naturalism did not mean a weakening of the sense of self, but actually a great intensification of the personality as the source of artistic authority. It was only in the long run, as this emitter too faded, that changeability was recognised as tenuousness and intermittence.

In the Cold War, the definition of propaganda relied on an authentic personality underneath the strata of conditioning. This idea of the hidden and abiding was structurally necessary for the whole discourse. But after hearing this proposition a million times it became wearying and lost credibility. The idea that poetry was there to deliver this hidden and infantile personality, as its essential burden and source of value, proved wearisome to many. Regression is authenticity? Repetition is pristine? The idea that the human species was notable for intelligence, and that this gave it the capacity to learn new patterns, was also discreetly voiced from time to time.

The concept of personality as a data object that appeals by its openness, responsiveness, rapid change, is quite the opposite of personality seen as something fixed from the outset, a text inscribed in some unknown hard material which unrolls over time and imprints its shape on every successive situation. The appeal of the former is that it changes all the time. Response is change; complexity cannot come about without the meaning-generator being written back to by the meanings generated. The 1950s vision of character as a difficult material, blemished by original sin and struggling for authenticity, is replaced by an intention of sinning in which traits are a personal style or sensibility enriching experience, and character is like a library of tapes to be eagerly played back and listened to. One makes experience repeat. One fractures itself into a million varieties whose differentiae display a whole taxonomy, its branches offering insights into a form-making process that lets us see and divine ever further back towards the 'first cause'.

The Critique of Subjective Experience

Most of us, despite all evidence to the contrary, still share the view of man which is a hangover from the individualism and rationalism of the eighteenth century and the hopes of the Renaissance and believe that the typical civilised human being is

an isolated individual, unique in his 'I-ness', seeking out others for love or company but essentially independent of them (...) The modern atom, however, is composed of many sub-particles, each of which is a whirlpool of energy rather than a material object in the accepted sense: (...) the more we look, the more it isn't there. So with the modern picture of personality; (...) In short, people are much more variable than used to be supposed, the boundaries of the personality much more vaguely defined (.)
(from J.A.C. Brown's *Techniques of Persuasion*, 1963)

Thus J.A.C. Brown defines by defining the instability of human attitudes even without propaganda, advertising, and so on. Brown continues,

The consciousness of self arises from messages coming in from the material environment, the sensations within our own muscles which inform us of changes in space, the sound of our voice, and, above all, from the way other people react in relation to us; in a real sense the self is made up from the reflected appraisals of others and the role it has to play in various social groups.
[...]
[T]he continuity is relative and dependent [...] on the persisting and consistent continuity of stimuli from our external and internal environment, and when these are changed [...] the self may be shaken to the core. [...] [T]he clusters of goals, values, and ideals which in some sense belong to the self are not all consistent with one another, all our potential roles cannot be played together(.)
(pp.241-6)

He specifies that our character judgements are wrong, partially because: 'It is often forgotten that the same person may show both honesty and dishonesty, shyness and boldness, aggressiveness and submissiveness, in rapid succession depending on the particular role he is playing and the circumstances he is facing' (p. 247). Our observations may be right, but we err by projecting them into the future, as if the living subject were frozen and incapable of variation. But a literary text is shot through with character judgements from one end to the other.

Brown explores the influence of social prompts on behaviour: 'It has been shown, too, that the idea that people can interact while remaining virtually unchanged in the process is untrue, that the boundaries of the self are much more vaguely defined than had previously been thought...' (p.248). The stability of the self might be at the level of following the rule, 'imitate what the people around you do', or 'do what they want': the rule remains constant, but the actions it specifies vary. What does this say about a poetry that defines the presentation of the poet's self as authentic because it is alone, in contemplation, and the poem as authentic because it is frozen, self-defining, walled-off from dialogue?

Brown even suggests a historical absence and then origin of this dependence: 'Certainly we can see how that individualism, so far as Europe and America are concerned, is characteristic of a certain historical epoch, not, as used to be supposed, the natural state of affairs.' One of the projects of the period since 1968 has been to travel back to the point of origin of uncontrolled individualism in art (as well as in property) and question and experimentally reverse developments that followed that dominant route.

Clearly, there are problems in making the self the organising principle of poetic works, or in making the poet's personality the commodity that sells the poems, when the constancy and autonomy of the self are so acutely in doubt. The closer the look we take, the more instability we find. Brown, incidentally, is taking a minimum position: other versions deny all possibility of stability and authenticity of the self. This is an example of a long-term process whereby rational study produces knowledge that competes with and undermines the information proposed as knowledge in poems. Poetry, captive of data, has responded by capturing prose texts, in a hundred ways.

Social contexts may be so stable that the variability remains latent, and character remains firm and real. Mechanisms in society and in the individual act to induce stability: our intelligence allows us to react quickly to new events but also to exploit our knowledge, which is only valid when there is some continuity between previous situations and new ones.

To see an object in the course of change, with forces becoming visible as they dynamically affect its structure, is more interesting than to see something that can't change shape. Emotions are important in art because they are produced by such moments of uncertainty and high potential. Allowing the self to vary in the way Brown describes, may not damage the nucleus of poetry, but actually expand its territory. The oscillation between separate and contrasted states of a single mind can itself become the action of poetry.

PROCESSUAL

The leftist example of the culture after 1968 was not friendly to individualism, so to possessive attitudes towards your feelings, so to extended (and even monumental) subjectivity. It was friendly to doubt. It was friendly to the critique of daily life. The location of the poetic work therefore shifted to the fine anatomy of how the verbal material is edited and how the critique (which has carried out the differentiation forming the detail of the word) is carried out. The fine handwriting is the anatomy of the work but is not essentially subjective; it portrays an intellect, as a personality function, rather than the subjective drives. Generalisation: the awareness of problems with the personality as controlling ego that means what it says has made itself known in poetry through the use of procedures that remove self-expression as the 'ruling class' of textual rules. A feature of certain modern texts is that none of the words come from the poet. This would apply to books by Tom Raworth and Adrian Clarke (subject to confirmation). The imprint of the poet comes exclusively from the editing- the blink rate, the edit rate, the shaping.

I have difficulty periodising this current. The Olson flow confuses its early history – this was documentary but invested energy in egoism rather than in conceptual thought. Clearly procedural poetry came out of documentary. The prehistory of the processual is in mid-century poetry which left literary confines to deal with the world of the working class and of economic processes. The critique of documentary film led to an acuter understanding of editing processes which led to the autonomisation of the editing process as the core history of the text. Pound was just an example of the engagement in the 1930s of modern artists with the world outside art, a product of the Great Depression which laid our political wisdom into question. He only wrote about history, not being the kind of guy to visit the working-class quarters. Yet writing about Renaissance tyranny, Confucius, and Henry Adams was his surrogate way of engaging in politics and with the structures of the public world. This was significantly parallel to Mass Observation documenting the life of 1930s Bolton, for example. These were huge projects and the gaping flaws which their size exposed led to a range of critiques that shaped the next generation of interrogation. Where Ezra Pound made long poems by struggling through long prose texts, the radical poets of the 1970s made long poems by struggling through structures of everyday life as revealed in news stories, advertisements, guides to the course of the River Thames, and the urban fabric as text.

Visual art in the 1970s was going through a different process of auto-critique, clearer in its design than what was happening in poetry. How does poetry fit into the conceptual project? Allen Fisher is the key figure but he came into poetry from the outside, having previously been involved in the conceptual visual art project, via Fluxus. In poetry, the emphasis is on taking source texts and mutating them. The mutations are programmed processes and these correspond to the processes of a conceptual artist. The legacy of Pound is a key component. His example was like a mass concentration that deflects flights by exerting gravity, so his treatment of source texts became the model for set experimental processes dealing with source information. The process that generated the poetic text as printed may be highly complex but it is not usually documented. You have to intuit it and normally you also have to reconstruct the old text that was mutated to achieve the one we have as end product. One example of this is Fisher texts that are created by mutating older Fisher texts. This process may be fairly transparent in parts of *Place*, from the 1970s, but has become less so as the methods of mutation became more sophisticated. The ability to identify with the act of mutating was a crowd pleasing element in the earlier work which becomes attenuated as *Gravity as a Consequence of Shape* develops (roughly 1982-2005; it runs to 720 pages in the collected version).

The poetic equivalent to the abolition of visual representation is the critique of the contents of everyday consciousness. This is the big woe, the thing that conventional readers miss and that defines new poetry as not being art. People want pictures. They want poems about beautiful people having beautiful experiences. It's like the ice-cream that is part of the visit to the cinema. Yet, imagine three people watching TV together. They watch advertisements and TV news and then verbally rip those visual texts apart, replaying and deriding them. This is something everyone does and doing it in poetry is populist. It's about as alien as going to a football match. We are all immersed in a morass of signifying chains, and it feels as if we are fathoms deep in all those seeps of words and to reach the surface even for five minutes would be a blessing. Conceptual poetry starts with this misery and deep dependency of immersion in propaganda, advertising and general symbolic effluent and takes that as its starting point, in the depths. We are all there. This is the serious part, where the project does the most difficult work and faces down the heaviest enemies. We can all relate to it. Few people could spend 12 hours watching advertising and listening to the speeches of politicians and corporate front men and consuming popular entertainment and not feel like contradicting what they are hearing, taking it as raw material and inverting it to produce something that has lost meaning but that releases the frustration. The mass media creates alienation. Fighting with it is populist. This part does not need explanation. The basic acts of a whole swathe of modern poetry are capturing, cutting up, collaging, composing. The raw material is the same mega-visual capitalist flow that everyone is sunk in the whole time.

The sense of doubt shows up as a tone of voice in the 1970s. That strange tone of voice may be related to this hinterland of critique and self-doubt. Does writing in a way which doubts itself get one past the problems of the split self that Brown describes? I don't think so. Language is potentially deceptive – consciousness potentially the 'silent utterance' of deception. No literary style gets past that abiding situation. Yet the responses of poets to these doubts are sometimes constitutive for the poems. The super-availability of data in the form of comparisons and then of self-images is one of the paths of breakdown into complexity.

It may seem as if the narrative that disappears from modern poetry made its exit in order to be replaced by endlessly dancing, elaborately advancing and retreating, doubt. What arrives is an idea of style as made of cognitive programs or gates by which a shared social symbolic flow of behaviour is transformed into a poetic text; in a kind of signal-processing procedure. These programs also allow for the different poets to mark boundaries between themselves – each with their own territory that yields a distinctive 'call-sign' to be imprinted on every passage of their work. A personalised doubt? The idea that this dance of doubt actually alters the relations between dominated and dominating seems to be doubtful itself.

Is reflexivity narcissism? The advance of reflexivity is a new form of the courtly ideal, the civilising process that typically means an increase in self-awareness and control of impulses. Is reflexivity the self-regard of the highly educated? Certainly the signalling of doubt became one of the differences between high and low in this period.

CONCEIT AND CONSPIRACY

A column by Professor Donald Michie in *Computer Weekly* quotes the MIT computer scientist Marvin Minsky: 'Consciousness. Some special place in the brain where everything comes together for instant introspection – there isn't really any such thing. Most of what goes on is thousands of concurrent processes below the thinker's awareness.' Also, a 19th-century physiologist, Francis Balton: the position of consciousness 'appears to be that of a helpless spectator of but a minute fraction of auto-matic brain work'. This seems to be popular with physiologists these days; a *New Scientist* review quotes a phrase from the book reviewed: 'the conceit and conspiracy of consciousness'. This agrees with what Brown claims. It is also strikingly reminiscent of Charles Rycroft's revisionist handling of Freud's theory of the unconscious:

> Concepts like the unconscious are unnecessary, redundant, scientistic, and hypostasizing – the last since the concept the unconscious insinuates the idea that there really is some entity somewhere that instigates whatever we do unconsciously, some entity which is not the same entity as instigates whatever we do consciously.

Rycroft points out that unconscious is an adjective, and can therefore only be a state of a named organ, not an organ in itself, bounded by some barrier. Any artistic process becomes unconscious with repetition: so that skill is closely related to making procedures unconscious.

The surface harmony of poets like Robert Graves, Richard Wilbur, or Norman MacCaig seemed increasingly like a smart coat of paint, the *politesse* of a waiter, detached from anything deeper, and concealing what might have ruffled it. This opens a large question of how you could write a poem that wouldn't impose a fictional completeness and wholeness on the material. The idea of decentralisation of functions to weaken the ego, the lost jockey, itself allows for a replenishment of the empty wilderness of the text with a new and expansive set of structures. At the time, there was an idea that the 'personality', as the subject of art, was only a thin stratum, a kind of superstructure. The lurking analogies with the ruling class (as thin stratum on top of the people), and capitalism (as a thin stratum of history) were linked as a theory about the nature of Cold War culture. The goal was a de-repressed culture.

The ideas offer a competitor to naïve self-awareness: zealots of the theories assume that the accounts of experience offered by writers are false. Radical writers of the 1970s assumed that all the inherited language of art was fictitious; the experience of the Cold War discredited art, overworked by both sides. The poetic equivalent of the 'dematerialisation of the art object' was to isolate or block out identification; it's much easier to deceive people if they identify with you. Any questioning of this process brought repining and wringing of hands from lovers of literature, who preferred to remain ignorant of this central thing.

Adherents of radical philosophy could only see the empathetic or introspective information offered by the writer as misrecognition, a decorous ideological surface under which they, reducing the writer to an ornamental decoy, could read the real processes. The metaphor of depth and surface was seductive at the time; surface being the ordinary person's awareness and depth being the mystically and eschatologically privileged ultra-modern objective knowledge of the initiate, who else but the speaker. Poets were bound to compete with this, admittedly psychotic and grandiose, idea. If the metaphor of repressed, dumb, explosive, forces posed itself sociologically as the working classes, politically as the real understanding obscured by false consciousness, psychically as the unconscious and its untapped sexual reserves, its literary disguise was as the unconscious rules of text generation, which it was felt the non-naïve writer could liberate and so shake out malign projections of capitalism, patriarchy, etc. Descriptions of these rules from non-partisan sources may be helpful. René Wellek and Austin Warren, in their 1949 *Theory of Literature*, remark:

> Even an apparently most realistic novel, the very 'slice of life' of the naturalist, is constructed according to certain artistic conventions. [...] we see how similar are naturalistic novels in choice of theme, type of characterization, events selected or admitted, ways of conducting dialogue. We discern, likewise, the extreme conventionality of even the most naturalistic drama not only in its assumption of a scenic frame but in the way space and time are handled, the way even the supposedly realistic dialogue is selected and conducted, and the way characters enter and leave the stage.
> (*Theory of Literature* p.15)

In the atmosphere of 1970, talk of 'rules' and 'conventions' immediately roused a crowd mustered to storm them. Meyer Schapiro, in his 1966 essay discusses the 'non-mimetic elements of the image-sign', where the frame, conventions of perspective, absolute scale, etc., advance to centre stage, while overt content is excluded. Schapiro remarks:

> In asserting with the support of scientists that there are no lines in nature and that we see only colors [...] [A] picture-substance ... that in several features is as arbitrary as the archaic black outline – I mean the visible strokes of paint and the relief of crusty pigment which violate both the continuity and texture of the represented surfaces.
> (from Meyer Schapiro, 'On Some Problems in the Semiotics of Visual Art: Field and Vehicle in Image-Signs' in *Semiotica* 1, The Hague, 1969, pp.223-242)

Since some of these elements are constant to all artists of an era, but change when the era does, it is tempting to see in them the key to how we are controlled and so the way to seize conscious control of history. Schapiro's discussion gets us close to understanding the relationship of style and time in art – the subject of my book, indeed. He says:

> Taken out of the image, the parts of the line will be seen as small material components: dashes, curves, dots that, like the cubes of a mosaic, have no meaning in themselves.
> (*ibid.*)

Looked at on a small enough scale – and the large scale is by definition a composite of the small-scale events – every picture is non-mimetic, just as the glass cubes or *tesserae* of different mosaics are all alike. In an era where record producers like Brian Wilson were using electronics to tweak the music and thicken up the sound a fraction at 18,000 Hz (let's say), it was tempting to believe that the study of linguistics would let you transcend both old-fashioned poetry and the immediate data of naïve self-awareness and let you liberate the text at the subliminal level. It's understandable that this excited poets more than it did the audience.

Descending to the subliminal level eliminates the individual artist. The deletion from the text of the figure you identify with is the precondition of writing this kind of (deliriously exciting) history. You can't write narrative without suffering the problems of the historian. Every advance of historiography since the early 19th century has depended on this deletion; adjusting the time-frame of the camera to pick up something material and opposed to consciousness, events either too large or too fine to enter consciousness or be recorded in naïve accounts. This reversal of figure and ground is just what we find as the basis of Schapiro's essay. Just as modern physiological psychology has found consciousness to be something attenuated and after the event, while the real processing is done by thousands of decentralised integrated modules, so history has switched off heroic narrative to allow an explosion of the experiencing subject. The primal act of the modern historian is comparing different accounts, with doubt as hero and detective, exposing the action of the narrators in distorting and schematising the truth. The distorting agent seems remarkably similar to verbal consciousness itself, and truth can only be reached through multiple points of view. Traditionalist poetry thinks it can evade these problems.

Schapiro points out, percipiently, that '[t]he picture sign seems to be through and through mimetic', a warning against treating the small scale as truly arbitrary. The discussion of the tiny dots, curves, and dashes must remind us of the work of Anton Ehrenzweig; which suggests to us that this small scale is the source of difference between a good painter and a bad painter (who both treat the same overt subject and feelings, for example the Deposition); since they are also one of the sources of stylistic difference, the possibility yawns open that they are the location of personality and its archaic world of self-referential, self-inventing, messages. The quantities in the artistic work that are open to the artist's free disposition, like the water a swimmer pushes around, are non-representational; but because they retain the patterns of the artist's swimming, writing the message that we as humans are able to read, they are also a representation, but of subjectivity.

This switching between scales is related to reading history, since it is endless repetition across time that makes small-scale acts significant (as, trivially, the small elements of a picture are made in short timescales while the overall picture is the product of a longer timescale as their sum). Self-consciousness is based on the account that memory offers, which is overwritten all the time and screened to remove contradictions; a record that remains stable and so shows you your behaviour over a longer timescale contradicts self-consciousness and shows you a whole set of patterns, perhaps of motives, that the inner conversation didn't catch. Structure becomes narrative, form becomes the hero. Timescale is like an envelope-skin containing a particular view of the self or of a social unit; altering timescale dissolves the coherence as new patterns or inconsistencies become visible. The extraordinarily obstinate instinct of grooming makes people harmonise whatever they know to be visible. Better recording methods give the observer the power to view behaviour over more or less any timescale, the very long or the very short; poetry starts dealing with life since the Pliocene and with fractions of a second.

If the self appropriates means of expression, and becomes visible in art by doing so, it is then a kind of distributional pattern in the minimal means, sounds or glass cubes or 'picture substance', of the work of art, which in virtue of their number exhibit all kinds of distributional patterns. What authorises us to say that one is the self and others are not?

Trying to sum up the propositions of radical thought after 1968 will get me into difficulties, because the underlay was the mass expansion of higher education and so of writers, and the impulse was to chase off in every direction. It is invalid to list a few writers when there were hundreds of influential books. The point I am making is restricted, namely that there was an amount of criticism of the authority of the author and that this affected the way that poets who read books wrote.

Decentralisation and Damage

You start with the *Hamlet* ballet where everything is flashing and flaring in one person's subjective world, and you end up with a state where there is nothing outside one person's subjective world and that world has been ransacked, emptied of all its content. The withholding of identification or enthusiasm was seen as politically intelligent even when it was indistinguishable from clinical depression. The wearing away of all glamour from the artist figure was seen as reducing illusion. The inspiring possibilities of a socialist future, of affection and cooperation in a shared task, and of an intelligent, selfless, and optimistic artist to talk to us, were seen as archaic and infantile. The mention of such a streak brings back unbearable memories of wet Sunday evenings in Camden Town facing a querulous and depressive 'non-illusory' artist. The positive energy of the artist was seen as oppressive to ordinary people, so the artist strove to be despondent, inconsistent, and insignificant. Actresses without glamour! Singers without a voice! Films without plot! Poets without ideas! Black greatcoats, slack jaws. Mortification. Bad drugs. Of course this kind of thing crossed over to popular art and became punk, a legitimate heir of Conceptual Art. This abolition of colour was not the result of Thatcher's victory, since punk rock arrived three years before that. It marked up the depressive sublime of Joy Division.

'Metal Box', by PiL (1979), sums up this atmosphere best. The exile of the Left from its State gave rise to a streak of miserabilism: 'up to here in drear', to use New Musical Express' phrase. Two stages in this were the defeat of Tony Benn in an election for deputy leader of the Labour Party, in 1982, and the second election of Thatcher, in 1983. However, the problem of grey anti-illusionist art is significantly older. It became almost a skill to withhold sympathy and participation. The critique of consciousness was productive. However, it could mean that poets saw any attempts to make the line of the poem clear, decisive, impressive, convincing, etc. as deviations from the truth. This could make things very drab. The stripping down of all sensuous, local, or decorative material may be a step on the way to abstraction. Abstract ideas have the power to change society. I accept this line, however if you are still producing art rather than critical philosophy then you have mighty theoretical problems to solve as you pursue disillusion. If the key is to understand everyday life then removing everything that belongs to everyday life is not a step towards that understanding.

THE ANTI-AUTOBIOGRAPHICAL

So, the distrust of the personality in the overpowering Cold War environment led to a method of composition in which poets withdrew from assertion to present texts as learning environments in which the suppression of potentially key assumptions of modern culture generated unheard-of sequences of situations that the reader is asked to explore as a learning environment; and in it they collect patterns of experience that are also not fixed and definitive, but which are part of a repertoire, added to those of a thousand other works of art. Tacitly, the fertility of this process exposes the old personality as a set of acquired patterns native to a legacy of old situations and liable to collapse in the future. Documentary was the path by which a new idea of art was reached, but is too static a concept to explain how poets capture data streams to build new environments from.

This is a beautifully clean statement of a decision process. Would poets agree that this is what they are up to? No, but they rarely agree to any definite statement by someone else. Is it plausible as an explanation? Yes, but it has to remain suspended in the air. I believe it but as the decision processes involved many people and were unconscious a clear utterance doesn't match. You can't get from the concrete instances to a schema.

Perhaps it is useful to be in a room where at a moment of a poem the autobiographical element is to the fore and the audience droop and lose interest. Autobiography. Memories. Feelings. Insights. Symbols charged with personal meaning. They don't want all that old furniture. They want part of the future.

An Era of Rising Property Values: Conservatism and Rollback

The Representation of the People Act, 1918, extended the franchise from about 30% of the adult population to about 80%, and was followed by 20 years of Conservative domination of politics. In modern times, the Conservatives have consistently won about a third of the working-class vote, adding up to about half of the votes which they receive. We are dealing with a conservative society, not merely a conservative minority in power. It is doubtful that an extension of the poetry audience is going to mean a more radical taste.

It is reasonable to bring on stage the fact that most poetry being sold is by poets who are dead. England is like a colony of the past. Modern poetry fits inside a much larger scene of people who like poetry but don't read the modern kind. I am not going to criticise what the majority do. Evidently indifference to modern poetry is a majority position, and it would seem to follow that much of the writing about modern poetry is by people who are radically indifferent to it and are merely putting down their preset position in words. Their position is too popular to be attacked and yet their concrete judgments about this poetry are hopelessly wrong and disoriented.

The Rollback

The recession of the early 1980s, with an industrial squeeze and millions of jobs being lost, made the possession of money much more desirable and removed most of the appeal of being a dropout or semi-dropout dedicated to creativity and to overthrowing the system. This was the end for most currents of post-1968 idealism and intentional poverty. (Meanwhile graduate unemployment gave a lot of people unlimited time for creativity and subversive discourse.) The need for poetry to sound like affluence became stronger than ever before.

The era was a restorative one, because in the first half of the 1970s the radicalisation of art, above all of new art and experimental art, reached a peak in which the ego attachments of the bourgeois were treated as confiscated assets, so that the cultured but comfortable middle-class audience became angry and took steps. This anxiety could also have been the nucleus of new energy, creative reshaping of symbolic holdings and attachments, in fact of a new life; its fall to earth as sloth, inability to form new concepts, hostility to new thoughts, as in fact the reverse of everything it intended, is surprising, but nonetheless true and decisive. There was a shared feeling of satiation and indeed rage at the sketchy, impossibilist, over-demanding, and repetitive nature of the radical art that was around at the time and which has now utterly vanished. David Caute speaks of half a million people being touched by the counter-culture, which is not the same as being given to it heart and soul. All the same these new people were numerous, and it became a central issue for the authorities in universities, government departments, magazines, and so on, to suppress and control them. I doubt that the New Right had as many committed activists – but it had an easier way into the institutions.

A friend of mine, an actor, was talking to me about life in a squat in King's Cross in the 1980s. The squat was collective, a whole block (at Peabody Buildings) and the committee was taken over by a Trotskyite group who wanted everyone else to be enrolled in their forward march. The cadres saw territory being lost all over the landscape. They wanted to exploit the remaining holdings more intensively. If your loyalty was part of that symbolic territory, it was going to have more intense demands made on it. The idea that you could follow your own wishes was no longer acceptable. The worse things got for the Left, the more authority the theoretical cadres exerted over the loyal. Eventually you were going to have a dictatorship in a single room. I didn't want someone else to tell me how to write. The pressure of a right-tilting world produced excesses. As Chris said, it is a good thing that Britain wasn't taken over by a Trotskyite government in the 1980s. I'm glad it didn't happen. The doses of ideological hardness that took over the channels in parts of the art world, for fleeting moments, were quite enough.

There is a Carcanet website where Michael Schmidt makes what looks like a position statement about Carcanet and *PN Review* when they started, around 1974, and he uses the phrase 'Left neo-conservative'. This is a really startling cluster of words, but we should delve into it. I think we could see the three decades 1980-2010 as one of a battle of a 'serious art continuing the modernist project' against an art that had essentially given up, either by writing about individual daily life in a banal way, or by slumping into an infantile avant-garde where chance, deliberate meaninglessness, and vacuous gestures of defiance occupy the frame. This project seems, from a certain angle, to be neo-conservative.

The classic neo-conservative cultural magazine was presumably *The New Criterion*, founded by Hilton Kramer (1928-2012), publishing its first issue in 1982. Kramer stated very clearly that he regarded modernism as the most important modern art and that the New Left, via identity politics, was the chief enemy of modernism in America. His magazine was there to promote modernism (and to find what in new culture lived up to its standards) and to attack the forces that wanted to dump it and replace it with a culture mixing agitprop with personal therapy. So roughly the idea was to conserve the European culture of 1930 and recover it from underneath the deluge of politicisation (and instrumentalism) that came about as a response to the Depression. This is a conservatism whose 'desired time' is 1930, or 1900-30. In 1980, neither civil rights nor anti-war protests were really at centre ground. It is possible that in 1980 high culture was the continuing line of modernism, and that it was not going to survive unless the culture of narcissism was driven from the field. I think the 1970s were a fertile decade but the complete pattern of what was going on included a number of aggressive currents that had to be stopped, and that should not be lost to memory. If Marxism has almost disappeared as a factor today, that tends to obscure the fact that a totalitarian vigilance was trying to take over British culture in the 1970s, and won major victories at many points. Just think of John Berger. If today culture is in good shape, that is partly because battles were won, in 1982 and at other times.

Reading Hilton Kramer's reviews, all of them dated, casts doubt on some of my careless views about the dating of processes in the recent history of culture. For example, I think of cultural 'roll back' as linked to the election of Thatcher in April 1979. But here is what Kramer says around 1975:

> Midway through the 1970s, it looks more and more as if the present decade is destined to become the graveyard of all those illusions and chimeras spawned in the radical culture of the 1960s. The signs of recoil and retrenchment, hesitant and uncertain only two or three years ago, now gather momentum with dizzying speed: the noise of recantation fairly fills the air. [...] When we open the pages of *The New York Review of Books* to find Susan Sontag generically rebuking 'the infantile leftism of the 1960s', we can be reasonably certain that we are in the presence of one of those geologic shifts that completely alter the ideological terrain on which we stand.

Because the mood of the cultured public was changing so rapidly, the exact dates are important. I suspect that each year of the 1970s had a specific atmosphere. Anyway, 'rollback' did not have to wait for the election of Thatcher, it was already happening in 1975. He goes on to say:

We are witnessing the final collapse of the great myth that dominated the aspirations of high culture in the West for more than a century – the myth of avant-garde intransigence and revolt that gave to all of modernist culture its aura of moral combat [.]
(both quotes from *Revolt of the Philistines:*
Art and Culture 1972-84, p.293)

The word 'final' claims a foreknowledge of history that is invalid. The excessively bleak art of the 1970s was a minority thing. It would hardly have been noticeable to someone who watched TV a lot, for example. To focus on it defines the observer as part of a small cultural group who were involved in the exploratory arts scene. If you think that scene is important you are already part of a minority. To compound that, the most excessive art has been edited out of memory precisely because it was excessive. The retrospective view of the 1970s does not habitually include the most anti-sensuous, partisan, and terrorist art. It is a problem to find it now. The 1980s were a decade of rollback.

The Black Rainbow

Key ideologues of the anti-modern would include Kathleen Raine, Peter Russell, W.H. Auden, Philip Larkin, Kingsley Amis, Philip Sherrard, David Holbrook, William Cookson, and Peter Abbs. Abbs has edited or written a long series of books attacking modernism. He edited and partly wrote *The Black Rainbow, Essays on the Present Breakdown of Culture* (1975) a statement of rejection of modernity which may give wider insight into conservative forces. It includes attacks on recent developments in architecture and land use, music, philosophy, the novel, and poetry.

We have a 1968 lecture by Herbert Read called 'The Limits of Permissiveness', Read names 1955 as when it all went wrong. But about 85 other dates have been nominated. It didn't go wrong, you stopped taking things in. Abbs has an essay on 'The Mechanical World-Picture'. The introduction says:

The refusal to recognise the limits of art is the reason why as critics we must withhold our approval from all those manifestations of permissiveness characterized by incoherence, insensibility, brutality and ironic detachment. [...] the media themselves have come to depend in various ways on the glittering, nihilistic mode of culture [...] the seductive images and vacuous slogans of

advertising [...] secure fame and fortune by publicly indulging their own tawdry interests in perversion and sadism [...] [I]t is important that we become aware of the nature of modern nihilism and barbarism [...] a space where a culture based on creativity and trust could again emerge [...] could not happen without a radical change in our present political and economic structure.
(from Peter Abbs, ed., *The Black Rainbow, Essays on the Present Breakdown of Culture*, 1975)

Read quotes Yeats saying on Pound that the nobility of his work 'is constantly interrupted, broken, twisted into nothing by its direct opposite, nervous obsession, nightmare, stammering confusion[.]' He continues:

[T]his stammering confusion is the characteristic of Pound's work that is now imitated by young poets who wish to be considered of his school. [...] They mirror a great confusion and call it the modern style. [...] the process of progressive disintegration is even more evident in painting and sculpture than in literature. [...] Their greatness *[of aged living artists]* lies in the past [.] The great creative period lasted from about 1905 to about 1955. [...] The artists who have come to maturity since the end of the Second World War (1945) are desperately striving to escape from the influence of the masters of the modern movement, but the more original they try to be, the more they are compelled to deviate arbitrarily from the prototypes.
(from Herbert Read, 'The Limits of Permissiveness in Art', in Robin Skelton (ed.) *Herbert Read: A Memorial Symposium*, pp.47-48)

Ian Robinson takes on two anthologies of pop or underground poetry (*Love Love Love* and *Children of Albion*) and wins:

the Children of Albion are not poets. It is necessary to defend the idea of poetry in our common language. [...] his underground is at least as much as Auden's itching to become the establishment, and well-equipped [...] to achieve its end [.]

The rainbow title comes from a Ted Hughes poem. With an inconsistency that is central to the project, Hughes is then subjected to an analysis that blames him for almost everything bad in the world (pp.32-54). The rainbow was a sign of God's covenant to mankind; Hughes' black rainbow is the darkened horizon of a larva under the soil, in nurturing blackness. The hatching is the arrival of a new culture, the theme of the book. In general the writers seem only to know about bad modern art, and to be trapped in it; they seem to sink into confusion, even suffering, and react with a hypertrophied building of paranoid and yet authoritative explanations of why everything has gone wrong. The strongest piece is a really terrific attack on aspects of pop music by Charles Parker, which says virtually everything that the punk rock movement was saying a year or so later. Parker is attacking capitalism in pop from a strong left-wing position. The writers come from D.H. Lawrence (filtered by Leavis) or from the anti-capitalist camp, which meant attacks on light entertainment and the resistance to infantilism and dumbing-down.

You could live through 1975 without noticing that there was any breakdown in culture. It was an elective position, of paranoia and thrilling isolation and wisdom. It was productive of speculation and the speculations became the stuff of culture. The whole punk movement started from there.

The Paranoid Conservative Trip

I think there is a specific cultural style that we can call paranoid conservative. *The Black Rainbow* calls for this term or a similar one, because its writers are in such a bizarre psychological condition. A special neurological malaise, a kind of music that hangs around in neglected spaces. *The Waste Land* is both the founding modernist poem and the definition of paranoid conservatism, the textbook. If you believe that, the day after *The Waste Land*, the lead character finds another young woman and the evil landscape vanishes like a dream, you are arguably less persuaded than someone who thinks that this is the condition of modernity and in the future everyone will be miserable and hallucinated. It means going further into *The Waste Land* to believe that it is real life, an abiding condition. That ability to detach from the pattern, to aestheticise striking situations of crisis and angst – it is there for people who enjoy modern art. This mechanism does not work for paranoid conservatives. They see modern situations and are stricken by them – trapped in the winds of a pattern you hate. Unable to detach or resolve. Besotted. This brings us to the important topic of bourgeois pain.

At the point of overload you can either panic or go into a high state. Anxiety is a neighbour of consciousness, a brain condition only evoked in crisis. The eyelids are locked open. *The Waste Land* resolved into an aesthetic form but is the source of paranoid conservatism. Why do you enjoy it? Being inside the waste land, without detaching and resolving, is a terrible state of mind. Something genuinely terrifying is resolved into an aesthetic experience. A paranoid conservative doesn't resolve it, it is for them a continuing reality, and they feel terror rather than pleasure and elevation. They gaze at modernity and feel intense and turbid emotions.

The problem with writing about modern poetry is dealing with the sector for which these reactions are their key artistic experience. You can't just take their votes away. There is a dividing line between the paranoid and the people who enjoy modern poetry, and the former have an inability to select out what is significant, to eject what is confused, to detach so that a pattern emerges, to clear the mind and move on. These are basic aesthetic functions. I suspect the inhibition in applying them has to do with territorialisation: the paranoid want to control and punish modern poets (or radicals in general) and their purpose is not to enjoy the art and reach a contemplative state. They are collecting evidence to win an argument. I distrust histories of modern poetry written by paranoid conservatives. It is just that the people who enjoy modern poetry should have the decisive say. However, as a critic, I have to persuade the reading public of the merits of this poetry – and paranoid conservatism is a popular style in this country. In some way you are defining your bad experience as a source of authority and knowledge – so you cling to it and acquire more of it.

The Black Rainbow looks partly at bad modern art. But people inside modern art discard the bad stuff and move on to find the good stuff. If you read *Children of Albion* and stop searching, instead halting to write elaborate explanations of why it is so bad – you don't get to the good art. So much of the reception of modern poetry by editors and critics has simply been paranoid conservatism. Obviously *Children of Albion* was a terrible book. But who reads the bad poetry of 1820?

Complexity is not only a function of modernity. Rather, society always was complex, but cultural forms produced simpler versions as a mechanism of defence. Modernity dared to break open those limits and let in glimpses of chaos. A modern art person deals with that hyperreality leaking in without panic. Freezing is though a basic mechanism. Not everything has an apex of winners.

One can only deal with complexity by framing limits. Armoured by formations of anxiety, the conservative is unwilling to improvise; fears chaos and collapse. As a balm and a refuge zone from these visions, he imagines and asks the artist to imagine frozen roles in a frozen picture. Characters go through sacrosanct and historic sequences of acts in rigid insensible poses. Society and art, struck by a thermal torpor, become predictable in almost every series; property values are preserved. The modern universe of multiple world-hypotheses, swirling unstably around a protean reality too complex for us to grasp, is unbearable, and excluded by a kind of cultural police action. The conservative, paralysed by problems in free associating, experiences energy peaks in rage at desecration of barriers and hallows. These peaks are a kind of high.

TOLERANCE OF MULTIPLE PATTERNS

I think we can detect two rival preferred patterns in artistic or imaginative activity, one based on neatness and one on complexity and irregularity. The underlying metaphor might be a wish for people to freeze into role, that is to act out a conservative vision; by observing inhibitions they protect property rights. This has far-reaching implications for the role of serenity and the sublime. The love of complexity, irregularity, spontaneity, simultaneous movements, uncertainty is constitutive for underground poetry. Dislike of it may express deep-seated pattern preferences, a wish to be undisturbed. Preoccupation with property may mean a dislike for instability and diversity in human behaviour, including art. Naturally the aesthetic preference for fixed patterns is a judgement like another and is to be respected. I just want to draw attention to the mobility of the line where complexity starts to be disorder: different people have different levels of tolerance for uncertainty and unresolved patterns. Incomplete patterns, and cognitive overload, are key areas for art.

The notion of freezing is key for conservative sensibility. A machine allows the laws of physics to operate undisturbed; the details of its design are largely to make the process, within a little artificial world, predictable and controllable. The wish for predictability precedes and makes possible the object that turns it into reality. Regulating human behaviour, within work processes, to make it predictable, preceded the machine age. The world of business, and of government, is a large set of boxes inside which variation can be excluded. It is hardly surprising if culture, too, represses variation. Artists, in a conservative society, tend to structure their working week, or their working year, like a job. The subjective result of realising that a situation is predictable is a reduction of awareness.

Read seemed alarmed by the lack of order in art movements after 1945. One element in this overload was the increasing number of people who know about art and who practice it; new countries arrived with entire art worlds teeming with painters and sculptors. Mass higher education is connected with mass artistic creativity. This is the way of the modern world, and it is a reflection of society as a whole becoming less repressed, more liberated, more vocal. To define this as overload seems egocentric.

It is likely that modern poetry reflects this higher level of complexity and subjectivity, and that this is part of its specific world-view – its definition of success. Someone who finds that high unpredictability disordered and threatening is likely to have a bad time with modern poetry across the board – and become a conservative.

So the art world is split according to how its members perceive times in which people and ideas pour across boundaries: one can either tolerate and enjoy this state of high unpredictability, or it triggers deeply-stored anxiety, alarm, and rigidity. One either tries to make art more complex, more adequate to the violent universe, or less complex: and more reassuring. What strikes me as lively and polyvalent strikes someone else as a 'bad chaos'.

Exclusion of variants produces a system of impoverished internal structure, unable to modify itself because all nearby states have been forbidden; it is bound to frustrate all groups except the narrowly orthodox, is unable to adapt, so fragile, and so a source of anxiety: whatever changes it, will bring about its overthrow. Change is not seen as progress, but as destruction, the loss of accumulated wealth. Literature is asked to record things as they were, to preserve them after their disappearance.

The Corporate 1980s

The decade saw a shift in the balance of emotional attention, and of control over economic resources, towards an old (late 19th-century) institution: the corporation. The idea of the 'good place' and sharing was widely replaced by aggrandisement, advance, calculation, marketing, and subordination. The shift in balance implies a contact boundary between the State, the corporation, and the family (or household), such that changes in the power of one affect the boundaries and prestige of the other two. This overall expansion of the corporate sibling was masked by unbearable pressure on individual corporations, dominated by competitions with others of their kind; the terms of the corporate job were largely redefined, so that far more people were unemployed, self-employed, or on limited contracts. This poverty and insecurity then affected the household. Worship of the corporate ideal ignored the fact of its limited scope; although the central institution of our society, the bearer of the values of modernity which had transformed society since the 16th century, it showed no desire either to employ most people or to fill most needs, and proved distinctly picky about proposed expansion beyond profitable limits. Analysis of poor regions, wards of towns, families, or individuals, as being short of corporate connection, was accurate. It didn't follow that unshackling the corporations would make the poor richer.

In history, the household was the main economic unit. A portion of the work done was drawn into the new system (growing since the 14th century) of money, but most, especially work done by women, wasn't. The employee evolved out of the servant, working for hire inside someone else's household, of which the family firm is the continuation. The industrial revolution wasn't funded by shareholding or even by bank loans. Analysis of ownership of land and shares might suggest that the corporation is just a mask for the continued prepotency of a few thousand families, its buildings just a new way of policing the work gangs. However, anyone who has held a low-paid job realises that a highly-paid job is a desirable thing, and reduces alienation; revolutionary politics made only a vague offer of more. Being made to feel inadequate and forced to internalise new values by your manager wasn't very different from having ditto and ditto done to you by a self-righteous commissar; all part of the modernisation process, I suppose. Since I joined the corporate world in 1978, I can say, personally, that it became a great deal more interesting in the 1980s. Things changed every few months, and the old, monotonous, clerical operations were progressively done away with by computerisation. An old belief that work was alienation and the family (marriage, community, congregation...) was simultaneously fulfilment and giving way to others, was ground down by criticism of the family and also by the new romanticisation of the 'job'.

The atmosphere of culturati, in those rooms where, we may suppose for lack of conclusive proofs, tastes are made and changed, was particularly labile. Fascination with corporate power poured out of women, the most mobile social group, because they were curious about this new world for them to conquer; preoccupation with the job might, in the 1950s, have been a way of boosting male self-importance vis-à-vis housewife and children, but it was by now the norm for women to work. Mostly, they were in low-paid jobs without union or security; but this was not so for the middle class, who are predominant in poetry.

Looking at the level of allegiance that an individual might be owing to their State, household, and corporation, we see that, while the corporation was tightening its grip on the employee, smashing the unions and continuously demanding more output, the family was stricken at its very foundations, and local or central government commanded only tenuous loyalty, cast as grumbling at politicians. Sentimental talk about the community disguised the fact that your employer and your household came first. The clear loser was the non-shareholding mass organisation, i.e. the unions and the Labour Party. The visible ineffectiveness of political work, measured against utopian expectations of ending the alienation of the masses, made committed people bored with it. Propaganda draws on the same skills as marketing and PR anyway, and makes dishonesty a virtue; the transition from being a radical designer on an underground newspaper to doing the same for an advertising agency or record company was almost painless. The cherished belief that capitalists were getting away with deceit and plunder led easily, in the anti-moral, bandit-loving, opportunism of the times, to envy and imitation: 'if I do it, it's OK'. Those who wanted leisure and pleasure found it through jobs, those who worked soberly and seriously at political work like research and leafleting found a job no more oppressive. The high tide of the New Right and deregulated hedonism in the 1980s did not find an asset value in poetry; it does not sell things, does not use shiny expensive gadgets, believes in individual conscience. It is inherently anti-capitalist; the atmosphere of the Thatcher/Lawson years affected everyone in the poetry scene as a cultural pressure in which emotional authenticity and belief in a community seemed less attractive. This showed itself as a loss of nerve; a migration away from critical and non-sensuous forms; repetition of previously radical gestures as loyalty tokens of the losing faction; the resurgence of insignificant culturally conservative poets; and perhaps the definition of the personality as a commodity, to be aggrandised without inhibition by the techniques of PR. New radical poets made very unimpressive careers in this decade. There is a whole world of conservatives that flourishes in an era of rising property values.

NEOCLASSICISM

So how do you write poetry in the absence of ideas? It is a mistake to confuse feeble archaism with neoclassicism. Those who have bet on neo-conservatism overestimate the emotional appeal of being unable to deal with the modern world, and of antique approaches to phrasing and rhythm. We have beautiful evocations of this from two German critics. Hermann Korte says about a certain contemporary German poet:

> (X) does not fail over metre and rhythm, but over the form itself, which he mistreats, as he wishes to bring back its long since sunken presence and yet only – in the image of the 'moist glances, which rest longingly on objects' – travesties their meaning, to pseudopoetic kitsch. [*my translation*]

Korte cites an article by Alexander von Bormann, 'The Regression to Form', which calls it 'a basic gesture of renunciation, of despair, of recognized pointlessness.' Michael Schmidt's 1983 anthology *Some Contemporary Poets* includes 167 poems, of which 57 use rhyme. Many English poets seemed in the 1980s to be running an antique shop, where battered objects from all eras were preserved, refurbished, and set out for sale. Of course these objects come more often from the households of aristocrats, and from churches, than from the dwellings of the poor. A patter adorned with picturesque old words flows over the wares and tries to restore them to life.

This sense of mourning may be reinforced by feelings of the old middle class that the whole path of history is undermining their social position, and that they are being drowned by a furious and competent new middle class. A class in decline may value the old for its own sake. We can distinguish this from the dealer's scale of values, where an old painting or vase acquires value just from being old. The fate of those who fail to emerge from the old is to become like the painters and artisans who create fakes for the antiques trade: a very highly skilled task, but the fake is not classicism. Conservatism today expresses a profound sense of inferiority. It is inexplicable that the study of history, i.e. of change, should lead someone to ask art to be frozen. The antiquarian version of history can ask 'how much is this object worth' but never 'why did it happen like this?'

Biedermeier

We have to ask what kind of poetry would please a paranoid conservative. Light can be shed on this by the text of an advertisement that appeared in an early issue of *PN Review*: 'X's plain and economical style blends feeling, thought and form with uncommon precision. He has a gift for memorable lines, for brevity and grace under pressure which make him a poet whose verse can be widely appreciated and understood.'

Empathy can let you down when the person with whom you are empathising wants you to act out a role of submission. There is a symmetry between threat behaviour (*Imponiergehabe*, in the German word) and appeasement behaviour, and the rage of conservatives gives rise to a specific poetic style of meekness that surrenders adventure because it could seem like defiance. It is hard to see how an advertisement like this would appeal or excite. Michael Schmidt edited (in 1976, 1980, 1983) three anthologies full of appeasement poems, not obviously neo-conservative but attuned to the absence of modernity.

The public face of poetry during rollback is reminiscent of Austrian culture in the post-1815 era of restoration under Metternich; everything serious is excluded from discussion; a traditionalist and anti-intellectual salon art holds sway, in which dissonant energies are pushed out into a fringe of manneristic decoration; poets are favoured for innocence, inanity, and stylistic regression; the withdrawal from public affairs leaves the way open for an enveloping domesticity. This style is sometimes called Biedermeier. Rather obviously the attack on political art meant that poets were not allowed to write seriously, and the result of not allowing adult affairs within the boundary of the poem was a regression to childhood by the poets who sought favour. The typical Biedermeier picture was one showing pretty and appealing children, within a family where authority was firm and sentiment and prosperity beamed out. In poetry, it meant domestic anecdote and writing about childhood. The ban on the Left hid itself behind prettifying evasions; neatness meant that a poem did not have any messy political implications and left everything the way you found it; egoism meant the lack of self-discipline of someone who wanted the system to be changed and who put his own opinion up against that of the great, the good, and the highly qualified.

The British resistance to modern art and ideas is tangled up with a nostalgia for the wonderfully and morbidly over-developed culture of childhood. British children's books probably are the best in the world. It has been remarked that children are naturally conservative, just as animals are. If you go to the same pastry shop every Saturday for 20 years, and eat the same cake each time, the prospect of this stopping may fill you with alarm; but also you are unlikely to perceive any single cake-eating event with any vividness, because it is so familiar.

The Property Metaphor

An era of rising property prices is also one where the price of art objects and cultural prestige rises. In a right-wing era, the commodity value of art is paramount. Because art is composed of ownable objects, fitting into an overriding *mise-en-scène* of prosperous domestic existence, artistic expertise is primarily that of valuing and authenticating these objects, and its discourse is the patter by which a shopkeeper commends a painting, or a wine, or by which the owner, so negligently and indolently, advises you of how wonderful his object is, and how it is too expensive for you. The book of poems is a collection of experiences, personal but which the author happens to be selling. The aura of art is for a conservative tied up with repetition, security, and the sense that other people are loyal to oneself – the idea of a treat tokening love and benevolence. The conservative does not wish to form new models, to hypothesise, or to think, in fact regards these tasks as a form of pain. These showings, because they are not monolithic, or monarchical, are defined as incoherent, and consequently as symptoms of neurosis, perhaps madness; anyway of unfitness to be heard. The poet who masters these rules can be taken up by the official poetry world.

The conservative English writer does not appeal to the reader, but tells them what their social duties are; and faithfully records social hierarchies, with all nuances of rank, insignia, numbers of buttons, family background, and past distinctions. This art is above all a series of acts of paying respect, with pleasure and choice playing no role; on the model of an 18th-century court, degrees of verbal respect taking up the whole of the waking day; elaborate language comes from this setting and poetry takes it over along with secret codicils. Because attention is an integral part of these formal social occasions, the individual must not direct attention by some private programme. The tasks of envy and admiration cannot be left up to private whim. The fulfilment of traditional tasks is invested with cultural value; writing a rhymed poem, or pastiching a 17th-century convention, is itself an act of respect and of self-effacement. Quality is thus a mode of repetition. Artistic forms are validated by their association with the senior and privileged, in a kind of primogeniture. Avant-garde writers are acceptable once they are over 70.

Tradition and Personal Art

If people change, update, their notion of your character all the time, that is a form of insecurity. Conservatism might mean freezing your idea of your own character so that it becomes solid, like a possession. If self-esteem were not wholly unstable it would not constantly be building defences.

If you write a poem in great haste, without reflection or close attention, it is likely to come out just like your last poem. This is why we say that someone original is putting their personality into the poem; the differentiation of every expressive and semantic level is apparently the mark of an individual psychology. But when someone writes the same poem a hundred times, they justify that too on the grounds, so reasonable, that it is their 'nature' to write so. Writing in the style of the generation before you were born is described as 'following your nature'. We can doubt, also, that development of technique is identical with the expression of personality. Writing in a conventional way is felt simultaneously to be natural, and so personal, and to be egalitarian, a refusal of bad subjectivity. The explanation of cultural preferences in terms of the sociology of prestige is doubly unwelcome because it suggests that the personality is part of a process: even this is not a possession. Indeed the preoccupation with personality (as an asset, as something unchangeable that stands still while generating changing forms) may correlate with downward mobility and be a denial of process. There is a problem with making personality the main content of art.

The only residual role of sensibility is to underpin high prices of scarce goods, for example of forgotten poetry books of the 1920s changing hands for large sums.

THE DECAY CURVE OF CULTURE

A group that acts as pioneers and leaders in setting anti-modern positions is the downwardly mobile elements of the middle class. Changes in income distribution mean that there are groups who are losing relative position; incompetence at a personal level means that some families or individuals, in any generation, are actually losing ground. Where these individuals possess the cultural attainments that are matching accessories to a high economic status, their natural tendency is to exalt the value of old cultural possessions and deny any value at all to new ones. It is hard for them to enjoy a process of development, one of whose outcomes is the realisation of their own economic decline.

The core of conservatism is ancestor worship: genealogies (on which claims to estates depend), retrieval of archaic patterns, glorification of great figures of the past. The past that refuses to go away may be the Gothic of our churches and public buildings, of saints and coats of arms, or the Elizabethan flowering, made sacrosanct by set texts and school plays, or the Victorian era, with its strange yearning for the Gothic.

The historian of the 'heritage industry' dates its take-off to around 1980. That is, the proliferation of museums is part of a withdrawal from a class-based telling of history. It is part of the rollback, and part of the eclipse of Marxism and intimately linked to the growth of inequality of wealth. The story 'in the past a few people had too much power. They held everyone else down, and built cultural institutions to do that. But history is made by the many and what happened was the rise of the many, the smashing of restrictions, and the draining of force of those institutions' was impossible to exclude from responsible books about history but didn't have to feature in costume dramas and tourist sites. The 1980s saw the rise of a new school of right-wing historians, which didn't even argue the wrongs of the past, but was merely antiquarian; virtuosic, Betjemanian, chattering agreeably like a vintner, but uncritical. Something cultured English people are good at is noticing tiny discrepancies in the rigging-out of cultural productions. Such expertise is only possible because we have enjoyed the same scenes too many hundreds of times, only valid because the scenes have lost their power to influence the living of life and have turned from ideas to objects. In order to realise that a button is missing, you have to accept and hold in stock the whole court ritual. One notices such details because of intellectual unemployment: the sense of being immersed in cultural being has vanished, the pool has dried up.

Perhaps fetishisation is an organic phase on the time curve of every kind of art, it only holds our attention because we have failed to move on. Perhaps every artistic scene starts as something immersing and boundless, and its breaking down into small, dead, separable, controllable bits of knowledge is a sign of age. It may be that all perceptions start to age as soon as they arrive, and that tedious poetry is simply filled with ageing and deteriorating perceptions, low down the unforgiving slope of thermal decay. Patterns of excitation decay all the time, they can only survive if they take in new materials.

A Deathlike Melancholia

Why is someone is so weak at forming new patterns of attachment – to modernist poetics, or, it might be, to a new and thick blanket? We could see conservatism as the symptom of aesthetic weakness; representing the corpse of a sensibility, or one that is undeveloped because it continually regresses to infancy and rejects the new experience rather than absorbing it. The old experience is damaged because its substance has been metabolised away, it is a ghost. But for such people the experience of the new is equally damaged, because of anxiety, inhibitions, or perhaps political resistances; they cannot release themselves into the new and alive; they cannot even understand what they are supposed to be enjoying.

There is a link between sloth and melancholia. One could classify conservatism as one species of melancholy; it could simply be the habitus of a sluggish sensibility, something cautious and slow that always responds too late, when the situation has already disappeared and is only recoverable as a memory or an object. The mind is full of dead objects because no live ones arrive to clear them away. One values oneself cheaply because one is full of low-value experiences, which interest neither oneself nor others. Perhaps the start is anxiety, which makes one avoid new and risky experiences. Since the movement of sensibility always goes from one thing to the next, the phase of detachment (i.e. loss) is experienced by everybody; but since it is only a transition, it need not cause pain. Debates on form do not alleviate deep psychological conditions. But the belief in cultural change can mediate a state of mind in which what was defined as the personality, something permanent and tragic, can be redefined as a temporary state, an 'affection'. Grief passes away. And so did Thatcherism.

THE 1980S: EGO-HISTOIRE

The death of the Movement was occurring during the 1980s. It is agreed that this clique of poets and editors or critics exercised a hegemony over English poetry after 1956. It is less clear when their rule ended. I suggest the mid-1980s. A lot of people went on being inhibited, but that is not the same as a coherent cultural formation. When Donald Davie (1922-95) published *Under Briggflatts. British Poetry Since 1960* in 1989, it was already obsolete and remained without influence. It is also striking that the accredited chief propagandist of The Movement could not find a group of successor poets to groom: instead he left out all poets who began publishing after 1960. This suggested that nothing had replaced The Movement. No doubt this is the message Davie wanted to send. At age 70 he still wanted to be 'best new poet'. But that pattern suggested rather that their moment of creativity had been incredibly brief and could not by any means be revived.

THE WORSHIP OF STYLE

Something that marked the decade was a combination of refinement (rejecting the coarse nihilism of the Movement) and orthodoxy (shying away from the innovation that had thrived in the 1970s). The stylistic research of the radical poets was rejected, in order to give the reader a surface which was apparently more yielding and undemanding; but this loss of inner autonomy had to be compensated by another withdrawal, the hint that the poet didn't mean what he was saying, or that some superior irony was evading the reader. So this 'courtly' style could be brief and overtly simple enough to be allowed into the 'culture spots' of High Street magazines as a basis for a career with a mainstream publisher; but this simplicity was also a loss of credibility and had to be compensated for by hints of a 'hidden' ambiguity. The courtly poet could suggest depth by withholding himself, by hinting at a trick surface of affability hiding detachment, disillusion, superior knowledge. An ancillary of this withdrawal is concern within the poems, for 'style', presenting characters so withered and externalized that they see themselves as objects on a screen. An example is James Lasdun's 'Vindice at the Oyster Bar':

> A parable: watch light blade down through blurs
> To tongue bright morning's tocsin from a jar

And coax a glass-hard tulip's metal scarlet,
The belling petals' aztec star –

One day you touch the flower, and each petal
Drops from the stem unblemished, hard, with all
Its moon-curve, pristine glaze immaculate
You almost hear them clatter as they fall.
    (from 'Vindice at the Oyster Bar', in *A Jump Start*, 1987, p.29)

Lasdun's fashion notes – filtered through the lethal vision of the Terminator-like hero of Tourneur's *The Revenger's Tragedy* – are the poetic summing-up of the consumerist 1980s: 'Bullion at flinty wrists… Silk scarves afloat on scalloped necks'. Lasdun holds identification and disgust in exact tension. Another example of 'Style Wars' flouncing is Jeremy Reed's poem 'An Age Bereft', in a volume dedicated to Lasdun:

They won't recall our panache, our finesse,
we're outsiders in an age without Proust,
James or Cocteau to notate how style is
a something not pronounced, minutiae of speech
[…]
  a mauve ink inscription on a flyleaf.
    (in *Selected Poems*, 1987, p.37)

Other characters from Tourneur's play are, of course, called Lussurioso, Spurio, and Supervacuo. The psychological focus vanishes into 'accessories' and then vanishes again, invisible even in those: the viewer is by definition not cultured enough to realise how expensive your clothes are. This idea that style exists as a meaning outside the audience observing it is, however, belied a few pages later:

the water reflections of ties
contrasting lapis lazuli with grey
shot silk – vestiges of a taste that lacked
courage to wear them, now exposed today

On counterpane and floor, a mosaic
to be boxed up and sent to charity
bazaars.
    (from 'Dead Hand', *ibid*, p.43)

This is a better description of the identical situation.

This shift of values from inner to outer is clearly the response to the total hostility of the cultural environment to poetry. The poem cuts its hair, buys a suit, does what the establishment commands. It no longer matters what the poet feels inside, only the surface – as suave, stylish, and wealthy as possible – counts.

> It bubbles underground, this throbbing vein
> of water in the cliff, then sparkles free,
> as though drawn through a needle's eye of light,
> each sun-flashed decibel of energy
> tooling the granite ledge to abalone.
> And eye in a peacock's feather, the sea
> transmutes the fine fleck of its rain
> to lapis. Whose winged foot has marked this stone?
> (Jeremy Reed, from 'Transformations')

Desuete literary figures come in as tributes to the crumbling but jealous literary power-holders. Landscape is chosen as a subject because it is old and crumbly and assiduous respect can be paid to it. When I read these poems by Reed in 1981 it was like a government announcement that poetry had ceased to be a zone of subjective openness and was now one of closed formality and struggle for office. One has to ask why poets, today, are counting lines and calling their (unrhymed) poems sonnets: surely the reason is a latent longing for rule-bound form and official acceptance.

Addendum 2016

I think the problem with this passage is that it is ambiguous about Lasdun's position. I wasn't specific enough that the poet was observing someone else and that the sharp comment was him about his 'Vindice', not me about Lasdun. It connects astutely to two phenomena of the time. The 'oyster bar' was a resort that was notoriously about spending lots of money in the visible pursuit of exquisite sensations, a place to find what were later called yuppies. The dwelling on clothes relates, directly or not, to Peter York's book *Style Wars* (1980), which was about self-adornment and grooming as a combat for position. The book was a front runner for depoliticisation: instead of cultural critique you have articles about clothes. The flip side of that was that it was quite frank about outright struggle. Dress to impress. Out for yourself. Solidarity cast aside. There was no community. People struggling in the jobs market might detest the economic policies that made them insolvent, but definitely wanted to win this outright struggle and achieve affluence. Concomitantly, suave style in poetry replaces ideological cut and thrust, the critique and construction of new shared meanings.

Vindice, in the play, builds up in secret to a dire revenge, and I would love to think that Lasdun's Vindice secretly harbours revolutionary passions – for the end of authority. Lasdun worked for a publisher and was one of the first people to read my long book of 1980-81. There was never any chance of him getting it published, but his criticisms were impressive and did define why I wasn't a mainstream poet – I didn't have that level of reflexivity at the time. Around 1980 is where my personal biography starts getting tangled up with the biography of poetry. The book came out in two parts in 1991 and 2001, and was finally reissued in one volume in 2013. I came in through the out door.

For a gay man, other men are lacking a beautiful organ that carries a sense, something like the skin or clothes but more beautiful and more sensitive. Naturally someone without that organ is to be seen as obtuse. But how similar this is to the sense that makes someone able to deal with the business and produce a book of poetry that is going to find its way into High Street shops and find its way out again as it sells. How much one wanted to clad a book in cultural raiment which would be like the hallucinatory outfits illustrated in *Style Wars* and armoured in elegance go out and be acceptable in the world whose rejection has the force of law.

The desuete figures were David Gascoyne and Kathleen Raine, important patrons for Reed at the time. (Of all the ways of getting Raine to publish you in *Temenos*, writing poems amazingly similar to hers was surely the best and most direct.) It is easy to write poetic history from the point of view of thousands of beautiful souls telling you why they didn't publish my lovely poetry, but you can also write it from the point of view of the management tier explaining why each book wasn't good enough and why it shouldn't have been published and how it could be better. Managers *do* play a delegated role for other readers – when the managers don't like it maybe the market doesn't like it either. Maybe the poetry-reading market is being let down every day by poetry that should be better. Legitimacy is not an arbitrary quantity but a real thing reflecting the judgments of bookshop managers, reviewers, editors, book buyers, poetry lovers – the fact that those wishes can change day by day as new information arrives does not mean they are unreal. Consecration by other people is not the same as consecration by yourself.

Cape did get Christopher Logue published and Vindice may be influenced by the weapon-fetishist figures of *War Music*. I decided to write my works rather than try to get them published. This is where I got my understanding of time. When I began hanging out at Sub-Voicive I met Adrian Clarke. Later, I began to edit a magazine with him. I was familiar with him as a figure at jazz gigs in Camden years before I knew who he was (the height, the shaven head), part of the chronotope of free jazz in pubs around the Lock and Gloucester Avenue. A world that, at the time, I aspired to. Something relevant to Clarke, even inspiring for him, is Paul Virilio and his dromoscopy, velocity as an autonomous form of perception, a speed lens through which everything becomes new. Something Adrian recalled for me was the argument for and against Coleman in English jazz circles around 1965. The speed might even come from Ornette Coleman playing alto sax in a field dominated by tenor sax – that greater speed, purity of tone, removal from the body. A line whose impetus rushed out into the unknown, defining space with melodic gestures rather than recurring to memorised patterns of knowledge or behaviour. Clarke has dismantled the syntax of his poems in such a way that overall semantic fields are identified by the way strings of nouns cluster, ideas are invoked by a kind of headline effect, but the articulation and determination that explicit syntax and parsing provides are simply not there. The rapidly moving verbal surface is rich in phantoms of meaning, shimmering without being resolved:

> isochemial homing tail in
> a scroll stable under
> centrepoint satellite capitals spat
> MOTHER in the Strand
> such a precursive scenario
> wouldn't get floor space
> from a Euclidian aesthetic
> idioglossia milked the pavement
> figuratively thick in expectance
> traffickers express photochemical atomized
> edged from a meaning
> effect the drift relocated
> estates vacant in strategic
> brilliance trajectory for agglomerate
>   (from *Obscure Disasters*, p.16)

This systematic use of montage is a development from a style most associated with Tom Raworth. In the poem quoted, each line includes exactly four words. This is not an abstract picture but a kind of insect-eye, a reflection of ambient metropolitan language in scraps, ruthlessly echoed, cut, sped up, played back. It's like call and response in jazz, Clarke may be playing back patterns rather than complete utterances but the original is still there and if you read it at speed involuntary memories of the sources flash up all the time. The imitation is scabrous, catching and exaggerating the unconscious gestures rather than the reasoned, planned ones. Virilio saw the blitzkrieg go past him aged about seven, and wrote ever after about speed. Let me quote from a handbook named *Military Space Forces*: 'Laser beam weapons, regardless of type (gas, chemical, excimer, free electron, solid state, X-ray), concentrate a tightly focused shaft or pulse of radiant energy photons on the target surface. The beam burns through.' The speed of modern domination makes the lightning of 1940 seem slow. Clarke's velocity reduces the integrity and physicality of perceptions in order to do to them something like what abstraction does to original experiences. Hollowing out local detail is like an unblinding which allows larger patterns to emerge. It is finance that uses super-speed to affect the order of daily life. Clarke filmed through a tube of vision sealed by velocity, a brass tunnel like the tube of a saxophone, where perspective shocks a tract of the world into order, an eyeball is briefly distorted, flowing off its shape, by the air velocity. Like a camera on the front of a train. Masses rushing towards it and diving away to either side. It was kinetic, held together by the beat, clean, almost metallurgically perfect.

The key event in the whole decade is where the New Right wave broke and stopped advancing and trying to wash everything away. This moment certainly wasn't visible to those living through it, but it changed everything. Between Nixon's victory in 1968 and some mystic point in about 1987, the New Right was advancing cell by cell. The Left thing was vapourware. Maybe the London stock market crash of 1987 was the point of halt. I had been given a job by the Stock Exchange and it was held up by the uncertainty after that crash. In about 1989, I used to hang out with D.S. Marriott (then working for the Bank of England) and talk about culture, money, and so on. Over about five years to 1984, I was learning Russian at evening classes. Some people in the classes were old Communist Party members, maybe even second-generation ones, who always struck me as remarkably stupid. Marxism didn't mean anything to me; it was a discredited salvation knowledge. Exploring a thousand phases of the disaster of Communist rule in eastern Europe was a feature of the time: everyone went through it. I read a lot of Russian dissident writing. Marriott and I were sure that if you had no understanding of business and made economics the primary thing in your understanding of history and politics, then your explanation of those things was worthless and your creative work would pour out through a great hole in the hull. This was at a moment when obvious industrial collapse and immiseration were making a left-wing analysis more and more desirable – that primary left-wing surge irrigating a landscape where politics and the media were solidly New Right. D.S. and I concluded that there was no point being neo-conservative unless you were rich. Many people realised this. This simple fact is what halted the advance of the New Right.

The title of 'style wars' was misleading (it was a derivation from the title of a film popular at the time). It was not 'style wars' because they weren't wars. What was happening wasn't warfare. It was narcissistic self-consecration. York didn't explain the meaning of clothes. Clothes have no meaning. He was just illustrating fantasies about impressing people. So the act of self-consecration had the implication that other people's opinions have no value. This was surely the unit structure of the New Right: a privatisation of the self. A currency with no collateral. A brand image.

I'VE GOT ME, BABE: CULTURE AS SELF-ESTEEM

You work all your life, you make a lot of mistakes. A high proportion of the people you meet dislike you. Other people are better than you at what you do. Then you die. This is not a popular message but politics has to be based on reality at some level. In 1968 the youth revolt persuaded people that these rules didn't apply to them. In 1988 the neo-con thing was persuading quite a few people that liberated capitalism would liberate them from these rules. Both kinds told people they could get away from this, it would cease to be true. Both fantasies were beautiful in their way but the Left and the Right utopias fell in on themselves. A key fact is that there was no neo-con literary project of grandeur to compare with the grand Marxist project. This asymmetry is a fact worth explaining. Maybe identity politics was the voice of the New Right, but it still didn't produce very much art. With the capitalist thing the visual presence of the ideal was already there: advertisements. You simply had to lose the bit of you that said no to them, that said worldly goods distract you from love and affection, and simply say yes. The ads show beautiful experiences happening to beautiful people. Maybe there was no need for neo-con poems: the visual and audible world in which we live was already saturated with this imagery.

If you believed that the world of glamorised photographs (in magazines, TV ads, films, packaging) was different from the real world you were cut off from Utopia. If you could watch an advertising film for a Porsche and feel whispers of doubt you were a crypto-Marxist, a deviant, a dissident.

I read that in the tomb of Tutankhamun there were 3,500 separate objects, presumably all expensive and more elaborate than the everyday ones. This Pharaonic plenitude is mindless, blissful, boundless. Reels of advertisements re-created it, endlessly yielding. It may be that you can write poetry without having this lavishness and variety, but it's better if you don't. 3,500 ornate verbal objects are as exciting as so many ones made of wood and metal. The 1980s quite noticeably saw a return to luxury and decoration.

European Conservative parties kept winning elections, and the Marxist camp developed from this a theory of false consciousness. This developed into a theory of constructionism: everything is constructed, so your desires and your feelings about yourself are illusions, constructed by socialising experiences inside symbolic forms designed by power interests. Culture, in fact, had no existence outside of propaganda. 'You don't really want that – you just have a constructed desire.' The effect of constructionist theory on political culture was this reasoning: there are no values; economic power is due to status, which is subjective; culture exists to give status; if we take over culture we can raise the status of our faction (e.g. women, black people, Irish); so culture and the media ought to be like advertisements for us. The premise is that the reader cannot see reason and has no rights to be given unbiased information. There was also a small-scale version of this, applied by individuals. This also set out from the proposition that 'the official assessment of me is inaccurate', and aimed to set up an alternative valuation, in which all the evidence came from the person being measured. This falsifies relationships, as it reduces the other people around you to objects to be manipulated.

'Identity politics' occupied the gross manipulative means of the capitalist media in order to make propaganda for factional interests, without any ambiguity or compositional tension at all. If a poem is saying, at the emotional level,

GREEK PEOPLE ARE WONDERFUL
I AM A GREEK
GIVE GREEKS MORE POWER
EVERYONE WHO DISAGREES WITH ME IS A BAD PERSON

then it is not more complex than an advertisement. Arguably, it is an advertisement. Arguably, we are so addicted to advertising that its methods permeate our way of thinking; even in lyric poems. A new political order without new processes for making, controlling, and sharing information would drift towards the anomalies and failures that exist in the present order. The belief that you can be whatever you present yourself as was oddly close to the clothes-worship of *Style Wars*, and not too far away from the idea that other people have no right to their opinions about you. The protocols of legitimation were violently shifting. You would wake up and find the boundaries had shifted.

One of the drivers was a feminist idea that all official cultural activity was made by men and that it was all projections of the ego and the wish to dominate. All you had to was flip this. Instantly the history of culture becomes simply the history of male fantasy and self-glorification. Obviously, this made study unnecessary. I recall one of the old Communists in my Russian class at PCL telling me that the history of English poetry was all works of praise for rich nobles who had been the patrons, and so that Soviet poetry chained to the State and to propaganda was exactly the same as Western poetry. This was an old Stalinist idea. Again, someone who knows the whole history of Western culture (in one lesson) is obviously better informed than someone who finds it complicated and only knows some parts of it. There was a turning point where critique of the self became making advertisements for the self.

Feminists deciding that all their experience was of a corrupt social order had to devise their proposed social order, whose Day One was today, out of the imaginary. Art could in fact be this imaginary. Proposing that 'conditioning by family and school left me with a set of behaviour tapes, which the real me firmly rejects' led to the other proposal, that these tapes could be seized, erased and re-recoded. A certain valuation of myth as the storehouse of social values led women to write mythological poems, and to attack existing myths, as if this would bring about a new society. (This could also apply to any other fraction rejecting basic tenets of society.)

There is a transcript by other people of the messages that you send and how you behave. The time saw delicacies in the transcript, a conflict over the legitimate version. There was a non-overlay of images. The blur, the vague area was where the *work* of culture took place. Other people wished to own the transcript of my judgement of their behaviour. Where agreement could not be reached, people simply pulled out; as the shared zone became ever emptier and less stable, the end result was privatisation. Once you don't accept that my opinion has any value the public realm is despoiled. It is broken up and territorialised.

Privatisation was a loss of belief in the opinion of others, in perception and judgment. These did not fit in with the self-consecration. Where the poem was a presentation of a self that was not present then authenticity vanishes from the message and the response could not satisfy. The suit had taken over. There is a difference between narcissism and authenticity.

Poets know the difference. It's like a false interpretation of the law. It may take weeks of work, great erudition, attention to fine detail. But if you're a lawyer you know the difference and a poet knows the difference. They just choose to ignore it. J.H. Prynne has insisted on this difference, all the time, over 50 years. The regard of the self is not self-regard. But the whole grey area between inauthentic and not quite inauthentic (between draft six and draft twelve?) was one of uncertainty in this period, when both legitimacy and authenticity were shifting rapidly around. It was easy to lose your footing. How far you fell was a matter of judgement.

'Theory', what the humanities call 'theory', was a leap away from fact and so susceptible to being turned into acts of self-consecration by ritual occupation. Liberation was loss of footing. The initial proposition that all social relations should be beautiful should have been resolved out, as an infinite quantity, by many steps of substituting in finite, real-world quantities. Notoriously, this substitution had not occurred, and the initial idealism, that double effect of blankness and blinding gleam, was still there, falsifying everything and constituting the source of attraction.

The rejection of conditioning postulates a distinction between the real me and my behaviour, including even my experience and my feelings. One has to ask whether this real me is not the product of envy inculcated by media representations of the good life. The proposal that everything which frustrates is oppressive is the infantile hallucination of omnipotence, it means that only gratification is authentic (which is the world-view of advertisements) and reduces poetry to a feature-less mythological bluster without sensuous grip. The rejection of conditioning is always an acceptance of conditioning in the sense that it defines behaviour patterns purely in terms of the application of psychological force to the exclusion of any material or social reality. I would propose that such poetry only reaches the status of art insofar as it (a) evokes autobiographical reality, and (b) liberates fantasy with artistic intent rather than being nailed to some spurious medical-political determinism. It emerges that the only interesting realism is dialectic realism, i.e. which starts by criticising reality and uses experience as the material of thought guided by revolutionary optimism.

Victims of Glamour

Lasdun persuaded Reed to abandon his Gothic and lexically exotic style in favour of something acceptable to the High Street, which indeed was published by Cape. This was symbolic for me; I thought the hushed and self-reverential manner was so bad that it absolved me from the effort of developing a style that would get into the High Street. Reed moved on, reaching much greater popularity as a poet of indulgence of fantasies, erotic and by preference perverse, for a large audience. Over about 50 books (who can count?) Reed has gone through multiple mutations. D.S. Marriott persuaded me, round about 1989, that the small-press world had something worth investigating, and reluctantly I began to uncover something hardly visible. Marriott's belief in the underground British poetry of the 1960s and 1970s was like St Paul with early Christianity; he organised it and gave it historical stature. One feature of the later 1980s is that committed English poets were no longer looking back to the American avant-garde of the 1950s as the horizon of the recent past which promised an immediate future, but rather to recent British poets, J.H. Prynne more than anyone else. This was partly the work of Anthony Barnett, as book designer and publisher, an associate of Marriott's. Reed often insisted that his sense of style stood for secret defiance, a line of messages incomprehensible to the outsider. This didn't seem to work for those 1980s books, where the style broadcast respect for older authority figures and conformance to legacy values of decorum. But again, that preoccupation with clothes is a notoriously gay thing, and does involve the transmission of messages that are only truly understood by those destined to understand them. The city was full of glamour magazines, seeing the *photograph* as where truth, the crystalline virtue of the lens, the straightness of the course of light, demonstrated a self-projection and took it out of the realm of fantasy. The photograph, descendant of the genre of portraits of nobles, replaced other forms of memory, reducing the past to re-enactments of rituals, and asked for glamour poems. Reed wrote:

> it's how most people think of poetry
> as buried slash, if there's meaning the feel
> is all of it, (I eat a lemon cake)
> between poems, polenta and drink wine
> out of the bottle neck
> (from 'White Bear and Francis Bacon')

'Slash' refers to a genre of illegal fictions that utilise existing settings and write new stories in them. An early form (around 1984) was Star Trek/gay, which involved stories about an affair between Spock and Captain Kirk. The slash is the oblique stroke which indicates appropriation. Reed is saying that culture works by inserting yourself into pre-existing stories and star identities, and that the act of reading involves inserting yourself in the roles offered by the poem (or pinup, etc.). *Vogue* did a feature on Reed sometime in the 1980s. I seem to have mislaid my copy of that one, but it was certainly a photo-spread plus adoring write-up. Is there any point in dealing with Reed except in the vocabulary of fandom? By worshipping glamour he reached a market to which modern poetry was completely unknown. After about 1990 he wrote perhaps a thousand poems that were like glamour photographs, moments of indulgence, intimacy, and consecration. D.S. Marriott wrote:

> Oblivion of heaviness opaque with
> dust a listless memory but choice
> of maple & green canticle. So,
> angled goodness past Dover till
> precious salmon gave tongue's
> counsel. Flood of winter for us
> & Northern bread. Till lighting
> scorches & elms lament.
>   We are struck dead, unsure of
> personal glory off last lights.
> 'Turn off' a circuit endeavours
> awash with cloud & wandering, in
> corporate Gloucester. You being
> a pastoral emptiness of Canterbury
> of regal limit. & despair cores
> all level habit, my swift love &
> final unction. Unsure – yes? Then
> why append a sacred power at Palos
> or Caracalla?
>   (from 'Sphere')

> Ventured into being as barren loneliness.
> The white, unclean cities, wounded by
> myths. It needs to be said: the Puritans
> from Saxony are like rich birds inside
> their solar plumage, trembling with vision
> & the possibility of pure sound, high in
> the fragrant courtyard.
>   (from 'In Darkness')

Marriott slash Prynne. Marriott did a doctoral thesis on Prynne and began writing classy Prynne knock-offs which were totally abstract and totally subjective, impossible to frame. Marriott translated Prynne into an asset, a wondrous technological lump of capital, and relentlessly acquired that asset for himself in an assertion of status. The style only emerged into view when schematised and imitated. Suddenly it was a software package: Grosseteste 1.0. The lack of ego boundaries was both dizzying and annihilating. Shining through the text was a figure of immensely organised erasure, the disappearance of anything not primeval to allow visibility to things exotic, idealistic and wrapped in philosophical abstruseness. The level of territoriality involved in this historicism did not suit me – I had socialist views about land ownership. Hidden behind the machinery of the Cambridge School stylisation was a compulsive and melancholic voice. It was the urge to dominate which was the most authentic thing.

ADDITION 2016

This has been written partly as ego-histoire (following the example of Lutz Niethammer). It's about me – but wasn't everyone who wanted to publish a first book in the 1980s facing the same ports of entry? The same security staff on the doors? Reed writing passionately and repetitively (in his great long poem 'White Bear') about how straight men couldn't understand colour and expression could be a response to what I wrote in *FCon*.

LUDIC POETRY

The legacy of the radical era, roughly 1968-76, was of a large scale. It involved a very large number of individuals. The new culture was forced to devise techniques for silencing and neutralising these individuals. An iron rule was that you couldn't present an idea: because the intelligentsia of the time were all Left beneath the skin and the idea was going to be cultural criticism and not aimed to preserve property values. Like chasing people off the estate.

During the 1980s, the High Street publishers produced big fireworks, for example Frank Kuppner, *A Bad Day for the Sung Dynasty* (1984); David Harsent's *Mister Punch* (1984); John Ash, *The Branching Stairs* (1985) and *Disbelief* (1987); Edwin Morgan, *Themes on a Variation* (1988); Jeremy Reed, *Bleecker Street* (1980); and John Hartley Williams, *Bright River Yonder* (1987). This represents brilliant decisions by individual editors going against the consensus of their colleagues. They would have been body blows to the underground (if the underground had noticed), and the list of new poets in the alternative sector may not be significantly stronger than this list. The features of intelligence, lightness, and beauty which we used to find in the underground seem to have migrated to this group and bypassed the venerable institutions of the small presses. They do not represent a complete renewal of the mainstream, because a great number of other writers were untouched by this new freedom. The word 'post-modernist' is often used; it is simpler to say that most of these poets, these books, showed the influence of John Ashbery. Beyond that, they are all ludic, or playful, except Harsent. The ludic style cut free of the need to moralise and to take a stand on everything, the most vital prejudice of English poetry readers. The route by which it became possible to write without schemas and consequences was the total ban by neo-conservatives on having your own ideas or trusting your own judgement on anything at all. You have students and long-hairs who have no values and *don't* want to protest, go on strike, occupy buildings, write essays explaining how power is unequally distributed? Fantastic. Give them what they want. You have poems that don't spell out that actions can have negative consequences and that citizens have duties to fulfil? Fantastic. Print them.

Poetry Review published reviews of Ashbery's books in 1978, 1982, 1986, 1988 and 1991. Those were probably the *only* reviews of avant-garde poetry they ran in the whole of the 1980s. Ashbery had nothing to do with anti-Vietnamese War protests and sounded suave, reflexive, affluent, courtly, decorous, dégagé, sociable, and educated. Actually, he sounded a lot more intelligent than the poets that the magazine was publishing. I think he changed the rules for English poetry. The mainstream wanted to sound like Ashbery. He became top poet, because everyone knew the mainstream poets were stupid. It was Ashbery calorie-lite, or cashbery. The conservatives had consecrated W.H. Auden and were quite aware that he had used an enigmatic style in the 1930s, in poems evoking an *unstated* set of facts which could have been either an economic recession, a political plot, or a set of homosexual relationships and feelings. Auden had been the chooser of Ashbery's first book for publication in a prestige series. He audibly continued early Auden by different means and the wave of attacks on him therefore never came. Reed had a deep envy of him. Later, Ashbery gave Reed plaudits, quoted on the jacket of the latter's book about Elvis. In order to bestow prestige, you have to possess it. Ashbery had that effect of making heterosexual men want to sound homosexual. He moved the zone to a place where that effect was unavoidable. There is a whole gay sensibility involving excess decorum as part of repressing what you do not want to hear. This was transferred to a neo-conservative cultural world which also did not want to hear what was almost inevitably going to be said, in a quite amazing way. That double surface seems to work better if you're gay and have had 30 years of experience of deploying it.

How does ludic relate to processual? That is, how does a poetry based on games relate to a poetry where generative structures are set up which run recursively and create stretches of language that are not foreknown to the poet but which are implicit in the rule-set and conformant to the rules? The two things sound similar and indeed Ashbery's poems are usually processual as well as ludic. Yet we cannot elide the differences to merge the two things. Surely the unstated and first rule of the processual line was that ideology reproduces itself and that generating language that escapes from preset intention is a model of generating behaviour that is free from existing property relations. The break-in of the unexpected reproduced a profound disgust with the way the rich expected their wishes to be reproduced, on and on and on. The aesthetically unattractive elements of processual poetry were connected to the critique that underpinned them, the undissolved memory of the bad things. The central feature of the post-modern poetry just described was its aestheticisation, it was charming, inconsequential, it spun a spell, you wanted it to go on and on. So there was a wide gap between ludic and processual even if logically a game is a process.

The critique of the unity of the self which we discussed in the 1970s evolved in the new Conservative regime into a personal politics concept in which the self was infinite and the issue was to get other people to accept this perfection. This narcissistic ejection of facts had a dark side of loss of belief in the substance and reality of the self, a condition leading naturally to depression. This tended to lock the individual into a relationship of dependence on the employer and on consumer pleasures. The abolition of realism led to a loss of belief in reality. Poetry had taken its main asset, authenticity, and used it as collateral for a foolishly acquired loan.

JOHN ASH (1948–) began appearing in small magazines such as *Rock Drill* and *Oasis* in about 1975, published two books (*Casino, The Bed*) with Oasis Books in 1978 and 1981 and made a meteoric rise into 'overground' publishing with a collection from Carcanet, *The Goodbyes*, in 1982, followed by a triumphant career (*The Branching Stairs, Disbelief, The Burnt Pages*). He remains a thorn in the eye of those who would argue that Carcanet is a completely reactionary and irrelevant organization.

My worry is that Ash has become commodified, astutely repeating the devices whose original merit was to be unexpected and rippling with uncertainty. New York provides an environment in which poets receive far more attention and rewards than is ever possible in Manchester; but the sheer number of poets makes for crude methods, as you can only break through the ambient noise by doing the same thing, in bulk, for several years, and then continuing to do the thing for which you are famous. Ash has achieved economic independence (he is a full-time poet) but has become new-yorkised as far as awareness of brand image and of promotional techniques is concerned.

Ash constantly uses classical music (including its theatrical role) as an analogy or backdrop in which to stage poems, but more important is the mystery of a woman's voice, the artificial and yet liberatory cadence into which every line fits. The trope of always being within a work of art (usually a bad and prolonged one) implies that one knows the rules and so co-operates with a fantasy of communicating on a non-verbal plane (a shared code not given to other speakers, i.e. being gay). This gives a wonderfully secure feeling. Ash was influenced by Ashbery and Auden but his poetry is not, like Ashbery's, reproducing the sensation of shopping, that pure freedom with miles of aisles stretching off in every direction, affluence as a realm of recondite sensations offering the possibility of self-definition, the designed absence of constraint, the opulence of mirrors. It's hard for someone from Manchester to be quite that free from realism, even in the face of a million swatches of textile. Ash's poetry has a character, it does not remain at the level of pure freedom.

This poetry perpetually regards existence as absurd and following a kitsch scenario, but this already points to a conspiracy of those who feel this way and can console each other; the reader's pleasure will depend largely on the reader being drawn to the 'happy few' (who could either be the intelligent, or the homosexual, or those who like poetry, or even possibly the English middle class). His favourite tropes include 'life seen as a novel (opera etc.)' and 'cultured exile complains of surreal and unpleasant nature of the country he lives in'.

I think a lot of Ash's appeal has to do with the old-fashioned carpentering of his poems; their continuity, concentration on the significant, strong characterization, decisiveness, plenitude, emotional clarity, recognisability. He has no real problems with his own character or with the character he has been creating on the page; he objects to various boring social situations, but (unlike other avant-garde poets) he has no objection to sociability and language as such, he only wants to find a room full of people who are amusing and who are fond of him. This is why he can actually write poems rather than making aleatory gestures of confusion and disapproval.

Ash's research is directed at finding the points in social space where conversation is interesting. Take this passage from the title poem of *The Goodbyes*:

> With things as they are it's difficult not
> to feel like a newly arrived exile

even though you've lived here for years.
Principal cities are renamed and history
slides into a dull dream of foreknowledge
in which past mistakes are cancelled.
Who are these heroes appearing in the false guise
of youth? these avatars of
expediency? No one is convinced. Even
the sky is discoloured
like the pages of a novel left open at a window, –
the plot so mechanical every word or sigh
fell with a thud to rot slowly where it fell,

staining the carpet at the place
where the corpse is marked in chalk.
(from 'The Goodbyes', in *The Goodbyes*, 1982, p54-5)

If Ash had expressed this malaise in terms of dissatisfaction with a lover or a social system, he would have excluded the reader, vanishing inside his own experience; by projecting his feelings out into these eccentric comparisons with a bad novel (and a foreign city and a 'dull' dream) he scales them down and makes it possible to play with them, while enlisting the reader as a co-conspirator and sympathetic ear. Flattery is an important element in his charm.

Even when he is evoking childhood (cf. the blurb for his first Carcanet collection:

Sonatas. Rain. Musical animals. Angels. Braided intersections. Architraves. Office buildings in sunsets. Those puppet theatres you used to be able to make up from the backs of breakfast cereal packets [...] Sexual encounters in modernized fairy-tales. Science Fiction and disguised nostalgia. Some portraits [...] Music, not painting, as paradigm. Large rhythmic units, not 'metrically exact lines', not iambics except as ancestral ghosts...
(from *The Goodbyes*, 1982, inner dust-jacket)

which is a classic moment of ickiness and embarrassment in most poets, it is forgivable because he was obviously an interesting child and would have been fun to teach, for example.

POÈME PSYCHOGÉOGRAPHIQUE

> 'There is only one possible location of Scotland: to the north of England.' (James G. Kellas, *Modern Scotland*, p.1).

> There is one city which is equidistant from all the capitals of North-west Europe. The centre of the circle whose circumference goes by Reykjavik, Stockholm, Berlin, Brussels, and Paris is Kirkwall in Orkney. Thus when affairs involve the whole of North-west Europe, Orkney is the strategic centre, with the added advantage that it commands both the east and west coasts of Britain [...].
> (from Ronald Miller, *Orkney*, p.10.)

The genre of defamiliarisation, eccentric erudition, and political critique of representation includes a number of poets from different parts of the country. In Scotland, I understand that the term 'Informationist' can refer to W. N. Herbert, Robert Crawford, Richard Price, Peter McCarey, David Kinloch, Alan Riach; born between about 1959 to 1964. Important influences would be Hugh MacDiarmid, W.S. Graham, Edwin Morgan, Ian Hamilton Finlay. An anthology and ideological statements can be found in *Contraflow on the Superhighway, an Informationist Primer* (edited Herbert and Price). I understand that the name aims to stress the poem as an act of information transfer. Implicitly, this is an attack on parochial poetry, which aims to record information the reader already has, manipulating sentiment and solidarity in fear of thought. The programme recalls the formalist dictum that the literary work is the sum of its procedures. Herbert and Crawford belong with the ludic line, so that the flyting between them is a game in verse and hyperbolic language (and in recalling 19th-century Scottish poems) rather than any real enmity. The estrangement both represents a feeling of alienation with mainstream English or American culture and its misrepresentation of Scotland, and is a try-out for what awareness would be like in a constitutionally different Scotland, an idea that seems strange when you imagine it but whose unfamiliarity and strangeness do not prove it to be a life you could not live.

An interest in information stems from an interest in the class structure; compare the Glasgow University Media Group (author of *Bad News* and *Really Bad News*, critiques of the TV news), and Alexander Graham Bell: who was enabled to invent the telephone by his investigation of the material nature of speech, stimulated by concern with the real difference between low-status Scots and high-status English pronunciation. The group is urban, and does not regard the city as corrupt; it is educated, and does not

believe that ignorance is authenticity. Its members write mostly in English.
I am informed that in an Informationist kitchen,

> The hob has a fractal element
> for instant boiling,
> Pictish spirals for neap-and-tattying,
> Just a saltire for a sullen/ simmer
> (fitted by Richard Price)

Herbert (1961–) has pledged himself to:

> deep sang, rowlit aroon thi rim of thi Hilltoon
> oanna Setterday nucht, lukean doon
> uts bluidblack thrappil, slit an flappan
> at thi lift, thi peopul dreelan lyk intestines,
> a belly full o beetuls an bitumen; thi tap
> oa ma heid cams off lyk a lick o herr

(*cante jondo*, rolled around the rim of the Hilltown on a Saturday night,
looking down its bloodblack throat, slit and flapping in the air, the people
teeming like guts, a belly full of beetles and bitumen; the top of my head
comes off like a lick of hair).

Part of the interest of this is its being written in the dialect of Dundee.
(Standard written Scots is basically the dialect of Edinburgh, where the
Court was.) Herbert's fight for lexicon, as the vessels in which the collective
past is stored, is like the search for '100 shadowy kings'. The suspension
of social identity and power relations, the phantasmagoric rewinding of
causal chains, and the psychogeographic drift through imaginary spatial
relations, throughout *Sharawaggi*, are in my view better than drugs.

> 'In all this he [MacDiarmid] anticipates with surprising accuracy
> the concerns of the Situationists in the '50s and '60s. For the
> Situationist, Capitalist society alienates the individuals within it
> by means of the Spectacle, or the endless parading of itself as the
> answer to their needs. [...] One of the Situationists' strategies of
> subversion was a remarkably playful tactic called the dérive or
> drift. Instead of plodding dutifully from home to work, or to
> the cinema, or any of the accepted forms of social movements,
> people should simply wander. The new perspective induced by
> such means could bring out 'The sudden change of ambience in
> a street within the space of a few meters; the evident division

of a city into zones of distinct psychic atmospheres... all very unusual and anti-Spectacular ways of viewing one's environs. [...] MacDiarmid is dangerous, then, [...] to the extent to which he operates as a doorway, or a series of doorways, between otherwise separate worlds.'
(W.N. Herbert, from the editorial to *Gairfish: Shibbo-lithos*, 1992)

For Herbert, therefore, geographical realism is replaced as a poetic doctrine by systematic geographical disconnection; a phantasmagoria. It is significant that he wrote his first book, the most distinguished ever written in Dundee dialect, against his home town. It is subtitled 'an exorcism':

> Whaur ur yi Dundee? Whaur's yir Golem buriit?
> [...]
> Ghaist of thi Thirties, Dundee whan thi Daith cam doon,
> grey sinders descendin, meldit wi claiths an dreams,
> Dundee whan Amerika fell,
> Dundee whan thi Depreshun cam owerseas
> an bidit, an restit in oor fathirs' braces –
> oor flatbunnits! oor bandylegs! oor rickets!
> Waulkin uppa street, a deid, a ghostie,
> a passedby, a damnit, a wurkir-
> ghaist restless and nivir kennin green.
>   (from 'Elephants' Graveyard', in *Dundee Doldrums*, 1991)

(The poems appeared in a magazine as early as 1983, though the book came out in 1991.) During the 1980s there were collaborations with Robert Crawford (also living in Oxford at that time, now in St. Andrew's), published in book form as *Sharawaggi*. This is a modern classic. From Herbert's comments it seems that he has doubts about nationalist positions. One of my favourite Herbert poems is 'Mappamundi', which draws on Peter Gould and Rodney White's classic *Mental Maps* (1974). They were geographers who asked people to draw their understanding of various spaces. These drawings revealed subjectivity and a lack of proportion in a striking way. Apparently naïve painting is how we really see the world. Real people have a mental map no more accurate than mediaeval world-maps (known as 'mappae mundi'). Obviously the willingness of everyone English to ignore the existence of Scotland 99% of the time lent itself to nationalist argument – Herbert could be making a nationalist point without wider intent, it was just one distortion among many he was satirising.

Whatever political differences may emerge between the collaborators, they are both interested in heterogenesis, in the critique of television and journalism as commodified versions of information, in decentring authority and prestige, and in phantasmagoria as a way of achieving this. Crawford writes mostly in English. Herbert's early poems are collected in *Forked Tongue* (1994). Heterogenesis is a phenomenon in biology where organisms alternate in generations, so that a parent gives birth to offspring which are different from itself, e.g. a sexually reproducing parent produces asexually reproducing offspring. More speculatively, it was used by the critical psychoanalyst Felix Guattari to describe homogeneous systems producing heterogeneous results. This could be extended to the creation of works of art with fundamentally incongruous components. This is an escape from the rigid harmonies of a classicising art that preserved decorum; it is associated with mediaeval forms and with Rabelais, as a late mediaeval writer. More recently, it is associated with MacDiarmid and with the linguistic clash of Scots and English in the mouths of Scottish writers. It may say, even, that Scotland is not part of decorous (or decorative) literature. Informationism has had enough intellectual rigour to avoid being submerged in the flood of mindless post-modernism; its interest in the still wooden and neo-mediæval lameness of common representations was fed by an interest in real social relations, i.e. the reality of Scotland. The thrill of Informationism was often the presentation of seductive and elaborate fantasies about Scotland (usually) which were inspired by dominant English-Westminster fantasies – they were a release into unseen worlds at the same time as being covert demolitions of what English politicians and cultural critics were drivelling. Disinformation as trip.

The Informationists are following the broad lines of cultural criticism laid out by Tony Benn in *Arguments for Democracy* (1981): 'Above all, we must allow the free flow of information, end secrecy and give everyone access to an education that will enable them to contribute to the decisions which affect their lives'. Benn's analysis (in chapter six, 'The case for a free press') of the monopoly ownership structure of the press and media, and the consequent narrowness of opinion in the media when measured against the diversity of opinion in the real country, the people, was truly frightening. This, in turn, was the climax of various left-wing critiques of the information available to the electorate, all of them (perhaps) inspired by an insight that the original struggle simply to make the people literate, had since the arrival of democracy been replaced by a new struggle, to give the people accurate information. The abstract means of control were summed up as Spectacle. The age of ignorance has been replaced by the age of data commodification, excess data, advertising. Information exists to deceive others as well as to inform oneself. As Benn demonstrates, corporate profit is not equable: 'When it folded the *Herald* was selling far more copies than *The Times*, *The Guardian*, and the *Financial Times* added together. It died because its readers were too poor to make them a worthwhile target for advertisers.' So they were too poor to be well-informed or to be linked to their political brethren by a shared newspaper.

The message is that participation in the mainstream media is a form of alienation, of diminished reality.

CULTURAL CONSPIRACY IN LEEDS

There was a specific atmosphere of hush that was part of the rollback. It connected with young people desperate to imply that they were not rebellious in any way. This was after the failure of revolt and after employers, university authorities, loan agencies were paranoid about the loyalty of anyone young to business values. It was influential because it redefined artistic innovation as being part of a revolt that would inevitably lead to being unemployed. Only the conformist were going to be allowed to study, to get jobs, to get published, to acquire the benefits of middle-class life. But part of the recession – which didn't even last for the whole of the 1980s – was that so many people were unemployed and had endless time. They didn't have to act deferential, they had time to argue, and, yes, this was productive for poetry. That way of life is the milieu for poetry as much as anything else.

There was a scene in Leeds centred on the English Department, with the magazine *Poetry and Audience*, and a readings series. Two poets living in Leeds were IAN DUHIG (1954–) and JOHN GOODBY (1958–). Both of them reached 35 or so without anything like fame, and with very little poetry in print even in magazines. The figure of PAUL MULDOON, a lesser writer who was very popular in about 1981, is behind the work of both of them at this time; he worked out the style or tone that they brought to fruition. The linguistic register behind all of them is that of the hedge-school, an Irish intellectual class of startling brilliance poured into vessels (Gaelic and mediaeval) that were alien to the English sensibility. One separates here three components: some traces of Gaelic idiom loan-translated into English; some flowers of bardic rhetoric, making this poetry considerably more interesting than anti-rhetorical Saxon glumness; and traces of Catholic (especially Franciscan) culture, with its pre-literate (oral) features such as stress on argument, feats of memory, quick exchanges, and readiness of wit. Further details on all this can be found in William Carleton's tales of the Irish peasantry, in particular the stories that describe hedge-schools and the learning that peasants desired for their sons.

Carleton came out of school, in 1815 or so, able to speak Latin better than he could English; the hedge-schools could reach extraordinary peaks of attainment, albeit in disciplines that hadn't really changed since the 15th century. In the context of an early 19th-century Europe in which business and manufacturing were making all the running, the Latinity and golden oratory of Carleton's school can in fact be read as a flamboyant waste of talent, to the loss of the island's economy. For writers born in the 1950s to take up this bardic-erudite approach implies a distantiation both oblique and deep. Goodby (some poems in *Before the Flood*, 1986, and Faber's *Poetry Introduction 8*) is writing about a Marxist-anarchist view of history, using brilliance and humour to make it readable, and shooting from a bizarre angle in order to establish bizarre causal lines and discredit (defamiliarise) the orthodox and impoverished causal lines of textbook (capitalist) history. Duhig (*The Bradford Count*, 1991; *A Mersey Goldfish*, 1995) is perhaps a less serious writer; his subversion is more immediate in its reactions, he is an upwardly mobile punk; the cleverness of his style is a reaction to its sarcastic scruffiness (and to the hostility of the Establishment to its prophets). His wish to discredit authority (as Conservative, anti-Irish, hostile to any attack on inherited wealth, etc.) is mixed with a protracted burlesque of Irish authority in its various forms of religion, poetry, nationalist politics, etc. Something like this is inevitable in an Irish poet brought up in England; it obliges him to know a good deal about the Irish past, and to show the admired Irish virtues (of wit, eloquence, learning, lightness of touch, etc.) to an advanced degree.

Take Duhig's poem about an Irish lad snatched by Algerian slave-traders:

> It is the Night of Power and the puppeteers
> are playing *Karaguez, Martyr to Chastity.*
> Nubian grooms are breaking cameleopards.
> Janissaries line their cloaks with lynx.
> [...]
>
> The Kizlar Aga was all sympathy,
> bruising almonds with myrrh for emulsions
> and poultices of medicinal sand.
> [...]

Castration has been a good career move.
I will learn to call the nightingales bulbuls...
(from 'The Irish Slave')

This is 'punk' because it points out how much of history we don't get taught. (Jean Monlau's *Les États barbaresques* gives details of these raids, stating also that the corsairs also made trips to Brazil at least once, and even Iceland.) This is really an attack on the media, but also has a punk-like annoy-the-priest angle because the hero becomes a successful and much sought-after catamite in his new Moslem home. This is not exactly the typical lachrymose song about the Irish emigrant driven from his cabin by the lough. In marketing terms, both Duhig and Goodby were acceptable because they sufficiently resembled Paul Muldoon – who was himself seen as a dumbed-down version of Ashbery and a harmless version of post-- modernism. The resemblances between their poems and Informationism are interesting. It is interesting, too, that their political attitudes were compatible with writing marketable poems and that they felt no urge to write stylistically alienated poetry to go along with the politics. The underground did not own radicalism. There was no need for critical poetry to attach itself to the legacy of the underground of the 1970s. The sector of resistance to the existing power order is about as likely to disappear as the island of Britain. But the poetic underground was by 1983 in danger of disappearing from the map of history and becoming a form of nostalgia. Because publishers came up with economic projects, refined objects, which put it back into High Street shops, this did not happen.

THE 1980S:
NEO-CONSERVATISM AND CHEAP INFORMATION

GOOD BOOKS OF THE 1980S

1980
Anthony Thwaite, *Victorian Voices*;
Harry Guest, *Elegies*;
Penelope Shuttle, *The Orchard Upstairs*.

1981
David Jones (d.1974), *The Roman Quarry*;
Adrian Stokes (d.1972) *With All The Views*;
Christopher Logue, *Ode to the Dodo* (poems 1953-78), *War Music*;
Peter Redgrove, *The Apple Broadcast*;
Allen Fisher, *Unpolished Mirrors*;
Ken Smith, *Fox Running*;
David Chaloner, *Hotel Zingo*;
Philip Jenkins, *Cairo*;
Jeremy Reed, *Bleecker Street*.

1982
J.H. Prynne, *Poems* (i.e. collected poems);
Ken Smith, *The Poet Reclining* (selected poems 1962-80);
Tom Raworth, *Writing*;
Allen Fisher, *Defamiliarising*;
Peter Didsbury, *The Butchers of Hull*;
John Hartley Williams, *Hidden Identities*;
John Ash, *The Goodbyes*;
Paul Brown, *Masker*.

1983
Peter Yates, *Petal and Thorn*;
George Mackay Brown, *Voyages*;
Asa Benveniste, *Lay Out the Life Line, Roll out the Corse* (poems 1965-85);
Ted Hughes, *River*;
Harry Guest, *Lost and Found: Poems 1976-82*;
J.H. Prynne, *The Oval Window*;
John James, *Berlin Return*.

1984
Anthony Thwaite, *Poems 1953-83*;
David Harsent, *Mister Punch*;
Gavin Selerie, *Azimuth*;
John Seed, *History Labour Night*;
Frank Kuppner, *A Bad Day for the Sung Dynasty*.

1985
Andrew Crozier, *All Where Each Is* (Collected Poems);
Allen Fisher, *Brixton Fractals*;
Barry MacSweeney, *Ranter*;
John Ash, *The Branching Stairs*;
Denise Riley, *Dry Air*;
Maggie O'Sullivan, *A Natural History in 3 Incomplete Parts*;
Kelvin Corcoran, *Robin Hood in the Dark Ages*.

1986
Christopher Middleton, *Two Horse Wagon Going By*;
Roy Fisher, *A Furnace*;
Michael Haslam, *Continual Song*;
Maggie O'Sullivan, *From the Handbook of That & Furriery,
    Divisions of Labour*;
John Wilkinson, *Proud Flesh*;
Kelvin Corcoran, *The Red and Yellow Book*.

1987
Alastair Mackie, *Ingaitherins*;
Colin Simms, *Eyes Own Ideas*;
Tom Raworth, *Visible Shivers*;
Peter Finch, *Selected Poems*;
Tom Lowenstein, *Filibustering in Samsara*;
Peter Didsbury, *The Classical Farm*;
John Ash, *Disbelief*;
Adrian Clarke, *The Ghost Trio* (as 1 book and 2 pamphlets, 1987-93);
Maggie O'Sullivan, *States of Emergency*;
Frank Kuppner, *The Intelligent Contemplation of Naked Women*;
D.S. Marriott, *Hours Into Seasons*.

1988
Edwin Morgan, *Themes on a Variation*;
Tom Raworth, *Tottering State* (new and selected poems 1963-87);

Adrian Clarke, *Shadow Sector*;
Maggie O'Sullivan, *Unofficial Word*;
Kelvin Corcoran, *Qiryat Sepher*.

1989
Christopher Middleton, *Selected Writings*;
Ted Hughes, *Wolfwatching*;
Peter Levi, *Shadow and Bone*;
Iain Sinclair, *Flesh Eggs and Scalp Metal*;
David Chaloner, *Trans*;
Allen Fisher, *Stepping Out*;
Frank Kuppner, *Ridiculous! Absurd! Disgusting!*;
Kelvin Corcoran, *TCL*.

Anthologies include: *Purple and Green* (anthology, no editor, Rivelin Grapheme, 1985, 33 female poets); *Angels of Fire*, ed. Sylvia Paskin, Jeremy Silver, Jay Ramsay (1986). *A Various Art*, ed. Andrew Crozier and Tim Longville (1987) is effectively the *Grosseteste Review Sampler*; most of it was written before 1980; *the new british poetry* (Paladin anthology, 1988, 85 poets); *Four Fife Poets: Fower Brigs ti a Kinrik* (1988).

THE UNDERGROUND IN THE 1980S

There is no folklore about what happened to the progressive interest during the 1980s. My impression is that the time saw a mixture of processes, of which the first would be the entry of poets collectively into the smothering embrace of academia, and the institutionalisation of the avant-garde as its members exchanged revolt for stability. As for politics, my impression is that ideas about political change include narratives about history, that changes in historical thinking (extending the number of subjects whose voices were heard, to put it crudely) made these narratives partly collapse, and that the vehicle had to leave the road while they were updated. The simple relationship with source texts whereby the poet as hero/reader took them on and proved them untrue underwent an inexorable development whereby the processing of information became more and more complex and yielded more and more. An idea of change as something simple, if conflict-ridden, and channelled by the radical Left, dissolved as change became total and not subject to anyone's control. The key processes mutated. Beyond that, there were opulent publications. The books by were the most overwhelming. Huge, beautifully designed retrospective

collections of Prynne, Douglas Oliver, Anthony Barnett, and Andrew
Crozier made the past of the Underground more sonorous and engulfing
than ever before while also tacitly making it clear that it was the past.
The anthologies, *the new british poetry* and *A Various Art*, were fabulous
publishing achievements. What was underground was looking more
like modern classic. Beyond that the poets gradually moved to deeper
penetration of the aesthetic field. Allen Fisher tells it like it is:

> Thus stage one projected and effected a text which could be read
> vertically and horizontally [...] and a textual parameter from a
> numerical interpretation of a music piece (which in this case was
> Ferneyhough's *Time and Motion Study 1, for Bass Clarinet* (Editions
> Peters, 1977). The textual parameter acted as word limiter, a
> spatial indicator (in terms of rhythm and visual presentation)
> and a conceptual model I wanted to radically change. In stage
> one the concern is to arrive at a new arrangement that can then
> be used in a set of seven lectures. The word sources for stage
> one were deliberately limited and deliberately used apparently
> incongruent materials, the main sources were articles concerned
> with planetary bow-shocks, radio windows & chorus emissions
> from galactic physics, following Einstein's centenary, and with
> perceptual science and art criticism with particular emphasis on
> the visual and aural, Art-Language's critique of *Ways of Seeing* and
> Flynt's *Blueprint*. Along with memoranda and references from my
> notebook/folder headed *Ways of seeing what or a future of Species*.
> [...] The language over this spectrum overlaps. Plasma carries the
> blood and surrounds the planet: windows, radio, oscillators, noise
> and so forth refer as much to the dance floor as they do to quasars,
> lots of things radiate.
>
> (from a letter printed in *Defamiliarising*,
> described as a text and letter project, 1982)

FORTRESS LEFT

Our democracy allows very little power to the losing side. Since the
Left was delivering very little in the way of government, legislation, or
improvements in working conditions, in this decade, energy was being
expended in the realm of ideas. Three trends can be isolated: a resolute
drift right of the Labour Party, somehow influenced by the departure of
its right wing for an ill-fated capitalist centrist party to lurch to the right

itself, craving for the centre ground, and energetically suppressing any new or radical ideas; an abandonment of politics in favour of lifestyle, defining social progress in terms of clothes, diet, or choice of music, rather than laws and property relations; and a flowering of theory on the part of the New Left, adapting completely to their academic habitat and loosening bonds to any conceivable change in the larger society. For the Left, it was a chance to get off the road, retest theoretical analyses, and to enjoy life, since the responsibility of running society was not to be had. The middle level of social life, life in small groups, was the sector that held the attention: where ideas were part of conversation, to the great benefit of poetry rooted in such intimate and speculative language. In these scenes the pressures either of communicating with people of different ideologies and attitudes, or of maintaining an alliance, or of government with all its sacrifices and disappointments, were lifted,

Feminism shifted the stress of social thought to the subject of women, presenting male leftists with the luxurious vista of being simultaneously the oppressors and the agents of liberation; right on the spot with a good seat. The belief that all men were guilty and parts of an oppressor class virtually stopped their radicalism in its tracks. Poets were not likely to articulate the new insights they developed if speaking for other people was seen as a form of engrossing social power and exercising covert influence.

The age-group most affected by the radical wave around 1968 was extremely unlikely to go into business. They were more likely to go into education or the welfare services, although a certain proportion 'dropped out' and pioneered a New Age lifestyle. The services for the poor were often staffed with people of leftist views; the poorer constituencies and wards were mostly Labour-voting, so that visible and face-to-face responsibility for those in want and distress rested mainly with left-wing people. The government in Westminster could quite well afford to let the welfare services come under unbearable pressure as the post-war social compact was broken, because it was their enemies who bore the psychological strain, and Socialist policies that were discredited as expensive and ineffective. Increasingly, the poor were like a fortress under siege, guarded by the Left: as council landlords, political representatives, social services staff, teachers, social workers. The Left was excluded from political power and yet bore all the worst psychological burdens of government. Being out of power ground down and exhausted the most idealistic component of society. This was the historic task of the New Left, to be immersed in the practical effort of holding society together but forbidden to apply any of their own ideas. Theoretical activity was a way of breaking out of this impasse and keeping hope alive. By withholding funds from Labour-controlled local authorities, the government could prevent them from carrying out their statutory duties and from bettering the lot of the poor. So you have huge council estates full of unemployed people who find that their visible enemy is the Labour council that demands rent and doesn't repair the houses. The authority that says 'no' to an application for a council house for the family's eldest child, who is still living at home, is also Labour, visibly saying 'no' and therefore seen as the oppressor. This weakened the collective spirit, because you could see that, if the other chap's bowl was filled, there was less in the pot for you. Personal politics can be seen as a series of denunciations, aimed to strike off people higher up the list than you, to get you closer to the flat, job, place at college, or whatever it is. This confrontation of middle-class Leftists and working-class clients was typical of the decade.

Society was split by a merely fiscal approach into two warring tribes: those who benefited from tax money and those who lost by paying it. The Left tended to become the tribal interest managers of the former – clearly a road to political failure, since it removed their freedom to manoeuvre and to attract the votes of the political middle.

By making these problems insoluble, a right-wing government could not only exhaust and wear down the Left, but also make the socialist project unglamorous and self-sacrificial. The Left needs to offer liberation to win, but has to demand sacrifice in order to bring change about.

The Labour vote was concentrated in the working class and in the industrial regions of the country, sections that could easily seem archaic while individuals were advancing into the middle class and growth was concentrated in the south-east and the services sector. The progressive elements of socialism could thus fade away from public imagination, while the idea of progress became identified with personal aggrandisement and intensified inequality. In fact, inequality was seen as progress.

The 1980s saw very little economic growth, except for inflation in the prices of houses, and were notable for the doubling of the number of people below the official poverty line. Waves of bankruptcies and mass redundancies destroyed the illusion of security and continuity, and made the self's props of status and possessions fragile and temporary.

Radical Philosophy

What occupied the academic (writing and debating) New Left in these years was something called 'post-structuralism' or simply 'theory'. I am not sure that this is a unitary phenomenon, but the terms refer to Foucault, Deleuze and Guattari, Derrida, Lacan, and their progeny. It tends to mean the theoretical activity of the French Left outside the French Communist Party and Socialist Party. None of these writers is primarily interested in the theory of art. This was the current of 1968. While conservative academics reacted to it as if it were a student occupation of their buildings, it also represented a withdrawal from political activity and the jettison of any mass movement. It involves a curious exchange of roles. The voice of magazines like *Critical Quarterly* and *PN Review* was raised against this whole line. There was a special issue of *PN Review* in 1985 doing just that and calling it 'the new orthodoxy'. Catherine Belsey seemed to be the Anxiety Figure. *PN Review* didn't run a special issue denouncing post-1968 poetry. Strangely, in the history of poetry this retreat also means poets being so outgunned as cultural critics that they couldn't keep up with the game. If terms like underground, British Poetry Revival, etc., seem out of date, it is due to the fact that no new term was in use because the literary world had forgotten this sector existed. Bourgeois fear is not about Prynne and Allen Fisher but about post-structuralism. The radical theorists, to an almost comic extent, ignored modern-style poetry.

'Theory' means philosophy; French students do a year of philosophy while still at school, while British literary critics never acquire fluency in it. The British response relies on envy and incomprehension. The recognition is shared by most of these philosophers that Marx and Freud were patriarchs who opened new fields of knowledge but tried to turn them into feudal fiefs and arrest open investigation of them. Terms of reference like 'breaking down large-scale generalisations into small accurate statements' and 'fracturing the apparent coherence and objectivity of bourgeois consciousness' underlie several different projects. The word 'theory' is used because British academics lack the philosophical fluency to relate these scintillating spirals of argument to any truth-tests. Instead of explaining things and merging with the observable data, they stay in a separate, glamorous, glass-walled, realm. They are attached to empirical, Anglo-Saxon essays in a neo-colonialist way, like an imported Chevrolet being drawn by a bullock-team: one studies 'theory' but does not learn how to theorise. The glamour is a little like that of French wine.

Another much-cited strand of theory comes from the Frankfurt School of the 1920s, especially Adorno, Benjamin, and Herbert Marcuse. This is called 'Critical Theory' (i.e. 'Marxism when practised by refugees seeking funding in America'). In later decades, it looked more like 'Marxism without politics'. It was either the ruthless politicisation of aesthetics, or the ruthless aestheticisation of politics; either the triumphal way of reason and hope, or the *joyeuse entrée* of religiosity and despair. The message still seems to be Hegel at third hand. The experience of reading this material is now a standard part of late adolescence: everything you know seems to be untrue, the world starts whirling around your head, you become hot and over-excited, you become dizzy with paradoxes, ideas seem to multiply and flow away. It is common practice to allege that 'modern-style' poetry is {+poststructuralism}, whereas traditional poetry is {-poststructuralism}: we have theory, you don't. But poetic theory is a set of rules for making decisions, or nothing. It is an elementary necessity for poetry to be as exciting as the philosophy of its era. The common element of the French philosophers mentioned is a reaction to the unrealised Sixth Republic of 1968, above all rejection of the French Communist Party, but then also to the defeat of its Maoist, Situationist, etc., successors. The appeal of the poststructuralists to Anglo-Saxon academics is that they represent the utopian project in undiluted form while also being clever or devious enough to undo the reductive and disenchanting arguments of the Right.

FEMINISM

The showplace of feminism certainly wasn't poetry but novels, popular sociology, interviews, TV serials, journalism, and even stand-up comics. In poetry, books like *Dry Air* by Denise Riley, *Poem for Guatemala* and *Flame Tree* by Judith Kazantzis, and *Tro'r Haul Arno* by Menna Elfyn (now partly available in English) show realised artistic achievement, to replace the speculations of year-one feminism. A partial list of effects on poetry would be:

(1) Larger numbers of women writing poetry (and editing, reviewing, etc.).

(2) Transformation of prestige objects into objects of contention and revindication.

(3) Suspension of public theories of human nature and need for individual poets to establish rules of behaviour within the text.

(4) Impossible to write poetry about love.

(5) Anti-authoritarian pathos.

(6) New ways of associating domestic life, fantasy life, economic organisation, foreign policy and warfare, etc.

(7) Curiosity about controversies creating an appetite for literature as evidence.

(8) A perceived separation between people's behaviour and social position, and their inmost nature.

The bibliography in the British Council's *Poetry Today* (1960), by Elizabeth Jennings, has 124 names, of which 17 are women (about 13.7%). The 1995 Bibliography of *Poetry in Britain and Ireland Since 1970*, also from the British Council, lists about 699 British names; of which 141 are women (just over 20%). In the 1980s, the proportion was probably rising rapidly. Point eight above should make simplistic marketing of a personality as commodity a non-runner, but precisely this was the swinish practice of most popular poets. It should have been easy to make the connection that suspending the personality as merely a set of complex processes of very variable outputs made the whole idea of political progress as the liberation of the personality dubious, but most poets seem to feel it doesn't apply to them. The island prejudice against intelligence in art inhibited the take-up of a number of techniques developed across the world for investigating this problem. The choice of mate must, in view of the length of time it takes to conceive a child and for it to reach independence, mean a long-term commitment – or plan for it; the calculation of this choice must rely on its data remaining valid for 15 years (a minimum figure). The idea that human behaviour does not remain stable for a year, and is in constant flux, makes the choice impossible or aleatory. The concept of social regulation failing to work is therefore unwelcome to a movement composed of women.

Committed poets of this period accepted that there is a primary reality of the senses and a secondary accretion of bourgeois guardianship, which makes invisible most of the possibilities latent in reality, and is composed largely of self-referential circularities. The words 'ideology' and 'propaganda' were popular; not yet replaced by their synonyms, 'marketing' and 'public image'. A feminist believed that women were an under-class whose labour is expropriated either for nothing or for the wages of penury, with the whole of art, political discourse, religion, and culture as a gigantic influencing machine making this relationship seem natural, and vilifying anyone who behaves differently. This official version was a compound of sorcery, perfidy, and artifice, to quote Andrei Sinyavsky. Feminist poetry was a voice seeping from underneath a dominant discourse, that could hardly avoid description as capitalist, patriarchal, and intolerant of alternatives. The core of the debate was the multiple *possible* interpretations. One of these was the path of the *authentic life*. These were admired either as a sign of liberation, as the underlying nature of reality, or as an artistic device for staving off boredom. Conversely, the motive for monotonous interpretations may not have been so much political conservatism as artistic conformism and incompetence.

The primary, the 'before', becomes a modern form of the sublime, misty, pristine, and yearned-for, but never quite imaginable. The primary language is an available flavour of unrepressed possibilities. This utopian bliss simultaneously opens a big trapdoor under its own feet: if the poem doesn't deliver any bliss, it becomes untrue as well as dull. *Cutlass and Earrings*, 1977, (a pamphlet only) is the purest version of radical feminist poetry, still in touch with the revolution, still amazed by the new ideas, before the slogans. Things moved rapidly after that, in the direction of staking out centre ground, and attacks humorous or otherwise receding towards the fringes. In 1985, a book is called *The Chatto Book of Post-Feminist Poetry*, a sneakily ambiguous title that can either mean 'feminism has gone away, phew' or 'this is the new heroic era post the start of feminism'. In any case, the commercial exploitation of feminism in poetry, a backwater genre, starts about six years later than in novels or film.

> [When I became a feminist] I did not stop writing poetry and plays, but I found, paradoxically, that the left-wing atmosphere, which disapproved of the arts as merely 'bourgeois', had communicated itself to the women's liberation movement. Poetry, I was told smartly on one occasion I will never forget, is 'moribund'. [...] [A]rt and politics did not cohabit easily in the radical politics of the late 1960s and early 1970s. [...] That changed, of course, during the 1970s.
> (Michelene Wandor, in *Once a Feminist*).

I think *Purple and Green* (1985) is the most impressive of the wave of feminist anthologies (listed in the first edition). These were the suffragette colours; the lack of an editor is a sign of non-hierarchical, consensual, collective decision-making, another early feminist ideal. The effect of 33 people talking in the same way, facing the same problem, makes the problem undeniable, tired and routine as oppression is, not tired enough to die. They are mutually supporting. The breadth of the subject makes the poems broad when they seem narrow in focus. The individual as boundary limits the poem but contains it like a jug. The themes of the poems include physiology and medical examination; being gazed at by men; the fruit of the womb; giving birth; the peace camp at Greenham Common where new and more provocative mobile nuclear missiles were being installed; literary ideals that fail to work; rejection of the mass media; passivity; incomprehension. There is a juncture point where general validity runs against close detail that would distinguish one person from another and which would sustain original language.

> Copulation and poetry –
> a man's game.
> What's the side
> of the fucked
> and the written?
> What do we feel,
> we, the created;
> we, who shed our clothes
> like stones and run
> our water fingers through
> the valleys of nature
> as we ourselves
> are the valleys,
> the water,
> the stones?
>   (from C.A. de Lomellini, 'Reading Paz on a Plane')

'What's the side' is like 'tell me your side', an account of an event involving more than one person.

'The Perfect Suicide' is close to Janis Ian's 'Insanity Comes Quietly to the Structured Mind' (1965), a singer-songwriter song amalgamated with a moody teenage annihilation song. A way of testing the idea that this colloquial-personal poetry is all close to the singer-songwriter thing. This is one of the great records of the entire 1960s – half Dylan, half Shangri-Las. Black and gold Verve label. Some of the poems regress to infantile language, which in its simple patterns remind one of playground rhymes – the voice of public opinion and also possibly of taunting and bullying. Those rhymes include public shame and that is the effect which most of these poems want. The suggestion that simplicity is a yardstick of truth may be a commentary on the simple language of most of the poems. Perhaps these are very simple situations or perhaps the writers are unwilling to deal with complex situations and feel safer in a refuge zone. The number of books is rather small; also, the number of women-only poetry magazines is vanishingly small. The separate distribution circuit for women's poetry seems to be illusory; the resources shared with men are the important ones, and this where the political contention comes in.

The fact that you dislike other people is inseparable from the fact that they dislike you. This cannot be reduced to a question of truth. Social liberation might make you more popular, or less popular and so less important. Equally, the image-making of the media is not usually subject to truth tests; the techniques, for example, by which a star is dressed, lit, made up, and photographed to seem beautiful, while not exactly sober, are not outright lies either. What is there to test them against? The artistic premise that 'all interpretations of this scene are equally possible' is the correlate of the political belief that 'everyone should have equal opportunities to become what they want to be'. In the exhilarating cavalry charge of dispersing thousands of artistic conventions, it could emerge that the rules being applied in art were also applied generative rules of consciousness; that if you imagined consciousness as a film (or an opera, or whatever), it also applied methods of composition, suppression, repeating gratification, unequal attention, self-mimicry, analogy, and so forth. One could not abolish moralising and sentimentality as merely literary.

The weakness of the women's trade-union movement remains one of the outstanding puzzles of British politics, and feminism can be seen as a despairing imaginary compensation for militancy in the workplace. A key part of Conservative economic strategy has been to swivel the economy onto a new base of docile low-pay female labour, under a white-collar sector with an individualistic ethos and no inclination to become unionised. If you compare the media hot cloud of masterful coutured power-women with the measurable reality of low-paid, low-skilled, non-unionised, mass female labour, it could break your heart. There is no question of feminism being too militant. Indeed, one wonders if this particular capitalist miracle could have got out into open waters without the media myth or pseudo-event of big-shouldered big-earning feminism to distract attention from it. The big difference between the new workforce and the old is the decline of unionism, i.e. of collective action and of a measured alternative to the dictates of the corporation. If feminism is the new radicalism, it is remarkable how it leaves the State and ownership of the means of production perfectly untouched. The new model of social progress through work promotion (quite irrelevant to the prospects of jobs that the huge majority of employed women do) involves higher output and longer hours, personal pay increases (so that the union has no place in the bargaining process), unconditional loyalty to the firm, admiration for your superior (and its converse), moral acceptance of the discourse of 'image' and display, acquisitiveness... what more could capitalism want?

This isn't what the founding Conference of 1970, with its loading of Trotskyites and other Leninists, had in mind. The 1980s saw the return of a positive valuation of power (of wealth, display, submissiveness of others to one's wishes, muscle, expensive clothes, sexual experience, psychological control, drug consumption, pride, bluster, indifference to the wishes of others) that had disappeared in the 1960s, if it had ever been there at all in a society that preferred to tone down differences of wealth. In the 1980s, class came back in a big way. The back path by which this manoeuvre was accomplished was feminism: feminists defined visible power as desirable. Radicals were inhibited from denouncing this, because it came from women, and the capitalists found it entirely laudable. Feminism demanded above all an outlet into spheres other than the domestic, and so provided willing employees. This bypassed the idea of taking collective control of the means of production, as a path to social change, and liberation was redefined as individual promotion through the ranks of capitalism: with the implications that moribund capitalism would be revitalised by women, to the defeat of Socialism, and that women's labour as commodity would be made more desirable to the market by use of the means of suggestion-assertion that advertising uses to promote the brand images of stars and commodities.

An early finding of the movement was that results had to be permanent. The win was to change public opinion – not to occupy some heroically exposed position. Further, the things that had to be changed were decentralised and part of everyday life. They involved learning rather than the seizing of citadels, dramatic dispossessions. The course of the singer-songwriter movement was to start with politics and protest, moving rapidly on to being egocentric and apolitical. There was a structural pattern that the new women's poetry evidently followed. The fraction which wrote poetry capable of abstraction stood out from a very large number of poets who were certainly pro-feminist but unwilling or unable to write something more than personal and anecdotal. Because the equality of women in the workplace and in the education system was the new reality, the success of feminism meant that successors were asking for something that was already there rather than being critical. The pivotal issue now is how to write poetry that mediates genuine critical thinking and re-imagination of how society works (and how a person came to be who they are). Reading a thousand radical poems jolting you out of your sense of normality unfortunately meant that the 1,001st didn't work. There was, though, ever more and more material for the learning project.

ANGLO-WELSH POETRY IN THE 1980S AND 1990S

Meic Stephens says, 'I don't think there would be much publishing of literature in Wales if it was not for subsidy from Government sources – the Welsh Office and the county councils via the Welsh Books Council and the Welsh Arts Council. The whole system depends on subsidy, without which it would collapse.' So the government, although staffed by treacherous

English imperialists, pays for everything. Who isn't interested? The Welsh public. The nationalist preoccupation with controlling the government is, paradoxically, amplified to an unbearable pitch by the generosity of the government and their total dependence on it. The 'second flowering', the poets who were around in 1967, had built an institutional base and certain poem-types had become institutionalised.

By the later 1970s, Anglo-Welsh mainstream poetry was in serious trouble. The people who had attacked the State so vigorously were now being paid to distribute its patronage. A pattern of what was identifiably Welsh had been located, and these rules presupposed their outcome within their initial structure. The development can be seen as a struggle between Robert Minhinnick and Peter Finch. Minhinnick (1952–) was clearly the most gifted poet of the new generation of Anglo-Welsh poets using a realist and un-elevated style. His work shows obvious talent but does not break out into anything really exciting by his first *Selected Poems* (1999). It is as if it took him 25 years to forgive himself for being Welsh. With *After the Hurricane* (2002) he broke out and wrote something unmistakably major – flamboyant, international, highly politicised, and what we could call post-modern. There is now a second *Selected*, accounting for this later, and far richer period. Finch (1947–) defies description because of his energy and diversity, but we can mention a starting game where he was using sound and concrete methods, and tapes – and being reviewed on the lines of 'this isn't poetry'. If we say that he was always treating language as a material thing then it seems to follow that he was reacting to the linguistic crisis of a country split between Welsh and English. I don't think this is true, although he has taken learning Welsh very seriously and even wrote what may have been the first avant-garde poems in Welsh ('Trowch eich radio 'mlaen", 1977). This is debatable as for example Euros Bowen's poetry of the 1950s may earn that title.

Language relies on fixed relationships of sound to sense, of words to grammatical rules, of implied intentionality, which means that good language is surrounded by millions of combinations which aren't right – a zone of the suppressed, you could say. One of his poems, a catalogue (frequent asyntactic Finch procedure) includes a song title, 'My hen laid a haddock'. I know about this because my mother used to sing this song. Anglophone primary-school children obliged to sing 'Hen wlad fy nhadau' sang 'My hen laid a haddock and had it for tea' instead. This is treating language as a material thing but also shows that Finch's linguistic de-suppression is linked to the world of seven-year-olds laughing at everything, endlessly creative, inclined to invent a million patterns that adult rules then write out again. Fighting Finch is like trying to prevent childhood. It is that basic.

Talus tectonic uplift erosion freeze thaw tree-line alluvium fossil image brittle streambed pattern weight joint anthracite great heat carbon felt pen weather chart cloud layer sun su sun grass box. Ley line power chi cloud stream wool hat flask walkng jkt boots hat ruck. Text in all pockets. Where the lines intersect.
[...]

Inside lan gua ged oes n't mea nCh opi ns partciles her ebu tad eep ern eur olo gic alf low Tor ran ced ecl aim ing wit hme ani ngh ang ing his coa tta ils lik ean old dog ack now led geh isb rot her sbu tdo n't bel ike the m man I chatter I prattle must slim this get lean and mean in the line tone and space and margin. Shoes like Woody Guthrie. No boxcars anywhere in the high Neath Valley. Man with a dog. Mist. Dope. Brychain.
(from 'Torrance' in *The Welsh Poems*, p.87)

This sped-up language includes a likeness of the geographically-oriented *English Intelligencer* poet and Neath Valley resident, Chris Torrance. Finch's work has an almost shocking energy where it seems that decentralisation of the linguistic ordinance has produced local autonomy and derepression for every part of the speech chain. There is nothing evacuated or alienated here. Once you unfasten the need to mean something, language flows out in every direction and becomes like mathematics. The same materialism captures endless concrete details of Cardiff – it is what the poet was seeing and breathing in every day, and where his poetry was constantly grabbing concrete details it was bound to scoop up a lot of Cardiff. Finch has a vein of ironic awareness that most Anglo-Welsh poets seem deprived of. At one level his poetry is about the automatic quality of Anglo-Welsh poetry, the regular recurrence of themes and images in a way that already seems the behaviour of a material rather than an organism. One definition of nationalism is that everyone says the same things in the same order every day. Always helped by Finch, a line of Welsh underground poets was emerging, naturally excluded from the subsidies: Philip Jenkins, Chris Bendon, David Barnett, David Greenslade, Graham Hartill. Elisabeth Bletsoe (1960–) has written some excellent poems about Cardiff (*The Regardians*), but her major work is about Dorset.

SCOTTISH POETRY IN THE 1980S AND 1990S

In Scotland, the absurd mismanagement of the Devolution Bill, abandoned despite the fact that it was the declared policy of both the major
political parties, ushered in an era where the Scottish consensus was pro-
Devolution, but the issue was boring and would probably continue to
bore until reform actually occurred. The rule at Westminster throughout
the decade of a confirmed, bigoted, Unionist was one of the factors that
destroyed the popularity of the Conservative Party in Scotland. Supporters
of the status quo became so rare as to cause difficulties to radical writers:
to restate arguments the audience already agrees with, to splash around in
ideas which the audience has long since tired of. To grasp the atmosphere,
one has to remember that someone could be nationalist, anti-capitalist,
anti-authority, and so enlisted in revolutionary change, and still be at
heart conformist, and have reached these ideas by imitating everybody
else, and without being much interested in thought or argument. The
government was frankly indifferent or even punitive towards Scotland,
seen as an unpacified territory where poverty could be painted in the media
as a punishment for voting Labour. The decreased prestige of England,
formerly a capitalist success but now a capitalist-authoritarian failure,
increased Scottish self-confidence and helped along a literary renaissance,
perhaps overrated vis-à-vis the general upturn since 1960, but still with
some classic writing to exhibit: by Alasdair Gray, Iain M. Banks, Irvine
Welsh, and Jeff Torrington, among others. Sociological changes towards a
leisure culture continued to operate, implanting Scottish literature more
thoroughly in universities' arts administration bodies, and local writers'
groups or classes, also letting flourish the real age of leisure, the retired. A
sterile and disintegrative decade in Scottish politics and even economics
saw a positive outcome for poetry, with the emergence of brilliant new
poets Frank Kuppner, Robert Crawford, and W.N. Herbert, and significant
books by Edwin Morgan, Alastair Mackie, and Sorley MacLean, among
others. Some important material by Morgan came out for the first time
in his *Collected Poems* in 1990. Increased self-confidence, sustained by the
decline of English prestige and influence, partially solved the *Sprachkrise*
and laid the basis for a boom, so that seven of the 20 poets in the *New
Generation* marketing exercise of 1994 were Scots. The new reading market
for Lallans was built by broadcasting, and by the prose writers James
Kelman and Irvine Welsh (from 1993), but splashed over onto poetry. A
quantitative surge in Lallans writing produced some striking poems (see
The New Makars, in the booklist), despite crippling lexical and stylistic

inhibitions; let's mention Raymond Vettese, Raymond Falconer, William Hershaw, and Harvey Holton.

The 1992 election returned 11 Conservative MPs for Scotland, eight more than the sum of SNP members elected; class politics remained more significant, if even more boring, than nationalism.

The 1994 anthology, *Dream State*, edited by the TV producer and poet Donnie O'Rourke, was only the second ever, by my count, to restrict itself to young poets, in fact those born since 1955. This represented a new overall strength and depth in Scottish poetry, in sombre contrast to the 1981 book *Seven Poets*, which included no-one born after 1928, and offered us a kind of poetic trip round the House of Lords, reverential and triumphal, if valuable for its interviews. Poetry is no longer seen as a tragic aristocratic conspiracy of virtual Jacobite lairds.

English Poets

Pulse strings out beat of intermittent presence: *Floating Capital – New Poets from London*, edited by Adrian Clarke and Robert Sheppard (1991). (The poets included were: Bob Cobbing, Allen Fisher, Gilbert Adair, Paul Brown, cris cheek, Adrian Clarke, Kelvin Corcoran, Ken Edwards, Virginia Firnberg, Peter Middleton, Maggie O'Sullivan, Val Pancucci, Robert Sheppard, Hazel Smith. *The timenow of this review is 1991*.)

Sociology. Over the past 15 years, an overlapping group of poets has patrolled the routes around Writers Forum, *Spanner* magazine and workshops, Eric Mottram's readings series at King's, and the Sub-Voicive readings. *Floating Capital* is a portrait of this precise group in the late 1980s. Sites included a meeting room run by an anarchist and the British Rail cleaning plant depot leased by the London Film Makers' Co-Op and the Musicians' Collective. These event spaces made it happen because they weren't there for academic assessment and certification: and there was a London Bohemia interested in all kinds of radical art for personal pleasure, not to gain course credits. A conspiracy of experimental gratification. A peer group of dancers, musicians, and film-makers, eager and excitable but easily bored and clueless about the authoritarian pieties of literary genealogy and 'theory', shamed and argued, thrilled and applauded. It was put up or shut up. A door and a metal staircase away from the cold blast of capitalism, something happened.

Rules: (1) Lay bare the beat. The primal event of style birth was the stripping down of language to noun strings: Paul Brown ('Apples Balloons/

beheading cases/ Cavities daggers/ Dancing Departure/ Dizziness') Maggie
O'Sullivan ('Words wiped out,/ shattering clasts,/ Summonses,/ Disturbed
Dimnesses, gorges./ Explicit compleynt./ Gust raiders, Doned Primaries,
Lurch Curatives'). This zone of pure potential exploded into a volley
of word clusters. Historically, perhaps, it was collective 'sound poetry'
outbursts or Phil Minton reinventing the voice next door at the Musicians'
Collective.

The most basic insight of the group is that long constructions act to
enfeeble the word-beat; stress, the propulsive force of poetry, is delayed and
so continuously denied by the 'long cadence' presented by long clauses,
long forms, and polysyllables. Rather than thinking of writing essays or
articles and overlaying a metric pattern, one should think of absolute
stress, dominating an empty space; and later hang formed words on it. The
stresses occur in patterns, happening I suppose in the diaphragm muscles.
It's institutions versus the body. The English language is phonetically
organised around peaks in the middle of 'word groups', not around line
breaks or on patterned repetition. You have to generate enough silence for
your stress peaks to be heard. Why not suspend the line in a show space;
caught in its own time, a complete cycle of start, anticipation, climax, and
release. Syntax is replaced by juxtaposition. We create our own space by
moving through it. The retreat to abstract ideas destroys the integrity of
the body and emaciates the space you create. Ideas can only be represented
if they burst out of strong sensuous imagery or from your whole way of
walking. The 'long cadence' of the discourse of the state and professions
is replaced by a pulse, something to do with blood and breathing: 'thickly
strewn pulse pervades' (Ulli Freer); 'The face is nobody's/ Salvage it copy/
Translation space become pulse vision' (Robert Sheppard). Something
sensuous emerges from beneath the shattered orders of learning.

Emphasis is a personal energy, and word-stress comes out of the poet's
vital pulses: a blaze leaving nowhere to hide. Detachment kills the beat:
what nobody's really saying isn't really speech. Being is becoming: you
cannot move without ceasing to be what you were: being is the draining of
the self in the name of energy. Waste in order to acquire. Forget in order to
perceive. Modernism is the loss of the self. The 'kinetic blur' soon reveals
who is being ironic ('this isn't really happening'), who is indeterminate out
of vagueness, and who is actually shaking with the impinging energies.

Rule (2): Blast away obsolete structural materials. You could make a
fake pulse poem by taking an existing poem and just deleting words and
syllables until the bare pulse was there. Wiping out detail in order to make
structure the area of maximum emphasis, forcibly freeing the poem of the

deathly grip of social manners and refined usage. The reader is no longer conducted as if by a tour guide but simply thrown into a violent surface. So speech becomes a tool for organizing and laying open experience.

Blasted genres: prefab socialism; Marxist alienation; moralizing; religion; bourgeois guardianship; soap operas about people with A-levels; wet lyricism; complacent *sensiblerie*; National Trust reverence poems. All this is simply cut away.

Maybe having to sound 'intelligent' is what drains your poetry of all meaning. A lot of this verbal decor has to do with claiming official status from institutions; not just 'sensitivity' but membership of a class, education, status, elite consumer habits, English tradition, whatever. These claims swirl around on a surface that is all delay and denial, merely allowing the decor to make its point. Such precautive rule-observance simply attenuates the signal. Once all this has been burnt away, anything you write is going to be interesting. Some people don't have, after burning, very much energy left; they are emotionally committed to dead literary apparatuses.

Rule (3): Disperse the personality. Why does language decay? One reason is the self as a blocking mechanism: weary avant-garde gestures of aversion and homage, genteel bourgeois gestures of suppressing 'unpleasant sensations' likewise emaciate the world in a 'consensual obliteration of the senses'. The personality is the prison of the poem, a maze of defence mechanisms and wilful distortions. Trapping the pure flow shuts out the personality. There are still people wearing a poetic style like a pair of jeans; the jeans are to show off your person and the voice is to show off your culture and sensitivity. The personality is a tautology, it only narrates itself with the shiny numbness of a snapshot. Trivial surface details detain us in minutiae; an eternity of low-energy gestures. Drains like class or politics or theory cut in too late in the cycle to show up in pulse poems: there is very little to link them to the cultural heritage. Personality shows up, instead, as simply a rhythm of blanks and pulses: the word-beat is the total trace of personality, thus viewed as a flickering kinetic blur, a scribble of sonic peaks and dips straggling along the time axis. Language as a wire connected to the muscles.

Noise and organs. Many of the group's outputs (notably, David Sellars' *Jjammin*) were blackened affronts, visual blare of all kinds squeezing out any white patches from the page in a yammer and jack that the words barged their way through. The poets took on the great mega-visual mega-audial river, the schizoid viral threat-display consciousness of capitalism, and shouted it down. In London, you've got to be assertive. These poets want to steal power, not make dulcet modulations. How did we ever fail to realise that the streets were so full of message that only a paralysed containing skin could keep poetry hushed and empty? The sound of what we were denying and euphemising fills these pages. Instead of a few cultured phrases distancing the poet from the urban environment, we find a total recreation of the street on the page.

Obvious weaknesses include a genre of feeble comments on the news. Fingers sliding across the blue screen cannot affect the image, remain frustrated. Passive, not subversive. Boring catachresis as pseudo-freedom. Pointless urban travelogues. Down those meaningless streets a man must go; a man who is not afraid to collate radio ads and call it modern art.

The surface of the city is overdetermined and meaningless at once; it is drained of cosmology, except for what you can hallucinate, geometrically fix, and overlay on it; you can't just photograph it, it's no longer a meaningful fabric. A lot of this poetry should have stayed in its own bedroom, listening to records.

Presence and decay. Irony: when someone says, 'this isn't really happening to me', it means 'this is all that's happening to me but I've drained my consciousness to retain control'. Lose control.

Language takes a few tenths of a second to decay. If reality is trapped at preconscious level, generalised statements and judgements haven't arrived; the pulse poets appear to be trapped in the primary sensuous world, drowned in it. The preconscious is not privileged. When primary awareness is fixed, it consists in equal parts of matter, projective wishes, undeciphered messages, and errors of the senses. The idiocy of the streets is the idiocy of the body. As ever, the gap between raw material and junk is magically effaced. 'From the fugitives, almost the rubbish, of society, from the abandoned monuments of a shrinking civilization, something new and excellent could be constructed.'

Categorisation and synthesis are the denial of presence. The act of reason destroys all the possibilities of a moment: the past has no possibilities, one must slow down the pulse of the continuous present in order to open up a potential space: as space flies up around the moving subject.

These pulses are rigorously stopped when their charge starts to fade; silence becomes a structural element as the poet completely halts the flow every one to three lines, drawing attention to the new idea and making the mechanical alternation of silence and signal as dramatic as possible. The poem is emitted as if it were being improvised one line at a time.

Decomposing every sense-stream into the single pulses of primary awareness before synthesis puts the poet through the appalling strain of shutting down at every line. The gesture finally gives back the energy it exacts. A high price is paid in passages of drift and babble.

Group reality is a distortion of the self and *vice versa*. Allen Fisher deliberately built the space in which this poetry would be possible, with a piece of chalk on a wooden floor. Even the people he invented can't write like him; more literal imitation would be a very good idea. Remote sensing; starlight jumps straight into the pupil as vessel which catches light reverberating from one inch, 100 inches, 100 feet, 2,000 feet away. No-one before Fisher has grasped this fact so lucidly; he sees a river where other people see a blank wall. He is the only artist documenting the mystery that surrounds the skin on both sides. He writes like a Frankenstein lashed to a mast in the midst of cosmic storms: 'no physical/entity escapes this surveillance./It frees all concern about issues/ of internal consciousness – violent/ motions, unknown forces, tortuously/ curved, even multiply-connected/ geometry.' This whole group exists in Fisherspace, although his approach to the beat is totally different. One exception: very early O'Sullivan reveals a clear debt to the hardly less titanic figure of Barry MacSweeney, in his late 1970s style.

I remember how scared I was of Maggie O'Sullivan's poetry when I first saw it in *Rock Drill*, bought at the British Rail plant depot around 1985. I didn't have the energy to form the motions it was calling: the shared surface drained by one side's personality blocks. Yet the personality is not the person, but the job, anxieties, traumas. The density of the beat threatened me with unconsciousness. I've had a similar experience with abstracts by Gerhard Richter and free jazz by Sonny Sharrock or Peter Brötzmann: the fear of being engulfed. Today, she's my favourite modern poet. Most poets could only reach this kind of energy for two or three lines, before being drained by it. I can't explain how these poems seem to be saturated in every dimension, and still flow with that dreamlike fertility and amplitude. Why, this is nothing less than the earth rising up to engulf us.

With Virginia Firnberg, the physiology of pulse has gone right through shaped language into singing, obviously not reproduced on the page; and the ripping of the envelope of personality has gone right through, to where perception is eliminated in favour of arbitrarily invented objects. Despite her random attitude to her own work, she simultaneously seems unaware that any reality exists outside it. While the most automatic and chaotic of the poets, she is also potentially the most suggestive.

(This review was originally published in fragmente *4, 1991).*

ADDITION 2016

The statement on 'Fisherspace' is inaccurate – I just wasn't familiar enough with the field. While it is true that Fisher incorporates just about all the stylemes used by other London writers, that doesn't mean that he originated them. I didn't understand where the pulse thing had come from, and the participants were unable to explain to me, with that lack of reflexivity that is typical for this group. I am reasonably certain that it comes out of the annihilation of language in sound or concrete poetry, and that this massive event led through nothingness to the greening over of a devastated space where mere chains of stain or signal had been. That dark cratered empty planet feel. Indeed the death of language led to a kind of infinite energy, unreduced by categories or articulation. The early stage of a rebirth of speech included short bursts with stress in simple peaks unspread by larger sense units. Hence its rhythmic power. These poets seemed to have a shared past including this death and rebirth. The pulse thing is post-concrete, post-nondiscursive, in incomplete transformation.

THE ESSEX SCHOOL

KELVIN CORCORAN (1956–) is an English poet, of Irish heritage, born in Worcester:

> In blue September between blue blinds
> I write and drink, thinking of money,
> thinking inside the physical forms of words
> for the pleasures of reification.
>
> The solid book of pictures opens like a new country,
> bevelled streets run to a silver point
> arranging the space in days, you do it with your hands,
> as if you would be given such secrets.
> (from *Lyric Lyric*, 1993, p.38)

In this set of parataxis, montage, lack of overt emotional or other framing signals, and the irony or distantiation of the whole, the principal formal influence is Tom Raworth, although Corcoran has spoken of Alan Halsey as someone he reveres, and wrote an (uncompleted) doctoral thesis on Peter Riley. Despite the denatured surface, much of Corcoran's poetry is extremely emotional, and the accumulation of evidence of the outside world just involves us more firmly in his emotions about politics, love, and family tragedy. What we may be seeing is a fundamental renewal of rhetoric, answering to a new generation with new expectations of artistic syntax, genre rules, and connectedness. Arguably, montage is a technique of film syntax, which we learnt to follow (from the TV) before we learnt to read. Poets born after about 1952 absorbed the TV kind of symbolic strings in parallel with acquiring language (although this was already true to some extent in the days of 'Saturday morning pictures' 30 years earlier).

Concentration on his technique could be a distraction; ultimately the method of organisation is less important than the fact that he is constantly reflecting back the world, this is poetry with a subject matter, and that is the society we live in, its human relations, urban landscapes, dispute over rules of association, its information media. Although the mix of elements is unique, it is hard to point to any feature of Corcoran's style that was not developed in the 1960s. It is hard to dismiss him as wilful or hot-headed. Involved in this avant-garde classicism are both the solidarity of the Left, the idea that only a critique that everyone can agree with is going to change society, as opposed to private and inherently frustrating fretting; and the historic blockage of the Left, its failure to achieve any goals since 1970. Local to Corcoran seems to be an undemonstrative, documentary, Midlands quality.

His lack of a framing commentary can be interpreted as a gesture of lack of solidarity with the ruling class. The naïve Leftist aesthetics of Martin Booth also regard interpretation as corruption and can advocate inarticulate 'primary' poetry as innocent and therefore true. Kelvin gives an analytical view of reality, and includes human attitudes and theories as part of the evidence, whereas 'domestic realists' omit essential information and make the point of view of the poem identical to that of the characters in it, preventing thought. Corcoran really doesn't believe that toasters and the colour of kinds of wood represent a hallowed and innocent level of pre-ideological reality. The office of supplying social semantics is the object of contention in a puzzling way, that people flee it as if afraid of being accused of arrogance; yet poetry is impossible unless the poet tells the reader what is going on. Indeed, the poem offers pure social semantics and not a situation at all.

Corcoran's success depends on finding the edge of social frames, choosing details that embody the significance of an event for the participants without asserting a textual authority. Perhaps the difference is that bad poets give visual and acoustic details, as if imitating television and making TV into the primary and unfalsified; whereas he gives all kinds of data, realising that the intentions and classifications of the actors in any scene are decisive. A reliance on objects finally means reliance on possessions, to the exclusion of relationships.

Mapped around the border
of what can be said about
the mind of the government,
which is to say nothing,
petrol air ribbons overlay
the dim plain burning;
a shopping arcade of mirrors
spattered with marble grain.
Reflected un examined action
we queue revenues decline
with dark and hollow mouths
nothing will ever fill.
 (from *Lyric Lyric,* p.18)

There were six books before this one: *Robin Hood in the Dark Ages, The Red and Yellow Book, Qiryat Sepher, TCL* and *The Next Wave.* Of these *The Next Wave* is much weaker than the rest, and *Robin Hood* is not yet absolutely sure in its technique.

Amid the distribution problems of the small presses, and with a certain generational rift, Corcoran also has the distinction of being the only 'small-press' poet to become established in the 1980s. There was a conservatism of the underground, as some people refused to admit that anything new could happen after 1977, a golden age of new poetry and revolutionary hopes. Other new poets had publication problems. The cutting-off of the underground from visibility between about 1977 to 1988 meant that neither new poets nor the audience shared in the cumulative results of poetic experimentation.

In the 1970s, the voice of bourgeois guardianship went on with its reassuring blather, but lost credibility and became mere words. Punk (which came along in 1976) was the cultural response to this, decoupled in some ways as is inevitable; the old pop world had been essentially a continuation of advertisements in its utopianism and wish to lead the good life, so punk was far more critical of authority in its visible form of the media than anything before. This was fuelled by a critique of personal relations; punk no longer used love songs or any expectation of nuptial bliss. This created a vacuum in which group relations, no longer sexual relations, reached the centre of attention: reaching politics, in fact. Politics rose up to dominate pop music because the political scene was going wrong, and Thatcherism was on its way. Corcoran's place in this is displaced, as one would expect of a poet: his specific trait is not to engage in the long disgusted angry rants which punk indulged in. The surface objectivity of technique flatters the general boredom with 'rage' (which set in at latest in 1981) while also withholding the complicity between poet and reader which dulls the critical faculty and is like the dual-narcissistic relationship between the maker of advertisements and the audience. The absence of emotional pointers foregrounds the composition of separate data as the key action of the reader. If you strip off the music from a film, the events become much more ambiguous; because the music hammers home a single meaning. (Punk was if anything the silencing of the music.) Corcoran cuts out all emotional prompts and 'frame markers', and is in the first place not writing poems of a predictable emotional-informational cadence. The act of composition, by which we get from raw sense data to a reading of the situation, is the centre of all his poetry because it is not given in his poetry.

In music, the reaction away from punk to suavity and beauty set in by 1982. In poetry, too, the music had been stripped away. That fake-collective, over-orchestrated programme music, was either replaced by a new music, of Marxism for example, or left an empty channel, underneath which the wordless ambiguity of the uninterpreted world sprawled, containing and denying all meaning; the core of *blank psychosis*, to quote André Green. Whereas Corcoran's work includes hermeneutic procedures that imply the possibility of a new social order, some of his contemporaries seem to be offering a parodic music in which all the elements are so jangled as to be merely comic. The empty music for the ceremonials has been filled up with long meaningless sequences; the procedures of variation, the imaged social process, have been reduced to scabrous and arrested parody, a toy march to a musical-box tune.

THE 1980S MAINSTREAM

The key opposition of the time had become between contestatory and non-contestatory. ALISON BRACKENBURY's (1953–) first collection, *Dreams of Power* (1981), seemed to me a perfect example of mainstream verse. It proves that it's possible for someone to write poems that aren't offensive to convention, aren't in revolt against anything, offer no difficulties to publication, etc., but which still have grace and artistic merit.

> But I would not betray
> The silence of you listening, you who are not there.
> The lime trees are in flower. Their leaves flash awhile,
> Tender the young twigs flower. The air is light
> With scent, and green and frail and stirred by bees

As every sense forgets. Yet it returns.
A footstep on the carpet shakes room warm
With presence. 'What of this?' your long ironic mouth
Demands me. And I ask you, say we salvage this from war,
This lost scent; though the lime-trees rise in storm.
>   (from 'Letter to No-one', in *Dreams of Power and other poems*,
>   1981)

The poem is about conflict, the breakdown of a relationship, nostalgia caught in sensations. It does not rise to any great heights, but is distinguished. A long poem, in this volume, is about Arabella Stuart, a victim of genealogy who lived most of her life in confinement at Hardwick Hall in Derbyshire. I have a problem with the choice of the 16th century (not the 20th), with an aristocratic heroine (too snobbish), with the romantic story (the reduction of politics to a romantic novel about the love-life of the royal family, what a disaster), with the obvious appeal of the poem to the English Tourist Board, but... it's a good poem. Unfortunately her second collection seemed to have lost all the distinction of tone and line that had made the first one interesting. An equally non-contestatory poet is ISOBEL THRILLING, (*The Ultrasonics of Snow*, 1985; *Spectrum Shift*, 1991), orthodox in every way (of course the orthodoxy is without rhyme and regular metre, today) but with an unfailing command of cadence, drama, and verse movement, to a much greater extent (even) than Brackenbury. Thrilling began writing poetry, the story goes, when facing an operation that might or might not have prevented the loss of her sight. Take this account of waking up after an eye operation:

>   Next morning
>   people fly down like birds
>   with enormous faces,
>   they feed me from huge hands.
>
>   Words slipping
>   their colours through voices,
>   speak about snow.
>   A mighty pane of sky cracks
>   into silver,
>   trees ring with crashed crystal,
>   a death of mirrors
>   breaking to sharpest quiet.

> I have been remade,
> odd creature
> whose hearing is immense,
> skin rewired
> to a spectrum shift.
>   (from 'Eye-ward', from *Spectrum Shift*)

This shows a number of modernist features. I would call this poetry tuneful, implying by that a minimal form in which every relationship is under stress and every one contributes to a perfectly memorable whole. These are poems of no theoretical interest, but they do make me feel how much 'aware' poets have lost by saying 'we don't do stories' or 'we don't do feelings' or 'we don't do landscapes', etc., and how easy it is for someone to outwrite them simply by writing about feelings within a situation, in such a way that every line reveals new essential information, and that the whole 'tune' creates tension and identification. Polarisation will wipe out almost every faculty except rage. I might prefer a situation like Hollywood in the 1950s where wonderful films, which were also humanistic and also about human feelings, were being made for a mass audience by directors like Douglas Sirk, Delmer Daves, and Howard Hawks, and 'difficult' films were a minority taste. I'd be glad if modern poetry weren't difficult, and much of this volume is an attempt to explain why almost all mainstream poetry is so bad, not to celebrate the fact. I find it depressing and alienating that the overwhelming majority of good poetry is on the 'modernist' side and comes out from small presses.

OBJECTIVISM

Related to George Oppen rather than Douglas Sirk, JOHN SEED (1950–) from a Catholic working-class family in Durham, has taught (after research, and some other jobs) social history in colleges of further education, in London from the early 1990s. He edits the journal *Social History*. He is no longer a party member, but was (in 1968 and shortly afterwards) in a group 'underneath' the New Left, critical of its excessively middle-class social origins and lack of linkage to industrial and electoral possibilities. He has left the Labour Party in disgust, perhaps more than once. He got into poetry through the Morden Tower bookshop in Newcastle, which then stocked books able to fire up young people. He read *Grosseteste Review*, a channel for Objectivism being assimilated to an English context. He has named his favourite poets as Wyatt, Shelley, and Oppen. An early book,

Spaces In (1977) formed about half of *History Labour Night* (1984), which was followed by *Interior in the Open Air* (1993).

                              headlights of the great lorries
                                    flashing
          speed and movement 'a kind of redemption'
               surging rhythm of the
                         engine in the empty
     streets
          a metaphysic   direction of events
                    second by second
     shines on passing windscreens   wing mirrors
          outward
          (untitled poem from *Spaces In*, in
          New and Collected Poems, 2005, p.13)

An explanation of Seed's work should follow an analysis of Objectivism, and precisely how the poems of Oppen, Lorine Niedecker, and Carl Rakosi work. Unfortunately, I can't understand why Niedecker's poems are so good, when the actual texture of the verse is so simple, the means of emphasis so sparing. The method certainly isn't infallible, a great deal of Objectivist verse is wilfully tedious. I can say that the discipline is like a kind of Chinese calligraphy where no corrections are possible, so that each stroke must be thoroughly thought through before the hand is allowed to move; but that is a comparison, no explanation. I could mention the Imagists, whom the Objectivists were certainly following; I could mention the so-called *ermetici* in Italy, a style developed at much the same time as Imagism, and also revelling in cutting poems back: I have the same problem explaining why a dozen syllables of Giuseppe Ungaretti contain more emotion than a hundred pages of someone else. We could even apply a phrase about him to Seed: 'the fascination of the images is in their refined and planned poverty'.

    Perhaps one could approach the problem from the other side. Take this passage of Henryson, describing Saturn as the spirit of Cold and apathy:

    His face frosnit, his lyre was like the leid,
    His teith chatterit, and cheverit with the chin,
    His ene drowpit, how sonkin in his heid,
    Out of his nois the meldrop fast can rin,
    With lippis bla, and cheikis leine and thin,
    The iceshocklis that fra his hair doun hang

> Was wonder greit [...]
> Atouir his belt his lyart lokkis lay
> Felterit unfair, ovirfret with froistis hoir
> [...]
> Under his girdill ane flasche of felloun flanis,
> Fedderit with ice and heidit with hailstanis.

Central to its effectiveness is its redundancy: it immerses the reader in winterness by repeating it in every word. Henryson doesn't really add any new ideas after the first line. This was an older way of achieving psychological depth. In order to say something only once, but create silence around it, one must be nearly silent; so creating texts that are scarce, sullen, verging on the barren. Worse, the poet can easily train himself to fix on a phrase for a long period, almost out of inanity, almost in paralysis, and fail to realise that the reader finds it banal and sees no need to dwell on it. Cutting and setting a dozen phrases that can still and satisfy the gaze, catching the deep silence, calls for the concentration of an oriental monk. Seed has this quality of almost violent patience and taciturnity, and his work brings me closer than anything else to a vision of the absolute, of the spirit of history.

Ungaretti exploits, perhaps, preset points of positional significance in emotional and linguistic space. I recall how they carry machine tools about, by putting a rope through a loop exactly at its centre of gravity: it's very stable and very easy to lift. Human affairs have such points of zero work, where the meeting of arrows of intensity mean that a few words carry ultimate force.

> in the morning isolate we
> Huddle in private bodies along the platform imaginary
> Subjects ghosts
> Of the structure of the
> Language of the circuit of capital...
> Imaginary keys to a real door locked iron
> Rails the bitter wind a mouthful of broken glass
> (from 'In the Sweet Dark', *New and Collected Poems, p.44*)

The parodic Objectivist poet writes a long text and strikes out words and phrases one by one until there is no redundancy. The traces of this are obvious. They would patiently reduce the Henryson passage to:

> leid
> With lippis bla

> flanis
>
> fedderit with ice

and consider this a far better poem. I would argue that there is information in the formal properties of a language string, and ignoring the
'emergent properties' of complex repetition is a form of reductionism. But
the 'paring down' is a monk-like act of self-mortification which in 99 cases
out of 100 misses all 'points of force' and is unmemorable. Writing poems
twelve words long doesn't make you Ungaretti. 'Poverty' may be a key
concept for Seed, the idea of simple repetitive physical tasks (this is social
history). One thinks of him sharpening the teeth of a saw, tiny parings off
the substance of tiny jags that stand in a certain relation to the felling of a
forest. How small is the cut in relation to the tree. How little energy the eye
needs, to redirect the hands. This is the poverty of the eye.

If we bear in mind what Basil Bernstein said about parataxis in
working-class speech, this rigour of style may have extra-poetic origins, and,
in the mouths of left-wing poets, a political intent. But Chinese poetry isn't
minimal because it was written by working-class people; if Seed suspends
lines without subordinating them to each other, it's because a field of
eight words allows much more complete control of weights and directions
than a field of 40 words. Oppen and Zukofsky didn't eschew legato and
hypotaxis because they lacked a knowledge of complex structures. There
is a concentration of poets writing like Bunting, or at least very simply
and musically, in the North-East. Great simplicity and great complexity
converge; the Hassidic rabbis recorded wisdom in incredibly compressed
form, perhaps because their illiterate followers wished to memorise sayings,
for lack of books. These sayings sometimes have the pithiness of Ungaretti
or Seed. However, these Hassidim are also close to Walter Benjamin, a
master of complex logical verbal structures and admirer of Buber and
Gershom Scholem; it is at the edge where logic lays bare the mysticism of
Benjamin's conceptions:

> Storm blowing from the beginning
>
> History history's angel
> Hurled backwards into future
>   tattered wings spread, ears deafened
> watches the debris climb skyward

                                        shattered
Crystal of human reason
    (from: 'After Walter Benjamin',
        in *New and Collected Poems*, p.35)

It is only when the founding of these conceptions registers in glimpses of irrational insight that one realises how much of classical Marxism is contained in Seed's fiery fragments.

Isolation and Fulfilment:
Poetry in the 1990s

Good books from 1990-7

1990
Edwin Morgan, *Collected Poems 1949-87*;
Alexander Hutchison, *The Moon Calf*;
Allen Fisher, *Civic Crime*;
Hilary Llewellyn-Williams, *Book of Shadows*;
Peter Finch, *Make*;
Brian Catling, *The Stumbling Block, its Index*;
Ulli Freer, *Stepping Space*;
Robert Sheppard, *Daylight Robbery*;
Robert Crawford and W. N. Herbert, *Sharawaggi*.

1991
John James, *Dreaming Flesh*;
D. M. Black, *Collected Poems 1964-87*;
Isobel Thrilling, *Spectrum-Shift*;
Tim Fletcher, *Firesong* (n.d.), *Derivatives*;
Brian Catling, *Soundings* (accounts of performance acts);
John Ash, *The Burnt Pages*;
Mimi Khalvati, *In White Ink*;
Ian Duhig, *The Bradford Count*;
W. N. Herbert, *Dundee Doldrums*;
Nicholas Johnson, *Listening to the Stones*;
Simon Smith, *Night Shift*.

1992
future exiles (selected poems by Allen Fisher and Brian Catling);
Tom Raworth, *Catacoustics*;
Wendy Mulford, *The Bay of Naples*;
David Barnett, *Fretwork*;
Pauline Stainer, *Sighting the Slave-Ship*;
Ulli Freer, *Sand Poles*;
David Greenslade, *Burning Down the Dosbarth*;
Jo Shapcott, *Phrase Book*;
Robert Crawford, *Talkies*;
Andrew Lawson, *Human Capital*

1993

F. T. Prince, *Collected Poems 1935-92*;
Tom Rawling, *The Names of a Sea-trout*;
Tom Raworth, *Eternal Sections*;
David Harsent, *News from the Front*;
David Chaloner, *The Edge*;
Denise Riley, *Mop Mop Georgette*;
the tempers of hazard (for Barry MacSweeney, selected poems);
John Seed, *Interior in the Open Air*;
Maggie O'Sullivan, *In the House of the Shaman*;
Graham Hartill, *Ruan Ji's Island and (Tu Fu) in the Cities*;
Kelvin Corcoran, *Lyric Lyric*;
Jamie McKefreerndrick, *Kiosk on the Brink*;
Robert Sheppard, *Flashlight Sonata*;
Caroline Bergvall, *Strange Passage*;
Moniza Alvi, *The Country at My Shoulder*.

1994

Francis Berry, *Collected Poems*;
Charles Madge, *Of Love, Time, and Places: Selected Poems*;
Roy Fisher, *Birmingham River*;
R. F. Langley, *Twelve Poems*;
Colin Simms, *In Afghanistan, Poems to Basil Bunting*;
David Barnett, *All the Year Round*;
Pauline Stainer, *The Ice-Pilot Speaks*;
Allen Fisher, *Scram, or the Transformation of the Concept of Cities,*
    Dispossession and Cure, Breadboard;
Nigel Wheale, *Phrasing the Light*;
Tony Lopez, *Stress Management*;
Vicki Feaver, *The Handless Maiden*;
Michael Ayres, *Poems 1987-92*;
W. N. Herbert, *Forked Tongue*;
David Dabydeen, *Turner: New and Selected Poems*;
Deryn Rees-Jones, *The Memory Tray*.

1995

Alan Ross, *After Pusan*;
Elizabeth Bartlett, *Two Women Dancing*;
James Berry, *Hot Earth Cold Earth*;
Judith Kazantzis, *Selected Poems 1977-92*;
Michael Haslam, *A Whole Bauble*;

Grace Lake, *Bernache nonnette*;
Brian Catling, *The Blindings*;
Chris Bendon, *Jewry*;
Robert Hampson, *Seaport*;
Ian Duhig, *The Mersey Goldfish*;
Alison Brackenbury, *1829*;
Niall Quinn, Nick Macias, and Nic Laight, *However Introduced
    to the Soles*;
Daniel Lane, *Wrecks in Ultra-Sound.*

1996

George Mackay Brown, *Following a Lark*;
Christopher Middleton, *Intimate Chronicles*;
Roy Fisher, *The Dow Low Drop: New and Selected Poems*;
Geoffrey Hill, *Canaan*;
John James, *Schlegel Eats a Bagel*;
Tony Lopez, *False Memory*;
David Greenslade, *Creosote*;
Rod Mengham, *Unsung: New and Selected Poems*;
Kelvin Corcoran, *Melanie's Book*;
W.N. Herbert, *Cabaret McGonagall*;
Tim Atkins, *Folklore 1-25*;
Vittoria Vaughan, *The Mummery Preserver*;
Andy Brown, *The Sleep Switch*;
Karlien van den Beukel, *Pitch Lake.*

1997

Barry MacSweeney, *The Book of Demons*;
Grace Lake, *Tondo aquatique*;
Peter Finch, *Antibodies*; *Useful*;
Alison Fell, *Dreams Like Heretics: New and Selected Poems*;
Frank Kuppner, *Second Best Moments In Chinese History*;
Kevin Nolan, *Alar*;
John Hartley Williams, *Canada*;
Mimi Khalvati, *Entries on Light*;
Rob MacKenzie, *Off Ardglas*;
Helen Macdonald, *Safety Catch*;
David Rees, *The London*;
Ian Taylor, *Ruins.*

Anthologies include *Floating Capital: 15 London Poets*, ed. Robert Sheppard and Adrian Clarke (1991); *The New Makars*, ed. Tom Hubbard (1991) is a convenient overview of some little-known poetry in Scots; *Dream State: The New Scottish Poets*, ed. Donnie O'Rourke (1993); *Ten British Poets*, ed. Paul Green (1993); *Contraflow on the Super Highway, an Informationist Primer*, ed. W. N. Herbert and Richard Price (1994); *Conductors of Chaos*, ed. Iain Sinclair (1996); *Out of Everywhere*, ed. Maggie O'Sullivan (1997). *An Aghaidh na Siorraidheachd* (bilingual anthology of recent Gaelic poetry) ed. Christopher Whyte (1991).

SPECULATIONS ON THE OUTLINES OF A GENERATION BORN IN THE 1960S

The time-now of this essay is 1996.

We can look at this group of poets only like a child running through a great darkened house, opening wardrobes and gazing at splendid clothes whose meaning we cannot yet understand and whose true outline we cannot clearly make out.

Magazines such as *Ramraid Extraordinaire, Active in Airtime, Angel Exhaust, Odyssey, Terrible Work*, and *Memes* have won our gratitude. Books offering glimpses of this generation would include: Caroline Bergvall, *Strange Passage*; Norman Jope, *Tors*; David Rushmer, *Sand writings*; Adam McKeown, *Bound*; Elisabeth Bletsoe, *Pharmacopoeia*; W. N. Herbert, *Forked Tongue*; Nicholas Johnson, *Haul Song*; Vittoria Vaughan, *The Mummery Preserver*; Karlien van den Beukel, *Pitch Lake*. The most finished work I have seen from this age group is by Bergvall, van den Beukel, Simon Smith, and Robert Smith.

The modern poet would like to be the columnist talking amateurishly about public affairs, banally about the small change of everyday life, and being witty and liked and trusted; the star as subject of wild fantasies and of energetic curiosity, whose every action is invested with significance, glamorous and mysterious; the scholar encoding rare ambiences, exposing authority, releasing precise information, carrying out feats of memory and eloquence, uncovering historical series; the spiritual healer who can decode the subtle signs of temperament and guide us to the paths of new growth, releasing tangles and blocks; the experimental scientist, the designer of ambiences, manager of a club where everyone wants to go and you can meet anyone you want to, devising a ritornellised space where the rules of normal behaviour are suspended and people are filled with curiosity, playfulness, and suavity; the hip consumer in-the-know about restaurants, clubs, clothes, foreign cities, foodstuffs, records, and clothes, filling poems with envy objects; the revolutionary upturning the structures of everyday life and revealing their artificial and unstable nature. It's not yet clear who is going to acquire these assets, conjured up by a collective longing.

At moments the instrumental, non-human sources of information scoop up what is more complex than our experience or internal images and thus explode the narrrowness of psychological patterns instated by monotony, conflict, and depression, and hurl these aside. Then, the perceivable world seems to immerse us in its inexhaustible immediacy and patternedness and novelty. The work of art can constitute such moments or sample them from the riches of observed knowledge. Such moments of excess and flooding of consciousness are fundamental in contemporary poetry; no doubt Peter Redgrove has written more of them than anyone else. They may resemble the trance moments of psychedelic drugs, happy dazes of the 1960s; they may take the thesis of attacks on authority, which invests in such limited cognitive systems or on organised knowledge. Awe at the teeming of life on the foreshore and in the rock pools may resemble awe at the diversity and strangeness of poetry itself. The word 'mind-expanding' is adequate for this state that funds so much activity.

I'm Gonna Tear Your Playhouse Down: The Loss of Mediations

The major topic of conversation over the past 20 years has been feminism. The liberation of women ('I'm gonna tear your playhouse down', Ann Peebles sang in 1975, a calm tale of annihilatory vengeance over a state-of-the-art Willie Mitchell backing) could damage the poetry of men where this was a form of self-esteem dwelling in myths of fascinating and dominating women, so that the straight version brought them crashing to the ground.

In about 1971 *Melody Maker* was talking about cock rock. The conversation of the time equated basic with sexual, saw every form of power and display as external properties of the phallus. Objects reinforced the ego, were stage properties for its display routines, were soaked with its scents. This excess analysis of the subjective meaning of acquired imagery, stupid and groundless and vulgar as it seems today, led, once the phallus was also identified as bad, to a breaking-up of the shared space, the loss of mediations. The recent history of poetry by men has been one long tale of trying to come to terms with a shattered world, trying to build up a poetic voice out of fragments, wallowing in anxiety and guilt. Poets who recede into a null-space where they are cut off from their feelings, from hopes, from other people, and from the symbolic world, generally go into a didactic stance: you're bad, I'm good. The symbolic transfer of power takes on the design of a political ceremony: the Governor General signs political power over to the natives as if this made him generous, or as if the power welled up out of him in the first place. It's hard to see that this misery and dumbness helps the cause of feminism.

Probably, Jimmy Page was playing a guitar rather than a penis. The influence of reflexivity was parallel, the allure of the academic stance that rules that, if you have no attachments or feelings, you are the manager. Going numb and playing dumb, the lumpish and languid see-through saints were trying on the attire of authority. The lack of sensations, held to throw the whole structure of society into question, to be superior and episcopal, was insensibility. The reader was expected to admire the triad of impersonality, vacancy, self-righteousness.

The uncovering of a dual subject inside the author of English literature, dual object among the reader of English Literature, of a female population underlying and splitting the social, put into question the rules of symbol formation; the pathways between the body and the vocabulary emerged into light as a separate component, which could be reformulated in new and experimental ways. It seemed that an intelligent network flowed between cultural forms and the cinema of fantasy, desire, and intention, a modulator where shaping or mediating took place.

Shopping for Power Objects

The period saw both a rejection of the moral authority of the universities and the intellectuals by the government in power, the expansion and institutionalisation of the university as a corporation to the point where students could forget about the outside world, the sinking of the intellectual or moral credibility of government to an all-time low, the threat of unemployment and poverty for people with a degree or even two, and a fashion in the media for extolling primitive self-aggrandisement. Power was the area of crisis. Ideas became a kind of power dressing, operated in seminars and articles with the adroit cynicism of a young manager operating business theory buzz words in order to shine and rise within a corporate culture.

The relapse of the 1960s attack on the 'whole structure of Western knowledge', to use a term of the time, was young academics losing interest in knowledge except as a means to advancement. The competitive element of intellectual debate, the duel, overrode the element of co-operation. The gesture of occupying the desired, envied, and vaunted verbal styles had multiple meanings, which could include a simple claim to succession to high office, to be candidate overlords. The gesture of giving away power was combined with lavish if stealthy gestures of claims of reprise, of the type 'I have here a vantage point where sexuality, class politics, and poetics all fit together' or 'this shell in my hand is not merely one among millions but one from which it is possible to speak about the seashell in general, i.e. the poem in general'.

The symbolic occupation of charismatic names like Heidegger, Derrida, Marx, de Man, Freud, Lacan, Hartman, Lévi-Strauss, explains the subterfuge with which the stylistic surface of J. H. Prynne or John Wilkinson was adopted and seized as a form of ostentation. Patriarchy is the keynote: the seizure of authority by occupying the awe-soaked regalia of previous authority figures, deified and drained of time. The father's body, torn up and eaten, is used as a trophy and badge of rank. This appropriation and status competition went along with the abolition of the personal speaking subject, the abnegation of secular appetites to leave a bleached, severe, acerb, sealed poetic surface. The academic left wing was disdainful of both culture and business, unfounding its own critique for lack of grist, and unable to utter communal feelings and life values. No doubt the argument is precisely that the latter ceased to exist after Thatcherism but since you can't have socialism without them, this leaves little scope for poetry. The counter-argument is that such poets are distancing themselves from their audience, emptying out their verse. Longing for an ideal of sexual authenticity, as unfulfilled as the longing for a radical Labour government, produces, perhaps, a poetry no longer about an authentic ground that is absent but about absence. The quality of their scorn and intransigence is welcome in a society not known for its ability to say no to anything. It seems equally impossible for academics to write about literature without dragging in psychoanalysis, Marxism, and the postmodern identity crisis, or to say anything intelligent and well-shaped that does scratchcard-score all those things. The discourse of sexuality, class conflict, linguistic materialism, and post-humanist epistemology seems to have been reduced to t-shirts or go-faster stripes: a cargo cult where aeroplanes are divine messengers and philosophical ideas are merely non-referential.

SCATOLOGY

I noticed *post factum* that issue 13 discussed W.N. Herbert's use of vomit, while 14 discussed Ian Duhig's use of shit. There is some cultural tendency towards defilement, justified by wearing baa-baa-Bakhtin t-shirts and talking about the 'grotesque body', but deriving from punk. These substances only acquire a semantic value through space; because there are social rules about where they can be, mis-locating them is a symbolic defilement of the rulemaker, an anti-authoritarian gesture. This act of scorn is related to the reduction of the individual through 'scientific' sociology, where at the outset the aesthetic feelings of the 'bourgeois' are assumed as wrong. The lack of an adequate theory of social agency leads to the loss of personality boundary as one refuses to identify with anybody else. The loss of external reference leads to boundless self-overrating, flights of megalomania alternate with a sense of psychic annihilation. The loss of validation from other people, reduced to ghosts, cancels out internalised subjective objects, and leads to the loss of a social tone in which things can be said.

The act of defilement is closely related to catachresis, the deliberate misuse and distortion of other people's words, cultural forms, and feelings; the bizarre forms of the avant-garde are oddly anticipated by the forms of caricature, more primitive than realism. The parody sketches of the early cabarets that were the avant-garde's first home could suspend coherence and reason because they were recognisable distortions. Punk was a collective experiment using all these styles and tactics; the influence on punk of the conceptual art of the 1960s and 1970s, via the art schools where so many of its creators studied, made it a crossbreed between popular culture and the radical avant-garde. The conceptual artist John Latham burnt towers of books as a protest against the ossification of cognition into organised knowledge, the sanctification of CIA-financed critics like Clement Greenberg into dictators. I wonder if there is some element of this in late Prynne, if he is not symbolically setting fire to the wings of English verse (and moral community, and respect for the past?) and releasing it on a downward spiral.

Two SUBLIMES

The choice between two sublimes structures the landscape. One achieves generality by receding away from concrete instances, throws out the freight of real experience in order to disappear into a misty 'before' or 'above'; it is philosophical, gladly soaks up atmospheres from Martin Heidegger, Theodor W. Adorno, or Ludwig Wittgenstein; it hopes that the truth may emerge from an emptied sight where we reject all the products of class society or of Western languages; it asks us to speculate as fogbound marshalling sites emerge in the space left by what has been banished, whose cognitive shapes migrate into abstraction, and are suspected to migrate further into 'valid being'.

The other sublime is a mythical and autobiographical one. The poet projects 'deep' internal structures onto the natural world, or even onto an imaginary set of symbolic structures; a difficult process of integration that is supposed to heal, as ritual completion of patterns soothes and cures the areas of damage and disorder; the timeless is supplied by archetypes or by the level of generality of the discourse, freed from realistic detail; the reader partakes of complexity by speculations about the grounds of being, in a landscape of ultimate origins and of transformations. On one side stand W.S. Graham and J.H. Prynne; on the other, Peter Redgrove, Robert Graves, and Ted Hughes. One purifies language by striking out teleology; the other by bending poetic space till it becomes total teleology, curved air, rendering the poet's personality where objectivity is a constraint.

Identification is the division between the two, as the mythic version is dependent on it and the epistemological variant tries to leave it out. Identification is like experiment because through it you become someone else for a few hours and explore new sensations. Obviously, watching a film of the 1930s is an experimental experience for me: I learn new things from it. Fantasy and speculation are two different modes of acquiring information. Identification is a suspension of the self, a solution of barriers where the self is both attenuated and aggrandised. Speculation is a similar suspension of the reality principle. Both variants desire the reader to create and modify new shapes, new associations: speculative doubt and mythical appropriation are similar and therefore compete. The two converge in trying to recover childhood stages of becoming; a project sited on the pristine field of the new and intact that is also a recapitulation and that is also the text. Left-wing, radical philosophy picked up, in the late 1960s, the project of recovering the stages of socialisation while trying both to abolish conditioning, to destroy class society within the individual brain, and to repossess it, so as to build a society of others among whom the utopian life can be safely led. This interest in retrieving moments of beforeness, where the child was acquiring personality sub-units, coincides with a Freudian, or Jungian, wish to do the same thing in a therapeutic session.

The intellectual faction has a queasy sensitivity about: metaphor; appropriation; feelings; projection; myth; spirituality; love. The inability to identify makes it impossible to write about other people.

THE PERIPHERY AS THE SITE OF AFFECT AND SUGGESTIVE CONTROL

John Stezaker wrote in the catalogue to a 1976 exhibition:

> [but] ideology is not communicated in the well-systematised cultural directives which we call 'ordinary' language, but in the outer periphery of unsystematised cultural directives, in connotation. Language is a system of our ordinary shared beliefs and those which are not shared are not systematised into the form of a particular culture-use, but exist in the transient zone outside syntax.
>
> (from a catalogue entry, British Art Today 1960-76)

Whether Stezaker was right about ideology being absent from the overt content of the founding texts is an open question. Anyway, the era of conceptual art subjected the inexplicit semantic framing of the cultural object/situation to searching scrutiny. Stezaker seems to offer, in a moment of heat, a division between meaning and rhetoric, as if by stripping away the latter we could begin to utter true messages to each other; a presumable rerun of the 'logical positivist' project, dominant in British academic philosophy. The term rhetoric implies that indirectly semantic elements of verbal emphasis and ornamentation are deceit, while the ideology of performance is that elements of ornamentation and emphasis that are carried out with the body (e.g. facial expression, suprasegmental features of speech, dance, clothing) are authenticity. The reverse would be equally convincing. This exacting process of foregrounding the unconscious, framing, elements of meaning matured, ten or 15 years later, in the ability to manipulate them to make beautiful linguistic objects. The publication of Peter York's *Style Wars* (1980), which dealt with the same marginal domain of the subliminal, elusive, and non-referential, symbolically saw the recapture of minutiae and the periphery for self-adornment and self-aggrandisement. Someone working in advertising could, just as well, develop detachment from meaning and perfect understanding of the impact of details. Contemporary poetry has or wants expertise in using suggestion, implicit instructions, contextual clues, deposits of prestige. Attention has shifted, not only to the nuances of arranging parts of a line, but to the overall context, the semantic framing of the space that contains the poem, the poet, and the reader. Both the smallest relationships and the largest are objects of conscious design.

The same exhibition catalogue describes installations by Tim Head that are simply light sources playing on a room. By defining space, he isolates the act of appropriation and calls the artist's personality into question. The difference between real and symbolic space is foregrounded even as it vanishes; the identity of the room, something deeply puzzling and yet important to how we feel and behave in buildings, reaches centre stage. Appropriating space is the most elemental and the most fraught gesture of modern poetry.

The situation of the visual arts, where the avant-garde entered the juries, received government patronage, got put on by the British Council, etc., is superior to that of poetry, where the sources of money and information were sealed off by a revanchist conservative group that fought a ruthless war against innovation. There is not a single book on the radical poetry of the 1970s. The discourse around the visual arts is roughly a hundred times more advanced. This lack of sophistication is probably reflected in the quality of the poets' artistic decisions. The politics behind the triumph of the mainstream await proper study.

Wanderings Inside the Body

As the collective and political themes of poetry of the 1970s dried up, deprived not only of the real power that deprived them but of the symbolic and conjectural space where their hopes grew and acquired features and animated art, the maximum defensible space came to be the self, explored following a map derived from New Age spiritualism and self-development psychology: the privatisation of a revolution. John Kenneth Galbraith spoke, 30 years ago, of private affluence and public squalor; the evaluation of public space as corrupt, by both the Left and the Right, was used by the latter to forgo collective responsibility, by the former to denounce corporate and government authority; flitting around the partial and unstable spaces of specialist markets, the artist no longer has a parish, a stable, capacious, external space where the behaviour of a community might find room. The isolation of the philosopher conforms to the narcissistic cossetting solitude of self-realisation. Each poet, then, goes through a drama of reopening, stabilising, and marking space, as the semantic expanse where two psyches can meet and exchange signs of agreed meaning.

Didier Anzieu, as quoted in *Angel Exhaust* 11, suggested that 'the group imaginary is a projection of the mother's body'. A certain wave of poets set out from the woman's body, or body-psyche, as the landscape within which everything occurs. The space immersing a performance is teetering between private, the depiction of merely internal events with a psychoanalytical slant, and public, where an imaginary future is opened up to the audience for making and modifying models. The word selfish, heard so frequently from all sides, has been a key to taste; art that is personal and subjective can only avoid being selfish by being superficial and inattentive to its own subject, and this has been a popular solution. As a generalisation, the aficionados of avant-garde neoclassicism are concerned with paternal power and the poets of performance and mythic ritual are concerned with feminine potency, emanating through the female body or through the landscape. This stress on plastic values brings also a crisis of the abstract and of ideas.

A shared subjectivity is strained by the regime of competition and ownership, which also promotes differentiation and experiment. Male poets of this age group also seem to suffer from a terrible sense of guilt at entering shared space, through public utterance or sexual advances, and simultaneously from a sense of exclusion because they do not enter it. The medical metaphor has been popular. Attention has been directed away from work and towards leisure. You can't reform the State but you can go jogging. The political defeat of the Left, both in national and local politics and inside the Labour Party, led to melancholia. One of the symptoms of this is hypochondria, which latched onto psychotherapy and the new concern with the body to produce a truly lethal boredom. Interesting conversation was simply not possible on this basis.

The terms of space and the body cannot be taken as literal or natural or permanent. Their emergence into currency fills the space left by the departure of the parish, as the shared imaginary of Anglican art, and of an ethical community, as demanded by socialist art. The radical artist broke a hole in the collective verbal-affective terrain because it was not collective enough; other social agencies then broke much larger holes. Any shared space, even a stage and its audience, threatens to become the utopian coast, the site where our affective reunion can start.

PERFORMANCE ACADEMICISM

Today, a poet has to perform in public in order to have a career, in order to make any money, acquire a following, or even get a book published. In the live situation, the voice and the body and its clothes can swamp the flow of words. If unused, they can make the poet seem psychically absent and the poem attenuated and of diminished reality. If the poet chases the values of live performance too adequately, the result is showbiz. The insecurity of the naïve poet about what to do with their hands and how to speak has led to the importation of learnt techniques for reassuring the audience (and the performer), hence to performance academicism. Any performer is surrounded by space in which the audience perceive them and has a body whose movements and exterior surfaces can become sign-bearing. Performance academicism teaches every student to think in terms of these two sources of meaning. This dyad resembles the confrontation of the perceiving self and external space, argued out in the terms of object relations. Actors are taught to think through their bodies, always to synchronise speech with movement, not to blank out their bodies in order to concentrate on the text, to respond to the movements of the other actors. In this way natural groupings are constantly achieved and the absence of a link between the actor and the present moment, and the playwright and the time of composition of the text, is hidden. Theatre people are made insecure by someone reading while standing still, especially in England, where actors have difficulty with body language and the literary tradition has tended to overwhelm the theatre. However, if you are going to write a poem you have to become totally verbal, you can't leave information out because it is still embedded in arm movements or the act of running or climbing a tree. So the whole momentum of actor training tends to damage the technique of poetry. The demands of showbiz led, during the 1960s, to a massive regression of poetry. The serious live poets only fill a fraction of the available space, which is dominated by semi-showbiz characters of unutterable banality. It was possible for a few seconds during the 1960s to believe that the stage and the audience represented the escape of high art from its cell of solitary thought into the realm of authenticity; the communion of liveness being the good society, the stable external space, which had existed for Anglican poetry but that had seemed to dry up and fragment as part of modernity. This illusion is used as a reproach against poets who explore the full capacities of language as if their conscious thought were responsible for the disintegration of the *socius* and the social democratic consensus.

It is implausible that dramatic heights can be scaled by a solo performer, without scenery, who is limited in physical manoeuvres by having to read a text. This bareness is imposed, equally, by economic limitations. The artistic impact of a poem may be enhanced by adding vocal and gestural inflections but the starting point was, after all, that its impact was diminished as uncontrolled semantic channels opened up around it.

The popularity of non-verbal techniques may be due either to the power of a world of subsidised performance, which dislikes poetry but has funding and its own internal formal debates, or to the inability of poets as readers. Caroline Bergvall and Aaron Williamson teach at Dartington Hall, where a course on performance writing is turning out graduates qualified to write what may be the standard average 'modern' poem of the next ten years. Poetry performance practices today owe a lot to a slightly older generation, such as Brian Catling, cris cheek, Maggie O'Sullivan, and Geraldine Monk.

Sound occupies, for elementary physical reasons, a volume of space. We can tell, for elementary biological reasons, the approximate age, state of health, and body weight of a speaker from the qualities of their voice. As the latter becomes sound, it also spreads out to fill space, from which it becomes inseparable. The dyad of body and space is artificial, they permeate each other.

Bergvall (born 1962, in Norway) in *Oblique View of a Room in Motion* (1990) documents the twin means of a solo performer, the demarcated space of the stage and the body as signifying object, which have become transformed and exalted into a charming erotic divertissement, where with insidious and old-fashioned slowness a house is described and the contact of two people evoked. A third figure, that of interfering authority, makes a phantom appearance as we discover that the lovers are two women. Bergvall works as a performance artist both with evocative and illusionistic texts, evoking mysterious landscapes with usually erotic intent, and confrontational texts, where semantic jumps evoke, perhaps, the protagonist moving through a multicultural and partly hostile society, its teeming and cyclically incomplete codes, while the first type is intimate, undisturbed, and involves two people. *Strange Passage* (1993), a choral ode, is a strangely tranquil and even stately work. Work in *Conductors of Chaos* (1996) is the chaotic and largely garbled or incomprehensible 'In Situ', presumably about sex, and 'Hands On Catullus', something with more semantic jumps than previous works but still effective in parts. The graphic signs of 'In Situ', possible instructions for a vocal performance but meaningless to the ordinary reader, are perhaps related to the difficulty of talking about the sexual act as a set of three-dimensional spatial relationships along with internal sensations mapped on other real but invisible spaces, to do with blood flow in the capillaries, muscle tension, and so on. Here space has collapsed, perhaps gaining in affective intensity as the curved and darkened surface of the lover's body expands to become space altogether and the diffuse maternality of the landscape becomes something warm and close up.

LAND ART

In land art the female body is expanded to be the whole landscape, the hospitable and encompassing Mother Goddess as evoked by an E. O. James or a Marija Gimbutas. Detailing her features is an act of piety and propitiation, an obeisance to the powers greater than the individual that also expands the poem to a divine magnitude; a walk gives the space a third dimension, unlike a picture from a single viewpoint, and the land goes on engulfing the poet and mocking the limits of what perception intakes, swallowing up the ego and offering a stable external space where every desire can be enacted. Its features are enrolled in a projective scenario of the poet, an impropriation carried out by making marks, but the resistance and integrity they offer is incomparably detailed, tonally variegated, and hard to damage. Where is an inner for such an outer? The goddess's far-flung and opened body, at once dominating, vulnerable, sensual, protecting, and containing, is seen sexually through the tantra and documented by the poet as wanderer, who maps landmarks onto grain edges of the higher symbolic space given by personal or oriental myth. This space is suprapolar in the theological sense. Submission is a political gesture, jettisoning autobiographical poetics along with the exploitative plan of turning natural resources into money and trying to live outside nature, having engulfed it. The schema was already carried out in Gavin Selerie's *Azimuth* (1984). The merit of this poetry is its scale, far larger than the human form, addressing the sublime in words, but scale and the movement of attention are then the problems. The issues are dealing with the psychotic (as one lover engulfs and destroys the other) and with life where forces much larger than the self reduce it to a conditional state.

I feel that Norman Jope's poetry, for example, suffers from an excessive ideological security. Wrapped in many layers of argument that seems perfectly true to the author, it is too slow and leisurely and does not do enough to fight off demons of doubt in the reader's mind. Its volume is not in proportion to its rate of aesthetic success. His campaign, with 'finding time', to rethink unemployment, recognise its permanent nature, and make civilised life more possible on it, has broken new ground and earns a particular debt of gratitude from this writer. The result of excess leisure is certainly the production of more culture by more people but not necessarily of art, whose pacing and balance are perfect. All children are selfish towards mothers and land art tends to eliminate other people. It can be the privatisation of imaginary space.

THE RADICAL POEM

The radical poem, where by withholding sympathy and identification the agent uncovers hidden assumptions of the social field and shows unconsidered symmetries, patterns, classificatory divisions, and interventions of power; where the reader slips wholly from the scheme of gratifying identification with a single player to perceive the shape of the game as a whole, a geometric affinity sense that makes system rules conscious and sees a new horizon of forms. Visualisations of alternative social structures, detailed, tenacious, resistant, able to be modified, shared, developed. Glimpses of the 'before' of all structuration. Touching the structuration, the rules, their arbitrariness, their effects. Why one person becomes different from another.

The revelation of switch points in the flow of personal experience and action, where conscious intervention permits a qualitative transformation of the patterns of everyday life; like a cook's lore understanding the chemical responses to heat, time and herbs of raw stuffs from the market. Reflexivity making the flow of experience more intense. *Menagère* skills of the study and the salon.

A challenge to authority. A verbal machine where the poet always wins the argument. The release of the personality by the overthrow and humiliation of those who judged and weighed it. You get to mark your own essays. Invalidating all judgments.

PERVERSION AND HYPOCHONDRIA

David Rushmer (circa 1964) is preoccupied with the 'other's' body as the source of space. *Sand writings* was reviewed in *Angel Exhaust* 11; a pamphlet, *Love Letters to the Dead*, came out in 1994.

> unreal men have spoken of god
> at such times
> i have tasted his absence
>
> in this young girls excrement
> and soiled his dead face
> in my own

> where is the heart of man
> when the cock spits
> into the filthied bellies of the betrothed
> (from 'The Guardians of Urine', *Love Letters to the Dead*)

Where the body is both the signifier and the signified, the loss of mediations no longer matters; the circuit of the communicative act shrinks down to micro level, almost without content or readership. Adam McKeown (circa 1968) writes about the body and the growth of identity in an idiom close to Rushmer's. He has published *Bound* (1993) and the prose murder tale *Further … Father* (1995). We are used to poets using physicality as an external solid medium that stabilises the sentiment and action. Basic to Rushmer and McKeown is however the instability of the grounds of feeling, surrounding the surface of contact and shared experience with vast extents of white space where the psyche, losing contact with its projection into the other, disappears altogether, falls silent. Rushmer named one of his pamphlets *Absence*. They are both gazing at a landscape of depression and isolation. The rules, derived from French antecedents such as Georges Bataille, Antonin Artaud, the painter Hans Bellmer, and Jacques Lacan, state that everything outside the body is unreal; the artist is only truthful when exhibiting and modelling heated and cyclic fantasies; perversion is strength, and dialogue or normal sex are dilutions, attenuations; the Other can only appear as a doll. The (male) artist is dependent on the female body, whose nature is only known through fantasy; symbolic thought is only possible through this desired body, which keeps withdrawing itself. Despite their in many ways conventional nature, these texts offer difficulties because of their extreme deletion of vocabulary, as if by purging the words by which experience is usually mediated one could discover a ground of intact purity, where communication would not be alienated and would not betray us. However, the dependence on various psychoanalytical texts mortgages the poetry to a set of predictable gestures. The formation, from internalised stores of observed and understood events in the world, of a lexicon that could be used for introspection, reassurance, relating, and writing, seems forbidden or inconceivable. Its lack makes their poetry appear monotonous as well as fragmentary. It is as despairing and frustrating as recording objects in motion with a camera nailed to the floor. At the same time the emptiness gives the reader a space to operate in.

Both in Rushmer and in Williamson we find the curious image of the book as a body:

[i]n the mean time the spine begins to form, congealing through its lacings of horn and nerve. A casing is thrown out, shot through with curved bolts. These ribs, curling within the pulp, are grooved through with the static of verbiage. They hold, out front as satellite to the spine, a surface of split ridges that gape and converge in the wind. The fore-edge: our sternum. Open and then close, dithering.

(from Williamson's *A Holythroat Symposium*)

This is pedantic and overripe at the same time; hypochondriac and Mannerist. In 16th-century Catholic religious symbolism it was the body of Christ that was a text. The withdrawal of sensuous reality is curiously close to the groundless language of mysticism, following the image of an early book by Jeremy Reed, *Saints and Psychotics*. With a lyric poet like George Barker, the affective body, the temperament, affected the external world of other people displayed in the poem. There was a dyad of poet and society, of I and the staging of experience. For the poets under consideration the demise of practical reason has destroyed the dyadic tension and spatial paradoxes result as the outside world collapses in on the person experiencing it. It either threatens the poet with psychic annihilation, or, incarnating itself as the object of love, develops affective instability of its own as a space containing the poet that is non-linear, buckling and withdrawing itself according to its own mysterious thermal cycles. The narcissism of the poet, offered as truth since the falsification or withdrawal of the outside world, is offered to the reader as a fulfilment, a toy, beckoning to the reader's narcissistic fantasy, as extremes of delusion are seen as merely a larger dose of the drug. The privatisation of experience, which the decline of an established Church left as a bolt-hole for art, has been pursued further along its own axis. From *preces privatae* and chamber music to adventures in your own bedroom.

To this, however, we have to add another strand of French literature, the ontological removal to an empty state where we are trying to piece together the language we have lost. This derives from the Catholic vision of the logos (*le verbe*) as creating the world, which brought the French poet to the threshold where language and the world are about to exist. Poetry then becomes the discovery of the world. This *via negativa* is curiously similar to Drew Milne and John Wilkinson, both motivated by an original emptiness and denial, a hysterical ejection of internalised objects, which is refilled with incomplete or affectively blank objects by means of an investigation. If none of them can represent other people in a satisfactory way, that is a by-product of being unable to represent themselves on the page except as a kind of fog. The area where objects become shared and allow communication with other people, so that the self acquires a definite engaged outline and can recognise other selves as real and continuous, has collapsed. We are being carried, perhaps, to an island where language is emptied out and can start again from the nameless and unmediated. The struggle of these writers for a stable and capacious external space, the one theorised by Adrian Stokes and Peter Fuller, is perhaps one that everyone engages in. Another reading of object relations theory shows how a healthy psyche can produce successful symbolic acts; the broader social space, the parish or *ecclesia*, remains closed or damaged.

The Exquisite Poem

The exquisite poem constantly varies, can see its own shape, is never heavy, never repeats itself, prefers complicity to simplicity, offers refined and pleasurable textures, has absorbed every lesson, knows the movements of our sensibility and follows them, knows all the ways in which poetry bores or loses conviction and avoids them, is not hypnotised by realism, is not punitive and religious, is not an exercise in sensory deprivation, is like a warehouse with swatches of every textile, acts by choice and not by compulsion, sees the arriving visual and temporal patterns of the world as mysterious and dithyrambic, is more preoccupied by the reader than the writer, is not didactic, is attenuated to the point where it never stops moving, does not take hypotheses for bricks, prefers multiple entrances and exits as an architectural principle, is not dogmatic or hectoring, shows tonal shading and a fine ripple in every direction of movement, is like conversation, has gaiety and equanimity, gets carried away all the time, takes anything on, is not trying to prove that the individual is an illusion, is stylistically upwardly mobile, thinks of nothing else except metrics, has a magpie's eye for bright sounds and textures, is not homemade, lives in a world of appearances.

Avant-Garde Neo-Classicism

The 1980s were induced by the political and poetic collapse of the radical 1970s, making a mockery of theories of devising and occupying the future. History did not move towards the future we had laid out. Another insurance against the fickleness of time was to seize on existing style modules as if by possessing the past one could take out a claim on the future; the gesture of avant-garde neo-classicism. It was around 1983 that the Fairlight made sampling big time and began the dominance of the producer within the creative team of the pop record. Accordingly, what we tend to find in new poets a few years after that is the apprehension of the past by sampling. This is a variant of the 'star fantasy': Milne is to Prynne as Reed is to Scott Walker. Sampling at cellular level. It is hard to separate the influences of academicism (graduate students acquire styles from the past in the same spirit as reading desuete texts) and of furious competition for prestige within the sexually tense and financially flattened society of students, which seizes on the style of Prynne, or whoever, as an asset for display. Among young poets, the avant-garde, in familiar form, does not seem to exist outside the universities.

One of the great publishing enterprises of the 1980s was the Allardyce Barnett series of huge marble slabs enshrining mainly Cambridge poets of the Grosseteste/Ferry realm. The republication by Iain Sinclair as an editor (1987-92) at Paladin Books of big volumes aimed at the High Street incensed those who weren't selected and depressed those who were when the whole series was pulped after Sinclair's departure. The grant application became the key document of the time and public manoeuvres were often consciously directed at that charter of power. These slabs embodied not only the splendour of objecthood but also whatever was exquisite, elegant, elevated, and intelligent in poetic style. Such assets led to one of the most striking phenomena of the last ten years: the reappearance of the 'Cambridge' style as a magnetic stylistic attraction for ambitious postgraduate students dissatisfied with the domestic-anecdotal mainstream. These would include Drew Milne (*Sheet Mettle*, 1994), Andrew Lawson (*Human Capital*, 1992), and D. S. Marriott (*schadenfreude*, 1989, etc.). The style has become much more visible now people are imitating it – a moment of self-awareness, I would hope. The arrival of a new generation doesn't necessarily represent an addition to the stature of the originals so much as a hint that they're obsolete. John James' influence was felt on the poetry of Daniel Lane and Andrew Webster, his students. Others latched onto Raworth or Objectivism.

Around 1976 the wave of free verse broke. Verse was no longer regular or rhyming but an approximation to spoken rhythms was felt to be no more than civil and amenable. The new wave of the late 1980s represents a return to syntax and verse movement as opposed to the endless stop-start of parataxis.

The institutional basis for the revived *Grosseteste Review*/Ferry Press ambience was the Cambridge Conference of Contemporary Poetry, an annual fixture from 1991, which allowed the experimental world to assemble in one room and be exposed to a barrage of poetry. The poets were published in the pamphlet series Equipage or by publishers like Reality Street, Prest Roots, and Boldface Press.

Why use the term 'born in the 1960s? Time seems a sufficiently negative concept but may call in too much; whereas some poets believe in the railway line of the new, others believe that one reaches the timeless simply by breaking through the emptied surface deposited by secular time. It seems that, the younger the poet, the closer they are to the forms of popular culture and the less original and contemporary in terms of poetic form.

These themes crop up in several of the poets examined and have no bearing on many others. The choice of themes is better than arbitrary and less than satisfactory.

Book publication of this age group still gives a sporadic and unsatisfactory picture, retouched, for me, by magazine publications, readings, and unpublished poems (which reach me in various forms): each mingling chance and excess. Little magazines seem to include no prose commentaries or to ignore anyone born after 1950. Thinking about poetry is a kind of geological process, taking place with decades of delay.

[This was the introduction to an anthology of new poets called *Bizarre Crimes of the Future* published in 1996.

The title came from a story in a comic called *2000 AD*. Other poets born in the 1960s would include Alice Oswald, Paul Holman, Mark Ford, David Rees, Andrew Jordan, Rody Gorman, Matthew Welton, Giles Goodland, Sean Bonney, Dan Lane, Mark Goodwin.]

THE END OF HISTORY?

This account of the problems to which young poets felt pressed to find solutions does not offer a cultural dominant for the 1990s because there was none. There was a poetry boom that affected every cell of the landscape but this just promoted divergence.

If things dissolve in time, then poems written in 1995 would have washed away in 2015, as I write. This is not so. But, that not being so, would it not follow that one could write a deeply conservative poem in 1995 that continued ideals of 1955 and yet was wonderfully successful in 1975 and still in 1995? Ah, so many questions. I feel tired.

It is clear to me that from the mid-1980s on there was a lack of style history to write. There were some fashions but the dispersal and dissipation, not to say territorial expansion, of poetry forbid a style chronology of the kind that applied in a slightly earlier period. It is as if the innovations related to inhibitions – and in a society that was chronically de-repressed and preoccupied with indulging appetites inhibitions were unusual. The landscape looked like one in which a liquid had flowed out to its natural boundaries and the vital fluid of poetry was spread everywhere. The origin of separation in multiple doubling gives birth to an archipelago. This is why the original edition of *FCon* contained no interpretation of style in the 1990s. Culture always involves convergence on a shared emotional object but if there are 12 different 'peaks' to converge on then the effect on the scene as a whole will be divergence: people are moving intently in 12 *different* directions. Where you have isolation, one can speak of islands, and the whole scene can be described as archipelagic fulfilment. We abandon the idea of a centre but people are getting what they want in diverse ways.

The accepted write-ups of the British Poetry Revival find it already happening in 1960. It represented stylistic thinking that was fully present then to poets born in the 1920s like Denise Levertov and Christopher Middleton. We have to ask whether the situation has changed for poets born in the 1960s. I have an impression of a boundless exploration of potential in the 1970s that did not clearly leave empty space for younger poets to colonise. For me, the period after 1990 shows a lack of forward movement – changes can be found within local groups but the range of poetological possibilities displayed in 1990 was so wide that most styles used since then can already be found within that range. There may also be a sector, little heard of, where programmatic innovation marches in step with limited artistic success – like target-driven departments, which hit criteria for success while actually failing. I expressed concerns in the first edition of this book about a lack of new innovations after 1980. I had a feeling that poets born in the 1950s, as I was, were in a difficult position in the de-repressed field, where there was no empty space to occupy and artistic development had to exploit delicate scales of feeling and imagination rather than heroic trips into the unknown. There was room for cultural critics to say that the underground sector of British poetry was conservative and recycling ideas from the past. After 20 years I am still unclear about this. I do harbour considerable doubts about the rather vitally conventional poets who are being talked up as the new innovators. Any answer to these questions is going to have to sink into the fine structures rather than the large-scale ones visible from the Space Shuttle.

We halt here. To help a retrospective view we can mention a few books that belong to the period (1960-97) but that were only published later:

Sinclair's *Red Eye* (and the extra material in the new edition of *Suicide Bridge*); the new poems in *The Ship*, by John Hartley Williams; *Black Russian: Out-takes from the Airmen's Club 1978-9*, by Jeremy Reed (2010); *Alto: London Poems 1975-84*, by Maggie O'Sullivan; 140 pages of George Mackay Brown's poetry published posthumously in his *Collected Poems* in 2005; and *Cabin in the Mountains*, by Paul Brown.

Bibliography

(1) GENERAL
I have not bothered to list the books (also periodicals) from which I derived
knowledge about British society, or about linguistics. Secondary sources that
are not hysterically opposed to modern poetry are remarkably few.

Akros 28 is a survey of Scottish poetry; *Akros* 29-44 then provided long
surveys of many individual poets.

For a map of the seven-volume work on modern British poetry:
http://angelexhaust.blogspot.co.uk/2009/08/affluence-project-central-ethos.
html

Reviews: there has been very little quality reviewing in the period but sporad-
ically excellent information appeared in *Poetry Information, Grosseteste Review,
Curtains, Spanner, Reality Studios, Angel Exhaust, PN Review, First Offense, Bête
noire, fragmente, Parataxis.*

(2) BY CHAPTER

What Just Happened?
    Booth, Martin, *British Poetry 1964-84: Driving Through the Barricades*
        (London: Routledge and Kegan Paul, 1985)
    Görtschacher, Wolfgang, *Little Magazine Profiles: The Little Magazines in
        Great Britain 1939-93* (Salzburg: Salzburg University Press, 1993)
    Homberger, Eric, *The Art of the Real: Poetry in England and America since
        1939* (London: JM Dent, 1977)
    Poet's Yearbook 1978 (Cleethorpes: Poet's Yearbook Ltd.)

Versions of the Chronology of Style

    Variations on a Time Theme
    Miller, Karl, ed., *Memoirs of a Modern Scotland* (London: Faber, 1970)
    Pittock, Murray G. H., *The Invention of Scotland: The Stuart Myth and
        the Scottish Identity: 1638 to the Present* (London: Routledge, 1991)
    Carmina gadelica online at http://www.electricscotland.com/books/pdf/
        carmina.htm

Form, Time, Fashion
    Gombrich, Ernst 'The father of Art History? The influence of Hegel',
        in Abbs, Peter, ed. *The Symbolic Order* (London: Routledge Falmer,
        1989)
    Watson, William, *The Muse in Exile* (London: Herbert Jenkins, 1913)

The Nonstandard Poem
Abse, Dannie, ed., *Poetry Dimension 2* (London: Abacus, 1974)
Sara, Ruby, ed., *Mandragora* (Brighton: Scarlet Imprint, 2012)
For an introduction to the British Poetry Revival, see the *Great Works* website: http://www.modernpoetry.org.uk/nrsh.html

The 1960s
Berger, Peter, and Luckmann, Thomas L., eds., *The Social Construction of Reality* (Harmondsworth: Penguin, 1967)
Crawford, Robert and Armitage, Simon, eds., *The Penguin Book of Poetry since 1945* (Harmondsworth: Penguin: 1999)
Esslin, Martin *The Theatre of the Absurd* (London: Eyre and Spottiswoode, 1963)
Glaser, Hermann, *Kulturgeschichte der Bundesrepublik* (Munich: Hanser, 1985)
Green, Jonathon, *Days in the Life* (London: Heinemann, 1988)
Middlemas, Keith, *Power, Competition, and the State* (3 vols., Basingstoke: Macmillan, 1986-91)
Nuttall, Jeff, *Bomb Culture* (London: MacGibbon and Kee, 1968)

The English Intelligencer
DeVoto, Bernard, *Westward the Course of Empire* (London: Eyre & Spottiswoode, 1954)
Pattison, Neil, Pattison, Reitha, Roberts, Luke, eds., *Certain Prose of the English Intelligencer* (Cambridge: Mountain Press, 2012)
Prynne, J.H.: see issue of *Jacket* online at http://jacketmagazine.com/24/index.shtml
Reeve, Neil and Kerridge, Richard, eds., *Nearly Too Much: the Poetry of J. H. Prynne* (Liverpool: Liverpool University Press, 1995)

The Counter-Culture
Brand, Jack *The National Movement in Scotland* (London: Routledge and Kegan Paul, 1978)
Bulpitt, Jim, *Territory and Power in the United Kingdom: an Interpretation* (Manchester: Manchester University Press, 1984)
Caute, David, *Sixty-Eight* (London: Hamilton, 1988), and Green, Jonathon, *ut supra.*
Coote, Anna and Campbell, Beatrix, *Sweet Freedom: Struggle for Women's Liberation* (London: Picador, 1982)

Davies, Hywel, *The Welsh Nationalist Party 1925-45* (Cardiff: University of Wales Press, 1983)

Davies, Wendy, *Early Mediæval Wales* (Leicester: Leicester University Press, 1982)

Edwards, Owen Dudley, ed. *Celtic Nationalism* (London: Routledge and Kegan Paul, 1968)

Marr, Andrew, *The Battle for Scotland* (London: Penguin, 1992)

Miller, W. S., *The End of British Politics?* (Oxford: Clarendon Press, 1981)

Morgan, Kenneth O., *Wales: the Rebirth of a Nation* (Oxford: Clarendon Press, 1981)

Rowbotham, Sheila, *The Past Is Before Us* (London: Pandora, 1989)

Rowe, Marsha, ed., *The Spare Rib Reader* (Harmondsworth: Penguin, 1982)

Sebestyen, Amanda, ed., *1968 1978 1988* (Bridport: Prism, 1988)

Wandor, Michelene, ed., *Once a Feminist: Stories of Generations* (London: Virago, 1990)

Scotland: more vital stuff on Scottish poetry at: http://www.pinko.org/30.html

Gothic

Akurgal, Ekrem, *Die Kunst Anatoliens von Homer bis Alexander* (Berlin: 1961)

Fuller, Peter: this paper reprinted in *Beyond the Crisis in Art* (London: Writers and Readers, 1980)

Kitzinger, Ernst, on asomatoi: *Byzantine Art in the Making* (London: Faber, 1977)

The 1970s

Barry, Peter, *Poetry Wars* (Cambridge: Salt, 2006)

Hodgkiss, Peter, ed., Barry MacSweeney interview in *Poetry Information 18* (periodical, London: Winter/Spring 1977-8)

Wales: interviews with almost all the poets mentioned can be found in issues of *Poetry Wales*.

Files of cuttings on the Poetry Society crisis held at the Poetry Library, London.

The Breakdown of Subjectivity

Brown, J. A. C. *Techniques of Persuasion* (Harmondsworth: Penguin, 1963)

Ehrenzweig, Anton *The Hidden Order of Art* (London: Weidenfeld and Nicolson, 1967)

Schapiro, Meyer *Selected Papers vol. 3* (London: Chatto and Windus, 1980)

Turner, Victor *Dramas, Fields, and Metaphors* (Ithaca, NY: Cornell University Press, 1974)

Wellek, Rene, and Warren, Austin, *Theory of Literature* (London: Jonathan Cape, 1949)

Rollback

Abbs, Peter, ed., *The Black Rainbow, Essays on the Present Breakdown of Culture* (London: Heinemann, 1975)

Kramer, Hilton, ed., *The New Criterion Reader. The First Five Years* (London: Collier Macmillan, 1988)

Kramer, Hilton, reviews from *Revolt of the Philistines: Art and Culture 1972-84* (New York, NY: Free Press, 1985)

The 1980s: Ego-histoire

Niethammer, Lutz, *Ego-Histoire und andere Erinnerungsversuche* (Vienna: Böhlau, 2002)

Reed, Jeremy, *Selected Poems* (London: Penguin, 1987)

York, Peter, *Style Wars* (London: Sidgwick & Jackson, 1980)

Cheap information: The 1980s

Clarke, Adrian and Sheppard, Robert, eds. *Floating Capital* (Elmwood, CT: Potes & Poets Press, 1991)

Lloyd, D. T., ed.: interview with Meic Stephens in *The Urgency of Identity* (TriQuarterly Press, 1995)

MacMullen, R. 'From the fugitives...' quoted from, *Enemies of the Roman Order* (London: Routledge, 1992)

'phantasmagoric realism' discussed by Martin Seymour-Smith in 'A Climate of Warm Indifference', printed in Tennant, Emma, ed. *The Bananas Anthology* (London: Quartet Books, 1977).

Purple and Green (Sheffield: Rivelin Grapheme, 1985)

Glimpses of the 1990s

Stezaker, John, cited from *English Art Today 1960-76,* Exhibition Catalogue (Milan: Electa Editrice, 1976)

Angel Exhaust 15: Bizarre Crimes of the Future, 1997 – you can compare the introduction with the anthology in its original setting, *Angel Exhaust* 15

For reviews of about 40 books appearing in the 1990s, see my *Legends of the Warring Clans*, online here: http://www.pinko.org/10.html

POEM CREDITS

Ash, John, *The Goodbyes* (Manchester: Carcanet Press, 1982);

Benveniste, Asa, *Throw Out the Life Line, Lay out the Corse (Poems 1965-85)* (London: Anvil Press Poetry, 1983);

Brackenbury, Alison, *Dreams of Power* (Manchester: Carcanet Press, 1981);

Brown, George Mackay, *Collected Poems* (London: John Murray, 2006);

Catling, Brian, in *future exiles* (London: Paladin Books, 1992);

Clarke, Adrian, *Obscure Disasters* (London: Writers Forum, 1993);

Corcoran, Kelvin, *Lyric Lyric* (London: Reality Street Editions, 1993);

Duhig, Ian, *The Bradford Count* (Newcastle: Bloodaxe Books, 1991);

Finch, Peter, *The Welsh Poems* (Exeter: Shearsman Books, 2006);

Fowler, Alistair, *Catacomb Suburb* (Edinburgh: Edinburgh University Press, 1976);

Freer, Ulli, *Stepping Space* (Peterborough: Spectacular Diseases, 1990) or *Rushlight* – uncertain but possibly in an issue of a Xerox magazine called *RWC*;

Harsent, David, *Selected Poems* (Oxford: Oxford University Press, 1989);

Herbert, W. N., *Dundee Doldrums* (Edinburgh: Galliard, 1991);

Hughes, Ted, *Wolfwatching* (London: Faber, 1989);

James, John, *Dreaming Flesh* (Cambridge: Street Editions, 1991);

Lasdun, James, *A Jump Start* (London: Secker and Warburg, 1987);

de Lomellini, C. A., in *Purple and Green* (Sheffield: Rivelin Grapheme, 1985);

MacBeth, George, *Collected Poems 1958-82* (London: Hutchinson, 1989);

Marriott, D. S., *Clouds & Forges* (Southampton: Torque Press, 1991);

Middleton, Christopher, *Two Horse Wagon Going By* (Manchester: Carcanet Press, 1986);

Mottram, Eric, *Peace Projects and Brief Novels* (London: Talus Editions, 1989);

Prynne, J. H., *Poems* (Newcastle: Bloodaxe Books, 1999 [expanded editions in 2005 and 2012]);

Raworth, Tom, *Collected Poems* (Manchester: Carcanet Press, 2003) (originally in *Lion Lion*, 1970);

Redgrove, Peter, *The Apple-Broadcast* (Routledge & Kegan Paul Books, 1981);

Reed, Jeremy, 'Infesting' from *Saints & Psychotics* (London: Enitharmon Press, 1979);

– 'Riddle of the Oak' from *Straight Lines* (periodical: London, 2, 1979);

– 'Three Devils Reef' from *Bleecker Street* (Manchester: Carcanet Press, 1980);

– 'Transformations' from *Temenos* (magazine, London, issue 4, 1983);

– 'White Bear' from *The Glamour Poet Versus Francis Bacon, Rent and Eyelinered Pussycat Dolls* (Bristol: Shearsman Books, 2014);

– 'An Age Bereft' and 'Dead Hand' from *By the Fisheries* (London: Jonathan Cape, 1984)

Rushmer, David: source unknown

Seed, John, *New and Collected Poems* (Exeter: Shearsman Books, 2005)

Shuttle, Penelope, *The Hermaphrodite Album* (London: Fuller d'Arch Smith, 1973);

Smith, Ken, *The Poet Reclining: Selected Poems 1962-80* (Newcastle: Bloodaxe Books, 1982);

Thrilling, Isobel, *Spectrum Shift* (Todmorden: Littlewood Arc, 1991);

Tonks, Rosemary, *Iliad of Broken Sentences* (London: The Bodley Head, 1967) [republished in 2014 in *Bedouin of the London Evening: Collected Poems*, (Highgreen: Bloodaxe Books, 2014)];

Wainwright, Jeffrey, *Selected Poems* (Manchester: Carcanet Press, 1985);

White, Kenneth, *The Most Difficult Area* (London: Cape Goliard, 1968).

Index

www.ingramcontent.com/pod-product-compliance
Lightning Source LLC
Chambersburg PA
CBHW020638030726
47498CB00002B/270